Maurice Hugh Keen was educated at Winchester College, (as a scholar, 1947-52) and won a scholarship in History to Balliol College, Oxford, 1951. He read history and obtained a first in Modern History 1957. He was elected Junior Research Fellow at the Queen's College, Oxford, 1957, and elected Fellow and Tutor in medieval history at Balliol 1961. He won the Alexander Prize (Royal Historical Society) 1961 with an essay "Treason Trials under the Law of Arms".

# THE LAWS OF WAR
# IN THE LATE MIDDLE AGES

# STUDIES IN POLITICAL HISTORY

Editor: Michael Hurst

*Fellow of St John's College, Oxford*

# THE LAWS OF WAR
# IN THE
# LATE MIDDLE AGES

*by*

## M. H. KEEN

*Fellow of Balliol College, Oxford*

LONDON: Routledge & Kegan Paul
TORONTO: University of Toronto Press
1965

*First published 1965*
*in Great Britain by*
*Routledge & Kegan Paul Ltd*
*and in Canada by*
*University of Toronto Press*

*Printed in Great Britain by*
*W. & J. Mackay & Co Ltd*
*Chatham*

© *M. H. Keen 1965*

# EDITOR'S NOTE

UNLIKE so many history series this one will not attempt a complete coverage of a specific span of time, with a division of labour for the contributors based on a neat parcelling out of centuries. Nor will it, in the main, be a collection of political monographs. Rather, the aim is to bring out books based on new, or thoroughly reinterpreted material ranging over quite a wide field of chronology and geography. Some will be more general than others, as is to be expected when biography is included alongside of detailed treatment of some comparatively short period of crisis like the appeasement of the Axis Powers. Nevertheless, whatever mode of presentation may have been appropriate, each work should provide an exposition of its subject in context and thus enable the reader to acquire new knowledge amidst things he knows, or could have known.

MICHAEL HURST

*St. John's College,*
*Oxford.*

# CONTENTS

vii

# PREFACE

THIS book was originally put together as a D.Phil. thesis, when I was working as a junior research fellow at the Queen's College, Oxford. To the Provost and Fellows of Queen's, who elected me to the fellowship, extended it for a year to allow me to complete the thesis, and helped to finance my work abroad, I owe an immense debt of gratitude. To my supervisor, Mr. K. B. MacFarlane, I owe equal gratitude, for his guidance at every stage of the work and for invaluable advice and criticism.

Much of the material on which the book is based comes from French archives. I should have found little there, but for the kindness of M. Pierre Géraudel, *conservateur* at the Archives Nationales, and the trouble he took to put me in touch with those who could best advise me. It was through him that I met M. André Bossuat, who directed me to many of the sources of which I have made most extensive use, and gave me much valuable advice on how to approach them. I also owe a great deal to Professor P-C. Timbal and to Mme. Josette Metman, for guidance on the study of the records of the Parlement in the fourteenth century.

I must thank Mr. C. A. J. Armstrong and Professor G. W. Coopland for allowing me to use MSS and microfilm in their possession. Mr. Michael Maclagan most generously lent me books from his library, which I needed to have by me and which would not otherwise have been available. For their assistance over the intractable business of reading the proofs, I am most grateful to Miss Jennie Robertson-Walker and Miss Margaret Bamford. I must thank the publishers and the Editor of the series for their continuous help and courtesy.

The errors that remain, and I have no doubt that there are many, are my own. But for those who have helped me, there would be many more.

M. H. KEEN

*Balliol College, Oxford.*

ix

# ABBREVIATIONS
## USED IN FOOTNOTES

| | |
|---|---|
| Arch. dep. | Archives départmentales |
| Arch. Nat. | Archives Nationales, Paris |
| Bib. Nat. | Bibliothèque Nationale, Paris |
| Bodleian | Bodleian Library, Oxford |
| B. Mus. | British Museum, London |
| C.C.R. | Calendar of Close Rolls |
| C.P.R. | Calendar of Patent Rolls |
| Cod. | * Codex Justiniani |
| Comment. | Commentaria |
| Decretal. | Decretales |
| *Dig. Nov.* | * Digestum Novum |
| *Dig. Vet.* | * Digestum Vetus |
| E.H.R. | English Historical Review |
| *Instit.* | * Instituta Justiniani |
| P.R.O. | Public Record Office, London |
| *Rot. Parl.* | Rotuli Parliamentorum |
| *Rot. Scot.* | Rotuli Scotiae |
| R.S. | Rolls Series |
| Rymer | Rymer's *Foedera, Conventiones et Acta Public,* Hague edn., 1745 |
| T.R.H.S. | Transactions of the Royal Historical Society |
| Usus Feud. | Usus Feudorum |

* In quoting from these sources, I have given the number of the book, the title (= Tit.), and the law (= l.); thus Dig. Nov., XLIX, Tit. 15, l. 24 means the 49th book in the Digestum Novum, titulus 15, lex 24.

*ADDENDA*

| | |
|---|---|
| Perche Orders | Earl of Salisbury's standing orders for his companies in Maine and Perche, 1427 (B. Mus., Cotton MS. Julius F IV, fo. 322 et seq.). |
| Melun *v.* Pomfret | Case of Melun *v.* Pomfret, tried before the Parlement of Paris, 1365–6 (Bib. Nat., MS. Fr. 21717, fo 144 et seq.). |

# I

# INTRODUCTION

Iₙ the year 1370 an English army, nominally under the command of the ailing Black Prince, lay before Limoges. Because that city's bishop, the Prince's one time councillor, had turned with his people to the French, the English commander had ordered that no terms for surrender were to be accepted, but that the town was to be taken by assault and without quarter. After a considerable siege the walls were undermined, and the city taken by storm. In his account of the fighting within the town, Froissart records a curious incident. Three French knights, who had defended themselves gallantly, seeing at length no alternative to surrender, threw themselves on the mercy of John of Gaunt and the Earl of Cambridge. 'My lords', they cried, 'we are yours: you have vanquished us. Act therefore to the law of arms.'[1] John of Gaunt acceded to their request, and they were taken prisoner on the understanding that their lives would be protected.

This passage in Froissart, together with a series of scattered references in other chronicles to the 'law of arms', the '*droit de guerre*', or the *jus belli*, poses a problem for the historian. What was this law to which the French knights appealed, claiming a right to quarter? The circumstances of the incident in Froissart give, it is true, certain general indications towards an answer to this question. The knights were clearly appealing to some sort of general code of military conduct, which they believed the combatants on either side in any war should feel bound to honour.

---

[1] *Oeuvres de Froissart*, ed. Kervyn de Lettenhove (Brussels, 1869), Tome VIII, p. 43.

Their words, and the scattered references elsewhere to the same law, argue the existence in the middle ages of some sort of prototype of the Geneva convention, a branch of international law governing the conduct of war.

This is the limit to what one can infer from the words of Froissart's knights. Nevertheless, there must be more to be told, for if a law can be heard above the din of battle, a certain precision in its rulings is implied. The object of this book will be to see how much more can be told. Its aim will be to establish what the 'law of arms' meant, and to study its application and working with reference to one particular war, the Hundred Years War between England and France. As a test of its legal effectiveness, this seems to be a sufficiently ample field for illustration; for this war was one which, at one point or another in its course, involved nearly every European state or principality west of Poland. The results of this enquiry should throw light on the general question of how far the middle ages had any idea of effective international law.

Fortunately, there is rather more than scattered references in chronicles to go on. There are other pointers as to the general directions which such an enquiry will have to pursue. From the voluminous writings of the great canonists and civilians of the thirteenth, fourteenth and fifteenth centuries, one can piece together the outlines of a well-developed theory of the 'just war', which was for them the only legitimate form of warfare. Certainly there are questions as to how far what they said on this matter can be treated as international law, because very often what they said applied to wars between private persons (as feudal quarrels) as well as to the wars of kings and princes. Their obvious preoccupation with moral issues suggests also another question, how far their theoretical views had any practical significance? Nevertheless, it is clearly important to establish what, if any, was the relation between the law of arms that Froissart spoke of, and the teaching of the canon and civil lawyers about the just war.

More obviously, it is important to establish the relation between this law and the contemporary cult of chivalry. Here the ground is a little firmer, for there is no doubt that the men who fought in the wars of the fourteenth and fifteenth centuries paid lip-service, at least, to chivalrous standards. But chivalry is a dangerous word. It can be used to describe the concept of the soldier as an individual whose vocation in a Christian society was to defend in arms the cause of faith and justice. The standards such a vocation would set are obviously high ones, and, if observed, would fully entitle the soldier's calling to the very high respect which it certainly enjoyed in the middle ages. To be a soldier then was to be noble, for 'arms enoble a man, whoever he may be'.[1] But as often chivalry is the word used to describe not the ideals but the social rituals of the military nobility, their passion for blazonry, tournaments, and courtly romance. It is often assumed that it was these trappings of chivalrous life, not its ideals, which really mattered to the soldiers and aristocrats of Froissart's time. Indeed, it would be reasonable enough, after reading his account of the sack of Limoges, to conclude that chivalrous ideals had little to do with the conduct of campaigns in the Hundred Years War. Unless, that is, some such law as the law of arms prescribed a formal minimum of humane and rational behaviour.

The demands of such a law would necessarily fall short of the highest possible standards, for it is in the nature of law that its rules are formal, not ideal. Even a formal minimum of chivalrous conduct, however, would if judicially enforceable add meaning to the 'chivalry' of the fourteenth and fifteenth centuries, which some have considered to be no more than an anachronistic pose. There are certain indications that there may have been just such a formal minimum. In the Hundred Years War soldiers, and not always soldiers of the highest character, frequently made contracts with aliens or enemies which they swore to observe on the faith of knighthood. A very large number of these contracts involved financial obligations, to fight at given wages, or to pay ransom, or to surrender forts in consideration for named sums. Even a hardened materialist need not question the significance of chivalrous oaths, when inducements of this nature were involved. Their currency reminds us of another factor too. Soldiering in this period had assumed many of the characteristics of a large scale commercial venture. Solid fortunes were founded on the chance issues of battlefields, as the careers of men like Sir Robert Knollys and Sir John Fastolf

[1] *Le Jouvencel*, ed. L. Lécestre and C. Favre (Soc. de l'histoire de France, 1887–9), Tome II, p. 81.

remind us. If one was going to make a living out of the profits of war, as these men did, one needed to be sure that one's enemies were going to observe the rules of the game, and that if they did not, there would be ways of forcing them to do so. An enforceable code of chivalrous laws, acknowledged by all soldiers regardless of allegiance, would have met just this need.

In the course of this book much more will have to be said about these matters which have been mentioned, about the theory of the just war, about chivalry, and about the regulation of military profiteering. As will become clear, there are good grounds for regarding all three matters as being closely connected. What a study of the law of arms should reveal is how their combined influence contributed to the development of the concept of effective international law.

# PART ONE

# The Legal Basis of the Law of
# Arms and its Administration

# II

# THE LEGAL BASIS OF THE
# LAW OF ARMS

THE problem which has to be faced at the very beginning of this enquiry is the question, what was the legal basis of the law of arms? This is not an easy question to answer. There had always, it is true, existed certain local, customary rules concerning war, such as the ancient law of the Marches,[1] which ran in the border country between England and Scotland. But the law of arms was quite different; it applied not just in one place, but in the words of one chronicler, 'wherever there was war'.[2] Yet it was not a code given upon authority, for in the fourteenth and fifteenth centuries no authority was recognised which could have laid down universal rules of war. Nor is there any record of any agreement between countries or kingdoms to observe a given set of rules. On what ground, then, could any law be accepted as having general application in all disputes arising out of war up and down Christendom?

This is really the selfsame question which the academic lawyers who wrote about the rules of war posed at the beginning of their treatises, 'from what law does war come?'[3] The answer given by the two most famous amongst them, John of Legnano and Honoré Bonet, is unfortunately at first sight rather

[1] *Acts of the Parliament of Scotland*, Vol. I, Appendix II, pp. 83–6.
[2] Pedro Lopez d'Ayala, *Cronicas de los Reyes de Castilla* (Madrid, 1779–80), Tome I, pp. 459–60, reporting the verdict of a court martial held in the Black Prince's army after the battle of Najera.
[3] E.g. Bonet, *Tree of Battles*, pt. 4, ch. 1 (Coopland's translation, p. 125).

unhelpful; 'war', they declared, 'is justified by all laws'.[1] This sweeping generalisation, however, was not made without due consideration. The two men in question were both professional lawyers, with considerable knowledge of theory and practice in their subject. Far from being an oversimplification, their answer is really a warning to us that in this matter we must take a wide view and examine the issues with care. We shall not go far wrong, therefore, if initially we take John and Bonet as guides, and attempt to follow the steps which led them to their conclusion (though we must bear in mind that their arguments are academic ones; a soldier might not see the matter in quite the same light).

As we might expect, in asserting the basic legality of war John and Bonet took their stand on what were to them the foundations of all law, divine authority and natural reason. War was justified in the first instance, they declared, by the divine law (*jus divinum*). The authorities were all agreed; Scripture, the Fathers, the *Decretum*, Aquinas himself. 'The Lord appointed new wars', wrote John of Legnano, quoting Judges V;[2] His people had known Him as the God of Battles, and He had even instructed Joshua in the means of laying an ambush for his enemies. Taking up this point, which a wealth of Old Testament references bore out, Bonet, and Christine de Pisan after him, remind us of its implication; we must not conclude from the evil consequences of war that war itself is evil. 'As touching the harms that be done above the right and *droit* of war . . . that cometh not of the right of war, but by the evilness of the people who use it evilly.'[3] The justification of war, it was pointed out, lay not in the manner in which it was conducted, but in its end; as Augustine had written 'war is waged that peace may be had'.[4] Here, behind the argument of the legists, one sees the belief, shared with them by nearly all orthodox theologians and philosophers of the Christian west,

[1] Bonet, ibid., 'Hence war in general is justified by all laws' (Coopland's translation, p. 126). Bonet is here summarising John's conclusions.

[2] John of Legnano, *Tractatus de Bello*, cap. 10 (there are a number of editions of this work: the most recent and most reliable being that of T. E. Holland, Oxford, 1917).

[3] Christine de Pisan, *Book of Fayttes of Armes and of Chyvalrye*, Book I, ch. 2 (Caxton's translation, ed. Byles, E.E.T.S., p. 10).

[4] Augustine, *Epistolae*, CLXXXIX, 6.

that war was part of the general struggle against evil. As such, there could be no question of its justification, and any incidental terrestrial miscarriages of justice could be written off against the ultimate achievement of the divine purpose.

From this position, John of Legnano went on to prove war in accord with the other great primal law, the *jus naturale*. This is a predictable step, seeing that for him the natural universe is no less than the divine creation; and it is already implied in his overall definition of war as something 'tending to destroy the displeasure which introduced it'[1]—the result, that is, of contradictions in nature. Nature sanctions the war of the beasts, which we witness daily; she sanctions, too, the wars of the elements, as when waters are dried up by the sun. Nature, animate and inanimate, is according to John driven by conflicting forces, for nature has implanted in each thing repugnance to its opposite principle.[2] But we must not conclude from this that the disorders which are the consequence of war are justified by the *jus naturale* any more than they are by the *jus divinum*. A war which has no justice in it is as unnatural as it is contrary to divine moral law, for equity is a natural principle. Such a war results from an unnatural failure in equity, since in the man who moves it the *intellectualis* is governed by the *sensitivus*. This, as Aristotle has shown, is contrary to nature, for it is against nature (i.e. unjust) for a higher principle to be governed by a lower one.[3] In fact unjust or unnatural wars are, says John of Legnano (making a distinction of a type familiar to an Aristotelian) not really wars at all. As his contemporary Baldus put it, they are not properly wars but *manifesta latrocinia*.[4]

The arguments so far rehearsed are theological and philosophical, and can prove no more than the ultimate legitimacy of war. Neither the *jus divinum* nor the *jus naturale*, as understood by the medieval lawyers, could provide enforceable rules of warfare. The *jus divinum* was binding only *in foro conscientiae*, and

---

[1] John of Legnano, *Tractatus de Bello*, cap. i.

[2] Ibid., cap. ii: 'Ex principiis naturalibus cuilibet enti naturali creato est insita inclinatio naturalis ad exclusionem cuiusque repugnantis suae naturali dispositioni'.

[3] Ibid., cap. 162.

[4] Baldus, *Comment. in usus Feudorum*, Lib. II, Tit. 28.

9

as was very properly pointed out in the Parlement of Paris in a case concerning disputed spoils of war, in which the justice of the war on hand was questioned, 'cy ne parle point *de foro conscientiae*'.[1] Secular courts were not concerned with moral lapses but with legal offences, and church courts could not consider the crimes of knights. Equally, natural law provided no basis for regulations covering the wars of men, for the *jus naturale* was common to men and all nature. In the words of the Digest 'natural law is what nature teaches all animals to do, for this law is not particular to the human race, but is common to them and all animals'.[2] Natural law is therefore really scientific law, and though in its context of Aristotelian natural theory this definition does not exclude any idea of justice, such natural justice clearly cannot be binding *in foro externo*. Negatively, men cannot be bound against its dictates, and no human law can override institutions, such as that of marriage, which are based in natural law. But in order to bind men positively, one must look to what St. Thomas Aquinas called a 'positive human law'.[3] Such a law the legists found in the *jus gentium*, the law which, in the words of the Institutes, is 'common to all men'.[4] Hence its name, for as Gratian put it 'this law is called the law of nations (*jus gentium*), because almost all nations obey it'.[5]

That this was the law which governed what we would call war between sovereign states ('universal corporeal war' to John of Legnano; '*guerre ouverte et publique*' to the knights who fought in it) no one denied. The authorities all agreed about this. 'Wars arise under the *jus gentium*'[6] said the Digest; Isidore's definition, which Gratian followed word for word, was to the same effect.[7] The authorities agreed further that the *jus gentium*, like the civil law, was a positive law;[8] indeed it was more, for

---

[1] Case of Giles Desmoulins v. Religious of Charterhouse of Le Parc, March 1433 (Arch. Nat., X¹a 4797, fo. 49 et seq.).

[2] *Digest*, Lib. I, Tit. 1, l. 1.

[3] Aquinas, *Summa Theologica*, I. 2ae, Q. 95, Art. 4, concl.

[4] *Instit.*, Lib. I, 2: 'jus autem gentium omni humano generi commune est'.

[5] *Decretum*, Pars I, Dist. I, c. ix, §1: 'hoc inde jus gentium appellatur, quia eo jure omnes fere gentes utuntur'.

[6] *Digest*, Lib. I, Tit. 1, l. 5: 'ex hoc jure gentium introducta bella'.

[7] Isidore, *Etymologiae*, Lib. V, cap. 6.

[8] Aquinas, *Summa Theologica*, I. 2ae, Q. 95, Art. 4, concl.: 'dividitur jus positivum in jus gentium et jus civile'.

it was immutable.[1] Its authority stood higher than that of any other human law, being derived from its conformity with natural law (and so with divine law, these being in eternal agreement). The derivation was direct; as Aquinas put it 'those rules belong to the *jus gentium* which are deduced from natural law as conclusions from principles'.[2]

The trouble arose over defining these conclusions from principles. The *jus gentium* was said to be a positive law, but no one was quite sure where to look for its positive rules. The Roman lawyers, from whom the medieval writers took their doctrine, lacked clarity in this matter. Bonet was quite clearly baffled by the problem, and simply fell back on authoritative statement. 'At the same time you must understand that we have another law, which we call in Latin the *jus gentium*. And it is not to be doubted that war is to be found therein, as the decretal and the civil law assert.'[3] But he was obviously very uncertain what it was that the decretal and the civil law were talking about. He extricated himself from the difficulty by falling back on a definition similar to that of Aquinas, that the law of nations is a law 'which covers everything which is according to reason in general'.[4] He went on to say that therefore the civil and canon laws could be called the law of nations, since 'they set forth and specify cases according to reason'. Thus in a single sentence Bonet spanned the seven league stride from the sphere of natural reason to that of written law. Clearly the position taken up by the medieval lawyer at this point needs careful examination.

As the medieval lawyers were following, or attempting to follow, the doctrines of antiquity, it is necessary here to go back and see what the Roman lawyers meant by the *jus gentium*. For them, this was the law which was common to all men, or rather those elements of law which were common to all known legal systems. The idea of such a law was in fact their response to the problem posed by relations between the multitude of persons subject to Roman rule who were not bound by the common law (*jus commune*) of Rome. The *jus gentium* was the common

[1] Bartolus, *Comment. in Cod.*, I, Tit. 14, l.4.
[2] Aquinas, *Summa Theologica*, I. 2ae, Q. 95, Art. 4, concl.
[3] Bonet, *Tree of Battles*, pt. 4, ch. 1 (Coopland's translation, p. 126).
[4] Ibid.

law of the empire, in the sense of the law common to all the peoples within the empire. The ultimate basis of this law was natural reason;[1] that is to say, it was based on those principles of honesty and good faith without which men cannot live as social beings. What this meant in the practical sphere of legal administration was that the written law of Rome was authoritative over persons who were not citizens only in so far as it expressed these principles in concrete form. This is the point after which Bonet was groping when he said that the civil law could be called the law of nations, because it set forth and specified cases according to reason. At the theoretical level, however, it meant that the *jus gentium* was simply an extension to human affairs of the *jus naturale*, common to all men within or without the empire. As Tryphoninus put it, it was the 'natural law of nations'.[2] We must remember, however, that this is the definition of a lawyer, not a philosopher, and that it accepts as natural those customary usages which the Romans found to be normally observed among persons of diverse nations, which usages do not have any necessary connection with principles of reason. On this ground, a number of legal conditions were described as *jure gentium*, some of which, such as captivity and slavery,[3] medieval Christian thought could not accept as natural.[4] A conflict was thus posed between the *jus naturale* and the *jus gentium*. A further problem was presented for the medieval lawyers by the fact that their antique authorities seemed sometimes to speak of the *jus gentium* as a law common to all men, and sometimes merely as the common law of the Roman empire.

The first problem they resolved in a manner typical of contemporary methods of argument. Rules such as that permitting the enslavement of captives, they said, might not be natural in themselves, but they could nevertheless be natural *secundum quid*,[5] in certain given circumstances. This position becomes

[1] *Instit.*, Lib. I, 2: 'quod vero naturalis ratio inter omnes homines constituit, id apud omnes populos peraeque custoditur vocaturque jus gentium'.

[2] *Digest*, XVI, Tit. 3, l. 31.

[3] *Decretum*, Pars I, Dist. I, c. ix: 'jus gentium est sedium occupatio, aedificatio, munitio, bella, *captivitates, servitutes, postliminia*'.

[4] Cf. Aquinas, *Summa Theologica*, I, Q. 96, Art. 4: 'in statu innocentiae non fuit tale dominium hominis ad hominem'.

[5] Cf. Albert of Bologna in Zilletus, *Tractatus Juris Universi*, Tome I, fo. 316.

much easier to defend if one believes, as they did, that one has an authoritative guide to the principles of nature, such as Holy Writ. It can then be argued that, 'given human wickedness', the enslavement of those who when free attempt to thwart the divine purpose (i.e. commit crimes against natural law) is justified in natural law.[1] Thus the unnatural appearance of certain conditions, as slavery, which were specifically described in law as *de jure gentium*, was seen to be deceptive. Given their sins, it was reasonable and legitimate to reduce those taken in a war against the infidel to slavery,[2] and, provided it had the Church's sanction, a war of conquest waged against them might even be said to be naturally just.[3] Because it sanctioned such actions as these, the *jus gentium* did not, according to medieval theory, run counter to the principles of natural reason; it merely added to them in specific respects. Taken in this sense, the medieval lawyers took the *jus gentium* to mean a human extension of natural law.

Clearly, however, in wars between Christians, rules such as the enslavement of captives could not apply, even though they were sanctioned by the *jus gentium*. As all were nevertheless agreed that this law governed the conduct of war, one could not simply turn back to the *jus naturale* to discover rules apposite to such wars. Whatever rules governed wars between Christians, they must be an extension of the *jus gentium*, just as it was an extension of the *jus naturale*.

Now when taken in its second meaning, as the common law of the Roman people, the medieval lawyers found that the *jus gentium* was not an inclusive description. 'The Roman people is governed in part by its own particular laws, in part by the laws which are common to all men.'[4] Thus the Institutes, and

[1] Ibid.

[2] Cf. Bartholomew de Saliceto, *Comment. in Cod.*, VIII, Tit. 51, l. 12: 'quaero, quid si unus rex contra alium . . . movet guerram? Respondeo, quod si alter eorum est barbaricae nationis, et sic infidelis, omnia dicta superius de servitute captivorum . . . locum sibi vendicant'.

[3] Aquinas, *Summa Theologica*, II. 2ae, Q. x, Art. 10: 'Potest tamen juste per sententiam vel ordinationem Ecclesie . . . tale jus dominii vel praelationis tolli; quia infideles merito suae infidelitatis merentur potestatem amittere super fideles'. Compare John of Legnano, *Tractatus de Bello*, cap. 12; and Bonet, *Tree of Battles*, pt. 4, ch. 2 (Coopland's translation, p. 127).

[4] *Instit.*, Lib. I, 2.

when one looked in them for a definition of what 'its own particular laws' meant, one found that this was the *jus civile*—the civil law of Rome.[1] Thus all who were subject to the emperor, it was concluded, were bound not only by the *jus gentium* but (in part at least) by the *jus civile* also. Unfortunately, however, the medieval empire was not, like the Roman, co-terminous with Christendom. What of the kingdoms of England, France, and Spain, which did not recognise the emperor's authority, and which possessed their own private legal systems? The answer was that although they were not, at least *de facto*, part of the empire, these kingdoms were nevertheless part of the Roman people, because the Roman people included all who obeyed mother church.[2] As regards such people, the Church had as a result of the *translatio imperii* inherited all the rights of the emperor, which rights were assumed on Gospel authority to be world wide, since by the decree of Caesar Augustus all the world had been enrolled.[3] Though, therefore, internally the subjects of such kingdoms might be bound by local custom and statute, in their dealings with the rest of the Roman people they were still bound by civil law. Moreover, since the Church had dominion and they acknowledged this, they were bound also by the law of the Church, the canon law.

Thus, in the sense that the *jus gentium* was the common law of the Roman people, the canon and civil laws could, as Bonet put it, be called the law of nations, for they were that same common law. The definition was indeed accurate, for the 'Roman people' meant not only the men of the empire but those of the independent *regna* and *civitates* also, and so a law which was common to it was genuinely a 'law of nations'. To the *jus gentium* in its broader sense of the natural law of all men, these two laws added for those within Christendom a further series

---

[1] Ibid., 'quod quisque populus ipse sibi jus constituit, id ipsius proprium civitatis est vocaturque jus civile'.

[2] John of Legnano, *Tractatus de Bello*, cap. 13: 'et per hoc infero quod omnes gentes fere quae obediunt sanctae Matri Ecclesiae sunt de populo Romano'.

[3] Ibid. 'Ecclesia ibi exercet jurisdictionem quam habebat imperium,' and 'si quis diceret imperium non esse dominium, diceret contra textum Evangelii, cum dicitur, "exiit edictum a Cesare Augusto" '. John is here following the argument of Bartolus, *Comment. in Dig. Nov.*, XLIX, Tit. 15, l. 24.

of positive rules, for 'beyond doubt the canon and civil laws add something further in the matter of war over and above the dictates of reason'.[1] Once again there was no question of any conflict of laws, for the equity of the canon and civil laws was the same as that of the *jus gentium*.[2] They too derived their ultimate authority from natural reason. The canon law was derived from natural law because it was derived from Holy Writ, and 'the divine laws operate in nature'.[3] The civil law was founded in natural law, because it was the accepted definition of civil laws that they were derived 'from the law of nature, by means of specific rulings on particulars'.[4] For the Roman people these two laws expanded the *jus naturale* and the *jus gentium* with a further series of specific rules, binding on all its members, but on them only. In dealings with *extranei*, as Tartars, Greeks, and Saracens, only the rules of the *jus gentium* proper were binding.[5]

Thus the *corpus* of the two laws, being law common to Christendom, was the basis for what was there accepted as international law. But this was not the end of the matter. There was another method of categorising laws; and according to this method, says Aquinas 'human law may be divided according to the categories of men who perform specific tasks for the common good, as priests who pray on behalf of the people, and knights who fight for their protection. And there are special laws apposite to all these people.'[6] The 'special law' of knights was the law of arms, and it was founded in the canon and civil laws, as were other 'special' laws such as the law merchant and the law of the sea. These special laws were extensions of the two great written laws (just as they in turn were extensions of the natural law and the *jus gentium*), adding particular rules binding only on persons of a particular class. The *jus militare*, according to Isidore's definition, governed such matters as military discipline, the payment of wages, the division of spoil, and military

[1] John of Legnano, *Tractatus de Bello*, cap. 11.
[2] Ibid., 'nam jus civile et jus canonicum non dicunt aliam aequitatem quam sit aequitas jure gentium'.
[3] Aquinas, *Summa Theologica*, I, 2ae, Q. xv, Art. 4, resp.
[4] Ibid.
[5] John of Legnano, *Tractatus de Bello*, cap. 13, following Bartolus, *ut supra*, n. 35.
[6] Aquinas, *ut supra*.

ranks and honours. It also governed certain formal matters, the signs of war and the legal forms of treaties, truces and alliances.[1] These are matters of a quite different nature to those which we have been discussing hitherto. They have very little, if anything, to do with natural equity, and rulings about them would be hard to find in scripture. Where then was one to look for authority in such matters?

Those parts of the *Corpus Juris Civilis* which dealt with the organisation of the Roman army did give a certain amount of guidance on some of these points. But as its rules were intended for internal, not international application, reference to them could not answer all the questions which might arise, even when, as often, they were liberally misinterpreted. The medieval *routier* might, for instance, wish to ask questions about his rights to compensation for losses incurred in the service of someone other than his liege lord, a point on which Justinian's laws were hardly likely to give specific rulings. In the absence of any other authority, such a matter would have to be decided by reference to customary practice. Professional knowledge here was the only available source for authoritative rulings. In complicated matters of military law, we find therefore that the opinion of heralds and of ancient knights was regarded as decisive.[2] Such men alone could state with authority which rules had acquired a sufficiently general acceptance to endow them with legal force.

Once again we are dealing not with a new kind of law, which may conflict with those already discussed, but with extensions of their rulings on particular points. On the issue referred to above, for instance, John of Legnano declares that a mercenary, who of his own free will hires out his services, has no action against the hirer according to written law, but that, in Italy at least, he would be able to claim for lost horses, since there such compensation is accepted as due by custom.[3] Custom however

---

[1] Isidore, *Etymologiae*, Lib. V, cap. 7: 'jus militare est belli inferendi solemnitas, foederis faciendi nexus, signo dato egressio in hostem vel pugnae commissio; item, signo dato receptio; item, flagitii militaris disciplina, si locus deseratur; item, stipendiorum modus, dignitatum gradus, praemiorum honor . . .; item, praedae decisio, et pro personarum qualitatibus divisio, ac principis portio'.

[2] For examples of reference to such authority in cases of doubt, see ch. III *infra*.

[3] John of Legnano, *Tractatus de Bello*, cap. 50.

could not run counter to written law, just as written law had
no force where it conflicted with principles of reason. So Bonet
rejects as unlawful the rule, which many knights affirm to have
customary sanction, that a town may be taken by escalade in
time of truce; for truce is a form of surety, and if such a rule
were upheld, surety would have no meaning.[1] As Nicholas
Rishton, the English doctor of canon and civil laws, put it: *in
jure caveatur respondere quod aliud est de jure, aliud est de usu armorum;
ista est fuga et refugium miserorum, non intelligentium.*[2]

With the addition of this body of customary usage to the
rules of the civil and canon law which concern soldiers, our
survey of the legal basis of the law of arms is complete. The
legitimacy of warfare in general was, as we have seen, regarded
as established by divine and natural law. The principles governing the conduct of human war were to be inferred from their
rules; these principles were called the *jus gentium*. In wars between states or kingdoms which were part of the Roman people,
the canon and civil laws, which equally had their origin in
divine and natural law, added a further series of specific rules
to the principles of the *jus gentium*. These two laws formed the
essential basis of the law of arms; to quote again from Nicholas
Rishton, *jura et usus armorum fundentur principaliter tam per textus
quam per doctores juris civilis et canonici.*[3] It should be remembered
here that for the medieval civilian the civil law included the
*usus feudorum*, whose rules were of some importance in defining,
for instance, the law of ransom. To these laws must be added a
further body of customary rules, observed from old times by
professional soldiers in the pursuit of their calling. All these
rules together formed the *jus armorum*, a branch of the *jus
gentium*, as added to by the precepts of the canon and civil laws
and by custom, and regulating the conduct of warfare within
Christendom.

There was no possibility of conflict due to the multiple

[1] Bonet, *Tree of Battles*, pt. 4, ch. 103 (Coopland, pp. 189–90).

[2] Letter of Rishton to the Duke of Burgundy's commissioners, dated 20 May
1405, at Calais, and complaining that the capture of the Bishop of Rochester
by the Burgundians was unlawful (Arch. dep. du Nord, B 18823, fo. 18).

[3] Ibid. Compare Paris of Pozzo, *De Re Militari*, Lib. I, cap. 2: 'quia non
possunt singula in stylo armorum comprehendi, oportebit tunc ad jura
civilia et imperialia confugere' (Zilletus, *Tractatus Juris Universi*, Tome 16,
p. 386vo).

sources of the law of arms, since the laws were not all essentially different but supplementary to one another in particular matters. Each was in turn governed by and contained within a higher law. It was in the manner thus dictated that conflicts of law were resolved in the courts, in cases arising out of war. In a case, for instance, brought in the Parlement of Paris in 1441, it was argued that one Denise de Bernardin could not be punished because she had gone to join her husband in English-held territory, since the bond of marriage, being founded in divine and natural law, overrode the bounds of territorial allegiance, which arose out of the *jus gentium*. Hence the French, though at war with the English, could not punish her for her loyalty, since *dei lex maior est legi principis*.[1] Similarly, in an earlier case pleaded in the same court, it was argued that the customary right of the Archbishop of Rheims as *seigneur* of the castle in that town could not prejudice the King's right to use the castle in war, because his right to do so was *de jure gentium ex quo bella et captivitates sunt orte*.[2] The *jus gentium*, being a higher law, overrode all customary right. In the same way, though a prince or commander could add regulations to the general rules of the *jus armorum*, these regulations could only bind those under his command; he could not alter the law of arms, because that was founded in the immutable *jus gentium*. So we find, for instance, Scottish soldiers serving in France objecting to a royal claim to a prisoner taken in Paris in 1417, based on the French rule that prisoners taken in an enclosed town belonged to the King. As foreign allies, they claimed, they were bound only by the general rules of the *droit d'armes*, and not by specifically French ordinances.[3]

[1] Case of Verrat *v.* the King's proctor and Prégent de Coitevy (Arch. Nat., X¹a 4798, fo. 285vo).

[2] Case of the townsmen of Rheims *v.* the Archbishop (Arch. Nat., X¹a 17, fo. 386).

[3] Case of David Margnies (?) *v.* Prévot of Paris; David's pleading: 'David replique et dit que le dit anglais fu prins par les diz Ecossais en son corps defendant et ainsi ils orent droit ou dit prisonnier . . . et ne sont pas les droiz d'armes telz que dit partie adverse, mais sont au contraire les usages; car prisonniers ennemis sont a ceux qui les prennent soit en ville fermee soit en dehors . . . et suppose qu'il y eust usage aucun sur ce a l'entencion de partie adverse, ce seroit au regard des subgez tant seulement et non mie des Ecossaiz ou aliez' (Arch. Nat., X¹a 4791, fo. 210).

In this last case precedence was claimed for the law of arms over other laws, but it is worth noticing that the same principles could militate in the opposite direction. Though it was founded in the civil law and the *jus gentium*, the law of arms applied in particular matters and to a particular class of persons only. Thus for instance a peasant could not claim rights in an enemy prisoner under the law of arms, because it applied only to military persons and therefore only they could sue for rights under it. If a soldier was captured by a civilian, the latter therefore could not ransom him, but must turn him over to the civil or military authorities.[1] As a branch of the *jus gentium* the law of arms had the same legal status as that law, but by no means the same legal scope.

The law was thus applied in the courts, and argued there by the professional lawyer, in a manner which accorded with those principles of legal theory which have been outlined. But how, one may ask, was the law regarded by the soldier himself? He had probably never heard of the *jus gentium*, and he was not likely to know much about the civil law. For him *jus militare* was a much more meaningful term, but he would probably not have described it in quite the way that Aquinas did, as a professional law. The word 'military' meant to him more than it does to us; 'chivalrous' would be a better translation. The *jus militare* therefore meant to him the law of chivalry. This helps to explain the scope of the law, for it applied in many matters which we would not describe as 'military', as for instance in judicial duels, and in armorial questions. Significantly, both the right to fight a duel and the right to bear arms were privileges of those of noble standing (so indeed, according to feudal theory, was the *droit de guerre*, the right to make war). For the soldier, therefore, *jus militare* did not so much mean a professional law, as the law of a certain privileged class, whose hereditary occupation was fighting.

This attitude had important effect in securing obedience to its rules. A great many of the matters most likely to be disputed

---

[1] See the statement in the trial of the dispute over the capture of the brigand Tassot by Robin de Beauques: 's'il (Tassot) eust este prins par gens d'armes estans au gaiges due roy, ils eussent eu tout ce qu'ilz eussent trouve sur lui, et si l'eussent mis a raencon'. Robin however, not being a soldier, could not claim ransom (Arch. Nat., X¹a 4796, fo. 270).

in military cases (agreements to pay ransom, to give safe-conduct and so on) could be treated in law as questions of contract. Contractual agreements were binding on all men, regardless of allegiance, because the sanctity of all voluntary pacts was a principle of the *jus gentium*, which no prince could alter.[1] But it was not for this reason, or at least not primarily, that the soldier kept his word once given. He did so because he had made an oath to do so on the honour of knighthood;[2] and if he broke such a promise, he did something much more damnable than simply failing to perform his part of a bargain. He had taken his knighthood in vain, and shown that he was unworthy of his honourable station; he was a 'false knight', which was as good as no knight at all. As his status was precious, on practical and social as well as psychological grounds, this was a name which no soldier would care to earn. Rules of honour impressed him in a way which the law of contract was never likely to, because the honour of the knight's estate was something he had been brought up to believe in. Even such agreements as indentures of war (by which the so-called contract-soldier was retained for a term of service) were therefore often guaranteed by oaths upon honour.[3] The lords who retained men in this way knew that the most effective means of keeping them to their word was to involve their pride of place in the matter. The fear of dishonour (in the formal sense of public reprobation) was the most effective sanction of the law of arms.

The difference between an obligation sanctioned by the law of contract, and one sanctioned by an oath upon honour is ultimately one of phraseology only. The rules respected by soldier and lawyer alike were the same, though the reasons for their respect were not. This difference was of attitude, and it reflected the difference of their respective upbringing and education. The lawyer had acquired his knowledge of the law through his legal education and in practice in the courts; the

[1] Cf. Bartolus, *Comment. in Cod.*, I, Tit. 14, l.4: 'pacta sunt de jure gentium'.

[2] For more detailed discussion of this point, see ch. X *infra*, especially the remarks on anathema clauses in agreements to pay ransom.

[3] There is a good example among the indentures preserved at Rouen, one between Bedford and William Mynors, dated 6 September 1434, in which Mynors undertakes his obligations 'sur son honneur et a peine de tous ses biens quelconques et aussi de son corps . . . selon l'exigence du cas' (Arch. dep. de la Seine Inférieure, Fonds Danquin, Carton 9).

soldier had picked his up in the course of a military career. If the lawyer was in doubt, he consulted his books, but the soldier respected different authorities (very likely he was illiterate). As we have seen, the people he would probably consult when doubtful on a point of military law were the heralds, who were esteemed the professors of chivalry. Whence then, did the heralds get their knowledge? The answer to this question will show that the authority on which the soldier relied was ultimately the same authority as that by which the professional advocate pleaded in the courts.

This answer is given explicitly by a contemporary. It is to be found in a heraldic treatise of the early fifteenth century, written in the form of a dialogue between a pursuivant and his instructor, an old herald. 'How shall I learn about the law of arms?' asks the pursuivant. 'I tell you,' says his master, 'that you will find it in a book called the *Tree of Battles*, and for this reason, you must get a clerk's learning; and you should also follow the wars, for there you will hear of the judgements that are delivered from time to time, which are not all mentioned in the *Tree of Battles*.'[1] The *Tree of Battles*, as we know, is none other than the work of Honoré Bonet, a professional canonist, who was very largely restating what had been said earlier by John of Legnano, who was a professor of civil laws at Bologna. The wheel has thus come full circle; when one seeks for the authority behind the knight's code of honour, it proves to be the same as that which Dr. Nicholas Rishton said was the authority behind the law of arms, the texts and commentaries of canon and civil law.

For heralds and soldiers, Bonet's book was a work on chivalry; that of Christine de Pisan, which was largely copied from it, was actually entitled the *Livre des Fays d'Armes et de Chevalerie*. But all Bonet had done really was to translate what John of Legnano and other professional lawyers had said into French, the language of knights, and to cut out their formidable array of academic references. He and Christine were relaying the lawyers' opinions to a wider public, and in a more popular and digestible form. The rules they laid down were respected by

[1] The treatise in question is to be found in several heraldic MSS. of the fifteenth century: see, e.g. Phillips MS. 10396 (in private hands), fo. 19vo; Bodleian MS. Ashmole 764, fo. 11; Bib. Nat., MS. Fr. 1968, fo. 64vo.

soldiers because they thought of them as the laws of the ancient and honourable order of knighthood. Equally, however, they were lawyers' rules, because they were founded in the canon and civil laws, whose currency was accepted as in some degree universal. It was this universality (which, as we have seen, had full theoretical justification) which was vital. Time-honoured local customs, such as the law of the March which the borderers of England and Scotland had long observed, had little meaning in the context of the great European wars of the fourteenth and fifteenth centuries, in which the same soldier might at different times serve half a dozen lords in as many countries. The law of arms, by contrast, was respected indifferently in all places, because it was founded in rules which all lawyers knew, and at the same time appealed to the social and professional pride which bound together all who bore arms.

The long process, by which this fusion of military customs, many of them originally of purely local application, with rules of canon and civil law had come about, lies outside the scope of a book whose object is to examine the working of the law of arms in practice. It forms part of a much larger story, the story of the reception of Roman law into the customary laws of Europe. What is important for the present purpose is that by the mid-fourteenth century, when records of cases begin to survive in sufficient number to make a systematic study of the working of the law of arms possible, a set of rules had been evolved which were accepted as decisive in the trial of disputes arising out of war, no matter where they were tried, or by whom.

# III

# THE TRIAL OF MILITARY
# CASES

No legal system has any true authority unless it can be enforced in practice. We have seen that the law of arms had its foundation in valid and known law; the next endeavour must therefore be to see how it was in fact administered. This question is one which at the outset poses serious problems. The law of arms was an international law, but the middle ages knew of no permanent international courts in which international cases could be tried. There was a time when the Papacy came near to establishing a right to try such matters, but before the beginning of the Hundred Years' War that time was past. The solution was that cases were moved in the courts of individual sovereigns. They were not, however, moved before their ordinary courts, because they were not covered by their ordinary civil laws. Cases under the law of arms presented a more complicated problem than ordinary legal disputes, because it was very likely that they would involve parties of two different allegiances. What courts then did try them, and what was their title to do justice?

In any attempt to answer these questions, two general points need to be borne in mind. The first is that the law of arms was not strictly a form of martial law, generally applicable only in time of war. For a case to be brought under it, there was no need for a state of war to be current. Peace was not regarded in the middle ages as the natural condition of states, and the signing of a treaty had no automatic effect on the rights of individuals arising out of the preceding war. Rather, it gave freer scope for their prosecution at law, as access to foreign courts became much easier. As disputes concerning rights won in war were more likely to be brought before the courts after the war than during it, and could even arise many years after it was finished, temporary expedients for dealing with soldiers' quarrels were not enough. There had to be some regular and permanent method of despatching cases under the law of arms.

The second point to be remembered concerns the position of the soldier, the potential litigant under military law. Soldiering in the age of chivalry was regarded as a Christian profession, not a public service. Though he took up arms in a public quarrel, a soldier still fought as an individual, and rights were acquired by and against him personally, and not against the side for which he fought. His native allegiance was therefore just as important as his military allegiance, because the latter might be temporary. If one wanted redress against him, his liege lord was much more likely to be able to give it, than the lord in whose service he was for the moment fighting. The subjects of the King of England and France could fight one another just as well under the colours of rival families in Brittany, or of the Counts of Foix and Armagnac, as they could in the service of their respective sovereigns. Nevertheless these sovereigns remained their liege lords, and their lands and fortunes were therefore in their jurisdiction; thus they were the persons who could give a suitor truly effective redress. Once again, the necessity for permanent and regular methods of trying cases by law of arms emerges, because such a case might be moved not as a result of the war of the sovereign in whose court it lay, but of the war of any sovereign.

We have posed the question, what courts did try cases by this law? In order to answer it, let us now, bearing the above points in mind, attempt to put ourselves in the position of a medieval soldier seeking redress under the law of arms. He need not necessarily be seeking redress against a stranger, but he very probably may be; let us suppose therefore that he has taken a prisoner in some hard-fought battle, who has promised to pay him a valuable ransom, say thirty thousand florins of gold and thirty-two suits of harness of the best Paris style, to mount thirty-two

gentlemen.[1] This man has now defaulted in payment, notwithstanding repeated summons. Our knight has good evidence to
back his claim; it will not rest merely on his prisoner's word of
honour given on the field, for he will also have a letter of
obligation under his prisoner's seal, promising to pay the precise sum mentioned, with all expenses thrown in, and invoking
terrific sanctions if the prisoner fails to be ready with his cash
at any of the terms. But now the money is not forthcoming. To
whom is our knight to turn for redress in his quandary?

His quandary is a real one. He has let his prisoner go home
on parole and the man has stayed there; and now, therefore, is
living comfortably in a foreign country, perhaps a hostile one
and almost certainly one which has been so until the last year
or two. Our knight cannot apply to the courts of his own land,
the procedures and methods of which he knows; he must apply
to someone who has authority over his captive and can distrain
him to make due payment. But he cannot apply to the ordinary
courts of his opponent's country either, for the judges there will
know nothing of him, or of the law under which he must prosecute his case. The obvious person for him to refer to is therefore
his prisoner's sovereign, the only person who has authority over
the man and who is also capable of independent relations with
external powers and people. He will go and present his case, if
he can afford it and if the rewards promised seem sufficient, to
the prince in person, and ask for justice at its fountain head.

In fact we shall find that, throughout the Hundred Years
War, a good many cases were taken up in this way, and brought
directly before sovereigns and their councils. At the end of the
first major campaign of the English in France, we hear of
Edward III's council considering the dispute as to whether
Berengar of Mont Blanc, taken in France by an archer, could
legally be a prisoner of war, seeing he was a clerk and so *hors de
guerre*.[2] After the end of its last campaign, Henry VI and his
council were dealing with the claim of Louis de Berthalot, a
Gascon squire, to a French prisoner, Olivier de Coitevy, whom

---

[1] This was a ransom actually demanded by Gaillart de Saliers, Wezeclan
de Waleran and Bascon de Mareuil in 1351, cf. Arch. Nat., X¹c 33, no. 80.

[2] Rymer, Vol. III, pt. I, p. 2. Berengar's captor, Nicholas de Stanweye
had explained that his prisoner's 'status, qualitas et condicio sibi fuerant
. . . incogniti'.

he and his companion-in-arms had taken in Talbot's descent on Bordeaux in 1452.[1] It was the English council again that in 1359 considered the complaint of William Lydell, a Scot, that he had been taken prisoner illegally and when he was riding unarmed and on parole for a previous ransom;[2] and which heard also the claims of the Navarrese to rights in the ransom of Olivier du Guesclin, taken outside Cherbourg in 1379.[3] Cases under the law of arms were heard similarly before the councils of the Duke of Burgundy,[4] of the Kings of France[5] and of Aragon,[6] and of the Black Prince as Lord of Aquitaine.[7]

To get a hearing before the prince and his council was however no easy matter, for they had more important things to consider than the claims of obscure soldiers of hostile allegiance. Our knight might have to bear with many delays, and that among unfamiliar men in an unfamiliar land, before his case was ultimately heard. As disputes over ransoms and such like were, after a long period of war, matters of everyday occurrence, and as ingenious men were ever ready with subtle excuses to cover their unwillingness to meet their commitments, our knight would very probably find that certain persons had been appointed to try just that kind of matter which he wished to bring up. These men would not be professional judges but knights, men who would understand just what difficulties he was in and what his arguments meant; they would in fact be the prince's official lieutenants in war, his Constable and

[1] Bentley, *Excerpta Historica*, pp. 214–15.

[2] Rymer, Vol. III, pt. I, p. 178.

[3] Rymer, Vol. III, pt. III, p. 90. Olivier du Guesclin had been taken by a Navarrese squire, Jean Coq, who was serving under the English captain of Cherbourg, cf. *Oeuvres de Froissart*, ed. Kervyn de Lettenhove, Tome IX, p. 96.

[4] E.g. case of Capdorat *v.* the Duke of Burgundy, heard before the Duke's council in 1448 (Bib. Nat., Collection de Bourgogne, Tome 23, p. 114vo).

[5] References to cases brought before the Parlement, many of which came to it direct, are too numerous to note: they are referred to throughout this book.

[6] E.g. case of Bertrand de la Popia *v.* Pedro Boil and Garcia de Oso, 1367, described in A. Gutteriez de Velasco 'Los Ingleses en Espana (Siglo XIV)' *Estudos de Edad Media de la Corona de Aragon*, 1950.

[7] E.g. case of Gaillart de Saliers *v.* Ingergier d'Amboise, heard before the Black Prince's council in 1367, and subsequently taken on appeal to Edward III, who appointed a commission to consider it (P.R.O., C61/81, m. 3).

Marshals. These men had permanent authority from the prince to try matters arising out of war by law of arms, and their courts would be open to those who wished to sue before them at any time in peace or war.

If he was a Frenchman seeking redress against an English captive, our knight's case would come before the Court of Chivalry of England, in which the Lord High Constable and the Earl Marshal presided as judges. It sat usually in the white chamber at Westminster, and we hear of its considering cases regularly at least from the middle years of Edward III onwards.[1] By the time of Henry IV enough business was coming before the court for it to be necessary, when the Constable was absent with the King, to depute other persons to hold his pleas in the normal place in his absence.[2] In France the corresponding Courts of the Constable and the Marshals of France were at the Table de Marbre in Paris, and we hear of cases being tried by them from the early years of the fourteenth century.[3] The Duke of Burgundy also had his Marshal, who tried cases arising out of war ex-officio,[4] and the Dukes of Anjou had their Marshal of Sicily.[5] John Chandos as Constable of Aquitaine tried military cases in the Black Prince's great appange in the brief period of its splendour.[6] John de Montfort had his Marshal of

[1] See G. D. Squibb, *The High Court of Chivalry* (Oxford, 1959), pp. 15–16.

[2] In 1405, when Henry was in the north and Bedford, the Constable, was with him, Thomas Arundel and Thomas Beaufort were deputed to hear cases in his court in his absence, cf. B. Mus., Add. MS. 9021, fo. 158.

[3] J. H. Mitchell, *The Court of the Connétable* (Yale University Press, 1947), pp. 7–8 and 13.

[4] Cf. case of Jean de Haplaincourt *v.* Jean and Gautier de Heusdam (January, 1454), brought before the Parlement on appeal from the Marshal of Burgundy (Arch. Nat., X¹a 4804, fo. 178 et seq.). Haplaincourt questioned the Marshal's jurisdiction; it was answered that he was a proper judge because the matter arose out of war and in Burgundy's dominions.

[5] Cf. case of Guillaume Boucher *v.* Jean Rougebec (July 1416), heard by the Parlement on appeal and arising out of a dispute in the Angevin host in Italy in (?) 1412 (Arch. Nat., X¹a 4791, fo. 119). The key sentence runs: 'pour ce que Harpedenne estoit Mareschal du Roy de Sicile et ce dependoit de la guerre furent mandez devant luy [les parties]'.

[6] Cf. Froissart's account of the complaints of soldiers of the free companies, assembling for the Castille expedition of 1367, against their French prisoners taken at Montauban, who refused to pay their ransoms on the ground that the free soldiers were excommunicate: 'si leur vint a grant contraire ceste ordinance dou Pape, et se complaindirent a monseigneur

Brittany,[1] while Charles the Bad of Navarre, typically, deputed military jurisdiction to a ferocious English *routier*, John Fotheringhay, who as his Marshal heard cases arising out of his wars in Normandy.[2]

The courts of these Constables and Marshals were permanent courts. Because they were permanent tribunals with settled jurisdiction, they were open to suitors who wished to bring cases at any time. But this does not mean that it was necessarily an easy matter for our knight to bring his complaint before such a court. Suppose him now an Englishman seeking redress against a Frenchman. In order to put his case he had got to cross the channel and travel through a foreign country, an expensive and probably dangerous journey. Before he went, he needed the king's permission to take up his suit, if he did not wish to make himself liable to the penalties of *praemunire* for pleading in an alien court. He might then need to purchase safe-conducts to travel in France, and he would almost certainly need to appoint proctors to put his case in proper legal form in the Court of the French Constable. And then there would be delays; his adversary would have to be summoned in the proper manner, and if he did not appear on the first summons, he must be given the normal delays before the case could be heard in his absence. Then the argument of the case itself might not be finished at the first hearing, and put off to a future date, or an enquiry be ordered. All this took time, and time always cost money, especially when one was a long way from home.

It might therefore be very much to our knight's advantage to bring his case, if he could, before some other judge who had jurisdiction in the matter, and whose court was less remote. Constables and Marshals were by no means the only persons who had jurisdiction over the law of arms. Royal lieutenants, acting as civil and military governors of provinces, nearly always

[1] Cf. the clause in the agreement between John de Montfort and Richard II in 1380, which states that in their combined hosts a Marshal of Brittany shall be associated with the Constable of the English host, to judge any quarrels over ransoms, etc. (Rymer, Vol. III, pt. III, p. 94).

[2] R. Delachenal, *Vie de Charles V* (Paris, 1909), Tome II, p. 6, n. 4.

Jehan Chandos qui estoit connestable d'Aquitainnes et regars pour droit d'armes sus tels besognes' (*Oeuvres de Froissart*, ed. Kervyn de Lettenhove, Tome VII, p. 140).

enjoyed similar powers. Such a man was the English Seneschal of Guienne. For a Gascon, whose case (let us say) arose out of the confused wars of the free companies in the south of France, he was the obvious person to refer to. He was nearer the scene of action than the Constable of England; and he would know a great deal more about local conditions, when and for what periods local truces had been taken, for instance, and what the standing of the combatants had been in any given siege or battle. Certainly he seems to have often tried military cases.[1] The French King's provincial lieutenants had similar powers;[2] we hear for instance of both the Marshal d'Audreham[3] and Jean d'Armagnac[4] hearing disputes as royal lieutenants in Languedoc. Another example of such jurisdiction would be that of the Scottish Warden of the Marches, to whose court cases arising in the border wars were referred.[5] In all these instances, of course, the jurisdiction of the lieutenant applied only within the area of his lieutenancy and in its frontiers. In this respect his jurisdiction was more limited than that of the king's Constable and Marshals, who were his lieutenants generally in all wars: but it was separate from theirs. Cases on appeal from the court of the Seneschal of Gascony did not go before the Constable of England as a higher military officer, but direct to the king's council. It was the same with appeals from the court of the

[1] See for example Edward III's order to the Seneschal to try the case of Ivo de Kerembars v. the Seigneur de l'Esparre 'secundum legem armorum' (Rymer, Vol. III, pt. I, pp. 143–4); see also the ransom cases considered by the Seneschal, e.g. Pons de Gordoun v. Arnald Amarys de Bergerac in 1359 (P.R.O., C61/70, m. 14), and Arnald Pellegrini v. Ademar de Ussello in 1361 (P.R.O., C61/72, m. 9).

[2] Cf. Bib. Nat., MS. Fr. 7492, fo. 5 (powers of John of Poitou in Languedoc, 1357); fo. 141 (powers of the Bishop of Beauvais, ibid., fifteenth century); fo. 187vo (powers of the Sieur des Cordes, ibid., 1482).

[3] E.g. Menard, *Histoire de Nîmes* (Paris, 1774–58), Tome II, Preuves no. 140 (prorogation by d'Audreham of a case arising 'ratione guerre sancte Spiritus'—the siege of Pont l'Esprit—until he can hear it in person, 13 October 1363).

[4] E.g. case of Jaques le Breton v. Louis de Cera, decided by a duel fought before Jean d'Armagnac in 1388 (Bib. Nat., Collection Doat, Tome 203, fo. 267 et seq.).

[5] The *Use of Merchis*, put in writing by the Warden's council in 1448, makes it clear that he had full jurisdiction over all cases under the law of arms, arising on the Scottish side of the March. (*Acts of the Parliament of Scotland*, Vol. I, Appendix IV, pp. 350–2.)

Captain of Calais, whose commission also was independent.[1]

If he was not satisfied with the justice he received in the court of the king's lieutenant, such appeal to the king and his council always lay, both for our knight and his opponent. Appeal would no doubt be a costly business. Nevertheless a good many appeals were brought, and they are in fact our only real guide to the number of disputes which did arise, for the records of the Constables' courts both in England and France have perished, as have those of all but a few isolated cases tried before provincial lieutenants. Even this picture, however, is very incomplete, for many other persons, besides those already mentioned, could in certain circumstances try cases under the law of arms. This posed a problem for plaintiffs such as our knight. It was most important for him to bring his case initially before the right court. If he did not, the defendant was always liable to complain that the court before which he had been summoned had no jurisdiction. This contention would at least need investigation, and that would mean further delays.

Our knight's ultimate decision as to where he should bring his case would depend largely on three considerations, the position of the person he was suing, the time at which he was suing him, and the nature of the redress he demanded. If he wanted redress of any sort, he had obviously got to apply to someone who could give it, which meant in the first place somebody who had authority over his opponent. The king's Constable or a provincial governor clearly had such authority. In addition, however, all military commanders had certain rights of justice over their own men *ex officio*. One hears of their holding and exercising such rights from the very first campaigns of the Hundred Years War on. Hugh Hastings, as commander of the English troops in Flanders in 1346,[2] was given power to try cases in which his own men were parties, and we learn of French captains trying cases in which their men were involved in the 1350s.[3] Probably these rights of justice have a much older

---

[1] Cf. the commissions of the council appointed to hear appeals from his court: e.g. C.P.R., 1405–8, pp. 113, 479; C.P.R., 1408–13, p. 97.

[2] P.R.O., C76/22, m. 36.

[3] See for example the case of Jaques Sermon, tried before the Captain of St. Jacques de Beuvron, February 1358 (Arch. Nat., JJ87, no. 25): see also p. 31, n. 4 *infra*.

ancestry than this. Certainly, however, they provided our knight with alternative authorities to whom he could turn for redress. From his point of view, the important questions were the extent of their powers and the kind of justice which they could give him.

A captain, naturally, could only hear disputes involving men under his own command and during the period of his office as commander. But within these limits his powers were very extensive. The dispute between Denis de Morbek and Bernard de Troye, as to which had captured John the Good at Poitiers, was not too high a matter for the Black Prince to consider under his powers as commander of the 1356 *chevauchée*[1] (it was only referred in the end to higher authorities[2] because the host which he had commanded broke up before the case was settled). Capital crimes were within a captain's jurisdiction; the count of Dammartin had no hesitation, after the battle of St. Jacques, about hanging in full armour a subordinate who had shown cowardice in the face of the enemy.[3] So also was treason.[4] What was much more important from our knight's point of view, disputes between his own soldiers and those of the enemy were equally within a captain's cognisance. The *Jouvencel* has two vivid descriptions of cases, in which claims to prisoners were lodged by Englishmen in a French captain's court. In one of these, moreover, in which the Englishman Estance the Herald appears to claim a man who has escaped from prison after giving his faith to his captor,[5] the case is, after due consideration, awarded against the Frenchman by judges of his own side. Clearly our knight had here at least a possible alternative authority from whom to seek justice against his prisoner. What, then, would be the advantages and disadvantages for him of choosing this line of action?

[1] *Oeuvres de Froissart*, ed. Kervyn de Lettenhove, Tome V, p. 468.

[2] According to Bernard de Troye's testament (ibid., Tome XVIII, p. 395), it was pending at his death before the council. It would seem that the Constable and Marshal had also considered the case, cf. Rymer, Vol. III, pt. I, p. 193.

[3] *Chronique Martinianne* (ed. P. Champion, Paris, 1907), p. 56.

[4] In 1359, for example, the captains of the Lombard company at Cloie did summary justice on traitors in the garrison, who had conspired to betray the fort to the English (Secousse, *Recueil de Pièces sur Charles II Roi de Navarre*, Paris, 1755, pp. 149–50).

[5] *Le Jouvencel*, ed. Lécestre and Favre, Tome II, p. 106 et seq., and p. 153. In the second of these two cases the Frenchman was ordered to return to his English captor, as his defence was inadequate.

In time of open war it was naturally extremely difficult to bring a case before the central courts of an adverse power. Occasionally someone did succeed in obtaining a hearing there, but it was rarely that they did so. If, therefore, our knight was suing a stranger for ransom and the war in which he took him was continuing, far and away his best policy was to apply to his commander for redress. There were, however, two disadvantages about doing so which he would have to consider. One was the danger obviously involved. Even if he did get a safe-conduct to come and state his case (which might be no easy matter), he was adventuring himself entirely into the power of his enemies. The judges who would hear him would be unlikely to be predisposed in his favour; and he would need to have a strong case and an honourable captain on the other side. Secondly, he could in any case only get limited redress by proceeding in this manner. A captain was not a powerful royal official, like a royal constable or provincial lieutenant; he was a mere military commander. This meant that he could only distrain a man in a military way.[1] He could seize his person, and hand him over to his captor or imprison him, or even execute him; he could impound his equipment (his horse and armour) or stop his wages. But he could not distrain his ordinary goods and chattels. If therefore our knight wanted to get the person of his prisoner returned to him or to see him punished for his default, he could sue him before his captain. If however, as was far more likely, what he wanted was money, he would do better to wait for the inevitable truce, and apply then to somebody who could distrain his opponent more effectively. The court of a royal constable or a provincial lieutenant could do what no captain's court could, put an arrest on a man's goods and so wring money from him. In this respect their justice was much more effective, because they had wider powers and could give more effective redress.

If however, our knight did choose to bring his case before a captain, it was of course entirely the captain's affair who then tried it. Often disputes were judged by the captain himself,

[1] Cf. the orders of Henry V and of Bedford delimiting the judicial powers of captains; the one in Rymer, IV, p. 24; and the other printed by Miss Rowe 'Discipline of the Norman Garrisons under Bedford', *E.H.R.*, Vol. 46 (1931), p. 204.

probably acting with his council (in this proceedings were like those in the permanent courts, where other persons often sat in judgment beside the king's Constable or lieutenant). In large hosts and major garrisons, however, officers were normally appointed to exercise all military jurisdiction; they were called constables and marshals, like the king's own lieutenants. Henry V in 1418 appointed his brother Clarence *constabularius exercitus* for his host in Normandy, to preside during pleasure in the *Curia Militaris* of his scattered army.[1] There is no question here of confusion with the office of Constable of England, since that was held at the time by the King's other brother, Bedford. As long before as 1356 Edward III had given identical powers to the constables of his host in France;[2] the appointment of such officials was a regular feature. On the French side, at least from the 1430s on, the powers of the marshals of France were limited to this sort of jurisdiction, over cases which arose while the host was still afoot.[3] For as long as a host was still in being, its commander or his officers had jurisdiction over the soldiers in it, and in the normal course tried their disputes.

A commander could, however, if he so wished, empanel a special court to try a case. When Le Mans fell to the English in 1425, so many quarrels arose over rights in prisoners that a special court martial had to be set up, under the presidency of Lord Scales, to deal with them.[4] When in 1367 the Marshal d'Audreham fell at Najera into the hands of the Black Prince,

[1] *Rotuli Normannie*, ed. T. D. Hardy (Record Commission, 1835), Vol. I, p. 316.

[2] Cf. B. Mus., Cotton MS. Titus C 1, fo. 50vo (Cotton's collections on the office of the Marshal): 'an order in ffraunce *anno* 1356 giveth "commissionem constabuli et marescalli personalium actionum inter eos qui capti bello fuerint" '.

[3] Cf. Bib. Nat., MS. Fr. 1983, fo. 37vo: 'item, si un debat vient entre gentilz hommes et autres les mareschaulx dient qu'ils en doivent cognoistre ou leur provost durant l'ost ... se l'ost estoit failly et le proces n'estoit commence devant les mareschaulx iceulx mareschaulx pourroient faire adjourner ceux qui leur auroient meffait devant monseigneur le connestable' (from a list of the rights of jurisdiction of the Constable, said to have been declared by Guillaume Le Cur, *président en Parlement*. He first appears as a *président* after Charles VII's return to Paris in 1436).

[4] The evidence for the appointment of this commission is the appeal against its sentence, taken to the Parlement in the case of Glasdale *v.* Talbot (Arch. Nat., X¹a 4795, fo. 324vo–5).

who himself wished to prefer a complaint against him for breach of parole, the Prince empanelled a court of twelve knights from among his host to judge the quarrel.[1] Similarly, John of Gaunt, commanding a host in 1373, and faced with a dispute over armorial bearings between Richard Le Scrope and 'Carmynau de Cornwall', put the matter before a court of seven knights of his own choosing.[2] In both these last cases, this manner of judging was chosen because delicate technical points in the law of arms were involved, and the commanders wanted expert opinion on them. Though they did not always observe its spirit, medieval soldiers were meticulous in their regard for the letter of their chivalrous code, and no one knew its detail better than experienced knights.

Hitherto we have been supposing that our knight had a strong *prima facie* case to put when he lodged his claim. But suppose that he had not, and that his case rested instead on his interpretation of some complicated point of military law—like the question discussed in the *Jouvencel*, as to who has the better right to a prisoner, the man who seized him by the right arm and took his gauntlet, or the man who first put his right hand into that of the fallen enemy.[3] Where a question such as this was involved, there was not much to choose between the various courts to which our man might have recourse; one soldier's view was in principle as good as another's. The whole problem would in fact be for him on a quite different footing. In the first place, what he would want in this case would not be redress in the normal sense, but a reliable decision in his favour as to what the law was. Secondly, he would presumably not be here pursuing a habitual defaulter, but a person with whom he had been in direct communication, and who had answered his demands for ransom, or whatever he was claiming, by pointing out that there was a potential flaw in his title. This man might or might not have further objections to raise later, but for the moment he was basing his opposition not on a matter of principle but on a disputed point of law.

[1] P. Lopez d'Ayala, *Cronicas de Los Rayes de Castilla*, Tome I, p. 459.

[2] Sir H. Nicolas, *The Scrope and Grosvenor Controversy*, Vol. I, pp. 49–50. 'Carmynau de Cornwall' probably means Carminow, a Cornishman.

[3] A case revolving round this point is discussed in the *Jouvencel*, ed. Lécestre and Favre, Tome I, p. 220.

Given that there was no international authority to whom they could appeal, the best option for two persons in this position was to refer their dispute to some arbiter whom they could both trust, and to agree to be bound by his decision. He would be asked to proceed on it as if it was a normal case in court, to hear the arguments of both sides, and to give a judgment. As the agreement of the parties to be mutually bound by his decision would almost certainly be validated by a notarial deed or a solemn oath in the presence of witnesses,[1] the successful one would have grounds for an ordinary civil action, if his opponent failed to act on the arbiter's award.

The object of arbitration in disputes under the law of arms was nearly always to obtain an expert opinion. Men resorted to it for this purpose much more often than in a search for equity. Hence the type of person to whom arbitration was normally referred. The dispute between Matthew Gournay and Johan de Lou on the one side, and Thomas Driffield and Johan de Bouch on the other, over the spoil taken at Arselay in 1359, was for instance referred to the decision of *chivalers et esquiers de valu*—in the event to William Felton, Robert Knollys and Michael Berkeley.[2] The dispute between Archambaud de Grailly and Florimont de l'Esparre, who claimed a half share in the ransom of Roger de Belfort as the brother-in-arms of his captor, Archambaud's father John, was referred in 1386 to a tribunal of four persons, two to be chosen by each side, and it was agreed that if they could not decide, it was to be judged by Gaston Phoebus of Foix.[3] In 1437 the dispute between Lord Scales and Galoby de Panassac, over the ransom of an English prisoner for whom Scales had stood surety to Galoby, was referred to the Marshal of France as arbiter.[4] In each of these

---

[1] For example, in the case of Matthew Gournay and others *v.* Thomas Driffield and others, referred to arbitration in 1359, the parties were 'jurrez aux Santes Evangiles notre seigneur' to abide by the arbitration (P.R.O., E101/68/4, no. 79): a long notarial deed lays down the conditions of arbitration in the case of Florimont de L'Esparre *v.* Archambaud de Grailly in 1386 (Bib. Nat., Collection Doat, Tome 203, fo. 40 et seq.).

[2] P.R.O., E101/68/4, no. 78.

[3] Bib. Nat., Collection Doat, *cit. sup.*

[4] Arch. Nat., X1a 69, fo. 141vo et seq. The case reached the Parlement, but had been commenced 'coram dilecto et fideli nostro Petro de Ruppeforti marescallo Francie *electo* judice et *assumpto* per partes infrascriptas'.

three cases complicated technical points in the law of arms were involved,[1] and the persons chosen to arbitrate were all the kind of men whose judgment in such a matter could be trusted. Felton and Knollys were soldiers of long experience and tried worth. Gaston Phoebus of Foix was a famous prince, whose court was thronged with soldiers and who was renowned for his knowledge and love of chivalry. And who could know the law of arms better than a marshal of France?

Over and above reference to arbiters on technical points of law, there is one further method by which cases under the law of arms were often judged, which has not so far been discussed. We have been taking it for granted that our knight wished to prosecute rights acquired against someone else in the course of a war. But suppose his case was entirely different, and what he wished to do was not to prosecute rights but to obtain damages, against a man who had despoiled him illegally or held him to ransom, when he was in some way immune from such action. In this situation he could, of course, proceed in any of the ways hitherto described, in just the same way as he could if he was seeking the benefit of rights which he claimed to be legal. Very likely, however, he would in this case be taking his stand on the ground that he had been taken or despoiled in time of truce. If this was so, and the truce still endured, the proper authority to judge the matter would be the commissioners or conservators of the truce in question.

Jurisdiction over truces was a very complicated matter, and we shall have to return to it again later. From our plaintiff's point of view, however, putting his case would mean appearing before an authority of one of two kinds. He might have to deal

---

[1] The issue in Gournay v. Driffield was whether Driffield and Johan de Bouch owed thirds of their spoil to Gournay and de Lou: this would depend on whether, at the capture of Arselay, the former were acting as lieutenants in the pay of the latter (see ch. IX *infra*). In the case of de l'Esparre v. de Grailly it revolved around the question of whether de l'Esparre was or was not fully quit of his obligations as a prisoner ('delivré de sa prison') to the Spanish, a point which could be highly complicated (see ch. X *infra*). De l'Esparre had agreed earlier that the main question, of his share in Belfort's ransom, should be postponed until he was so quit. In the Scales v. Panassac case, Scales was claiming that he was not bound for Cusac, the man he had pledged, because 'dictus Cusac subtili ingenio secundum jus armorum abire licite et impune potuerat'.

with a conservator appointed by his opponent's party to keep
the truce. The jurisdiction of such an official differed in no
important way from that of an ordinary military lieutenant
who had rights to distrain goods as well as persons. It was
limited in the same way, by the powers granted to him in his
commission (which normally included criminal jurisdiction
over breaches of the truce), and to cases which arose during
the truce and within the area for which he was appointed conservator. Appeal lay from him, either to the sovereign who
appointed him, or to some person or persons agreed in the
truce, possibly to a commission including members from both
sides. Before such a man, our plaintiff would proceed in very
much the same manner as he would if he were bringing his case
before a normal military court.

Conservators of truces however were not always subordinate
officials. An independent third party might be appointed to
superintend them, or it might be laid down that alleged
breaches of the truce should be referred to a commission with
members from both sides for judgment. Amadeus of Savoy was
for instance appointed conservator for both sides in a series of
truces taken by the Burgundians and the French between 1425
and 1435.[1] In the same way, representatives of the Council of
Basle judged breaches of certain truces between the Austrians
and the Burgundians in the early 1430s.[2] The advantage of
employing such third parties as conservators was of course the
improved prospect of impartial justice being done (ordinary
conservators were notoriously inefficient). A commission of both
sides secured the same result, and was sometimes employed as
an alternative. When for instance a truce was agreed in 1389
between the Count of Armagnac and the free companies led by
Ramonet de Sort, judges from both parties were appointed to
decide all outstanding and new quarrels between their soldiers.[3]

[1] Cf. Dom Plancher, *Histoire de Bourgogne*, Tome IV, Preuves nos. XXVII,
LXVII, etc.

[2] See, e.g. the letter of the Abbot of Vezelay to the Chancellor of Burgundy about the disputes to be raised before the Council's representatives
at Montbéliart, dated 1 June 1431 (Arch. dep. de la Cote d'Or, B11942,
no. 121). It is clear that proceedings were to be judicial as the Abbot states
that the Austrians have undertaken to produce certain Burgundian prisoners
on the day, who will plead their case 'ung chacun d'eulx pour tous eulx'.

[3] Bib. Nat., Collection Doat, Tome 203, fo. 282: 'Item, per la part

A year later, the same expedient was used in a truce between the Marmouset's official, Jean de Blaisy, and the free companies.[1] In the 1420s there were two truces between the English and Scots in which similar arrangements were made, referring cases to a commission of eight judges, four from each side.[2] But the most complicated effort of all in this pursuit of impartiality was certainly the arrangement of the Austro-Burgundian treaty of 1453. Here it was agreed that any disputes between persons of the two allegiances were to be sent before tribunals, each of five judges selected for the occasion, two to be chosen by the plaintiff from his party and three by the defendant. The opinion of a majority of the judges was to be decisive, provided this majority included members of both parties.[3] I do not know the details of any cases tried in this manner; one suspects however that on this occasion the quest for impartiality may have put any hope of final judgment out of court for ever.

From our plaintiff's point of view there were two important considerations to be duly noticed where a truce was supervised by a third party or an independent commission. In the first place he could not obtain redress from them direct, as he could from an ordinary conservator. Their title to jurisdiction was different; they had not been deputed to act in a subordinate capacity. Their position was much more like that of modern international courts, resting on the agreement of the powers involved to be bound internally and externally by their decisions.[4] They gave judgments, therefore, but they did not execute

[1] Cf. text of the agreement, printed in A. Jacotin, *Preuves de la Maison de Polignac* (Paris, 1898–1906), Tome IV, no. 707.

[2] Rymer, Vol. IV, pt. IV, p. 148 (truce of 1429); from a letter dated 12 March 1427 it seems that the same arrangements had been made in earlier truces (Nicolas, *Ordinances of the Privy Council*, Vol. III, p. 264).

[3] Plancher, *Histoire de Bourgogne*, Tome IV, Preuves no. CLXIV.

[4] Cf. the terms of the truce of 28 September 1424 between Burgundy and France, of which Amadeus of Savoy was conservator: 'et seront tenues les dites parties, leurs feaulx hommes, officiers et subgets, de obeir aux commandemens et cognoissances qui seront faites par mon dit Seigneur de Savoye ou son depute, et feront les amendes et reparations qui seront ordonnes par mon dit Seigneur ou son depute'. (Plancher, op. cit., Tome IV, Preuves no. XXXVII).

---

deldit Conte et yssiment per la part deldit Ramonet seran mes jutges per conoysse et jutgar totas mercas e rancunas d'una part et d'autra'.

them; and in order to obtain execution our plaintiff would have to refer to his adversary's officials, who were bound by the terms of the truce to implement the conservator's judgments.[1] Besides this, the jurisdiction of this kind of conservator was unusual in that it was a final jurisdiction. No appeal lay from him, because there was no one to appeal to. To quote from the treaty of 1453 between the Austrians and the Burgundians mentioned above: 'who-ever is in the wrong shall pay all damages and expenses ... without any means of redress or protest'.[2] This point is made still more clearly in the truce signed by Louis XI and Maximilian in 1478:

> ... the judgements and sentences of the said conservators ... shall be put to full execution, and the subjects of both parties shall be constrained to obey them, regardless of any protest or appeal which they may make, and there shall be no method of their obtaining any redress against them whatever.[3]

Our plaintiff would need to be very sure of his case if he was going to appear before men with such powers. It might well be in his interest, if he could, to settle his dispute out of court.

This more or less completes the list of authorities before whom cases under the law of arms were normally tried. There is however one matter which would be of very great importance to our knight or plaintiff, who wished to move a case under this law, which has not yet been mentioned. This is the form which legal proceedings would take in whatever court he chose to raise his complaint. Broadly speaking, there were two alternative ways of proceeding at his disposal, ordinary legal process and trial by battle. We must now therefore examine the factors which would decide the method to be followed in his particular case.

[1] For an example of this system's working, see the actions of the Council of Basle in supervising the Austro-Burgundian truce in 1431, to redress infringements by Humbert de la Roche, Count of Villers-Sexel. The complaint was referred to the Council by the Austrians (Plancher, op. cit., Tome IV, Preuves no. LXXXVI), and the matter taken up with Burgundy 'en esperance de reparation adigne avoir' (25 November 1431): on 27 November the Council ordered restitution, and informed Humbert by letter (ibid., no. LXXXVII); and at the same time wrote to the Duke of Burgundy's *bailli* of Amont, ordering him to distrain Humbert's goods if he did not comply (ibid., no. LXXXVIII).

[2] Plancher, op. cit., Tome IV, Preuves no. CLXIV.

[3] Ibid., no. CCLXXXVI.

Ordinary legal process could be of two kinds, summary or formal. Which procedure was followed depended largely on the nature of the case; our knight would know by which method his suit would be likely to be tried, but he would not himself have much choice in the matter. Summary procedure was always allowed in military cases,[1] and the power to do summary justice was mentioned often in, for instance, commissions to conservators of truces.[2] It was most usually employed, however, where cases were tried directly in the field. If our knight brought up his complaint a day or so after a battle, claiming perhaps that a fellow soldier was attempting to deprive him of a prisoner justly won, all that his commander would need to do would be to establish the facts concerning the man's capture and award the prize to him who had justice on his side. There would be nothing harsh or unjust about proceeding upon such a case *summarie et de plano, sine strepitu et figura justicie, solum facti veritate inspecta.* But suppose the case was not thus, but that it arose long after the battle, perhaps years later when memories of the scene were blurred and all sorts of transactions between captor and captive had complicated the issue. To judge summarily would then indeed be over-hasty: the case would demand formal proceeding and the careful weighing of intricate legal arguments. If these were the circumstances in which he brought his case, our knight would apply to a permanent court, and he could be pretty sure that it would be judged with the circumspection its complexity demanded.[3] Indeed, he would probably be less worried

[1] Cf. statement of the Marshal d'Audreham, in an order of 13 October 1363, to hold over a case till he could hear it in person: 'hujusmodi negotiam ad statum guerre pertinet, in quo procedi debet simpliciter et de plano, et sine longo strepitu judicii et figura' (Menard, *Histoire de Nîmes*, Tome II, Preuves no. 140).

[2] See, e.g. *John of Gaunt's Register* (Camden Soc.), Vol. II, p. 400, no. 1223 (powers given by Richard II to Gaunt to deal summarily with breaches of the truce on the Scottish March, 3 May 1381); Rymer, IV, pt. II, pp. 59–60 (agreement, 1 May 1414, of the proctors of the English and Scots that lists of complaints of breaches of the truce be compiled, and cases dealt with summarily at the next March day); Plancher, op. cit., Tome IV, Preuves no. LXXIX (summary powers of justice granted to conservators in a truce between the Duke of Burgundy and the Dauphin, 8 September 1431): ibid., no. CXXIV (similar powers given to conservators of the treaty between René of Anjou and the Duke of Burgundy, 7 February 1437).

[3] The proceedings of the Court of Chivalry illustrate this point aptly. In

about the prospect of a hasty judgment, than of the possibility of the case dragging on so long that all his profits would be wasted in litigation before it closed.

A case under the law of arms might also, we have said, be decided by a judicial duel. If he thought it to his advantage, our knight could throw down his gage of battle and demand his right to prove his case on his opponent's body in the lists. This would be a risky and adventurous step on his part, and it was not one to be lightly resorted to. The Church frowned on duels, and they were only permitted in certain circumstances. For a duel to be allowed it had to be shown that the honour of at least one party was at stake, that both parties were entitled by rank to fight one, and that there was not sufficient evidence to judge the case by ordinary process of law.[1] It might not be easy to satisfy all these requirements. When William Felton wished to fight a duel with Bertrand du Guesclin, whom he had accused of breaking his faith as a prisoner (to a third party), the long and learned arguments aimed to establish whether or not a duel lay took up more time than the entire argument of an average case at law, and it was finally decided that it did not.[2] Recourse to a duel did not by any means automatically dispense with the need for professional legal assistance, and there was a serious chance that a challenge to fight one would be disallowed.

Nevertheless duels were fought, and frequently.[3] The reasons

---

[1] See Philip the Hardy's ordinance concerning duels (*Black Book of the Admiralty*, R.S., Vol. I, p. 330 et seq.). Compare John of Legnano, *Tractatus*, caps. 175–6, and Bonet, *Tree of Battles*, pt. 4, ch. 130.

[2] Case of Felton v. Du Guesclin (Arch. Nat., X²a 7, fo. 145 et seq.).

[3] See for examples the numerous references in the Rolls of Scotland to duels, arising out of incidents in the border wars: e.g. *Rot. Scot.*, Vol. II, pp. 103, 104, 106, 129, 178, 205, 206, 207, 212.

---

a complex case, for example that of Hawley v. des Roches in 1402, which centred round alleged spoliation of merchants under safe-conduct, it proceeded with all formality, and the judges consulted carefully with doctors of civil law before giving sentence (P.R.O., C47/6/4, Roll 4). The court could however also try a case summarily; powers to do so are mentioned explicitly in the Constables' commissions in the time of Edward IV (see L. W. Vernon Harcourt, *His Grace the Steward and the Trial of Peers*, London, 1907, p. 392). This was not then an innovation; it had tried cases summarily long before, e.g. that of Henry Boynton, a traitor taken in arms in the field, in 1405 (see Keen, 'Treason Trials under the Law of Arms', *T.R.H.S.*, 5th Series, Vol. 12, 1962).

for this were probably twofold. Firstly, duels were popular
occasions, offering all the attractions of a tournament with the
spice of added risk. Chroniclers nearly always give details of
any duels of which they had heard.[1] That fought between
Jacques Breton and Louis de Cera, whom he claimed as his
prisoner before the Count of Armagnac in Rodez in 1386, was
clearly the great local event of the year in Rouergue.[2] But quite
apart from this aspect, the alternative of fighting a duel really
did, in certain circumstances, offer a man like our knight, who
had a right against another which he wished to prosecute, as
good a hope as any of obtaining justice. In a time of open war
and in a case where the facts were disputed, he was not likely
to get more than partial justice in the court of a hostile captain,
even if he could get a safe-conduct to appear there and state his
case. Great as its risks were, a duel gave him an even chance of
success, and his challenge would at least ensure his case was
heard. Its wording solemnly proclaimed his opponent a traitor
to his faith, impugning his honour as a knight and a Christian.
After this, the enemy were very unlikely to refuse him a safe-
conduct to come and take up his challenge, for they could
hardly deny a soldier in their own service the chance to clear
his reputation of blame.

At this point the outline of some sort of system of deciding
cases under the law of arms seems to be emerging. Given the
details of his case, we should now be able to say where our
knight would be most likely to bring it, and how and by whom
it would mostly likely be tried. In deciding where to institute
proceedings, he would consider in the first place the position
of the man he wished to prosecute. Whoever he appealed to, it
must be to somebody whose authority could bind his opponent,
or to some arbiter whose decision this opponent had agreed to
observe. In the second place, the time at which our knight

---

[1] See for example the accounts of duels fought between Perrot de Lignaige
and the Sire de Montravel, before the latter's captain, Louis de Bourbon,
during the siege of La Roche Sennadoire (*Chronique du Bon Duc Loys de
Bombon*, ed. A-M. Chazaud, Soc. de l'histoire de France, 1876, pp. 98-9);
and between Guillaume Barillet and John Carnicon (? Carmion) before
Charles VI at St Martin des Champs in 1409 (Monstrelet, *Chronique* ed.
L. Douet d'Arq, Tome II, p. 5). Both these duels were fought over breach
of faith.

[2] See Bib. Nat., Collection Doat, Tome 203, fo. 267 et seq.

brought up his complaint would influence the matter. If he brought his case in time of open war against a man serving on the other side, he would apply to his opponent's commander, who had jurisdiction of his person. If the case was brought during a truce or in time of peace, the man in question might not have a commander; therefore our knight would have to present his case before some judge who had a settled jurisdiction which entitled him to consider military cases. He could apply to his opponent's sovereign, or to his Constable, or to some provincial governor; which he chose would depend very much on his own judgment and convenience. If however, it was not only a time of truce, but also the basis of his complaint was an offence against the truce in question, then he would apply to the conservator of truces, whoever that was. In the third place, our knight would have to take into account the kind of redress he wanted. If he wanted ransom money or damages, it was no good applying to a field commander, unless the sum was very small indeed. Instead, he would have to apply to some court which could put an arrest on his opponent's goods If he wanted to distrain a man by his lands he might have to take his case further still. The Constable of England could not distrain a man's freehold, because it was protected by the common law and his was not a common law court.[1] In this case our plaintiff would have no alternative but to bring his case before the King's council. He could also bring his case before the King's council on appeal, for in every case appeal lay from the lower courts to the higher, from a court in the field to the court of the Constable or some provincial lieutenant, from his court to that of the sovereign. The only persons from whose judgment he could not appeal were arbiters whose decision he had agreed to accept as final, and independent conservators of truces.

How his case would be tried would depend largely on its nature. If it was tried in the field and revolved about a matter of fact, it would probably be tried summarily. If it arose long afterwards, and the legal validity of documents and actions was involved, it would be tried formally, with all the usual paraphernalia of argument and legal procedure before a carefully weighed judgment was delivered. If a technical point of chivalrous law was involved, expert opinion would probably

[1] See *Rot. Parl.*, iii, p. 473.

43

be consulted; either the case would be tried before a court of knights, or experienced knights associated with the judges to advise them on their decision. If the honour of a party was at stake and the facts of the case could not be established, a duel might be fought to decide the issue. Very often duels were fought before captains, but they could equally well be fought before the sovereign, or his Constable or lieutenant, or a chosen arbiter. Again the matter would rest largely on individual choice.

It may at this point sound as if the administration of the law of arms, both as regards the courts to which cases were referred and the manner of proceeding in them, was relatively comprehensible and systematic. The chaotic anomalies which arose in practice show that this picture is misleading. It leaves too many problems unsolved. What for instance was the Parlement of Paris to do when it found itself faced in 1364 with a claim to outstanding local ransoms, which was based on the terms of the will of Henry of Lancaster, a document drawn up by aliens in a foreign country in accordance with the rules of a foreign law?[1] How was it that the court of the Constable of England in 1446 managed to find itself executing a sentence passed in the court of a marshal of France?[2] How was it that a definition of case law given by a court martial assembled by the Black Prince in Spain came twenty years later to be quoted as a definitive ruling in the Parlement of Paris?[3] There are so many puzzling anomalies like these that they cannot be dismissed as mere eccentricities. They make it clear there are still a good many questions to be asked and answered before we can claim to understand how the law of arms was applied in practice.

[1] Case of Thomas de Uvedale v. Pierre Tournebu and others. The French defendants questioned whether Uvedale could claim legally to collect local ransoms owed to Henry of Lancaster, who was dead and whose will and testament 'sub sigillis incognitis et extra regnum erant confecte' (Arch. Nat., X¹a 21, fo. 73).

[2] B. Mus., Add. MS. 9021, fo. 222.

[3] See ch. IV infra.

# IV

# THE AUTHORITY OF
# MILITARY COURTS

THE problem behind most of these eccentric cases just mentioned is the same. It is the problem of the judges' title to jurisdiction. The reason why this problem arises at this point, is that so far we have been looking at things solely from the point of view of the litigant. It has also been assumed that, probably, this litigant's action would be a civil one, for payment of a ransom or for restitution of goods plundered unlawfully. In these circumstances, no real problem arose over jurisdiction; a plaintiff in such a case would naturally apply to the defendant's lord, or his officers, since only they could give him redress. But the law of arms did not only apply in civil actions such as these; it governed also questions of military discipline, and matters of honour. It is with regard to these that the thorniest difficulties arise, especially where, as on occasion happened, military courts tried soldiers of enemy allegiance for criminal offences. Their right to do this is not easy to explain. In order to make the problems involved clearer, it may be useful to quote some examples.

For this purpose two cases may be selected which seem to be in certain ways particularly relevant. The first of these is the trial of Walter de Selby in 1346. In that year, Walter was captain of the town of Liddell for the English, and he was captured when it was stormed by the Scots. He surrendered himself, it is said 'to be kept for ransom', and he was therefore allowed quarter 'according to the rules which the victors customarily observe in the wars against the French and the Scots'.[1] Nevertheless, David of Scotland had him put to death for treason. It is not easy to see, in the first place, how the King of Scots could have had any right to try the treason of a native-born Englishman. The comment of Geoffrey Le Baker on the affair makes it still more puzzling: 'I have never heard it said of this knight,' he writes, 'that he had ever committed treason against the King of Scots or any Scotsman.'[2] How could an Englishman have ever committed treason against a Scottish king, let alone against some individual Scotsman?

It is a pity that the precise charge against Walter is nowhere mentioned. In the second case, however, this is known, and it is significant. This is the case of Jean d'Angennes, a Frenchman who was sentenced to death by Henry V in 1418. Jean had been one of the French captains in Cherbourg, which town was surrendered to Humphrey of Gloucester, after the English had lain before it for several months, and when relief was clearly not forthcoming.[3] The story goes that it was Jean d'Angennes who negotiated this surrender, and that the English gave him money for his part in it. They also gave him a safe-conduct to travel back to the land of his own allegiance. He made his way to Rouen, and he was still there when that town too fell to the English. His safe-conduct was still valid, and, as far as is known, he had not broken it by taking arms against the English. As soon as it expired, however, he was put on trial by Henry V, 'because he had taken money for the surrender of Cherbourg when it was still well stuffed with supplies and artillery'.[4] On these grounds he was convicted and executed as a traitor.

[1] *Chronicon Galfridi Le Baker*, ed. E. Maunde Thompson (Oxford, 1886), p. 86.

[2] Ibid, p. 87; compare *Lanercrost Chronicle* (Bannatyne Club, 1839), p. 345. Le Baker's details are not entirely accurate, as he states that both Walter's sons were also put to death, which is incorrect (see Maunde Thompson's notes, p. 264); thus the Lanercrost confirmation of the main point is valuable.

[3] For the terms of surrender, see Rymer, Vol. IV, pt. III, p. 64.

[4] Waurin, *Chroniques*, R.S., Vol. II, p. 244; Monstrelet, *Chronique*, ed. L. Douet d'Arq, Tome III, p. 243. Both these chronicles call d'Angennes the captain of the town, but this appears to be incorrect, as Jean Piquet is styled captain in the terms for surrender in Rymer, *cit. sup.* The traitor's exact name is also in some doubt; Monstrelet calls him Jean d'Angennes (followed by Wylie and Waugh, *Henry V*, Vol. III, p. 110), and Waurin

There is nothing remarkable about this charge. As we shall
see later, to surrender a town while it was still supplied and
armed was generally accounted a treason by law of arms.[1] It is
the judge, not the charge, that surprises. For how could Henry
V have had any right to punish a man for a treason, committed
against his own capital adversary, and by which he himself was
the gainer? It would certainly be amazing today if an English
court claimed the right to try, say, a Russian citizen who was
guilty of betraying Soviet secrets to the British, but this would
be on a par with what Henry did. What is more, contemporaries
accepted his action as legal, and even applauded it.[2] The decision in this very case was quoted as sound legal precedent by
Mowbray when, in 1453, he charged the Duke of Somerset with
treason,[3] because he had surrendered Caen and other towns to
the French without enduring formal siege.[4] No one at the time,
clearly, questioned Henry's right to do what he did.

The implication of these two cases seems to be clear. It is
that military tribunals at least claimed cognisance of the
offences not only of soldiers of their own side, but of soldiers
generally, even those of the enemy. This is a very striking
claim, but it alone will explain how Henry V could try Jean
d'Angennes, or David of Scotland Walter de Selby (though

[1] See ch. VIII *infra*.

[2] Waurin says that the French were very joyous when they heard of the
sentence, 'pour ce que par convoitise de pecune, il (d'Angennes) avoit ainsi
vendu la dite place au grand préjudice du Roy de France'. (*Chroniques*, R.S.,
Vol. II, p. 245).

[3] *Paston Letters*, No. 191 (ed. Gairdner, London, 1872, Vol. I, pp. 260–1).
Mowbray declared that 'it hath be seen in many royaumes and lordshyps
that for the loss of touns and castells wythoute sege, the capitaynes that hav
lost theym han be dede and behedede, and her godes lost; as in Fraunce one
that lost Chyrborough'. This can only refer to d'Angennes. Fenn noted it as
part of a speech of Mowbray in the Lords; but the charge is in the form of a
signed bill, and more likely was put forward as a petition to the Council.

[4] Blondel says that Somerset insisted on a long delay before the final
surrender of Caen for fear that this charge would be raised: 'ne per suam
ignaviam, verum per subidii armorum subtractionem, ut defectu suc-
currentium, non suo, tam potentem villam, validum castrum et arcem
ornatissimum ab Anglicis perdidisse, laesae majestatis accusetur'. (Blondel,
*De Reductione Normannie*, R.S., 1863, p. 223).

---

Jehan de Jennes; but the treaty is sealed, among others by Nicolas de
Gennes. This is presumably the man.

here there is too the additional problem of how Walter could have committed treason against the Scots). The next step, therefore, must be to see whether any legal basis can be found for a claim to such remarkable powers. Two further cases, both in their time *causes célèbres*, seem to throw some light on this matter, and they thus demand examination in detail.

The one which shall be considered first is the famous trial of the Seigneur de Barbasan, once again before Henry V, on the charge that he had been implicated in the murder of John the Fearless. Barbasan was by no means the only man tried for this.[1] Philip the Good had taken it as a charge on his honour to avenge his father's death, and Charles VI had declared all those privy to the murder guilty of *lèse-majesté*.[2] The feud was pursued relentlessly, and as Barbasan had been one of the Dauphin's chief councillors, it was virtually certain that if he fell into enemy hands, he would be put on trial. In 1420 he was captain of Melun when it was besieged by the English. After a fierce resistance, during which he had personally fought with Henry V in a mine under the town walls, he was forced to surrender, and was duly charged.[3]

Details of his trial are recorded in a single chronicle only, the English life of King Henry V. Its author learnt them from the Earl of Ormond,[4] and he tells us what otherwise we would not know, that Barbasan was actually condemned to death, but was spared because he appealed successfully against this judgment. 'He appealed' we are told

> from the judgement of the king to the judgement of the officers of arms, and that alleged to be lawful cause of his appeal, that no man having his brother-in-arms at his possession and at his will ought not to put him to death for any displeasure or occasion, and that he was brother-in-arms to the king by arms; and ap-

[1] The Seigneur de Guitry, for example, was charged with complicity in the murder, when he was taken at the fall of Montereau, but was acquitted (Waurin, *Chroniques*, R.S., Vol. II, p. 321).

[2] Plancher, *Histoire de Bourgogne*, Tome III, Preuves, no. CCCX.

[3] Even the dead were not spared. The corpse of the Count of Narbonne, killed at Verneuil, was quartered and hung because of his part in the murder (Waurin, *Chroniques*, Vol. III, p. 117).

[4] For a detailed analysis of Ormond's contributions to this chronicle, see Kingsford's introduction thereto (C. L. Kingsford, *The First English Life of King Henry V*, p. xvi et seq.).

proved that he had fought with the king hand to hand in the mine as is aforesaid; which battle was held by the heralds of arms in like strength as if he had fought with the king body to body within the lists. And his appeal was by them for that cause approved, and they judged that by law of arms they might not put him to death, wherefore he was adjudged by the king to perpetual imprisonment.[1]

On all the points where Ormond's story might be questioned, it seems to stand up to tests. Chastellain too tells of the encounter between the king and Barbasan in the mine.[2] Titus Livius mentions the trial, though he gives no details,[3] and Barbasan certainly was imprisoned; he was found at Château Gaillard nine years later when the French recaptured it, 'enclosed and environed' in a cage of iron in one of the dungeons.[4] It is further clear that fighting in a mine did have a special significance according to the laws of chivalry. Two other stories are in fact strikingly similar to this one. One is Froissart's tale of how, at the siege of Limoges, John of Gaunt fought hand to hand with Jean de Villemur in a mine.[5] When the city was stormed, this Jean was one of the three knights to whom Gaunt granted quarter, in spite of the Black Prince's order that none should be spared.[6] The other is the story of how, at the siege of Verteuil, Louis de Bourbon fought incognito with the captain of the town, Regnault de Montferrand, in a mine. At last, struck with admiration at the courage of his opponent, Louis asked his name and gave his own. Regnault, a mere soldier, was so overcome by the honour which the duke had done him by fighting him body to body, that he immediately surrendered the town on the sole condition of receiving knighthood at his opponent's hands.[7] The final point in the Ormond story, that no man having his brother-in-arms at his will might put him to

[1] Ibid., p. 170.

[2] Chastellain, *Chronique du Duc Philippe*, ed. J. A. C. Buchon (*Choix des Chroniques et Mémoires sur l'histoire de France*, 1837), p. 53.

[3] Titus Livius, *Vita Henrici Quinti*, ed. T. Hearne, pp. 89–90.

[4] Kingsford, *First English Life of King Henry V*, p. 171.

[5] *Chronique des Quatre Premiers Valois*, ed. S. Luce (Soc. de l'histoire de France, 1872), p. 209.

[6] Froissart, *Chronique*, ed. S. Luce (Soc. de l'histoire de France, 1878), Tome VII, p. 251.

[7] *Chronique du Bon Duc Louis de Bourbon*, ed. A-M. Chazaud, pp. 151–2.

death, can also be confirmed. Normally such a man was indeed obliged not only to help his brother pay his ransom if he was captured,[1] but also, if they were serving on opposite sides and he took him himself, to set him free without ransom.[2]

Thus confirmed, Ormond's account assumes great significance. For it shows that in a matter tantamount to a war-crime (Titus Livius describes the murder of John the Fearless as *contra fidem et jus gentium*)[3] appeal lay from the judgment of the sovereign who was claiming the right to try the case. The nature of the appeal is also striking, for it was not an appeal to equity, to the natural moral law whose authority was higher than that of sovereigns' laws. It was an appeal based on a technical point in the rules of honour. The men appealed to were the heralds, members of an international order, and the acknowledged experts in the lore of chivalry,[4] the rules, that is, of the international order of knighthood. They gave their verdict according to the law of arms, which was binding on Henry V not as a prince but as a knight and a soldier. One must not, of course, confound the heralds who on this occasion gave a judgment with a final court of appeal. Such a court did not exist. But since the law of arms was founded in the *jus gentium*, which even a prince could not lawfully flout, the opinion of those expert in it was binding on any man who bore arms, no matter what his status. It was the law, and not any man or any court, which was truly sovereign.

The details of the second case which has been mentioned enable one to take these conclusions a little further. This was the already mentioned dispute between the Black Prince and the Marshal d'Audreham. The facts of the affair were as follows.[5] At the battle of Poitiers, d'Audreham was taken prisoner

---

[1] See Keen, 'Brotherhood in Arms', *History*, Vol. XLVII (1962), p. 9.

[2] Cf. Bartholomew of Saliceto, *Super VIII Cod:* Tit. 51, l. 2.

[3] Titus Livius, *Vita Henrici Quinti*, ed. Hearne, p. 78.

[4] Cf. the words of Dame Prudence to the heralds in the *Debat des Heraults de France et d'Angleterre*: 'Beaux Sires, vous avez ung tel office que toutes nobles doibvent amer et priser. Car a vos rapports et relations les Roys, les Dames, les Princes et autres grans Seigneurs jugent des honneurs mondains.' (Ed. L. Pannier & P. Meyer, Paris, 1877, p. 1.)

[5] All the details of this case given here are taken from the chronicle of P. Lopez d'Ayala, the only one to give a full and accurate account (P. Lopez d'Ayala, *Cronicas de Los Reyes de Castilla*, Madrid, 1779–80, Vol. I, pp. 458–61).

by the Black Prince, and when his ransom was fixed, he gave his promise to be a loyal prisoner, and not to arm himself against the Prince or the King of England until the ransom was paid, unless it were in the company of the King of France or one of the princes of the Fleur de Lys.[1] At Najera in 1367 d'Audreham was armed in the company of Henry of Trastamare and Du Guesclin against the Black Prince, and in the rout of their forces fell once more a prisoner into English hands. The Prince, seeing that the Marshal's ransom was still not fully paid, charged him with treason, because 'he was false to his faith and perjured upon it, since he had not fulfilled what he promised on his honour in this matter'. The Marshal asked leave to defend himself against the charge, and the Prince agreed that their case should be tried by a court of twelve knights, chosen from among his host. Since 'this was a matter of knights and of war',[2] the Marshal, it was said, could speak freely before such a court, notwithstanding the Prince's high estate.

The point here is clear. Since this was a matter arising out of war, the Prince and the Marshal were equally bound by the laws of knighthood before a court of knights (though we must note that it was the Prince who empanelled the court; this was not a case of arbitration, but a criminal trial). The arguments brought before the court were technical ones about the rules of honour. The Prince's case was straightforward; the Marshal had broken his faith as a prisoner, given upon his honour as a knight, by arming himself in the company of Henry of Trastamare,

---

[1] E. Molinier, in his *Etude sur la Vie d'Arnoul d'Audreham* (Paris, 1883, p. 181), suggests that this agreement was void in 1367, since d'Audreham was one of the hostages for John the Good, and under the Brétigny terms these hostages were to be quit of their own ransoms, *unless* they had made definite agreements for their payment before 3 May 1360 (cf. Rymer, Vol. III, pt. II, p. 4; item no. 15). He therefore questions Ayala's reliability. But it is clear from a letter of d'Audreham to the Estates of Languedoc, quoted by Molinier himself (op. cit., p. 77, n. 1) that the Marshal had made a definite agreement: 'pour aucunes haines que les Anglois et Gascons m'avoient, j'ay este mis a greigneur finance que en aucune maniere je ne pourroye payer'. Molinier dates the letter, which mentions no year, to 23 February 1360, others to 23 February 1357; in either case, it is clear that a definite agreement had been made before 3 May 1360, so that the clause in the Brétigny treaty discharging hostages from the ransoms would not have operated for him.

[2] 'Este era feche de Caballeros et de guerra' (Ayala, op. cit., p. 460).

who was not of the line of the Fleur de Lys, and when his ransom was not yet fully paid. The Marshal did not deny the Prince's facts. He claimed, however, that he had not armed himself against the Prince as a public person, since the Prince was not the 'head of the war', but had entered it as a captain and at the wages of Pedro of Castile. The Prince therefore had been present at the battle as Edward Plantagenet, a private person, and the Marshal had armed himself against this Edward's master, Don Pedro, not against the Prince. Thus he claimed to be free of the charge on his honour. The twelve knights acquitted him on these grounds, and we are told that all, the Prince included, were rejoiced that such a noble knight had thus escaped the sentence of death, which, if proved, his treason would have merited.

Judging by the formal language of his account, it looks as if Ayala, the Spanish chronicler who described the trial, must have had before him some sort of official account of it. Several important points seem to emerge from his story. The first is, as has been said, that the case was treated as a matter 'of knights and of war', and that in these circumstances the Prince and the Marshal had equal standing before a military court. The second is that the case was taken as constituting a legal precedent, for henceforward, says Ayala, 'all cases were judged in accordance with this sentence wherever there was war'.[1] This is a striking remark; it shows that the ruling of a court of knights on a matter governed by the law of arms was valid not in one host only, or in one kingdom or for one campaign, but wherever knights were going about their military profession. This was in fact accepted even by the civil lawyers: Paris of Pozzo, for example, quoted the ruling of a court of knights, which judged the case of Robert of St. Severino, as definitive with regard to certain obligations of a captor to his prisoner [2] This very ruling of the twelve knights of the Black Prince's host was, indeed, quoted in the Parlement of Paris twenty-three years later. Garcia

[1] 'e por esta sentencia se libraban despues qualesquier pleytos semejantes deste en los partidas do avia guerra' (ibid., pp. 460–1).

[2] Paris of Pozzo, *De Re Militari*, Lib. IX, cap. 2 (Zilletus, *Tractatus Juris Universi*, fo. 421vo). In cap. 6 it is made clear that the judgment was by a court of soldiers on campaign: 'ita alias fuit judicatum, in persona illustris domini Roberti de Sancto Severino, in castris per capitaneos, milites, et conducterios'. (Zilletus, fo. 422vo.)

Raimond d'Aubeterre, an ex-mercenary, was suing the Count de Longueville, Bertrand du Guesclin's heir, for the repayment of loans made to Bertrand, when both were serving Henry of Trastamare in Spain.[1] Garcia had sworn to serve Du Guesclin in Henry's cause, but he had left him when summoned by the Black Prince, his sovereign, who had joined the other side. The Count alleged that for this 'treason' to Bertrand, all debts owing to Garcia were confiscate. Garcia could not claim that the Prince's summons took precedence over his oath to Bertrand, he said, because in this war the Prince had fought as a private person: 'le prince estoit soudoier du Roy Pietre, si [Garcia] ne faisoit point de son chief le mandement'.[2]

The other really striking point about the dispute between the Black Prince and d'Audreham is the nature of the charge against the Marshal. Essentially, the case revolved around a private agreement between two knights, for the payment of a ransom. Yet the charge was treason, and, if pressed home, would according to Ayala have involved the death penalty. Clearly d'Audreham's crime cannot have been the public crime of *lèse-majesté*, since he was not of the Prince's allegiance. The treason was not to the Marshal's liege lord and sovereign, but rather to his faith and his knighthood. The second item is here important, since breach of faith alone would have been straightforward perjury and triable in the church courts; it was the breach of a chivalrous obligation which brought the case within the view of military authorities. Though no public allegiance was betrayed, the rules and obligations of the military calling appeared to have been, and this could constitute a treason every whit as damnable as the crime of *lèse-majesté*.

The implications of this case and of the trial of Barbasan before Henry V are thus the same. War was fought by knights, and in war the rules of honour applied universally, binding princes and men at arms equally. Offences against these rules could therefore be tried by anyone who had a right to try the offences of soldiers, whatever the offender's allegiance. This resolves many of the problems presented by the anomalous cases discussed at the beginning of this chapter. There was no

[1] The details of the case are printed from the Parlement registers by Molinier, op. cit., Preuves nos. XCIII–XCVI.

[2] Ibid., Preuve no. XCV (plaidoirie of 16 January 1391).

reason why, for instance, an Englishman should not have been found guilty of treason towards the King of Scots, or some Scotsman, though this treason would not, of course, have been a crime against the state. Nor was there any reason why Henry V, as a knight obliged to uphold the honour of his calling, should not have tried and condemned one who, by selling a fortress to his enemies, had committed treason not only to the King of France but also to the faith of knighthood.

This leaves only one major problem unresolved, how the right of a prince, or his officers, to try crimes against military law committed by those who were not his subjects nor in his service, could be justified in legal theory. In order to clarify this point, it is necessary to examine the matter of treason to the faith of knighthood a little further, for it was not only in exceptional cases, such as those which have been so far under discussion, that the charge was brought.

The essence of this treason was the breach of a solemn oath, made to a particular person. This reflects an older, more feudal idea of treason than the public crime of *lèse-majesté*, as defined in Roman Law. According to this definition, the breach of any solemn personal oath could be regarded as treason of a sort; hence the breach of any promise made on a soldier's honour could be a treason to his knighthood This was the view in fact adopted. Where persons guilty of ordinary treason to their sovereigns were convicted in military courts, their sentences accordingly imposed not only the ordinary capital penalty for this crime, but also degradation from all knightly honours. Thus Andrew de Harclay in 1323 was sentenced to have his sword broken and his gilt spurs, the insignia of knighthood, hacked from his heels:[1] Ralph Grey in 1464 was sentenced by the Constable of England to be led to execution in a coat of his arms reversed;[2] and Lord Audley, convicted of treason in the Court of Chivalry in 1497, was led to death with 'a coat armour of paper on him all to torn'[3] Abroad, the chapter of the Golden

[1] *The Brut*, ed. F. W. D. Brie (*E.E.T.S.*, 1906), Vol. I, p. 227.
[2] The sentence is printed in *Warkworth's Chronicle*, ed. J. A. Halliwell (Camden Soc., 1839), notes, pp. 36–9.
[3] *Chronicles of London*, ed. C. L. Kingsford (Oxford, 1905), p. 216. See also L. W. Vernon Harcourt, *His Grace the Steward and the Trial of Peers*, pp. 414–15.

Fleece condemned Jacques de Crèvecoeur to the same penalties of dishonour for treason to its sovereign, the Duke of Burgundy, and they would have passed sentence of death too, if he had not been safe in the service of Burgundy's enemy, Louis XI.[1]

Significantly, this same procedure of exhibiting a man's arms reversed or broken could also be followed when a soldier was charged with treason to his knighthood, because he had failed to pay a promised ransom.[2] Essentially, this charge was similar to an ordinary charge of treason against a soldier, because it too involved the breach of a solemn promise made on his honour. The right of a captor to dishonour a man in this way, if he defaulted, was often mentioned in letters of obligation to pay a ransom; the prisoner agreed in such case to be held a traitor, false and perjured on his faith, in every court and country in Christendom.[3] This stigma of disgrace was thus universal, because the order of knighthood in Christendom was a single universal order. In order to dishonour a man lawfully, however, official permission was required. Here a most important point emerges. For the authority usually accepted was the license of the *plaintiff's* sovereign or of his lieutenant in war.[4] When, for instance, Galoby de Panassac wished to dishonour Lord Scales, for failing in his obligations as the pledge of a prisoner, it was to the King of France, Charles VII, and to his Constable that he applied for leave to do so.[5] Thus the Constable of France could apparently give a decision against an

---

[1] Baron de Reiffenberg, *Histoire de l'Ordre de La Toison d'Or* (Brussels, 1830), pp. 123–4.

[2] For examples, see ch. X *infra*.

[3] See for instance the clause in the agreement of the sureties of the Seigneur de Derval, 7 July 1358, with Edward III: 'et voulons et grantons aussi se riens soit fait au contraire de cestes choses avanct dites . . . que lors nous soions tenuz faux, parjurs, de foy menties en touz lieux et devant tous personnes, et sur ce audience nous soit denie partout' (Rymer, Vol. III, pt. I, p. 171). Compare the obligations agreed by the Court of Vendosme, 1417 (Rymer, Vol. IV, pt. II, p. 196), and by Artus de Richemont (Rymer, Vol. IV, pt. III, p. 112).

[4] Cf. statement in the case of des Termes *v.* Chateauvillain, July 1441: 'par raison et par l'usage de guerre ils ne doivent proceder a deshonnoirement . . . sans autorite de souverain ou du seigneur' (Arch. Nat., X¹a 4798, fo. 376vo). Chateauvillain was claiming that des Termes' reversal of his arms was illegal for this reason.

[5] Cf. statement in the case of Pannassac *v.* Scales (1437): 'dictus actor

Englishman in a matter of honour, though he clearly could not, as a result of a civil action, put an arrest on his goods (as he could for instance on those of a French soldier).

What this seems to imply is that the military officers of a sovereign, when they considered cases under the law of arms, acted in a kind of dual capacity. The very name of the court of the Constable of England confirms this suggestion: it was the Court of Chivalry, at once a court of knighthood and honour, and the court of the highest military officer in the realm. The association of experienced knights with the professional judges of the French Parlement, in cases where judgment involved rulings on technical points of military law,[1] would seem to have been aimed to secure, in these circumstances, the same sort of double authority. The Parlement had full power to judge men as subjects of the King of France, but only soldiers could adequately judge their conduct as members of the profession of arms.

It is, of course, much easier to explain a military court's title to the one jurisdiction, over soldiers under allegiance, than to the other, over matters of 'knights and war' generally. But the difficulty here is only apparent. It arises out of the difference between the modern point of view which thinks of a soldier as a member of a specific military force, and the point of view of a man like Bonet, who thought of him as a member of a Christian profession. Where we therefore assume the chief function of military courts to be the enforcement of discipline internally in armies, he and his contemporaries regarded as their first duty the enforcement of the 'discipline of chivalry'. For them constables and marshals, whom they could see everywhere judging cases by military law, were the lineal descendants of the Roman

---

[1] For example, they were called in in the cases of the Seneschal of Hainault v. Rifflart of Flanders, 1367 (Arch. Nat., X²a 7, fo. 336 et seq.), and of Tyrel v. Rayneval (Arch. Net., X¹a 22, fo. 259 et seq.). Both these cases involved technical points about breach of a prisoner's parole, in the one case by Rifflart himself, in the other by Simon Burley.

---

(Pannassac), ut contra defensoris honorem, prout de jure armorum fieri decebat, prosequi posset, nobis necnon constabulario nostro et magno consilio nostris certam supplicationem porrexerat, quod per nos concessum eidem extiterat' (Arch. Nat., X¹a 69, fo. 141 et seq.).

*magistri militum.*[1] Equally, they regarded chivalry as in origin a Roman institution. They believed that it was 'the valour and warlike skill of the votaries of chivalry' which had won the Romans the *imperium* of the world.[2] The key to the triumphs of Henry V, the conqueror *par excellence* of the Hundred Years War was his strict adherence to Roman standards: 'well he kept the discipline of chivalry, as did the Romans in former times'.[3] If they wanted to know more of chivalry, they turned to Vegetius, whose work for them was a 'book of chivalry', discussing 'knighthood and battle'.[4] Heralds traced back the pedigree of their office to its institution by Julius Caesar,[5] and argued the rules of armoury from the law of Justinian, which knew nothing of them. Even the ritual degradation of those who were traitors to the rules of honour, which has been discussed above, was traced back to Roman practice: 'when one who bears arms is to be dishonoured for treason, or cowardice, or breach of faith, then his arms should be portrayed reversed, for faith is to be kept even with the enemy, according to the *civil law* and the law of arms'.[6]

It is this ascription of the customs of chivalry in general to Roman origins which, I believe, reveals just how the judicial powers of military officers were regarded. The law of arms was

[1] Cf. Bonet, *Tree of Battles*, pt. 4, ch. 9, on the powers of the *Constable*; he is here following John of Legnano, *Tractatus*, cap. 19, on the powers of a *magister militum*, and the ultimate source is Vegetius. See also Upton, *De Officio Militari*, Lib. I, ch. 16 (ed. Bysshe, p. 32): 'Ad officium insuper Ducis Belli pertinet de contractibus et delictis militum cognoscere, quod eciam pertinet ad specialem magistrum militum . . . sed hodie omnia ista predicta pertinet ad officium constabularii et marescalli.'

[2] Monstrelet, *Chronique*, prologue to Book II (ed. L. Douet d'Arq, Tome IV, p. 125).

[3] Waurin, *Chroniques*, R.S., Vol. II, p. 429.

[4] Jean de Meun's translation of Vegetius was entitled *L'Art de Chevalerie*; that of Jean Priorat, *Li Abrejance de l'Ordre de Chevalerie*; the English verse translation is called *Knyghthode and Bataile* (edited for the E.E.T.S. by Dyboske and Arend, 1935). Translations such as these were very popular, and Vegetius was used by all the expert writers on chivalry; by Ramon Lull, by Christine de Pisan, and by the author of the *Rozier des Guerres*.

[5] See for examples Julius Caesar's 'ordinances for heralds', in Phillips MS. 10396, fo. 1 et seq. (This MS. is in the possession of Professor G. W. Coopland, who kindly allowed me to use it.)

[6] Johannes de Bado Aureo, *Tractatus de Armis* (ed. Bysshe, London, 1654), p. 44.

an international law, but it was not universal international law, for it applied only to wars between 'nations' which were part of the 'Roman people'.[1] Its foundations were in the canon law of the Roman Church, and the civil law of the Roman Empire. But by the fourteenth century the secular authority of the Roman Empire was no longer regarded as vested in a single authority: kings and princes had parted it between them, and ruled each as 'emperor in his realm'. Anyone who had no secular sovereign, could claim imperial authority; as Bonet said of the Count of Foix, 'in his land of Béarn he is Emperor, for he holds it of God and by the sword'.[2] A *magister militum*, in order to act judicially under Roman law, had to be appointed on imperial authority. The Constable of any sovereign prince, therefore, was a *magister militum*, with public authority among the Roman people, for the Roman people remained one, even though secular authority was divided. As such, he could do justice wherever Roman military law ran, that is throughout Christendom.

It does not matter that the medieval lawyers had here confused the standards of training and efficiency set in the Roman army with the standards of moral conduct for the Christian warrior class: the fact is that they did so. As a result, for them any soldier serving any sovereign was a soldier of the Roman army, and this at once gave him a certain social dignity, and bound him to certain rules of honour. He could be held responsible for upholding this dignity, and observing these rules, by any officer with Roman authority. Thus a constable, who derived his power from the commission of a prince exercising imperial rights, could consider any matter arising out of war, wheresoever it was done and by whomsoever, because war was governed in Christian society by universal rules, the Roman 'discipline of chivalry'. Just as a prince's patent of nobility made a man 'chivalrous' and entitled him to the privileges of

[1] See ch. II *ante*. This was not just an idea of the legal theorists; it was a point on occasion quoted in the courts, e.g. in the case of Buxton *v.* Dorot (Arch. Nat., $X^1a$ 4797, fo. 215 et seq.), *plaidoirie* of Dorot: '[les Francais] *non sunt hostes populi romani*, dont parle les lois *de captivis*'. (Dorot's object was to show that a French prisoner was not strictly a slave, since it was only in wars against enemies of the Roman people that prisoners could be enslaved.)

[2] Bonet, *Tree of Battles*, pt. 4, ch. 16.

a noble not only in his own land but throughout Christendom,[1] so a prince's commission to judge matters of 'knights and war' gave his *magister militum* power to judge soldiers of any allegiance for dishonourable actions which offended against the code of knights. Naturally enough such an officer had no civil jurisdiction over a man who was not in the service of his sovereign. But where civil redress was not demanded, contemporary notions of chivalry and its rules gave him much more extensive powers. It was the duty of every prince to ensure that these rules were observed by all, and his business was to help his master in carrying out this duty.

[1] See for example King Richard's patent of 1 July 1389, making John Kingston a gentleman and esquire, so as to give him the status to take up a challenge from a *Frenchman*, i.e. a status which will be accepted in all places (Rymer, Vol. III, pt. IV, p. 42).

# PART TWO

# The Just War and its Conditions

# V

# THE LEGAL THEORY OF
# JUST WAR

W HAT has emerged from a study of the courts which
administered the law of arms is that there was only
one limit on their powers which can be regarded as general.
They could judge only matters of 'knights and war', since these
were the only matters in which the law of arms, which they
administered, applied. This limit now poses a problem of
definition: what does war mean in this context? The Court of
Chivalry's jurisdiction was over 'deeds of arms' generally,[1] but
clearly there was no need for an official state of war to exist
before men could perform martial acts. There was plenty of
blood shed in the horrors of the French Jacquerie, and gallant
deeds performed on both sides, but when the Marshals of
France claimed the right to consider disputes which were con-
sequent upon them as being *dependencia ex guerris*,[2] were they
or were they not outstepping their legal rights? Was the rising
of these peasants, armed with what they could lay hands on, to
be spoken of as a war, or was it a civil commotion, tragic perhaps, but something quite different to war in its true sense?
And if the latter was the case, did the law of arms apply in

---

[1] 13 Richard II, Stat. 1, c.2.

[2] Arch. Nat., X¹a 17, fo. 223. The Marshals claimed that 'ad ipsos spectat
et consueverunt cognoscere nomine nostro de omnibus et singulis casibus et
dependenciis que ex guerris et rebellionibus inter subditos nostros oriuntur'
(22 January 1362). Their claim that this included the Jacquerie was not
allowed.

such conditions, or not? In order to answer these questions, we shall have to make another excursus into legal theory, to try to establish what was the accepted legal definition of war.

This problem is rendered more serious by the fact that in the middle ages one could not, as one can now, apply a common-sense distinction between times of peace and war. War did not mean an exceptional period of international strife; it was the endemic condition of West European society. The distinction which the medieval lawyer had to draw was not therefore between war and peace, but between one condition of war and another. One could quite well have war in the land, with its full accompaniment of pitched battles and violent deaths, without interrupting an official time of peace. The judgment passed on Thomas of Lancaster after Boroughbridge was reversed in 1326, on the ground that he had been tried summarily and that such trial was not allowed in *peace-time*;[1] nevertheless he had been taken in arms and when his men were arrayed for battle, and all the signs would have led one to suppose that a war was being fought. Conversely periods of actual peace and of legal peace did not necessarily coincide, for many of them were no more than times of truce, suspensions of hostilities which put a stop to warlike acts but not to war itself.

In spite of these difficulties, any quest for legal definition must start with a distinction between war and peace. The essential standards of medieval lawyers were those of reason and justice; 'hence it is seen,' wrote Cynus, 'that one thing is just in time of war and another in time of peace, for one defines as just what is appropriate to existing conditions.'[2] The great Pistoian lawyer here put his finger on the centre of the problem, for the first principle of the legists was that only a just war could have legal consequences. His statement bridges in one step the gap between this theoretical and moral principle, and its practical application. The question, as he puts it, ceases to be one of whether such and such an action is of itself just and lawful, but whether conditions render it so. An example may make this point clearer. Raymond of Pennaforte, dealing with the crime of arson, defines incendiaries thus: 'an incendiary is one who, out of hate or ill-will or for the sake of revenge sets fire to a town, or to a village or to a house or vines or anything

[1] *Rot. Parl.*, ii, p. 5a.　　[2] Cynus, *Lectura super Codice*, Lib. VI, Tit. 50, l. 1.

of that kind. But,' he adds, 'if he does this at the command of one who has the power to declare war, then he is not to be judged an incendiary.'[1] It was the same with other crimes, such as spoliation of a man's goods. In time of peace this was robbery, but in time of war it might be the basis of a legal title to possession, because in war it is not unjust or unreasonable to despoil the goods of the enemy. The justice of a war could not only render acts, which would otherwise be crimes, legitimate, it could also endow them with legal consequences.

All kinds of criminal acts could therefore be defended on the plea that they had been done under the right of war. Since, as has been said, war was an endemic condition, this meant that in such cases the question was not whether the act involved had actually been done in time of war, but whether the war in question was a just one. A war which was unjust had no standing in law, and those who took part in it had none either: 'knights who take part in a war without just cause', wrote Nicholas of Tudeschi, 'should rather be called robbers than knights.'[2] But this was not the end of the problem by any means. The legality of actions was to be judged in accordance with the justice of the cause in which they were done, a matter which, as Cynus's wise remark suggests, could only be judged in relation to particular circumstances. The foundation of justice was reason, which should influence judgment *sicut lex*.[3] If therefore two wars were just for different reasons, different conclusions were to be drawn as to what they justified, and the law must take account of this. It thus became important not only to distinguish just from unjust war, but also the causes which rendered a war just.

Once again it is necessary to take a step back, and to consider what causes could render a war just before going on to consider what the consequences of its justice might be. As justice is a moral concept, one will find that this question was discussed most fully by the canonists and theologians. The ultimate sources of most of their opinions were Augustine and Isidore.

---

[1] Raymond of Pennaforte, *Summa de Poenitentia*, Lib. II, cap. 5 §5.

[2] Nicholas of Tudeschi, *Lectura Super V Libros Decretalium*, 2 Decretal., Lib. II, Tit. 24, ch. 29.

[3] Paris of Pozzo, *De Re Militari*, Lib. I, cap. 2, 'dictum rationabile debet judicatum movere sicut lex'. (Zilletus, *Tractatus Juris Universi*, Tome 16, fo. 386vo.)

It was Augustine who laid down the first principle: 'the final object of war is peace'.[1] This reveals that in its very origin the Christian apologetic for war was legal in intention: the object of war was not to chastise sin but to restore harmony by the redress of wrong. 'Wars are defined as just', wrote Augustine, when their aim is to avenge injury, that is when that people or city against whom war is to be declared has neglected either to redress the injuries done by its subjects, or to restore what they have wrongfully seized.'[2] Isidore's remarks were to the same effect, though his authorities were different; he looked rather to Roman law, and behind it to Cicero's Republic, than to the fathers and the Greek philosophers. 'Just war must be waged on valid authority, either to regain things lost or to drive out invaders',[3] he wrote, and his definition passed into Gratian's Decretum,[4] and thereafter into the writings of most of the canonists. The remarks of these two doctors on the unjust war were again to be the basis of a good deal of subsequent commentary. Isidore put the principle: 'Unjust war is that which results from passion, not from lawful reason; as Cicero explains in his Republic, unjust wars are those on which men enter without good reason'.[5] Augustine defined the consequence in legal terms: 'unjust war is no more than robbery on a majestic scale'.[6]

It was these opinions of Augustine and Isidore which the canonists later extended into a full scale theory of the just war. Most of them had their own particular point of view, but their basic position was first and best defined by Raymond of Pennaforte,[7] whose definition of justice in war was repeated by Hostiensis,[8] by Monaldus,[9] by John of Legnano,[10] by Baldus de Ubaldis[11] and many others. Raymond laid down five prerequisites for a just war. It must be just with regard to the persons engaged in it (that is, it must be fought by laymen, since clerks cannot justly engage in war); it must be just with

[1] Augustine, *Epistolae*, CLXXXIX, 6.
[2] Augustine, *De Civitate Dei*, Book 19, ch. 7.
[3] Isidore, *Etymologiae*, XVIII, i.
[4] Gratian, *Decretum* 2, Causa XXIII, q. 2, c. 1.     [5] Isidore, op. cit.
[6] Augustine, *De Civitate Dei*, Book 4, ch. 1.
[7] Raymond of Pennaforte, *Summa*, Lib. II, cap. 5 §17.
[8] Hostiensis, *Summa Aurea*, Lib. I, Rub. 34, 3.
[9] *Summa Monaldi*, de bello justo (Lyons edn., 1516, fo. xix).
[10] John of Legnano, *Tractatus*, cap. 76.   [11] Baldus, *Consilia*, Cons. 439.

regard to its object (that is to say, its aim must be to redress some injury or other, whether to right or possessions or person); it must be just with regard to its cause (which means that this must be a necessary cause, and that there must be no alternative way of achieving the object, other than by recourse to arms); it must be just in intention (that is to say, the person levying it must be moved by a genuine desire for justice, not by hate or cupidity); and it must be waged on valid authority (that is to say, on the authority of the Roman Church or of a sovereign prince). John of Legnano, besides repeating these standards of justice, gives a series of further definitions,[1] which come to very much the same conclusions, but are phrased in a rather more practical way, probably because they were in fact borrowed from Cynus.[2] He here divided just wars into four categories. In the first place there is Roman war, waged on the authority of the Church against infidels. In the second place there is war which is just according to written law, which seems to mean war levied on the authority of a prince. Thirdly, there is war which is levied on the authority of a judge, a definition which gives some sort of standard by which the justice of the objective can be guaranteed in practice (and which also presupposes that the adverse party has refused to abide by judgment). Fourthly, there is necessary war, that is, war waged in self-defence. Antithetically, John divided unjust wars into three categories, but only one of these, what he calls voluntary war, is of importance, and this will be discussed shortly.

The canonists, from Raymond onwards, thus had a series of standards by which to judge the justice of war. The question remained whether, for a war to be called just, it had to satisfy all the requirements, or only some of them. Clearly a war waged by clerks would never be just, but was princely authority, for example, required in every instance? Clearly it was not. 'It is lawful for every man to move war in defense of himself and his goods',[3] wrote Innocent IV, and Raymond was of the same view; 'it is always lawful to meet force with force'.[4] Other

---

[1] John of Legnano, *Tractatus*, cap. 76.

[2] Cynus, *Super Dig. Vet.*, I, Tit. 1, l. 5.

[3] Innocent IV, *In V Libros Decretales Commentaria*, 2 Decretal., Rub. 13, cap. 12.

[4] Raymond of Pennaforte, *Summa*, Lib. II, cap. 5 §18.

lawyers agreed; Johannes Andreas,[1] Baldus de Ubaldis,[2] Henry of Gorinchen,[3] and others all discuss just wars which are waged without authority and are just '*ex sola causa*'. That they should take this view is not surprising. In a society in which large scale violence was an everyday problem, it was essential for individuals to be guaranteed a right of self-defence, and public authorities a right to enforce their decisions by arms upon recalcitrant persons. But here the lawyers drew a distinction. There was an obvious difference between wars waged in self-defence or with the object of enforcing judgment, and a public war waged on the authority of a prince. In the case of a war fought to enforce judgment, those who resisted clearly had no right to do so and were to be regarded as rebels, not enemies. In self-defence it might be lawful to resist and even to kill, but the matter was still within the view of the ordinary courts, where the injured party could defend his violent action by the '*exceptio paris criminis*'.[4] But though he could resist he had no further right to extra-legal vengeance, and he must be careful not to impair his defence by seeking it. The aggressor's unjust actions did not create a state of war, with its drastic accompaniment of legal consequences. Nor did resistance to lawful authority, and armed action to enforce it was, according to Henry of Gorinchen 'to be regarded rather as the exercise of justice and jurisdiction than as war'.[5]

In the last resort the lawyers were very unwilling to admit that any war other than one levied on the authority of a prince was a war in the true sense of the word. At least, it alone was a '*bellum hostile*',[6] a war in which the adversaries could regard one another as lawful enemies. This idea of just war, as being the war of a sovereign prince, goes back like so much else to Augustine. The purpose of the secular power in the terrestrial world

---

[1] Johannes Andreas, *Super II Decretal.*, Tit. 24, cap. 29.

[2] Baldus, *Comment. in Decretal.*, 2 Decretal., Rub. 24, cap. 29.

[3] Henry of Gorinchen, *de Justo Bello* (*Tractatus Consultatatorii venerandi Majestii Henrici de Gorychum*, Cologne, 1503, fo. 50).

[4] Innocent, *In V Libros Decretales Commentaria*, 2 Decretal., Rub. 24, cap. 29.

[5] Henry of Gorinchen, *de Justo Bello*, Prop. 10 (op. cit., fo. 56vo).

[6] Cynus, *Lectura Super Codice*, Lib. VI, Tit. 50, l. 1: 'dicitur et bellum hostile quod populus Romanus vel princeps indicit hostibus suis . . . et istud vocatur justum bellum'.

was to uphold peace; therefore 'the natural condition of mankind, which is attuned to peace, demands that the decision and authority for making war should lie with the prince'.[1] From this it is only a small step to the statements of Bartolus that 'only he who has no superior can declare a just war',[2] and of Nicholas of Tudeschi that 'wars which are not declared by a prince are not properly wars'.[3] The legal theory behind this view, as expressed by Innocent IV[4] and Johannes Andreas,[5] seems to be that since war alters the effect of the civil laws, it cannot be declared except by one who is above them, which the Prince alone is. A prince could not, of course, alter the laws under which wars were fought, for these were founded in the *jus gentium*, a branch of natural law, and 'the Prince cannot do anything which is contrary to natural law, because it is immutable'.[6]

The importance of this limitation of just wars proper to those levied on the authority of a prince emerges in Cynus's remark that such a war alone is a '*bellum hostile*'. Under any other conditions, there must be some superior authority to whom resort can be made, which means that the civil laws are still in force and that a final judgment can be given as to who is in the wrong. He can therefore be convicted of a particular civil crime. Bartholomew of Saliceto makes this point very clear: 'What then shall I say of those companies of men at arms, who overrun the territory of our cities? I reply that there is no doubt about their position, for they are robbers, . . . and therefore as robbers they should be punished for all the crimes they have committed.'[7] But where a war was levied on the authority of a prince, there was no superior to whom recourse could be made in order to

[1] Augustine, *Cont. Faust.*, XII, 75.

[2] Bartolus, *Tractatus de Reprisaliis*, III, 2.

[3] Nicholas of Tudeschi, *Lectura Super V Libros Decretalium*, 2 Decretal., Tit. 24, cap. 39.

[4] Innocent, *In V Libros Decretales*, 2 Decretal., Tit. 13, cap. 12. 'Item, ubicunque per alium rem suam et jus suum prosequi non potest, licitum est auctoritate superioris arma movere et bellum indicere . . . tamen si Principem super se habet, eius auctoritate hoc faciat et non aliter, *quia nulli licet jura temperare sine auctoritate conditoris juris*.'

[5] Johannes Andreas, *Super II Decretal.*, Tit. 13, cap. 12. 'Inde est, quod princeps sine auctoritate hominis, cui non subest, et *sine auctoritate juris, quo non astringatur*, movet bellum.'

[6] Andreas de Isernia, *In Usus Feudorum Commentaria*, Lib. II, Tit. 56.

[7] Bartholomew of Saliceto, *Super VIII Cod.*, Tit. 51, l. 12.

judge on whose side right lay, for enemies are by definition out-side one's jurisdiction. Because there was no one to judge the cause, the only practical standard of justice which could be applied to such a war was the fact that a prince had declared it. In this case it was to be presumed that both sides believed that justice lay with them, and until arms had settled the issue, both were entitled to the benefit of the doubt.

This meant that such a war was not only a just war but also a public one, to whose conduct the laws of public war, founded in the *jus gentium*, applied. In it alone adversaries were con-sidered enemies. This was an all important distinction, because all the lawyers were agreed that it was only in such a war that there was no limit on the taking of spoil and prisoners. Bartolus, having dismissed wars levied in self-defence and in execution of judgment, continues thus: 'thirdly, there is public war, which is declared by the Roman people, or by the emperor on whom their entire authority has been conferred . . . and in such war captives can be enslaved, and goods taken in its course become the property of the captors'.[1] Johannes Andreas, on behalf of the canonists, echoes him,[2] and the authority of Gratian[3] and Aquinas[4] is behind him. The point which the lawyers were here making was not, however, just a theoretical one. It was a defini-tion of first importance to the professional soldier, for half the lure of his occupation was the prospect of rich gains of war. It is true that it was generally admitted that in wars between Chris-tians the law which permitted the enslavement of captives did not apply, but as this only meant that the rule was modified in favour of the right of ransom,[5] this did not matter much to him. What mattered to him was that in public war and public

[1] Bartolus, *Comment. in Dig. Nov.*, XLIX, Tit. 15, l. 24. Note also his remark here that 'istud bellum (Sc: war without authority) licet sit licitum, non est publicum, et ideo non dicuntur proprie hostes adinvicem, et quae ibi capientur non efficuntur capientium, quia requiritur quod bellum sit publicum'. See also John of Legnano, *Tractatus*, chs. 59 and 60; Bartholomew of Saliceto, *Super VIII Cod.*, Tit. 51, l. 12.

[2] Johannes Andreas, *Super II Decretal.*, Tit. 13, cap. 12. 'Bellum autem verum, in quo capti servi fiunt, et quod vere et proprie bellum dicitur, solus princeps, qui superiorem non habet, potest indicere.'

[3] Gratian, *Decretum*, Pars II, Causa XXIII, q. 5, c. 25. Gratian reserves all spoils taken in war to the king who has conquered.

[4] Aquinas, *Summa Theologica*, II. 2ae, Q. 66, 8 ad 1.

[5] John of Legnano, *Tractatus*, cap. 60; and see ch. X *infra*.

war alone he had the right to make himself rich on the spoils of victory.

Of course, in theory the canonists insisted that for these rights to be valid, a public war must satisfy the other standards of justice, besides that of authority, which made it public. In practice however, a just war (in the proper sense of war) and a public war meant the same thing. In any war both sides would be sure to claim justice was with them. 'It is tacitly assumed that it is in the nature of war waged by kings and lords, that it is public and general on both sides.' Thus Bartholomew of Saliceto.[1] The same point was made very clearly in a case before the 'English' Parlement of Paris in 1433, between one Giles Desmoulins and the Carthusians of Le Parc.[2] The French had carried out a raid in their locality, and in the process captured a fine booty of cattle, some of which belonged to the Carthusians and some to Desmoulins. Subsequently the Carthusians bought back some of these, which Desmoulins claimed to be his. The Carthusians argued that the French had acquired them as booty, and so they, the Carthusians, had bought them from their legal owners. Desmoulins replied that the French could not have acquired such title.

> Suppose qu'on di que ce que nous prenons sur noz ennemis soit nostre *in judicio nostro*, pour ce que nous reputons *bellum nostrum justum*; mais pur ce ne disons nous mie que ce que les ennemis prennent sur nous soit a eulz acquis, *in judicio nostro, quia non agunt bellum justum*, et ainsi le bestail ne povoit estre acquis aux pillars ou ennemis.

The Carthusians made hash of this smart argument. Known French captains had taken part in the raid; hence it could not be suggested that the beasts had merely been stolen by brigands.

> *Latrunculi dicuntur a latrando*, et *hostes dicuntur qui publicum bellum indicunt*; or dient ils que a la prise du dit bestail estoient les capitaines de Chartres, de Rambouillet et autres; et pour ce on doit

[1] Bartholomew of Saliceto, *Super VIII Cod.*, Tit. 51, l. 12. Compare with this the statement of Angelus of Perusia, *Disputatio, inc. 'Renovata guerra'*: 'aut quilibet asseret se prius insultatum et se pro defensa sui juris facere dictam guerram, quo casu propter dubium ex utroque latere dicere possumus guerram justam'. Angelus' disputations were published at Pavia, *c.* 1490; the volume is unpaginated.

[2] Arch. Nat., X¹a 4797, fo. 50.

dire que ce que les ennemis prennent sur nous est a eulz acquis, ainsi que nous est acquiz ce que nous prenons sur eulz, *etiam in judicio nostro aliter judicium claudicaret*.

For all practical purposes it was agreed that the test of the justice of a war, and of its public nature, was whether or not it had been declared on the authority of a prince.

The trouble in practice about this standard was not that its validity was disputed, but that it was not easy to arrive at a satisfactory definition of what sovereignty for this purpose implied. The idea of the absolutely sovereign prince, whose powers were untrammelled by any law, was alien to medieval thought, legal or political, for all princes were subject to law (though not necessarily to all laws). There was a further problem, too, to complicate matters, a problem this time of genuine conflict of laws. So far we have been dealing with the views of canonists and civilians, who tended, because their authorities did so too, to limit the right of levying war to princes without any secular superior. This principle necessarily came into conflict with the old established feudal right which entitled any person of noble status to levy war. If one turns from the canonists and civilians to, say, Beaumanoir, one finds a quite different theory about the right to wage war. For him it is the privilege of all gentlemen to settle their disputes by arms if they so wish,[1] and it is clear that he regarded barons at least as entitled for this purpose to employ mercenaries and take prisoners.[2] What he says of feudal war is very similar to what other lawyers say about public war; he too, for instance, speaks of actions which would be civil crimes being covered by the '*droit de guerre*',[3] of truces being merely interludes in the war and of the right of those excluded from them to continue hostilities.[4] The difference is however seen clearly when he talks of a '*quievetaine de guerre*', which the lawyers would render in Latin '*dux belli*'. Such leaders have the same kind of rights according to both parties,[5] but whereas the

[1] Beaumanoir, *Les Coutumes du Beauvaisis*, ch. 59 §7, 'gentil home puissent guerroier selonc nostre coustume'.
[2] Ibid., ch. 58 §22 (prisoners), and ch. 59 §21 (mercenaries).
[3] Ibid., ch. 59 §2, 'en tel cas me metroie je en la guerre par mon fet. Dont se mal me venoit puis de l'averse partie . . . il se porroit escuser de droit de guerre.'
[4] Ibid., ch. 59 §11.   [5] See p. 79, n. 1, and p. 79, n. 2 *infra*.

canonists and civilians intend by their phrase a sovereign or his lieutenant, Beaumanoir clearly means the principal or the head of the family engaged in the war.

The Church had always been opposed to private war, and as time went by its view, limiting the right of war to sovereign princes, gained ground, while the ancient feudal right to levy private war fell more and more into desuetude. This kind of thing could not happen overnight, however, nor was it the Church which was in the long run to be the gainer by the process, but the secular prince. In fact when the whole case comes to be examined, it will be found that there are not just two possible points of view involved, but three, the feudal view, the view of the canonists and most of the civilians, and the view of the apologists of the rising secular states. Because the question of the right to levy public war was a matter of practical importance to the professional soldier who hoped to acquire gains of war, these views must be examined with some care.

Feudal custom varied enormously from place to place and from time to time, but the feudal principle was clear. Any person who was of military status, any gentleman that is, had the right to defy his enemies and levy war upon them, given lawful cause. By the period of the Hundred Years War this cherished right was ceasing to operate.[1] There were a variety of reasons for this. The moral effect of consistent ecclesiastical censure no doubt had something to do with it: so also did the increasing study of Roman Law, whose doctrine of *lèse-majesté* could put the actions of a contumacious vassal in the ugly light of a capital crime. But most important of all was probably the growth and centralisation of the power of the secular monarchies. This cut at the classic excuse for feudal war, '*déni de justice*'. Denial of justice worked very well as an excuse for war, as long as all rights were regarded as private rights, but the concept of a public authority introduced a third party into the dispute. One can see the effect of this idea of public weal even in Beaumanoir, tolerant as he is of the right of private war.

---

[1] In England it is true that private war was always technically illegal outside the Marches. The events of the reigns of John and Stephen, however, show that this position was not fully accepted for many years after the Conquest; and significantly, levying war, even against the King, was seldom construed as High Treason before the reign of Edward I.

If one gentleman kill or wound another, when there is not open war between them, and the lineage of both parties wish to put the matter to the test of war, the justice (i.e. the *bailli*) should not on this account neglect to pursue the malefactors and put them on trial for their misdeeds, for the malefactors have not only done offence to the adverse party and their lineage, but also to their lord whose duty it is to superintend and judge their affairs.[1]

The attractions of private war were clearly diminished if one was not only liable to be defeated by one's private enemies but to be punished by public authority as well. The growth of the idea of public authority was moreover accompanied by claims to the precedence of the public weal over all private right. During their great struggle with England, a long series of ordinances of the French Kings forbade all private defiances while the kingdom was at war.[2] Though these ordinances were never fully effective, they helped to bring the feudal right into further disrepute. It was a right which could not in the long run survive the emergence of an idea of public authority and of a common weal.

At the opposite extreme to the feudal view, there was the view of those lawyers who were the protagonists respectively of papal and imperial claims. For them Christendom was a society with a single head, be he Pope or Emperor. They accepted, therefore, the limitation of the right of war to the prince who had no superior, and they interpreted this phrase in the narrowest possible sense. The clearest statement of the extreme papalist position is probably that of Henry of Gorinchen; 'neither kings nor emperors can make war with one another, unless their rights have been reviewed before their superior, that is to say the Pope, who wields the swords of both spiritual and secular power'.[3] The weakness of Henry's position is made clear by his own reservation that he is speaking '*secundum forum conscientiae*'. Written in the years of the great conciliar experiment, his words can from a practical point of view be regarded at best as hopelessly idealistic. The same is true of the imperialist thesis. It is

[1] Beaumanoir, op. cit., ch. 59 §7.

[2] E.g. *Ordonnances des Rois de France*, Tome II, pp. 511–12; Tome III, pp. 525–7 (bans on defiance of 17 December 1352 and 5 October 1361).

[3] Henry of Gorinchen, *De Justo Bello*, prop. 9 (op. cit., fo. 55vo).

put both by Bartolus[1] and John of Legnano[2] (who is largely copying), but lamely, with reservations in favour both of the papacy and of other secular princes. Their view is that public war can only be levied on the authority of the Roman people, whose power has devolved by translation to the Emperor, and subsequently (probably) to the Roman Church. These powers alone, therefore, are entitled to levy war. The two difficulties which faced John and Bartolus in squaring their view with practice, were the facts that by their time ecclesiastical authority had been effectively banished to the forum of conscience, and that imperial authority had been demonstrably rejected by the majority of the so-called Roman people. Bartolus resolved the difficulty posed by the independent *regna* and *civitates* by stating that they exercised sovereign powers *de facto*, but not *de jure*.[3] John of Legnano followed him to a point, but he clung to the last to the view that in strict law their wars were unjust. The third of his categories of unjust wars was the voluntary war, 'which is the kind of war which the princes of our time wage, without the authority of the Emperor. And this war is unjust, for one may not even carry arms without the Emperor's licence.'[4] The whole course of the Hundred Years War is a refutation of John's view, but it was one which died hard. For Jacob Meyer, writing after the beginning of the sixteenth century, the great struggle of the English and French still appeared not as a true war, but as a furious civil commotion which was a blot on the reputation of Christendom.[5]

Midway between the view of the feudalists on the one hand, and the papalists and imperialists on the other, stood a third party, the apologists of the rising *regna*. The greatest among these

---

[1] Bartolus, *Comment. in Dig. Nov.*, XLIX, Tit. 15, l. 24.

[2] John of Legnano, *Tractatus*, cap. 13. This is very largely copied direct from Bartolus.

[3] Bartolus, op. cit.

[4] John of Legnano, *Tractatus*, cap. 76.

[5] J. Meyer, *Commentaria sive Annales rerum Flandicarum* (Antwerp, 1561), p. 136: 'Bellum Anglicum exordium habuit, quod omnium longissimum atque atrocissimum fuit; quodque per intervalla centesimum excessit annum. Seditio potius domestica, quam bellum dicendum. Christiana Respublica unum regnum, unaque domus est; quaecunque in ea geruntur bella cum magno dedecore geruntur; nec si verum fateamur bella sunt, sed turpissimae seditiones.'

75

were the lawyers of France and Sicily, and the foundation of their view was the doctrine that the King is Emperor in his realm. 'There are those nowadays who declare that the law with regard to *lèse-majesté* applies only to the King of the Romans, that is the Emperor, because all the laws which speak of royal majesty are speaking of the Emperor,' wrote Andrew of Isernia, 'but this position is not tenable in law, for the King's law is mightier in his kingdom than the Emperor's in the empire, and kings in practice distrain traitors by their persons and their goods.'[1] This is a thesis which Bartolus would have stamped as heresy.[2] In their search for arguments to support it, the apologists of the *regna* showed indefatigable ingenuity. Andrew of Isernia found a reference in an English chronicle to the confiscation of Becket's lands to the fisc during his quarrel with Henry II; as the fisc was a sign of *imperium*, the English king must clearly have imperial rights.[3] The compilers of the *Somnium Viridarii* went to natural law for relevant material; other animals than men were social, they pointed out, but the Queen Bee was queen of one hive only.[4] A body politic cannot do without a head, but there can be more than one body politic among men as among bees. This view received, besides, some considerable support from the papal apologists, who were much happier to see secular power concentrated in many hands than in those of a single, world wide emperor.[5] The trend of political thought also was running this way: Aquinas's *Summa Theologica* itself provides the philosophic basis for the theory of the independent secular state.[6] But most of all the theory gained ground because it related more closely than any other to existing conditions. When Andrew of Isernia,[7] or William Duran-

[1] Andrew of Isernia, *In Usus Feudorum Commentaria*, Lib. II, Tit. 56.

[2] Bartolus, *Comment. in Dig. Nov.*, XLIX, Tit. 15, l. 24. 'Et forte si quis diceret dominum Imperatorem non esse dominum et monarcham totius orbis, esset haereticus.'

[3] Andrew of Isernia, *In Usus Feudorum*, Lib. II, Tit. 56.

[4] *Somnum Viridarii*, Lib. II, cap. 36.

[5] See, e.g. the remarks of Innocent III on the jurisdiction of the Kings of France, *Registrum*, Lib. VII, ep. 42. The absolute temporal sovereignty of the French Kings was publicly acknowledged in the bull *Rex Gloria* of Clement V.

[6] Cf. A. P. D'Entreves, *The Political Writings of St. Thomas Aquinas*, Introduction, esp. pp. xiv–xv and xxiii.

[7] Andrew of Isernia, *In Usus Feud.* Lib. I, Tit. 17.

THE LEGAL THEORY OF JUST WAR

dus,[1] or the Compilers of the *Somnium Viridarii*[2] said that only a prince who had no superior could levy public war, they meant a king; and it was kings who did so in practice.

Nevertheless they too for the time being had to compromise. But their compromise was not, as might have been expected, with the papalists and imperialists, with whom they shared most of their arguments on the subject of war (except only a redefinition of the meaning of the word '*princeps*'). It was instead, in practice at least, with the feudal view. This again was a compromise dictated by the shape of existing conditions. The new Europe of nation states was not born overnight; anomalies, dating from an earlier age and arising out of a different order of things, lasted many centuries. The King of England might or might not be Emperor in his realm, but was he not the vassal of the King of France for his Angevin inheritance? He certainly did not wish to be, but the only means by which he ever looked like winning a title to independent sovereignty in these domains was by bargaining for it his claim to the French throne, whose justice force of arms had failed to settle either way. A still more puzzling position was that of the Duke of Burgundy. He had not one superior but two, the King of France and the Emperor, but he ruled his lands as one principality. If he wished to levy war and to employ all his forces, must he ask the leave of one sovereign, or of both, or of neither? And would his war be a public war, in which spoil and ransom could be taken?

The effect of difficulties such as these can be seen when one turns to Christine de Pisan's *Livre des Fays d'Armes et de Chevalerie*, a work used for practical guidance on the rules of war. 'And without doubt, according to law and right, the right to do battle or levy war for any cause whatever belongs to sovereign princes, such as Emperors, Kings, Dukes, and other secular lords who are lords principal of secular jurisdiction'.[3] As dukes and other secular lords are not usually without superior, Christine seems to be here extending the meaning of the phrase 'sovereign prince' in order to fit the facts of her day. Much the

---

[1] Durandus, *Speculum Iuris*, Lib. II, Partic. 1, de 2 Decret., §5 (Frankfurt, 1612 edn., p. 135).

[2] *Somnium Viridarii*, Lib. I, cap. 109.

[3] Passage quoted by A. M. Vanderpol, *La doctrine Scholastique du droit de Guerre* (Paris, 1919), p. 79.

same sort of compromise seems to be attempted, among the professional lawyers, by Bartholomew of Saliceto. He asks the same question as other legists—to which wars do the laws of captivity and *postliminium* apply? But he asks it with regard to different antagonists. Whereas they are speaking of the wars of a 'prince', he is speaking of the wars of 'kings and barons'.[1] Barons by definition were persons who acknowledged superiors.

The key to this compromise position lies in Christine's description of sovereign princes as persons who are 'lords principal of secular jurisdiction'. As has often been pointed out, sovereign is in origin the same word as *suzerain*. Sovereignty in the middle ages was therefore a loose term. It could mean anything from the possession of high and low justice to the possession of final secular jurisdiction, and Christine's loose phrasing could at a pinch be taken either way. Henry of Gorinchen, whose work is roughly contemporary with hers, makes it clear that in his time and locality the possession of high and low justice was regarded by many as carrying with it the right to levy public war.[2] Though he himself rejects the claim, it is not hard to see the reasoning behind it. Public war, as Bartholomew of Saliceto pointed out, was so called because it was fought for the public weal;[3] this is what set it apart from wars fought over purely private issues. The very existence of a right of high and low justice indicated the existence of some sort of public weal; the lord who possessed it had subjects and was responsible in some sort of way for the administration to them of impartial justice. This made him a sovereign of a sort: 'every baron is sovereign in his own barony,' wrote Beaumanoir.[4] Moreover, he made it plain that this sovereignty gave the wars of such a baron a prior right, overriding the private interests of his subjects.

The count (he is speaking of the Count of Clermont) and all

[1] Bartholomew of Saliceto, *Super VIII Cod.*, Tit. 51, l. 12. 'Sed pro ampliatione materiae, quaero, quid si unus rex contra alium, vel unus baro contra alium baronem, vel civitas contra civitatem movet guerram?' and later 'tacite inest, ex natura guerrae a regibus et baronibus indictae, cum tunc guerra sit *generalis* et publica ex parte utriusque territorii etc.'

[2] Henry of Gorinchen, *De Justo Bello*, prop. 7 (op. cit., fo. 52vo–53vo).

[3] Bartholomew of Saliceto, *Super VIII Cod.*, Tit. 51, l. 12. 'Item est sciendum, quod est quaedam alia guerra, quae sit a privata persona contra privatam, *quia nullo modo ad utilitatem publicam* etc.'

[4] Beaumanoir, op. cit., ch. 34 §41.

those who hold baronies have on account of their sovereignty the undoubted right, that if they have need of the fortresses which belong to their subjects for the purposes of their wars, whether to put garrisons in them or to keep their prisoners there, or simply to guard them, or for the *common weal of their country*, then they may take them over.[1]

This is a particularly interesting right, because, just less than a hundred years after Beaumanoir wrote it was being claimed as a right of the King alone, in a case before the Parlement in 1363.[2] This case revolved about the rights of the Archbishop of Rheims, as seigneur of the town, over the supervision of its defences. The royal position was put thus:

Ad nos, qui regnum nostrum pure a deo sine alio superiore tenemus solus et insolidus super omnes alios, pertinet protectio et defensio regni nostri et habitantium in eodem, modus etiam resistendi et ordinatio guerriandi seu guerram inimicis nostris et regni nostri faciendi; ad nos etiam per consequens pertinet constructio et defensio fortaliciorum in regno nostro *solus et insolidus*.

The King in 1363 was claiming these rights over fortresses as sole and absolute sovereign; what Beaumanoir makes clear is that a count or baron, in time past at least, had possessed the same rights as a sovereign, although he undoubtedly recognised superior authorities.

In the fourteenth and fifteenth centuries the possession of high and low justice does not seem in practice to have carried automatically the right to levy public war. Equally absolute sovereigns had not by any means established their exclusive right to do so. Practice continued for the moment to reflect a compromise over principle. Two points, however, which had important practical consequences do seem to have become established. One was that rights to spoil and ransom could not arise out of a private war, at least if it was fought between two subjects of the same sovereign. This seems to be quite clear; one might quote, for instance, the arrest of the Parlement of Paris of 15 July 1391, in the case of the Count de Longueville against Garcia Raimond d'Aubeterre.[3] This declared that

---

[1] Ibid., ch. 58 §22.    [2] Arch. Nat., X¹a 17, fo. 386 et seq.

[3] Printed by E. Molinier, *Etude sur la Vie d'Arnoul d'Audreham Maréchal de France*, Pièces Justificatives, no. XCVI.

Garcia could not claim debts in respect of the ransom of a prisoner, who had been taken in a war levied by Charles of Artois, 'because both the parties (in the war) were subjects of our kingdom, and therefore it was not right to ask anything of the said prisoner by way of ransom'. Or one might quote the plea of William de Ferté thirty years before,[1] that his war against his lord, Sir Peter de Crassey, was a lawful war, because Peter had denied him justice; because his defiance was legitimate, since it was a time of peace; because he had not taken any *prisoners*; because he had wasted land but not *burnt it*; and because he had retained no *spoil*. What he was, in fact, claiming, was that he had fought his war entirely as a private war, without in any way using rights confined to public war. It is clear from examples such as these that though the feudal right of war persisted, the principle of the lawyers, that such private war conferred no right to seize the enemy's goods or put men to ransom, had been accepted. Those who levied war which was *'couverte, non publique'*,[2] were anxious to prove that they had not done these things.

The other principle which seems to have been established was that a public war required sovereign authority on the part of the person declaring it, though there was room for debate as to just what sovereign authority meant in this instance. Kings

[1] Arch. Nat., X¹a 17, fo. 98 et seq. (19 June 1361.) Peter de Crassey's case was partly based on an accusation that William and his men 'ceperant ad modum hostium regni in prisonarium suum quandam hominem vocatum Strabonem de Chinillaco'. William's case was that Peter had attempted to levy an undue *péage* on him, and he had defied him because he would not do him justice. The prisoner, he said, had been taken by way of reprisal because he had himself been taken unduly by Peter's men; and he had given no cause for an action in his conduct of the war, 'neque ob hoc incurrerat aliquam penam in corpore sive bonis videlicet vastando bona absque igne nichilque sibi applicando de ipsis'.

[2] This phrase comes from the case of Tremoille *v.* Lafayette and others, before the Parlement of the Bourges Kingdom, 18 January 1425 (Arch. Nat., X²a 18, fo. 60). Tremoille stated that 'les guerres de Picardie soient couvertes et non publique', and complained that no defiance was allowed in time of open war. He, like William de Ferté, was anxious to show that in resisting he had not abused the right of war; a ransom which was alleged to have been taken from a priest was in fact, he said, payment of a debt, and 'aux quarant vaches de Montboistier . . . dit que ne vindrent de pillage mais les donna Jehan de Montboistier a Arnotin et Messire Betrand de Rochefort', both of whom were of his party.

and their advisers naturally and consistently advanced the idea that the right was limited to absolute sovereigns, because they, and they alone, represented public authority in their kingdoms. So one finds for instance, the King's proctor in France denying any *ex officio* right of justice to the Duke of Burgundy's Marshal, because he had not been assigned jurisdiction in military cases by a public person.[1] The only person in the kingdom of France who could license a war, he urged, was the king himself, and therefore only he could license a man to judge cases arising out of it. Victor's rights to ransom and spoil, which could not be acquired save in a public war, were not however denied, either by individuals or the courts, after such battles as Bulgneville and Auray and Launac. Though they were not sovereigns without superior, the leaders engaged in them, men such as the Dukes of Burgundy, Brittany, and Anjou, and the Counts of Foix and Armagnac, were nevertheless great secular princes. They were all men of sufficient status to come at least within Christine de Pisan's definition of sovereign princes as 'lords principal of secular jurisdiction', and to levy wars which the chroniclers could describe as '*guerre de prince*'. Such wars would be public wars in which all rights allowed under the law of arms would apply, because they were 'open wars', disrupting time of peace in a way which the 'covered wars' of the feudality did not. In disputes arising out of such wars only persons with military jurisdiction could judge. It is to this kind of war, the only kind of war which can be properly so called, that the statutes and ordinances defining the powers of constables and marshals refer, and it was in its course alone that spoil and ransom could be freely taken.

[1] Arch. Nat., X¹a 4804, fo. 178 et seq. (22 January 1454), Jehan de Haplaincourt *v.* Jean and Gautier de Heusdam. The case, which arose out of Burgundy's war against Ghent, had been heard by his Marshal. It was pointed out that 'le mareschal a cogneu de la cause comme mareschal', and requested that 'au regard des procedures faictes devant le mareschal ne sera foy adjouste car n'est juge ne celui qui les asigne n'est personne publique'. Simon, the King's proctor, said that the Marshal could not judge the King's subjects in a military case, since 'nul ne peut induire ne faire guerre en ce royaume sans le congie due roy'. This was a very clever position, as it laid the Marshal open to prosecution for usurping justice and Haplaincourt for having taken men prisoners of war without the King's leave (the Ghent war was not a public war), so the King could recover damages (at least) from both.

# VI

# THE PROBLEMS OF ALLEGIANCE
# AND OF ILLICIT WAR

The problem which the legal theory of just war posed for the soldier is well expressed in a letter of the famous *routier* captain Perrinet Gressart, giving instructions to his nephew Francois of Aragon, whom he was sending to interview the Marshal of Burgundy. It is dated 24 December 1425, when a truce was on the point of being agreed with the French. 'Tell my Lord the Marshal', he wrote, 'that if he includes this town (La Charité-sur-Loire) within these truces, that he must find for me and my companions some means of living: otherwise it must not be included in the truce, for without wages we cannot sustain ourselves unless we make war.'[1] Perrinet's problem was, quite simply, that he was a professional soldier in an age when standing armies did not exist. As long as a state of war existed, it was not a matter of great moment to such a man that he was not on any official payroll. An able commander would have no difficulty in obtaining an adequate living from his gains of war in the way of ransoms and spoil, and from the tribute of the countryside (*appatis*) which he extracted by threats of devasta-

---

[1] H. de Flamare, *Le Nivernais pendant la guerre de Cent Ans* (Paris, 1913 and 1925), Tome I, Pièces Justificatives, no. XX. Compare Chandos's orders to Perducas d'Albret in 1369 on the outbreak of war: 'vous recuilleres vos gens et vous remetteres ensamble, et vous monterez amont sur les marces de Limozin et d'Auvergne et feres la guerre, car *sans guerre vous ne poes ne saves vivre*'. Froissart, *Chroniques*, ed. Luce, Tome VII, pp. 154–5.

tion with fire and sword.[1] But from the moment war ceased, his legal right to burn and pillage and take prisoners ceased also. As most medieval treasuries would not sustain the upkeep of a paid army in time of peace, this meant that he was cut off from the possibility of earning a legal livelihood. A good many soldiers in such a situation chose to fight on regardless, but from the moment the war ended the same actions which had won them renown and profit in its course would stamp them traitors and outlaws.

Though this did not usually deter the soldier from continuing to fight, it doubled the risks he ran. If a war ended, a professional soldier was therefore necessarily looking for a legal excuse for remaining in arms. As has been said earlier, it was not difficult for him, in the fourteenth or fifteenth centuries, to find a new cause to fight for. When the English signed a truce with France in 1357, many of the English companies in Normandy turned Navarrese overnight; similarly, in the 1420s a good many of Perrinet Gressart's Burgundian fellow-soldiers turned English for the time being when the truce of Bourbon-Lanceys put a temporary stop to Burgundy's part in the war with France. The problem for the professional soldier was not, however, simply to find a new cause, but to find a cause which was legal. There were plenty of petty lords in, for instance, the south of France in the 1360s, who would be quite willing to offer him service in wars which were not. The object of this chapter will be to show first what practical considerations decided whether a soldier could or could not justly and legally engage in a particular war, and what risks he ran if he fought illegally.

In order to answer the first of these questions, we may start by looking back to the canonists' standards of justice in war. Two of these were obviously important and relevant. In the first place, the war must be waged for a just cause, in the second, on lawful authority. The professional soldier paid lip-service at

---

[1] Cf. *Le Jouvencel*, ed. Lécestre and Favre, Tome I, p. 95: 'Et s'ainsi est que, pour avoir d'autres affaires ou moyennant le conseil d'aucuns, il (le Roi) soit trouble et desconseille en maniere qu'il ne nous puisse donner provision de payement ou de gaiges, il nous faudra lever de nous mesmes vivres et finances, tant sur ceulx de notre obeissance comme sur nos ennemys.'

least to the first of these standards. To quote Jean de Beuil's *Jouvencel*:

> . . . let the young man keep his honour and his duty to God always in mind, and make sure that he does not engage in any quarrel but a just one. For I believe that every man who risks his life in a just cause, to succour his sovereign or his kinsman in justice and in his right, accomplishes thereby God's will.[1]

No doubt Jean was here echoing what had become a platitude of chivalry, but the expression of such views is not limited, outside the writings of the canonists, to romance. The treaty which Seguin de Badefol concluded in 1361 with the chapter of Lyons, under Urban V's mediation, says things to much the same effect. Once he had been paid an indemnity of 32,000 francs and received full absolution for all his crimes, Seguin promised that he and his companions

> . . . would depart out of the realm of France and never make war there, unless it be just war and in the cause of their proper lords, nor would they fight anywhere else in Christendom except in a just war.[2]

The same anxiety over the justice of the cause in war may be seen in the terms of the Anglo-Armagnac alliance of 1412, by which the Armagnac lords undertook to 'expose their lives and bodies for the cause of the said King of England in all his just quarrels'.[3] They further specifically agreed to recognise as one such just quarrel his claim to the Duchy of Aquitaine.

One must of course beware of reading too moral a sense into the word 'just' in these passages. Arguments based on the absolute justice of a cause would not have impressed a Seguin de Badefol. When Knollys met Perducas d'Albret in 1370 and over dinner talked him into deserting the French cause, it was not moral arguments that he appealed to, but to the advantages of service with the Black Prince, 'who loved him so much and had advanced him to such honours'.[4] The word just must be taken not in a moral but in a legal sense—what mattered to the soldier was that he should fight for a cause which had some sort

[1] Ibid., Tome I, p. 118.
[2] G. Guiges, *Les Tard Venus en Lyonnais* (1886), pp. 120–1.
[3] Rymer, Vol. IV, pt. II, p. 13.
[4] *Oeuvres de Froissart*, ed. Kervyn de Lettenhove, Tome VII, p. 360.

of legal colour, of hereditary or prescriptive right or as the cause of an injured party. In an age when the manipulation of 'peculiarly tangled jurisdictional and tenurial relationships'[1] was the stuff of politics, such justification was not hard to find. The really important question, from the soldier's point of view, was therefore not the justice of a cause, but whether a given lord had a right to levy public war in its pursuit. It did not really matter to d'Albret whether he fought for the King of England or the King of France, because he had been born on land which was in dispute between them, and both were lords with an established right to levy war. There were, of course, plenty of those who did not trouble themselves over legal niceties. The companies who won the battle of Brignais fought for themselves, owning no lord and no allegiance. But the absurd lengths to which some men would go in order to give some colour of authority to their actions may be illustrated by the story of John Verney, an English *routier* who in 1365 was levying open war as the official lieutenant of a lunatic who believed himself to be the rightful King of France.[2] Few, no doubt, and least of all the victims of his depredations, were much impressed by John's claim, but it is significant that he should have troubled to make it at all.

In a war fought under the avowal of a sovereign prince, the soldier could fight, and had a legal title to his gains of war. But the problem of taking part in a war did not end here. A third standard, suggested by the canonists, was also relevant to the soldier's position: the war must be just with regard to the person engaging in it. Given that it satisfied other legal standards of justice, he still had to decide whether he personally could justly participate. What he had to consider here was whether his personal connections, feudal, chivalrous or otherwise, did or did not impose prior obligations which would preclude him from justly taking up arms.

---

[1] G. Templeman, 'Edward III and the Hundred Years War', *T.R.H.S.*, 5th series, Vol. 2 (1952), p. 78. This article gives an excellent résumé of the type of legal problem about which, in the fourteenth century, the question of levying war revolved.

[2] Baluze, *Histoire de la Maison d'Auvergne*, Tome II (Preuves), p. 441. On this pretender, whose true name was Joannino Gueci, see Vaissette, *Histoire de Languedoc* (Toulouse edn.), Tome IX, p. 723, n. 3.

This was far from being an easy question to answer. In medieval times men treated with great seriousness any sort of personal relationship. Connections which carried all kinds of implications could be contracted in the most casual manner: we have seen already how an accidental encounter in a mine could create a close bond between two soldiers.[1] To receive gifts, let alone honours or a pension, compromised a man seriously. Hence, for instance, the Black Prince's angry insistence that the Captal de Buch return the gifts which Charles V had made him, when he released him from prison after he had been taken at Cocherel.[2] Hence, again, the strict rule in the statutes of the Order of the Golden Fleece, that anyone entering it should renounce any other order or association which might interfere with his obligations.[3] This rule was one which had to be modified early in the history of the order, which is an indication of how complex this problem of personal connection was.[4] It was all too possible for a soldier to be faced with a problem of directly conflicting loyalties, and he had to judge for himself, on the basis of particular circumstances, whether such conflict put him out of the war, or whether prior obligation brought him in. He had another problem too, perhaps more serious; suppose he decided that he was entitled to fight, certain connections notwithstanding, would the enemy also regard him as so entitled if he had the misfortune to fall into their hands?

Although almost any kind of connection might affect a man's just title to take up arms, the most serious were those which involved oaths. Among these, the bonds of feudal and sovereign allegiance had the most obvious importance. This is indicated by the fact that these loyalties were normally reserved in instruments which established other relations between soldiers,

---

[1] *Ante*, ch. IV, p. 49, n. 6, 8.

[2] *Oeuvres de Froissart*, ed. Kervyn de Lettenhove, Tome VII, pp. 79–80.

[3] See statutes, in Léfèvre de St. Rémy, *Chroniques*, ed. F. Morand (Soc. de l'histoire de France, 1881), Tome II, p. 212. A similar rule is laid down in the statutes of a confraternity of Quercy knights in 1380; see L. D'Alauzier, 'Une alliance des Seigneurs du Quercy en 1380', *Annales du Midi*, Vol. 64 (1952), pp. 149–51.

[4] The statute was modified at the 1440 chapter, to the effect that a companion could continue to bear an order of which he was himself head, *Régistres de la Toison d'Or*, i, fo. 27vo.

in the statutes of orders of chivalry[1] and of confraternities of knights,[2] for example, as also in contracts of service[3] and in agreements between brothers-in-arms.[4] Even the most hardened of freebooters, indeed, were careful about these two prime obligations. The Archpriest refused to fight at Cocherel, because he held lands of the Captal de Buch, who commanded for the King of Navarre.[5] Perrot le Béarnois would never take service with the Count of Armagnac, though almost all his fellow *routiers* in Auvergne did so, because the count was the capital adversary of his sovereign lord in Béarn, Gaston Phoebus of Foix.[6]

Even these relations, however, did not always make a man's position clear. A man was not normally regarded as entitled to wage war if his liege lord was a principal on the other side, unless it was in his own cause and he had formally defied him. The ruling in the case of Garcia Raimond of Aubeterre and the Count of Longueville in 1390, which has been quoted already, was however that by law of arms this embargo might not apply when the liege lord was not a principal—as in this case, when the Black Prince, Garcia's lord, was said to have fought as the paid soldier of Don Pedro.[7] Equally, there could be a clash of loyalties because a man held land feudally of more than one lord, or because two lords claimed the same allegiance from him, or because there was a conflict between allegiance to his

[1] Léfèvre de St. Rémy, op. cit., p. 217.

[2] See statutes of the Quercy confraternity, op. cit. (n. 11): and compare the statutes of the confraternity of the Golden Apple (founded in Auvergne in 1395), and printed by A. Jacotin, *Preuves de la Maison de Polignac* (Paris, 1898–1906), Tome II, p. 172 (no. 283).

[3] Cf. for example Ramonet de Sort's exception of the King of England in his contract with Armagnac, January 1389, Bib. Nat., Collection Doat, Tome 203, fo. 286; and John de Salazar's exception of the King of Castile in his contract with Philip the Good, June 1442, Arch. de la Côte d'Or, B 11740. The English indentures, among the Exchequer Accounts Various, are not of much importance in this instance, as nearly all are made with English subjects.

[4] See the compact of brotherhood between Thomas Duke of Clarence and Charles of Orleans, November 1412, in L. Douet d'Arq, *Pièces inédites sur la Règne de Charles VI* (Soc. de l'histoire de France, 1863), Tome I, p. 359, in which Clarence carefully reserves his allegiance to Henry IV.

[5] Cherest, *L'Archiprêtre* (Paris, 1863), pp. 246–50.

[6] Cf. J. Rouquette, *La Rouergue sous les Anglais* (Millau, 1887), pp. 345–6.

[7] See *Ante*, ch. IV, p. 53, n. 1 and 2.

liege lord and his sovereign. Enguerrand de Bournonville, claimed in 1414 that he was defending Soissons *jure guerrarum* for his lord, John the Fearless (who clearly exercised some sort of sovereignty), against John's capital adversary, the Duke of Orleans.[1] Charles VI, however, was in the Armagnac camp, and when the city fell Enguerrand was put to death as a traitor, who had appeared in arms against his sovereign, the King of France.[2] The problem facing a soldier in such a case had no easy solution.

There were many other bonds, besides these, which might affect a man's position if he was considering arming himself in some given cause. He might have taken a solemn oath to another to be his prisoner, or his brother-in-arms, or have taken his personal order, or he might be his pensioner or hold office from him.[3] Any such connection laid on him powerful obligations, and his betrayal of them might be construed as treason. The most important of these bonds other than those of ordinary allegiance were probably those of kinship, and those of a sworn prisoner. This latter was not one which presented frequent problems, because a prisoner was not always able to fight, but it could do so, especially where a ransom was discharged by service.[4] This then presented a major clash of allegiance. One must remember that being a man's prisoner was, in idea at least, an honourable relationship; hence the anxiety of noblemen and princes over the status of their captors (John the Good at Poitiers, for instance, chose in the mêlée to give his faith to Denis de Morbek because he was a gentleman).[5]

[1] *Chronique du Réligieux de St Denis*, ed. M. L. Belleguat (Documents inédits sur l'histoire de France, 1844), Tome V, p. 298.

[2] Ibid., Tome V, p. 329.

[3] A good example of the importance of office is given by Denifle, *La Désolation des Eglises*, Tome II, p. 261. When the companies invaded papal territory in 1359, Innocent VI requested the King of Aragon not to retain in his service any longer John Ferdinand de Heredia, as he was Captain General of Papal troops and therefore required to serve about Avignon.

[4] A fair number of persons—especially men of humble rank—seem to have discharged ransoms in this way. This involved fighting against their own side, technically a treason, and one therefore finds records of such ransoms in the French chancery registers, among pardons for this offence, e.g. Arch Nat., JJ 87, no. 167; JJ 90, no. 237; JJ 108, no. 329; JJ 173, no. 21.

[5] *Oeuvres de Froissart*, ed. Kervyn de Lettenhove, Tome VI, p. 454. John would not surrender until Denis assured him he was a knight.

Like other sworn relations, as that of brotherhood-in-arms or companionship in an order, it created a bond of fellowship, to break which seemed, in contemporary eyes, deep treachery. The betrayal of fellowship, of whatever kind and however created, could not be easily forgiven. Twenty years after Najera Du Guesclin's nephew still had hard words to say of the soldiers who had left his uncle to join the Black Prince in Spain; the wound was not closed.[1]

Two further points deserve mention in connection with this matter of private relations, both of which emphasise further the importance of purely personal connections. One is that even if these were overriden by a prior allegiance and a man took arms in spite of them, their effect was by no means entirely null. Thus a man could not, in strict law, keep his brother-in-arms a prisoner,[2] while a companion of a chivalrous order, though he might without dishonour take the part of his sovereign against the head of the order, must release a fellow member without ransom if he took him in war.[3] The second point is that there was a considerable difference between fighting against a party in which one had close connections, and fighting when one's connections were present in person. A good example may be seen in the terms of the contract, signed in 1433 between Jean de Vergy and the Duchess of Bar. Vergy took her wages, and agreed to make war on the English in Bar and Lorraine, in order to drive them out. Nothing, he promised, would force him to desert her cause or to cease to serve her against these enemies 'unless the King of England or the Regent come to these parts in their persons'.[4] Vergy, like so many Burgundian

---

[1] Molinier, op. cit., Pièce Justificative, no. XCIV. Longueville claimed that all the debts owed to Aubeterre were confiscate for treason, because in Spain 'le sire (d'Aubeterre) estoit jure Messire Bertran, et se tourna contre lui'.

[2] Bartholomew of Saliceto, *Super VIII Cod.*, Tit. 51, l. 2; otherwise, he declares, their association 'non potest dici bona societas et fraternitas'.

[3] Cf. statutes of the Golden Fleece, Léfèvre de St. Rémy, op. cit., p. 218.

[4] Dom. Plancher, *Histoire de Bourgogne*, Tome IV, Preuves no. LXXV. Compare with this the terms of the agreement between Robert de Fiennes, Constable of France, and John Dalton and Dakyn Hatton, the English captains of Regennes and La Motte de Chaulay, 1 December 1359, Rymer, Vol. III, pt. I, p. 190. John and Dakyn agreed to evacuate for 26,000 *moutons d'or*, and thereafter not to take arms against the French for a year,

leaders, had close connections with the English, and while he could fight their soldiers in the Rhineland, he was too closely connected to them to arm himself in the personal presence of Bedford or Henry VI. In very much the same way the arrival in 1439 of the personal heralds of Charles VII and the Duke of Bourbon, with the news that their masters had entered the war of René of Anjou against the Count of Vaudemont, caused something like half the companies which the count had hired to change sides in mid-campaign.[1]

It must by now be clear that on this question of the right to engage in war certain guiding principles could be laid down, but that the rules were not clear cut. Even on central issues opinion could be uncertain, and there could be sharp disagreement between two sides as to whether given individuals could take up arms. The Captal de Buch in 1369 clearly thought himself bound to arm in the English cause; but Charles V equally clearly thought he was bound not to, and when he was taken prisoner refused absolutely to allow himself to ransom himself.[2] In such a case, one may doubt if all the legal wisdom of western Europe could have found one clear solution. This being so, it is time to turn from the question of a soldier's title to take

[1] A. Tuetey, *Les Écorcheurs sous Charles VII* (Montbéliard, 1874), Tome I, p. 69. The letter presented by the herald to Antoine de Chabannes has been copied into the *Chronique Martinianne*, ed. P. Champion, p. 29. The whole incident is clearly parallel to the events of 1366–7, when the Black Prince joined Pedro the Cruel, and summoned back the companies of his allegiance who were serving Henry of Trastamare. Another similar incident took place in 1432, when Artus de Richemont came to the aid of his liege lord, John of Brittany, and joined Scales, Fastolf and Willoughby at the siege of Pouancé, although elsewhere he was fighting for the French against the English. All the companies at the siege were in Brittany's pay and avowal; see E. Cosneau, *Le Connétable de Richemont* (Paris, 1886), p. 187.

[2] *Oeuvres de Froissart*, ed. Kervyn de Lettenhove, Tome VIII, pp. 400 and 402. Compensation was paid by Charles V to the Montmor brothers, who had bought the Captal for ransom from the Spaniards who captured him. See *Chroniques des Règnes de Jean II et Charles V*, ed. R. Delachenal (Soc. de l'histoire de France, 1920), Vol. III, pp. 162–78.

but this embargo was not to apply if they were serving in the personal company of Edward III, his lieutenant, or the Duke of Lancaster. Again, in the affair of the Black Prince and d'Audreham, discussed *ante*, ch. IV, the Marshal, though a prisoner, was said to be entitled to arm against the Prince if in the company of the King of France or a prince of the Fleurs-de-Lys.

up arms to the question of the risks that he ran, if he decided to do so.

In the case of a man of single allegiance, let us say an Englishman like John Fastolf or Mathew Gough, there was no problem. In the struggle against the French he was to them a legal enemy, and ran no more than the ordinary risks of war. The case of a man like the Captal or Enguerrand de Coucy, who had connections with both sides, was much more complicated. He might, as Enguerrand did, choose to stay out of the war, and if he did so he stood a reasonable chance of achieving recognition for his purely private neutrality.[1] But he might, as the Captal did, choose to make war under the avowal of one or other of the principals. If his connections with the other side were merely personal, he would be expected to disclaim them before entering the war (the records of the various orders of chivalry give a good many examples of persons who renounced membership on these grounds).[2] If, on the other hand, he held lands of someone in the opposing party, he would be treated, as far as these lands were concerned, as guilty of treason. This did not mean that he would be treated as a traitor if taken. If the opponents recognised his avowal and his obligations to the side for which he fought, he would in that case be treated as a genuine enemy, and allowed such privileges as the right of ransom.[3] But his lands and goods which were within their actual or asserted jurisdiction would be confiscate, and for treason, from the moment he took up arms. Thus the Parlement

---

[1] Cf. *Oeuvres de Froissart*, ed. Kervyn de Lettenhove, Tome VIII, p. 291.

[2] See, e.g. Enguerrand de Coucy's renunciation of the Garter when he joined the French side in the war, 1377 (Rymer, Vol. III, pt. 3, p. 68); Francois of Aragon's renunciation of the Garter, after the taking of Fougères had been disavowed (Stevenson, *Wars of the English in France*, R.S., Vol. I, p. 276); Lord Duras's renunciation of the Garter on doing homage to Louis XI, 1476 (Anstis, *Registers of the Garter*, Vol. I, pp. 78 and 202; but note his Garter was not apparently returned but offered at the altar of a church in Calais); Chateauvillain's renunciation of Bedford's order in 1433, Plancher, *Histoire de Bourgogne*, Tome IV, p. 170. Plancher wrongly refers to the Order as the Garter.

[3] An example would be the Earl of Kendale, who had extensive lands in France, all of which were confiscate; but when taken a prisoner in 1451, was still allowed to ransom himself. As he had little fortune in England, he was ruined by the payment. See Anstis, *Registers of the Garter*, Vol. I, p. 78, n. 1.

of Paris in 1436 adjudged that all Bedford's goods were confiscate because he was *crimineulx de crime de lèse-majesté*.[1] The
judges rejected, however, the ingenious plea, made against this
decision and aimed to reduce it to absurdity, that if this was so
then the Kingdom of England was confiscate for the same
offence.[2] They did not deny that Bedford had had the status
and privileges of an enemy. They claimed only that in so far
as his goods were in their jurisdiction they were the goods of a
traitor, which was in that age a very reasonable way of getting
over the endless problem of the multiple allegiance not only of
men, but of land and property too.

But suppose a man took up arms in a quarrel which his
opponents did not regard as legally justifying his action, what
then? Such a case involved a number of problems, both from
their point of view and his, which must be considered in turn.

It has been said that taking a part in legally unjust war
doubled the risks which a soldier ran. This was because if he
did so, he was automatically guilty of *lèse-majesté*. If he took up
arms in despite of binding allegiance, this was obviously so. It
was so in any other case too because only a sovereign prince
could levy public war, and if a man levied public war without
the licence or avowal of such a prince, he was usurping sovereign
authority and injuring majesty. Thus he was a traitor, and could
be taken and treated as such. He might, of course, defend himself on the ground that he had not committed any act of public
war, such as burning or taking spoil, but judges were likely to
be sceptical about this, and rightly. Accusations were usually
carefully worded, listing individual acts committed *ad modum
hostium regni*, or *ainsi que la guerre fut ouverte*[3] in order to bring
home the charge.

---

[1] Arch. Nat., X[1]a 4799, fo. 222.    [2] Ibid., fos. 228vo and 230.

[3] Cf. for example the Regent Charles's order to the Bailli of Macon, 1358,
to proceed against Henry de Montagny, who had attacked Brignais 'more
hostili' (Guiges, op. cit., p. 231); accusation, 1361, against William de
Ferté that he had taken prisoner a man of Peter de Crassey, 'ad modum
hostium regni' (Arch. Nat., X[1]a 17, fo. 78); accusation against Berthon de
Signey and John de l'Essarges, 1365, that they had fought 'ad modum acie
et guerre' within the Kingdom (Arch. Nat., X[2]a 8, fo. 110 et seq.); against
Gerard de Bucy and Bernard de Lissade, 1369, that they had fought 'more
hostili et predonum guerre' (Arch. Nat., X[2]a 8, fo. 118); and for a later
example, the complaint of the Duke of Somerset, February 1448, that the

The seriousness of this legal position, from the soldier's point of view, must not however be exaggerated. The solemn anathemas of Edward III on the free companies,[1] and of Charles VII on the *écorcheurs*,[2] banishing them and disavowing them as traitors and rebels, were not very effective. A great many soldiers committed unnumbered acts of war without a shred of legal title, and got away with it. There were two main ways by which men avoided the consequence of such actions. In the first place, soldiers frequently managed to obtain royal pardon, either by purchase, or because a king regarded their allegiance or service as a valuable asset against some more important enemy. There are endless such pardons preserved among official records in France.[3] As most of these cover all acts done before the pardon was granted, a man who obtained one was probably secure in such profits, at least in goods and chattels, as he had made in the course of his illegal enterprise.[4] The only inconvenience he had to suffer was, therefore, that he could no longer pursue any claims to unpaid ransoms, *appatis*, and so on, because his actions were admitted to be outside the law, and no legal claim could arise out of an originally illegal act. This was in fact one of the regular defences against a claim to ransom money. One might instance the case between the Duke of

[1] Rymer, Vol. III, pt. II, p. 50. Order dated 18 November 1361 to John Hound and Richard Imworth to go to France, and seek out those who were English subjects and were occupying themselves 'de piler et rober les gentz, prendre prisons et ransoner, occuper forteresses, si en avant come en temps de guerre'; to give them a term to leave France, and arrest them if they refuse; or if they were not able to arrest them to report their names to the Council.

[2] Cf. Tuetey op. cit., Tome I, p. 127, n. 1. The opening words of Charles's order are worth noting: 'Comme de raison nul ne puisse ou doie assembler gens et soy mettre sus en armes . . . sans nostre auctorite, congie et licence, et s'aucun fait le contraire, il se rend criminelle de crisme de lese mageste'.

[3] A representative selection of examples may be found in the additional documents, printed at the end of Tome X of Vaissette's *Histoire de Languedoc*, in the Toulouse edition (1872–6), e.g. nos. 624, 640, 641, 683, 688, 693, 694, 698, 717, 734, 749.

[4] An example of pardon being pleaded against claims for damages is the case of Ferté *v.* Crassey, quoted earlier (Arch. Nat., X¹a 17, fo. 98).

men of the French garrison of Lonniers were raiding in English land 'tout ensi que la guerre eust este et fust ouverte' (Bib. Nat., MS. Fr. 4054, fo. 83).

Burgundy and the Pursuivant d'Amour in 1368, in which the
Duke alleged a debt to be null because his money was promised
the Pursuivant to pay an illegal ransom, and the King of England
was quoted as having disavowed the Pursuivant's war.[1] This
did not mean that the Pursuivant was likely to be accused of
high treason. His crimes seem to have been long forgotten, but
since his war had been technically illicit, he could make no
claim, even though he had a letter of obligation sealed in the
proper form to back it.

A further inconvenience of levying war without the avowal
of a prince was that it was technically not only an offence to
take spoil or ransom in such circumstances, but also to pay it,
or indeed to communicate or traffic with enemies of this kind
in any way. For this offence innumerable pardons are entered
in the French chancery registers.[2] They reveal the disadvantage
of this rule, that it was impossible to implement effectively.[3] In
a period (the 1380s) when it could be said of the whole province of Rouergue that it was 'more or less appatised by the
enemy'[4] (that is, by the free companies), most local people had
a far more healthy fear of a *routier* captain than they had of the
king's law. If they paid their ransoms and *appatis* to the soldiers,
the most they were likely to suffer was the payment of a fine for
a pardon if anyone afterwards raised the matter. But if they
took their stand in law and refused to pay such ransoms, they
could be fairly certain that drastic reprisals would follow; their

[1] Arch. Nat., X¹a 1469, fo. 265.
[2] E.g. Arch. Nat., JJ 90, nos. 184, 187, 201, 215, 220, 224, 257 (all
pardons for trading, or communicating with Navarrese and English companies in N. France). For pardons given in the south of France, mostly by
the King's lieutenant in Languedoc, see Dom Vaissette, *Histoire de Languedoc*
(Toulouse edn., 1872–6), Tome X, cols. 1453, 1685, 1686, 1687, 1814, 1824,
1826.
[3] The researches of the Abbé Rouquette throw some interesting light on
the difficulties here involved. He quotes, for instance, a letter of the Bishop
of Paris to the Bishop of Millau, ordering him and his clergy to absolve those
who had fallen under Urban V's excommunication because they had traded
with the companies, because it was *impossible* for them to avoid doing so.
(*La Rouergue sous les Anglais*, Pièce Justificative, no. 30.) He also notes large
payments mentioned in the Archives Communales de Rodez, for the right
to trade with the free companies (ibid., p. 299).
[4] Vaissette, op. cit., Tome X, p. 909, n. 4, quoting French Chancery
register for 1382.

lands and crops would be overrun, their vines burnt, and their neighbours and kinsmen carried off as hostages.

Herein lay the root of the problem of the free companies. The administrative, financial and military problems of mounting a royal expedition in sufficient force to mop up the companies, especially in country such as Rouergue and Auvergne, were virtually insurmountable. This gave the *routier* his other chance to get away with unlicensed war, and that not merely scot-free but with substantial profit. Everybody knew that the companies had no alternative to living off the country, and everybody knew equally that it would be costly and dangerous to attempt to dislodge them. Much the simplest thing to do was to pay them a sum down to quit; by which means, after twenty years of abortive effort, the Marmouset official Jean de Blaisy finally cleared the central provinces of Auvergne, Rouergue, Gevaudan and Velay in 1392.[1] By that time most of the captains there had been bought off the country, or specific parts of it, half a dozen times at least.[2] Usually, unless they thought their position was weak, they insisted on full payment of all outstanding ransoms and *appatis* over and above the capital sum for departure.[3] Although such ransoms were extracted illegally, in this case the law would be on their side, for no one was more anxious to see the last of them than the government and its officials. The Parlement of Paris in 1373 had no hesitation in forcing the men of Senlis, who had agreed to help pay off one

[1] Cf. J. Monicat, *Les Grandes Compagnies en Velay* (Paris, 1928), p. 87 et seq Blaisy's agreement with Armagnac about the terms they were to offer the English are printed in Jacotin, *Preuves de la Maison de Polignac*, Tome IV, no. 707 (pp. 263–4).

[2] The first major effort to clear the companies was made by d'Audreham as royal lieutenant in Languedoc in 1362 (Molinier, op. cit., pp. 108–9). A few years later (1367) the efforts of the English seneschal of Rouergue to raise money to pay off the companies in his area was one of the causes of the quarrel between the Black Prince and Armagnac (Rouquette, op. cit., pp. 110–14). Further major efforts to pay off the companies were made by Armagnac in 1376 (ibid., p. 284); in 1379 (ibid., p. 303); in 1380 (*Preuves de la Maison de Polignac*, Tome II, no. 252); and in 1387–8 (Monicat, op. cit., p. 84). Besides these, of course, there were innumerable treaties and agreements with individual commanders to leave given localities.

[3] Careful arrangements for the trial of cases arising out of such claims, before two judges, one chosen by the companies and the other by the French, are among the terms agreed between Blaisy and Armagnac in 1390 (n. 1 *supra*).

Sancho Garcia, to meet their obligations.[1] The lengths to which officials would go in this matter is well illustrated by an ugly little story from Anjou in 1358–9. In order to get the companies away, all prisoners who had escaped were ordered to return to their captors. Some were so terrified by this prospect that they took to the hills, and hid in caves. In his anxiety to meet the province's creditors, the seneschal himself pursued them, and when they would not leave their retreat he ordered his men to smoke them out. One man was suffocated, and the seneschal obtained a pardon for his death, which he had caused in the conscientious pursuit of official duty.[2]

The real answer to this problem of the freelance soldier was only found at the end of the Hundred Years War, in the organisation of standing armies. By the 1420s the English in France were becoming anxious to ensure that every man-at-arms appeared on some official muster roll;[3] while Charles VII's ordinance of 1439 virtually founded the French royal army.[4] The severe measures taken against those who were not mustered made it, from these times on, steadily harder and harder for the independent *routier* to find a living. But even before this there were plenty of occasions when the law took its due course, and imposed the full penalties on those who had waged illicit war. The list of those who suffered for this crime is long, and many names on it are those of men who in their own way were illustrious. Pierre de Saquainville, 'who was in his time a good esquire', was beheaded at Evreux after Cocherel.[5] Enguerrand

[1] Arch. Nat., X¹a 23, fo. 224.    [2] Arch. Nat., JJ 89, no. 468.

[3] Cf. Bedford's ordinance of 1423, printed Miss Rowe 'The discipline of the Norman garrisons under Bedford', *E.H.R.*, Vol. 46 (1931), which orders that 'gens sans adveu ou retenue de capitaine' are to find captains at once, or leave the calling of arms (pp. 202–3); also Salisbury's Perche Orders (1427), which order that 'no man of arms no archer of what estate, condicioun or nacioun that ever he bee that they abide not nor hold them under the colour our said lord the erle, but that theire captens be in this present assemblie and compaine, and that they mustered and muster at all times that they be required' (B. Mus., Cotton MS. Julius F IV, fo. 322). The whole question of the reorganisation of the English armies in this period is admirably reviewed by A. Newhall, *Muster and Review* (Harvard Historical monographs, no. 13; Cambridge, 1940).

[4] *Ordonnances*, Vol. XIII, p. 306 et seq.

[5] *Chronique des Quatre Premiers Valois*, ed. S. Luce (Soc. de l'histoire de France, 1862), p. 149.

de Bournonville, who had been the idol of the French companies in Lombardy, was condemned to death because he had defended Soissons in arms against Charles VI.[1] Sir Henry Boynton was condemned to death by the Constable of England, because he had defended Berwick against Henry IV.[2] The Bastard of Bourbon was tied in a sack at the order of the Provost of the marshals of France, and thrown into the Aube.[3] Many others received equally short shrift. As their trials were normally summary, accounts of them seldom survive. One trial is however recorded in detail, that of Mérigot Marchès, a genuine *routier* and a famous one.[4] It may be useful to conclude this chapter with some account of this process, as it illustrates how the issues discussed here were likely to be raised in a court of law.

Mérigot Marchès was one of a group of *routier* captains who operated in southern and central France in the 1370s and 1380s, fighting sometimes in the name of the King of England, sometimes for the counts of Armagnac and Foix, and often enough for themselves. Along with a good many of his companions, he came into the truce organised by Jean de Blaisy in 1390. After its signature, however, presumably because he found John's payments to quit slow, he seized the fort of La Roche Vendeux, and levied open war around it. The fort was besieged, and though when it fell Mérigot was absent, he was surrendered to Jean de Blaisy by his cousin, the castellan of Tournemine, with whom he had taken refuge. He was sent then to Paris, and was tried at the Chatelet in July 1391.[5]

In the course of the trial Mérigot spoke at length in his own defence, and his arguments were considered and answered by his judges. These two viewpoints reveal what issues were in

[1] *Chronique du Réligieux de St. Denis,* ed. Bellaguet, Tome V, p. 329.

[2] B. Mus., Add. MS. 9021, fos. 8–9.

[3] Gruel, *Histoire d'Artus III Comte de Richemont,* ed. Michaud and Poujoulat (Nouvelle Collection des mémoires pour servir à l'histoire de France, Tome III, Paris, 1837), p. 216.

[4] Duplés Agier, *Régistre criminelle du Châtelet de Paris 1389–92* (Paris, 1861–4), Tome II, pp. 177–213.

[5] For further background of the case see Maurice Chanson, 'Un procés criminelle sous Charles VI', *Revue d' Auvergne,* Tome V (1888), p. 87 et seq. I have taken these details from his article, but corrected the date of the trial from July 1392, which he gives, to July 1391, as in the Register.

question. Mérigot's speech is the less consistent (he had probably been subjected to torture), but its general drift is clear.[1] His first object was to establish his English allegiance. He had been left as a child, he said, in the care of the English, when his native Limousin was ceded to them at Brétigny; at the age of sixteen he had done homage in person to the Duke of Lancaster, 'and swore to serve the said Duke and the King of England well and loyally for ever'. Since then he had served continually in the English cause, and had 'done all those things which a man can and ought to do in a just war, as taking Frenchmen and putting them to ransom, living on the country and despoiling it, and leading the company under his command about the realm of France, and burning and firing places in it'. As additional evidence, to show that the French had recognised his avowal by the English, he pointed out that he had three times been captured by them, and had always been allowed to ransom himself.

So far Mérigot had been making clear his general position in the war, and up to this point his case seems to have been fairly strong. It was when he came on to defend himself on the particular charge, that he had continued to make war after he had come into the truce arranged by Jean de Blaisy, that its weakness became apparent. Sometime in August 1390, he said, a commissioner of Richard II had arrived at La Roche and had ordered him to leave the fort, on pain of being banished as a traitor and a rebel (the usual form of disavowal). This had been said publicly; in private, however, the commissioner had told him to defend the place as best he could. He also claimed that about the same time he had received letters from Lancaster, saying that he was to defend the fortresses in his power to the limit of his ability, and that the Duke would shortly be mounting an expedition against France. These two stories were clearly intended to suggest he had avowal for his actions since the truce. As a further alternative defence, he submitted that he had seized La Roche as surety for a debt outstanding from the Count of Armagnac for his wages when he fought for him in Aragon, and that its seizure was therefore excusable as an act of legitimate reprisal. The claim was empty, as Armagnac had already granted him the fort of St. Gariers, but it was probably

[1] Merigot's statements occupy pp. 184–200 in Duplès Agier.

98

meant to buttress a shaky defence, since the stories of English avowal were quite unconfirmed.

The judges, in their review of the case, answered Mérigot point by point.[1] They first sought to establish that he was a native subject of France; his father's liege lord had been the Bishop of Limoges, who was of the French party, as too were all Mérigot's kin. He had fought continually against the French, burning, robbing and pillaging, all acts of open war and so forbidden to a French subject. The judges' view here was a little tendentious; Limousin was disputed land, and in the past Mérigot's English allegiance had been always recognised. On the particular charges, however, their case was strong where his was weak. He had done acts of war since the truce as well as before it. He had no confirmed avowal for these acts from the King of England, whose commissioners had publicly forbidden them, and so they were *sans cause et raison*. Nor could he defend his actions on the ground of reprisal (reprisal, in law, technically required princely authority). The judges summed up as follows:

> Against the said prisoner, who is not the head of a war, the king can have no formal war and has no defiance from him. Rather has he (the prisoner), by way of treason, taken, raised, and levied *appatiz* and ransoms in the king's realm, and has done so since the truces were cried.

Therefore they were of the opinion that Mérigot was 'a great traitor to the king and his realm, and a great robber, murderer and incendiary, and as such he merited solemn execution'. Mérigot was therefore condemned to die as a traitor, and was beheaded in Les Halles at Paris.

Nearly all the issues discussed in this chapter seem to have been raised at this trial. It revolved essentially round certain actions which, Mérigot claimed, a soldier 'can and ought to do in a just war', but which the judges defined as the crimes of treason, murder, robbery and arson. Which view was correct depended on whether or not the war could be regarded as just, and the evidence quoted was intended to be conclusive on just this point. The questions were whether, in the first place, Mérigot had the avowal of the English; whether, in the second, this avowal could entitle him to make just war in France, seeing

[1] Duplés Agier, pp. 205–10.

he was the feudal man of the Bishop of Limoges, a Frenchman; whether, in the third, even if it could do so, it could cover his acts done since the signing of the truce. Since on this third and decisive count he could produce no adequate defence, and as he had not the standing to make 'formal war' in his own name,[1] Mérigot was guilty of treason, and as a traitor he was executed. He was perhaps less fortunate than many of his fellow-soldiers, but the law was clear enough; it was only circumstance that saved them from similar disaster.

[1] Compare this with the statement made by proctors in the Parlement of Paris with reference to William Bulmer, an English *routier* condemned in the 1360s: 'Boulemer n'estoit que pillart et ne pouvoit faire guerre, et fu execute pour ses demerites' (Arch. Nat., X¹a 1471, fo. 293). See also the account of the treatment of the 'English' prisoners taken at Vignée by Guillaume de Merle in 1365, *Chronique Normande du Quatorzième Siècle*, ed. A. and E. Molinier (Soc. de l'histoire de France, 1882), p. 166: 'et assez tost apres les fist Guillaume de Merle tous noyer . . . pour cause que ilz faisoient guerre de compaignie et n'avoient point de tiltre de seigneur'.

# VII

# THE SIGNS OF WAR

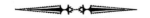

MÉRIGOT MARCHÈS was perhaps unusually unfortunate among men of his class. It so happened that at the time when he seized La Roche Vendeux there was only one major war in progress on French soil, and in that war hostilities had been halted by a truce. This was not the usual state of affairs; one might for instance contrast it with the conditions of the decade following the peace of Brétigny, when also the Anglo-French war had been halted. These ten years saw at least three major wars in France, the war of France against Navarre which ended at Cocherel, the war of the rival houses of Blois and Montfort in Brittany, and the war of the Counts of Foix and Armagnac. Besides these there were innumerable minor feudal wars in the kingdom, and two major ones on its frontiers in which both French and English were involved, one in Provence resulting from the tangled quarrels of the Neapolitan dynasties, and a straight war of succession in Castile. Throughout this period, large areas of France were overrun by the free companies. How, in these conditions, could one tell whether a given captain was engaging in a technically just war, or simply plundering on his own account?

The conditions of the 1360s were not exceptional in the period of the Hundred Years War; those of the first three decades of the fifteenth century, for instance, were very similar. In such circumstances, genuine and honest errors were easily made. In 1353, for instance, one Miles d'Argenteuil found himself being sued in the Parlement for the spoliation of two

Lombards, whom he had taken under the impression they were lawful prey. Luckily in this case his honesty stood him in good stead; he had released them and restored their goods when he realised his error, and therefore the court ordered that he be pardoned, 'because he would not have done this if he had not thought it was in open war'.[1] Where honest errors could be made so easily, it was not hard for men whose single quest was spoil to contrive them to their own advantage. There were a great many ways of doing this, some of which will be discussed in later chapters. From the point of view of the unfortunate victims of such trickery, however, one great difficulty could be proving that they had been unlawfully injured. What, for instance, were the men of Crevant to do about Estienne Oyn, who in the years 1358 and 1359 was putting their lands to ransom, seeing that no one knew what his allegiance was?[2] Resistance could be dangerous, not only martially but legally. The men of Chablis, for instance, who hunted and killed a band of men at arms, who had pillaged their land and refused to state their allegiance, found themselves being sued for their action before the marshals of France. Louis de Sancerre, having heard their cause, gave them a sealed pardon; but they were lucky to have a fair judge. It was just as well for them they did, for the Marshal's pardon cleared them when in 1370 they were sued again over the same affair in the Parlement.[3]

These men of Chablis were facing a charge of homicide. Their alleged crime was that they had defended themselves against soldiers whose allegiance they did not know, and who were ravaging their countryside. If such anomalous situations were to be avoided, it was necessary to have some simple means of establishing the identity of men-at-arms. To some extent, no

[1] Arch. Nat., X¹a 15, fo. 214. Compare the pardon to Enguerrand de Monstrelet, 1422, for the capture of some merchants of Abbeville, under the impression they were 'bon butin'. He too made restitution, Arch. Nat., JJ 173, no. 13.

[2] Secousse, *Recueil de Pièces sur Charles VII Roi de Navarre* (Paris, 1755), p. 126. There was at this period great confusion as to which side persons were fighting for; cf. for instance the case of Athesans v. Fardel, Arch. Nat., X²a 12, fo. 98, in which each party claimed he was a loyal Frenchman, and the other Navarrese.

[3] Arch. Nat., X¹a 22, fo. 188vo–191. All the details of the case are taken from this record of the proceedings in the Parlement.

doubt, this was achieved by the rules of formal chivalrous etiquette. An army on the march through a kingdom would be met by heralds, who had been sent to challenge it and enquire its business;[1] similarly a commander, before commencing a formal siege, would always summon a town, in his own name or that of the 'head of the war', to admit him.[2] But such exchanges seldom did more than make a situation, which was already clear, explicit; and sometimes the exigences of war made even these formalities impossible. A captain who planned to take a town by escalade at night did not send a herald round in the afternoon to announce his intentions. It was necessary to have some method of indicating them which was clear and direct, but not tactically embarrassing.

To meet this need, a kind of language of war evolved, which was generally recognised by combatants of any party. This language was largely one of signs and cries, that is, of the usual accompaniments of martial ceremony and savagery. But here they were adopted to a more important end; to furnish legal evidence of the manner in which soldiers had conducted themselves and of their title to do so. Such evidence could be crucial in a case where, for example, the legality of a ransom was disputed. As time went by, and the language grew, forms of words were found which showed what rules would be observed in almost innumerable situations, and whose significance became part of the body of customary military law. Some of these signs will be mentioned later. Two matters, however, where the signs themselves were of first importance, must be discussed immediately. In the first place, they were used by soldiers to indicate to their opponents what rules they would observe in battle. Secondly, and from the legal point of view still more

---

[1] Heralds were for example sent by John the Good to meet the army of Henry of Lancaster to offer battle, near Verneuil, in 1356 (*Robert de Avesbury*, R.S., p. 464); by Buckingham to offer battle to Burgundy, near Troyes, 1380 (*Oeuvres de Froissart*, ed. Kervyn de Lettenhove, Tome IX, p. 266); by the Constable d'Albret to meet the army of Henry V on the way to Agincourt, 1415 (*English Life of King Henry V*, ed. Kingsford, p. 48).

[2] Cf. for example the summoning of Soissons in 1414 by Mountjoy King of Arms (*Chronique du Réligieux de St. Denis*, ed. Bellaguet, Tome V, p. 298); summoning of Coursant by heralds, 1433 (Lefèvre de St. Rémy, *Chroniques*, ed. F. Morand, Tome II, p. 277); there are many other examples in, e.g. Froissart's account of the Galician campaign 1386-7.

importantly, they were used to indicate the allegiance of a host or company, and so its title to make war.

Let us turn to the first of these matters. There appear, in our period, to have been four possible conditions or states of war which could be signified. In the first place there was war to the death (*guerre mortelle*). This was what the lawyers called Roman war, fought by the rules which in antiquity had applied in the wars of the Roman people. There was no privilege of ransom; the conquered could be slain or enslaved. Secondly, there was public or open war (in legal Latin, a *bellum hostile*), that is the war of one sovereign Christian prince against another. In this men might take spoil, and captured enemies had the right to ransom themselves. Thirdly, there was feudal or covered war (*guerre couverte*), in which men could wound and kill without blame, but could not burn or take spoil. Fourthly, there was war which may seem no war at all, that is, a truce. Although in truce no hostile act was lawful, it was nevertheless, a condition of war, not peace, for 'when a truce is over, one should not say that a new war has begun, but that the former war continues'.[1]

There was a good deal of confusion about the distinction between the first three conditions of war I have mentioned. This was largely because the earlier middle ages (the eleventh and twelfth centuries) had little experience of international war between Christian princes. The endless local struggles which disrupted northern Europe were almost all wars technically between lords and vassals; even the struggle of the Capetians with the house of Anjou was a feudal war in name.[2] The only international war which the men of this earlier period really knew was the crusade, and this was a Roman war in the true sense. The result was that in the later middle ages men were still confused as to what 'war to the death' meant, hence for instance the long argument in a ransom case in the Parlement of Paris in 1433, as to whether the Hundred Years War was a *guerre mortelle* or a *guerre guerriable* (a war fought under the feudal *droit de guerre*).[3] In fact of course, it was something between the

[1] Martin of Lodi, *Tractatus de Bello*, Quaest XXIX; in Zilletus, *Tractatus Juris Universi*, Tome 16, fo. 324vo.
[2] Cf. R. Fawtier, *The Capetian Kings of France* (transl. L. H. Butler, Macmillan, 1960), pp. 65–7, 139–46.
[3] Buxton *v.* Dorot, Arch. Nat., X$^1$a 4797, fo. 215 et seq.

THE SIGNS OF WAR

two, for it was not a feudal war, and war to the death in its proper sense meant war without the privilege of ransom. Phrases such as *guerre mortelle* or *bellum mortale*, however, could be and often were used loosely.

Inside Christendom, this condition of war to the death was uncommon, at least internationally. In civil strife, quarter was frequently refused, but technically it was doubtful if civil strife merited the name of war at all, any more than did the war of unavowed companies. Its repression was justice, not war. In other instances, where quarter was refused, there were sometimes special reasons, as at Montiel, where Du Guesclin is said to have ordered that no prisoners be taken, on account of the numerous Jews and infidels in Don Pedro's army.[1] But occasionally ordinary engagements were fought to the death too. The French at Crecy, for instance, had orders to give no quarter;[2] and Joan of Arc, in an open letter to the English commanders, told them that she was a *chief de guerre* and that her followers would take no prisoners.[3]

The usual sign of war to the death was the carrying of a red flag or banner. Thus in 1293 English sailors, who had been involved in a clash at sea with the French, reported that the enemy had been flying *bausons* or streamers of red sendal 'which everywhere among mariners means war to the death without quarter'.[4] Le Baker declares that at Crecy the French displayed a fiery banner alongside the King's standard, which meant that no one was to take any man alive, on pain of death.[5] This was the Oriflamme, which in the fourteenth and fifteenth centuries seems only to have been unfurled at moments of dire necessity and when no quarter was to be given. It was displayed again at Poitiers, when Knighton calls it 'the red banner which is the sign of death'.[6] It was unfurled also at Roosebeque, according to Froissart after much deliberation and because the Flemings were considered to be no better than enemies of the faith.[7] With

---

[1] *Oeuvres de Froissart*, ed. Kervyn de Lettenhove, Tome VII, p. 266.

[2] *Chronicon Gaufridi Le Baker*, ed. E. Maunde Thompson (Oxford, 1889), p. 82.

[3] B. Mus., Add. Ch. 3642 (n.d.).

[4] Cf. document cited by J. H. Ramsay, *The Dawn of the Constitution* (London, 1908), p. 402, n. 7.

[5] Le Baker, op. cit.   [6] *Chronicon Henrici Knighton*, R.S., Vol. 2, p. 89.

[7] *Oeuvres de Froissart*, ed. Kervyn de Lettenhove, Tome X, pp. 167–8.

obvious anger, Lefèvre de St. Rémy tells us that it was again carried, 'as if against the Saracens', by the Armagnacs when they invaded Artois in 1414, but on this occasion it was not unfurled.[1] Nicholas Upton says that in heraldry red was the colour signifying cruelty and ferocity, as of a prince against his enemies;[2] no doubt this is why it was the colour which signified that no mercy would be shown to men in arms.

The second condition of war was public or open war, the war of a Christian sovereign. This was sometimes called war to the death, but properly it was not so, because quarter was given and prisoners were permitted to ransom themselves. It was, however, war with fire and sword, for as Albert Achille of Brandenburg put it *der Brand ziert den Krieg, wie das Magnificat die Vesper*.[3] Some stories even tell of its being proclaimed by a herald who bore in his right hand a drawn sword and in his left a flaming torch.[4] But the usual sign of such war was the display of the banner of the prince in whose name it was fought. Once his banner was unfurled, he had given a challenge to combat and a state of war legally existed.

From this moment on, the laws of war were in force. This is clearly the point which, in 1322, the younger Despenser was urging on Edward II when he advised him not to unfurl his banner, 'for', he said, 'if your banner, my lord King, be displayed, such universal war will shake your land, as you in your time may hardly be able to still'.[5] What he seems to have meant was that if the royal banner was displayed there would be a state of open war in the realm and the subjects' protection through the common law in part suspended, with unforseeable consequences.[6] After banners were displayed, any opponent (provided he was not a subject) was free to act as in public war. Thus when in 1365 Jean de Melun protested before the Parlement that the Englishman Henry Pomfret, who was suing him for a ransom, had taken him in time of truce, Pomfret's reply

[1] Lefèvre de St. Rémy, *Chroniques*, ed. F. Morand, Tome I, p. 170.

[2] Upton, *De officio Militari*, ed. Bysshe, p. 110.

[3] Quoted by Denife, *La Désolation des Eglises*, Tome II, p. 1.

[4] B. Mus., Add. MS. 9016, fo. 165 (Anstis's notes on heraldry. I doubt if this story is very reliable).

[5] *Chronicles Edward I and II*, R.S., Vol. II, p. 75.

[6] See Keen, 'Treason Trials under the Law of Arms', *T.R.H.S.*, 5th series, Vol. 12 (1962), p. 102.

was that 'Meleun et ceux de sa compaignie chevauchoient a
penon desploye qui estoit vraye signe de guerre entre les gens
d'armes . . . et par ce fut loisiblement pris'.[1] The same point
was made by Richard Aston, lieutenant of the Captain of
Calais, in 1405, when he complained to the Vidame of Amiens
that the Count of St. Pol's men, despite the truce, were making
war 'so plain and open' that they had ridden in English
territory with pennons displayed and taken prisoners.[2]
The display of banners or pennons had thus considerable
legal significance, because deeds done in these circumstances
were performed '*in actu belli*'. It could therefore be used as
evidence for two important purposes, to prove effective breach
of a truce,[3] or to prove that public war had been levied by
unauthorised persons.[4] But it had also further significance. A
banner or a pennon was a man's personal emblem; therefore
when it was displayed he was committed on his honour to

[1] Bib. Nat., MS. Fr. 21717, fo. 144 et seq., assembling scattered references
to this case from Arch. Nat., X¹a 1469 into a full account.

[2] Archives du Nord, B 18824, fo. 231: 'seigneurs de France nous font si
plaine et ouverte guerre que vendredi darrein passe vindrent devant le
chastel de Guysnes un chevalier nomme le Sire d'Asne, Messire Baudwin
de la Conchie etc. . . . et plusieurs autres a panons desploiez et illecques
escarmucherent, prindrent, et navrerent tant de nos gens comme eulx
peuvent.'

[3] Cf. for example the above case; also the complaint of the Earl of
Douglas, 1425, that the English of Cumberland and Westmorland were
raiding in Scotland against the truce 'par playne chivauche de jour od
estandars desployetz' (Nicolas, *Proceedings of the Privy Council*, III, p. 353);
complaint of Perrinet Gressart that the Count of Clermont was fighting
'avec son estandart sus' in time of truce in 1427 (Flamare, *Le Nivernais
pendant la guerre de Cent Ans*, Tome I, pp. 328–9, Preuve no. LXV).

[4] Cf. for England the stress laid on their display of banners in the sentences on those condemned for treasonable war in 1322, *Parl. Writs*, Vol. II,
pt. 2, Appendix, pp. 261a, 262a, 264a, 265a. For French examples see for
instance, among the evidence of criminal acts of war in the case between
Guibert de Martenac and the men of Aurillac, mention of the fact that
Guibert and his relatives had fought 'vexillis erectis et bannitis explicatis'
(Arch. Nat., X¹a 21, fo. 414); the accusation against Loudin de Salignac
(1352) that he had fought 'prodictorie vexillisque erectis per modum
hostilitatis' (Arch. Nat., X²a 6, fo. 62); or the accusation against Jean de
l'Essarges (1368) that he had fought 'armis discoopertis et vexillis arectis
ad modum aciei et guerre' (Arch. Nat., X²a 8, fo. 110 et seq.). All these
cases concern private or feudal wars, and this is why the display of banners
is quoted as criminal.

battle. So Diego de Valera, in his book on chivalry, warns kings and princes that their banners should not be unfurled, except in the sight of the enemy and when they intend to combat him formally in the field.[1] Moreover, because a banner was a sign of high social status (any knight could carry a pennon), a battle in which banners were displayed was a much more serious affair than one in which only pennons were shown. Thus, in 1433, the Seigneur de Montagu was expelled from the Order of the Golden Fleece, because he had left the battle of Anthon, where banners were displayed.[2] In 1471, however, the charge against Jean de Neufchastel, that he had retreated in face of the French at Buxy, was withdrawn because only pennons had been unfurled.[3] The banner of the Duke of Burgundy, in whose name and service he was fighting, had not been unfurled, and so his retreat had not blemished the honour of the Order and its sovereign. This kind of class-distinction about battles is significant; it reminds us that we must beware of treating the law of arms as if it were a modern international law. Though its rules and signs had legal significance among men of different nations, it was observed by them because its regulations were rules of honour, rather than for any rational or humanitarian element in them.

Very little can be established, with regard to the fourteenth and fifteenth centuries, as to what, if any, were the signs of feudal or private war. As has been said earlier, the wars of the greater feudal princes, like the Dukes of Burgundy or Brittany or the count of Foix, were reckoned as the public wars of sovereigns. The wars of the minor feudality, in the normal

[1] Diego de Valera, *Tratado de los Rieptos y Desafios* etc. (Madrid, n.d., *c.* 1500), fo. 19vo. Diego de Valera was a widely travelled knight, and this book is said to discuss rules of arms and ceremony of the English, the French, and the Spanish. He was an acquaintance of Olivier de la Marche.

[2] Régistres de la Toison d'Or, i, fo. 2vo.

[3] Régistres de la Toison d'Or, iii, fo. 18vo. The form of the charge was that 'combien qu'il y eust *penons* desploiez et quilz fussent approchez jusques a combattre et qu'il y eust des mors d'ung coste et d'autre, toutesvoyes finablement . . . les bourgignons se retrahirent par petite conduite'. The reply of Neufchastel was that 'au lieu ou l'aventure estoit advenue n'avoit nulles banieres desployes, que l'entreprise pour laquelle les gens d'armes de bourgogne se mirent a champs ne fut oncques en esperance d'avoir bataille, etc.', i.e. that this was not a full scale battle. I owe this reference to Dr. J. Armstrong of Hertford College.

course of events, attracted attention only when the courts had to consider them, because parties had outstepped their rights by burning, or taking prisoners, or displaying banners in the field. A great many of these petty quarrels were in any case pursued under the cover of greater ones; thus a favourite defence in the French courts against a charge of illicit war was that one's opponent had employed the English or the free companies in his service,[1] and that hostile acts were thus legally done as against the King's enemies. As far as can be made out, the rules of private war remained otherwise what they had always been; a man could arm himself in his own coat armour, he could presumably use his own cry of arms, and provided that he had lawful cause and had defied his enemy, he could fight and kill in his own name. But he could not burn and ravage or ride about the land with unfurled banners; his war was not open but muted, a *guerre couverte*.

The signs of the fourth condition of war, a truce, were of considerable legal importance. This was because a truce, though it suspended hostilities, did not necessarily suspend them generally. It could be quite local, putting some piece of land in the middle of a campaign area temporarily out of the war. Or it could apply to persons instead of places, and they might have to journey through country where war was afoot. Recognisable signs of a truce were therefore essential, and just as red was the sign of war to the death, so white was its special colour. Heralds, according to Anjou King of Arms, carried white flags in sign of truce;[2] they also carried white wands, as a sign of their personal immunity from war.[3] In the same way, in battle, prisoners and

---

[1] See for example the accusation against Pensard de Marsac and others (1368), that they had attacked the men of Albi, aided by diverse men-at-arms 'tam de regno nostro quam *aluinde* oriundi', i.e. free companies (Arch. Nat., X²a 8, fo. 56); accusation against John de l'Essarges (cit. ante p. 107, n.4), that he had employed in his war 'quamplurimos anglicos et alios extra regnum nostrum oriundos'; accusation against Guillaume Dirga and Gaubert David (1391) that among their soldiers were 'englois et autres ennemis du Roy' (Arch. Nat., X²a 12, fo. 131vo et seq.); accusation against the seigneur de Barbasan (1395) that he had employed the English in his war against the Count of Perdiac (Arch. Nat., X²a 12, fo. 282vo). In all these cases the plaintiffs against these men held that the employment of English and other foreigners justified their own hostile actions.

[2] Bodleian MS. Rawlinson C 399, fo. 4 of Anjou's treatise.

[3] B. Mus., Add. MS. 9017, fo. 4 (Anstis's notes).

other persons who were in surety sometimes carried a piece of white paper in their head-dress.[1] But probably the most common sign of truce was the carrying of a white baton, which was regarded as an adequate safe-conduct. Garrisons which had surrendered towns on condition of being allowed free passage back to land in their own allegiance normally marched out of a city carrying these batons in their hands, which gave them security against attack for as long as they were in hostile territory.[2] They were usually given a small escort, possibly just a herald or pursuivant; and strikingly, there are not many examples of persons marching in these conditions being attacked or despoiled.

An alternative, and much less satisfactory way of signifying personal security was to give the person secured a sign or emblem, similar to those which soldiers wore on their coats (the St. Andrew's cross for Burgundy, as it might be, or the cross of St. George for England). Thus, under the year 1418, Monstrelet tells us that 'the Normans now generally wore the red cross, which served them as a passport to go wherever they pleased in security'.[3] But this was a dangerous kind of passport, as it was very easy for persons bearing such signs to be taken for enemies by their own side. There was for instance a long wrangle in the Parlement in 1433 as to what construction should be put on the fact that one Michel de Tillaye had been seen in the Kingdom of Bourges wearing the white cross of Armagnac.[4] Henry VI's proctor took it that he had joined the enemy, and defended the confiscation of his goods as a traitor. His wife and children on the other hand pleaded that he had put on the white cross only for security while a prisoner, as the Armagnacs had

[1] *Le Jouvencel*, ed. Lécestre and Favre, Tome II, p. 236, where a prisoner carries in battle 'ung papillon de papier sur sa teste . . . et estoit l'enseigne que les prisoniers et gens a sauf-conduit portoient pour le temps'.

[2] Cf. account of the evacuation of the garrison of Rouen in 1419, who went out 'le baston au poing' (Waurin, *Chroniques*, R.S., Vol. 2, p. 262); of the evacuation Montaiguillon in 1423, whose garrison went out 'chacun un blanq baton en leur main' (do., Vol. 3, p. 33); of the evacuation of La Roche in 1423 (do., Vol. 3, p. 234). The earliest reference I have found to the use of the white baton is in d'Oronville's account of the evacuation of the English garrison of Saint Angel in 1375 (*Chronique du Bon Duc Louis de Bourbon*, ed. A-M. Chazaud, p. 104).

[3] Monstrelet, *Chronique*, ed. L. Douet d'Arq, Tome III, p. 313.

[4] Arch. Nat., X[1]a 4797, fos. 102vo, and 181, 185 and 186.

ordered all prisoners to do so after a number of captives had been killed in error for lack of some sign of their position. De Tillaye was therefore being faced with ruin on one hand and ransom on the other. Still, he was more fortunate than another prisoner, who in 1376 was cut down by the men of Randon de Polignac outside Fortunet, because his captors had dressed him in their cloth with the red cross, as a passport.[1] Though it was used often enough, this method of giving security was very unsatisfactory. The trouble was that the same sign was being used for two purposes, as a passport and also as a sign of allegiance.

This was, in fact, the other really important function of these signs, that they denoted allegiance, and thus the title under which a soldier made war. For this purpose both banners and badges or coats were used: the only difference being that to display a banner meant war, whereas to wear a coat or uniform did not. A third method of signifying allegiance was the use of a cry of arms. This had very much the same significance as a banner, for a cry, too, was the personal sign of a particular lord and hereditary in his family.[2] It, too, was only given *in actu bellicoso*,[3] but whereas banners displayed showed that one was offering battle, the cry was the signal to advance. This mean that great care had to be taken about the use of cries, and the standing orders of armies accordingly imposed very severe penalties for those who raised them without authority.[4] In an age when any campaign would be accompanied with a good deal of parleying, a cry raised at the wrong moment could cause disaster. There was an ugly incident of this kind at the surrender of Fronsac in 1451. The town had been given

[1] Jacotin, *Preuves de la Maison de Polignac*, Tome II, p. 69 (no. 250).

[2] For a full discussion of cries of arms and their history, see Du Cange, *Dissertations sur l'Histoire de St. Louys*, nos. XI and XII (*Glossarium*, ed. Favre, 1887, Tome X, pp. 38–47).

[3] Cf. allegation of certain sailors of Dieppe, who were claiming that a cog which they had taken in the year 1369 was lawful prize, that the men on the cog had been heard 'clamantes Sancte Georgi Sancte Georgi quod est signum Anglicorum in actu bellicoso' (Arch. Nat., X¹a 22, fo. 219vo et seq.).

[4] Cf. Richard II's Durham ordinances, 1385, cl. ix, x, xi (*Black Book of the Admiralty*, R.S. Vol. I, pp. 456–7); Henry V Mantes Orders, cl. 10, 11, 12 (ibid., p. 462).

up to the French by *appointement*, peacefully, which meant that it was not to be plundered. While the senior French commanders were at dinner, however, two pages appeared on the walls, shouting the one 'St. Denis', the other 'St. George'. At the same time someone stampeded some horses, which rumour quickly inflated into a force of cavalry. The French soldiers flew to arms, the town was escaladed, and by the time their officers got onto the scene looting was in full swing, and there was not much they could do except join in. No doubt they were quite willing to do so, but if they had not arrived there might easily have been a massacre. There was no doubt, when an enquiry was ordered, that the whole thing was contrived by someone who was anxious for a lion's share of plunder, but nobody was clearly implicated. The only moral left to be drawn was the danger which the raising of a cry could create.[1]

Except in this one respect, a cry had the same significance as a banner or a badge. From the moment a soldier adopted such signs, he made clear in whose name he was fighting. Thus their use could be of considerable political importance. When, at dawn on 5 September 1451, Francois de Vaulgrigneuse took the Burgundian town of Romenay by assault, with a cry of *ville gaigniee! Savoye et Daulphin*, a serious diplomatic situation was created. Burgundy and Savoy were not at war, but because Francois had used his cry the Duke of Savoy was compromised.[2]

---

[1] Bib. Nat., MS. Duchesne 108, fo. 35 et seq. (report of the commissioners, Guillaume Juvenel des Ursins and Jean d'Estouteville, into irregularities at the taking of Fronsac). The raising of the cries of St. George and St. Denis is mentioned in the evidence of Jasper Bureau, Maitre d'artillerie (fo. 41), who declared that it was at this moment the soldiers moved forward.

[2] Arch. dep. de la Côte d'Or, B 11930. There are four documents in this *liasse* concerning the taking of Romenay, (i) the evidence given to Jean de Loisy and Guillaume le Mareschal, investigating the affair for the Duke of Burgundy, 11 September 1451, (ii) their report to the Marshal of Burgundy, 12 September, (iii) a further report to the Marshal from the Bailli of Macon, 17 September, (iv) the Marshal's letter of protest to Savoy stating that 'aucuns eulx disans vos officiers . . . se sont par agart et voye de fait boutez a force dans la place, bourg, et chastel de Romenay . . . et ont oste les armes de nostre tres redoubte seigneur et y mis et esleve les votres et mesmement votre banniere armoyee de vos armes a plus hault de la grosse tour en manière de place gaigniee par voye de guerre'. The evidence of the cry of Savoy is in (i). The matter seems to have been finally settled by negotiation, but could easily have led to war.

If he did not disavow his man, it would be his own honour that would be cheapened by taking a town in time of peace without any warning and with all the signs of war. The honour of a prince was not something which a mere *routier* could afford to treat lightly. It was for this reason that in the confused fighting which broke out after the taking of Fougères in 1449, the French companies fought under the cry and banner of Brittany.[1] Charles VII moved with deliberation, and months passed before it was known whether he would consider the truce with England broken. Until then, no one dared to compromise him by adopting the cry or the colours of the King of France.

It was where, as in this case, truces were involved that cries and banners had their most important legal significance. One of the simplest lines of defence, when a breach of truce was alleged, was that those said to have broken it were acting under the avowal of a party not in the truce. Thus, when the Seigneur de Chateauvillain (a Burgundian) routed the troops of Francois de La Palu late on in 1431, he was able to defend himself on the ground that he was in the pay of the English, and that as La Palu was serving the Duchess of Lorraine, an ally of France, he was entitled to attack.[2] His men had worn the red cross.[3] So did the Burgundian soldiers who assaulted Belfort earlier in the same year, and the Duke was therefore able to disavow them and claim the truce unimpaired on his side.[4] In the early years of Henry IV's reign, Frenchmen used just the same subterfuge,

[1] Robert Blondel, *De Reductione Normannie*, R.S., pp. 26–30. The most important actions carried out in the name of Brittany were the captures of Pont de l'Arche, Conches and Gerberoy. Compare Berry le Herault's account, printed with Blondel in the R.S. edn., pp. 250 and 253; he makes clear that the cry given was 'Bretaigne et St. Yves'.

[2] Arch. dep. de la Côte d'Or, B 11942, nos. 181 (complaint of Varembon, 8 January 1432, to Marshal of Burgundy), and 189 (reply of Chateauvillain to the Marshal, 15 January 1432).

[3] Ibid., no. 205 shows that Chateauvillain's men were wearing the red cross at this period.

[4] Ibid., no. 143; letter of Nicolas Rolin, dated 15 June 1431, to the Councillors at Basle, who were conservators of the truce between the Burgundians and the Austrians, who in this area were French allies. Belfort had been taken by Burgundians, but he protested that 'hoc factum extitit pro guerra et nomine domini nostri regis et non nomine seu mandato vel consensu dicti domini mei ducis Burgundie nec factores advocavit seu advocare intendit'.

answering English complaints against breaches of the truce with the assertion that the actions in question were done under the name and colours of the King of Scotland and under Scots officers, who as allies were allowed free movement in their country but could not be summoned to judgment because they were not subjects.[1] It is easy to see how confused issues could become in these circumstances. No doubt this was why Richard Aston in his complaints about the assault on the castle of Mark in 1405 was so careful to stress that the attackers had displayed the banner of Flanders, because the English had a firm truce with Flanders, but not with France generally.[2]

These cases were all fairly straightforward; the question at issue in them being whether or not goods despoiled should be restored and persons compensated. Questions much more complicated than this could revolve around the use of signs and cries, especially when private individuals were suing in the ordinary courts. I will give just one example to illustrate this point. Sometime, either in 1357 or 1358, the castle of Poix was taken by English *routiers*. Later, in 1359, their garrison was induced by Ralph de Rayneval to evacuate the place for a large ransom, and he along with several others gave them his bond to pay this. The seigneur of Poix, Jean Tyrel, was absent at the time, but later agreed to pay a substantial portion of the ransom, giving Rayneval his bond to do so. He subsequently learnt that Edward III had confiscated the debt owed to the garrison, because the agreement to evacuate had been made without his

---

[1] Cf. Arch. Nat., J 645A no. 20; instruction to the French commissioners with reference to the forthcoming meeting at Leulinghen, April 1403, to repair the truces, that they are to deny responsibility for the acts done under the Earl of Crawford, since though he is based on France he is not a subject and cannot be adjourned. Also *Royal and Historical Letters—Henry IV*, ed. Hingston, R.S., Vol. I, pp. 218–9, letter of R. Aston, 18 March 1404, complaining that 'les gens de Harefleu . . . soubz umbre et couleur d'un ou deux escotz demourans et en heritez entre eulx se mistrent a la mer ou prindrent et robberent des marchans et subgies du Roy plus que C mille livres d'esterlungs par dessus les rancons des marchans et mariners par eulx amenez au dit lieu de Harefleu . . . et mis a destresse comme en nom et en la guerre du Roy d'Escoce non prenans regard a l'article desdites truces'.

[2] Arch. dep. du Nord, B 18823, fo. 26: 'le Conte de St. Pol homme lige et vassal du dit duc (de Bourgogne) et ysant de son pays de Flandres vint assieger le Chastel de Merk accompaignie de plusieurs baneres des quelles l'un estoit et encore est des armes de Flandres'.

consent; and he accordingly paid 5,000 *moutons d'or* to the royal commissioners at Neufborg. When later Rayneval began proceedings against Tyrel to make him pay according to his bond, he produced Edward's quittances, but Rayneval refused to accept them. Rayneval deposed that the town had been captured under the cry of Navarre, and that therefore the King of England had no right there; Tyrel answered that it had been held by Englishmen in the name of their king. Rayneval said it had been captured in 1358 when the truce of Bordeaux had suspended hostilities with the English, and therefore the ransom money was owing to Rolin Walton, the captain who took the town; Tyrel that it had been captured in 1357, and that therefore the debt was to the English, and to Edward if, as their king, he pleased. The court in the end decided for Tyrel, as one would hope, seeing he had paid cash down.[1] But by that time there were five conflicting claims to either the castle or the ransom, that of Tyrel, that of Rayneval, that of Rolin Walton, that of Edward III, and a fifth from the Count of St. Pol, to whom Rayneval had made an abortive attempt to sell the castle of Poix when Tyrel refused to pay Walton. All these complications arose because it was not clear whether the castle had been taken under the cry of Navarre or of St. George.[2]

This case of Tyrel *v.* Rayneval indicates something besides the importance in law of signs and cries, that is, their drawbacks and deficiencies. If Rolin Walton had been a soldier of fixed and known loyalties, the case need never have arisen. He was one of those Englishmen, however, who soldiered in

[1] Tyrel's main submission was however incorrect, as the castle apparently *was* taken in 1358, when there were truces between England and France, but not between France and Navarre; cf. *Chronique des Quatre Premiers Valois*, ed. S. Luce, p. 87.

[2] Arch. Nat., X¹a 17, fo. 275vo, et seq. With this case can be compared that of Tremoille *v.* Lafayette (1425), in which Tremoille alleged that his opponents had used the cry of Burgundy, and that this excused his hostile actions (they claimed they were acting in self-defence) (Arch. Nat., X²a 18, fo. 60 et seq.). Also similar was the case of Chesnel *v.* Anjou, in which Anjou alleged that Chesnel had taken his town of Luc with the cry of St. George, and that as his liegeman Chesnel was not entitled to fight against him for the English; Chesnel replying said that he had taken the town in the name of Brittany, whose liegeman he also was, and to whom he had the prior obligation (Arch. Nat., X¹a 4804, fos. 101 and 115vo, and X¹a 82, fos. 166vo-7).

northern France under the colours of Navarre and England indifferently, as it suited his convenience. With men of his stamp about, the truce of Bordeaux was virtually worthless. So in fact was the ruling of the international law of arms, which forbade acts of war done without princely authority, because such authority was too easy to come by. The enforcement of the rule by the courts became infinitely problematical, because allegiances could be changed too quickly. To give an example, when in 1364 the Navarrese war broke out anew, it was too easy for the companies in central France to discard their pennons of St. George and take the cry and banner of Navarre;[1] thus their war, hitherto nameless, became a just quarrel on the instant. How could the courts be certain whether the same soldiers, from the same fortress, took a man prisoner on Wednesday when it was treason or on Thursday in lawful war? The idea behind the law was no doubt a noble one, sanctioning the right of the Christian soldier to take part in any quarrel he considered just. In practice the law could be reduced to absurdity by men like Walton, or the Breton *routiers* of St. Denis who, we are told, wore 'sometimes the cross of St. Andrew, and sometimes the white upright cross of Armagnac, so that they could call themselves Armagnacs or Burgundians just as they pleased'.[2]

It would be unfair, however, to conclude here with the suggestion that the law and the signs whose use it sanctioned were worthless. The trouble was not here; it was that though the wars of the later middle ages were in fact wars of nations, men had not yet adjusted their ideas to the exigences of international war. They had no more constructive idea of a national war than some kind of clumsy cross between a crusade and a purely private quarrel. As a result, the laws which they applied

[1] Cf. letter of the Consuls of Puy-de-Dome, dated 30 August 1364, Molinier, *Étude sur la vie d'Arnoul d'Audreham*, Pièce Justificative, no. LXXXVII: 'avem auzit, que en l jorn deven esser devan lo Puey et aqui deven leyssar lo peno di san Gorgi, lo qual portaron, en prendre la banieyra de Navarra'. Compare with this the letter of the Consuls of Millau in 1369, reporting that the Companies under Anjou and Trastamare, who for the last year had been fighting a covert war against the English 'eran venguts a Roquacesierra e avian combattut la tore e portavo lo pano desplegat del rei de Fransa'; Rouquette, *La Rouergue sous les Anglais*, p. 179.

[2] *Chronique du Religieux de St. Denis*, ed. Bellaguet, Tome VI, p. 156.

did not adequately distinguish between, say, an English army raised in England and led by English lords, and a band of adventurers of all sorts and races who took advantage of using the same cry and the same colours. In the long run this problem was solved by the appearance of national armies, and the successful enforcement of the rule that no man should take up arms unless he was in the pay of a prince and entered by name on his official muster rolls. In the meantime a great deal of disorder had to be tolerated, largely because rulers tolerated and even encouraged the activities of unpaid *routiers*, who provided a cheap way of backing up their sporadic martial efforts with a constant war of attrition. In any case, the royal expeditions were often just as disorganised as the ravages of the free companies; indeed they were bound to be so for as long as plunder continued to offer infinitely greater rewards than pay. The problems which these conditions engendered were part of the contemporary *mise-en-scène*; they were far too wide for the law and its formal-minded advocates to cope with.

What the lawyers, quite properly, were much more concerned about were the kind of matters which were likely to come before the courts. Most of the cases which they had to argue concerned private rights acquired in the course of war. These rights were property rights for the most part, and what they needed was evidence of title to property. In the heat of battle it was clear enough that the kind of evidence which could and should be produced to support title to, say, land, was unobtainable. The customs of the military profession however provided a series of signs and forms of words whose significance was generally recognised, and these were therefore adapted to the legal purpose of furnishing evidence in matters arising out of war. Their great advantage for this end was that they were immediately recognisable and not too ambiguous.

From the use of these signs, the lawyers developed the important doctrine that in battle words and signs had the same force that legal instruments had in ordinary law. As Simon, advocate in the Parlement of Paris, put it in a case which revolved about the sale of a prisoner in the field: 'the deal was done verbally, which is quite sufficient in the field of battle'.[1]

[1] Arch. Nat., X¹a 4801, fo. 399 (Yvo de Puy *v.* The Count of Maine, February 1448).

The theoretical lawyers were of the same view: 'the simple words suffice' was the comment of Bartholomew of Saliceto on contracts made in the course of an engagement.[1] No doubt such words were less sure in their effect than a written document, but the chaos of war does not naturally conduce to clarity, and they were probably the best kind of evidence which could be got. Gradually a whole vocabulary of military usage grew up, governing many more matters than have been discussed in this chapter. Indubitably, however, the most important signs were those we have examined, which indicated the allegiance of soldiers and the rules by which they intended to fight. These did not prevent confusion, particularly over allegiance, but in an age when war was endemic and few questioned the right of soldiers to involve themselves for private ends in quarrels in which they had no other interest, confusion was unavoidable. In these circumstances, signs and recognised cries at least made it possible for the law to preserve a little order in great chaos.

[1] Bartholomew de Saliceto, *Comment. in Cod.*, VIII Tit. 51, l. 2. The only limiting factor on the sufficiency of words was that, where a contract was involved, some sign of assent must be given; cf. Paris of Pozzo, *De Re Militari*, Lib. IX, cap. 20 (Zilletus, *Tractatus Juris Universi*, Tome XVI, fo. 424vo).

# VIII

# SIEGES

THERE was one condition of war, which was fought under special rules, which was not mentioned in the last chapter. This was siege warfare. From the strategic point of view, this was a very important kind of warfare, which presented particular problems. The art of defence was one which had been very highly developed in the later middle ages, and it took time, skill, and a great deal of expense to batter down the imposing walls of a fourteenth or fifteenth-century fortress. The stories of great sieges, such as those of Calais and Rouen and Orleans, therefore loom large in the history of the Hundred Years War; in fact they are its turning points. Perhaps this goes some way to explaining what is most striking about the laws which governed siege warfare, their unusual and savage severity.

From the legal point of view, there were two methods by which a town or fortress could be taken. It could be taken by assault; either by escalade or ambush, that is, or stormed after its defences had been breached by cannon or siege engines. Or it could be surrendered by an *appointement* or treaty. Both these different methods presented special legal problems, and, according to the means of capture, the rules differed also. Alternatively, both sets of rules might be invoked at a single siege, for a siege had at least three stages, the reduction of the suburbs, of the town itself, and of the citadel. In the case of the capture of Carentan in 1450, for instance, it was claimed in court that in law the suburbs were taken by assault, but that the town was surrendered by *appointement*, a point with important

119

consequences with regard to rights in spoil taken at the siege.[1]

By whatever method a town was ultimately reduced, however, formal protocol demanded that the first step of a commander, whose forces appeared before it, was to send it a summons to surrender. A messenger, very likely a herald, would go forward under surety, and formally demand admittance in his master's name.[2] This gave the garrison and the townsmen an opportunity, if they so wished, to make a treaty on the spot. This messenger also gave them due warning of what the consequences of refusing his summons would be, which served as an added inducement to them to make terms. For this part of the message would probably not be very palatable. When Louis de Bourbon appeared before Moléon in Poitou in 1381 he sent his marshal to summon the town, whose captain refused him entry. 'Then the marshal replied to them, that since they would not see reason and surrender the fort, let them take warning that there would be no further talk of terms being given; and if they were taken, they would be dealt with so that others should learn by their example, for the Duke of Bourbon would hang every man of them by the neck.'[3] This threat so terrified the garrison of the fort that they made terms at once.

There was, however, nothing exceptional about Bourbon's threat to the soldiers of Moléon. He was simply making it clear that if entry was refused him, he would invoke all the sanctions permitted by the law of arms in a town taken by assault. These were extremely rigorous, and could be enforced as from the moment that a formal siege was begun. The sign of its formal commencement was the firing of the besiegers' cannon, or of their siege engines,[4] and from then on it was in the discretion of

----

[1] Arch. Nat., X¹a 4804, fo. 250 and vo. This would mean that the goods of the burgesses were lawful spoil if taken in the suburbs, but not if taken in the town.

[2] For examples, see *ante*, ch. VII, p. 103, n. 2.

[3] *Chronique du bon Duc Louis de Bourbon*, ed. A-M. Chazaud, p. 143. Compare the similar threat of Henry V, before he set siege to Tonque, reported in *The Brut*, ed. F. W. D. Brie (*E.E.T.S.*, 1908), pt. II, p. 383.

[4] This seems to be made clear by various references. Philip the Good, in a letter written in 1436, disclaimed having laid siege to Calais, because he had not fired his cannon: 'nous ne nous y meismes que par maniere de logis, et non de siege comme dit est, ne y feismes asseoir ne tirer aucunes bombardes et aussi ne feismes point sommer ceulx de dedans' (Arch. dep. du

their commander to offer or accept terms. Unless he chose to do so, the rule was war to the death without quarter (though the rule could be waived for anyone, and a prisoner who could pay a good ransom was likely enough to be spared). So, when Henry V's army was fighting to enter Caen, we are told that his men showed no mercy, except to women, children, and priests;[1] for the rule of no quarter held good not against soldiers only, but against all the able-bodied inhabitants of the town. Even messengers attempting to leave or enter it could be put to death, for, as Commynes says, 'when a prince has laid his siege to a place, and has fired his artillery, anyone seeking to enter it to comfort or assist those within is worthy of death, according to the laws of war'.[2]

In a city taken by storm almost any licence was condoned by the law. Only churches and churchmen were technically secure, but even they were not often spared. Women could be raped, and men killed out of hand.[3] All the goods of the in-

---

[1] Titus Livius, *Vita Henrici Quinti*, ed. Hearne, p. 39.

[2] Commynes, *Mémoires*, Bk. V, ch. 6 (ed. B. de Mandrot, Paris, 1901–3, Vol. I, p. 376). Commynes says that this rule was observed in the wars in Italy, but not normally in France; but there are other examples of its being invoked, besides the hanging of Cifron at Nancy by Charles the Bold. At the siege of Ponteaudemer in 1356 a messenger of Philip of Navarre was captured trying to enter the town; 'pour quoy le dit messagier fut decappite et escartele, puis fut pendu devant le chastel' (*Chron. des Quatre Premiers Valois*, ed. Luce, p. 39). For another instance, at the siege of Soissons in 1414, see *Chron. du Réligieux de St. Denis*, ed. Bellaguet, Vol. V, p. 319.

[3] I have found no legal authority for these rules, but the chronicles make clear what they were. Cf. Monstrelet on the spoliation of Chartes in 1431: 'quand est de parler de ravissemens, violacions, et autres besognes extraordinaires, il en fut fait selon les *coutumes de la guerre*, comme en ville conquise' (ed. L. Douet d'Arq, Tome V, p. 25); and on the capture of St. Valery, 1433, 'si y furent de grans maux par iceulx Francois, selonq la coustume de la guerre en ville conquise'. (Ibid., Tome III, p. 56.) Compare Waurin on the assault of Montereau in 1437 'la ville fut prinse d'assault ... et quant est au regard des asseigies, en furent mors environ trente hommes

---

Nord, B 18842, pièce 29521). The fact that neither cannon nor engine had been fired was used as evidence to show there had been no siege by the men of Carentan in 1450: 'contre la forteresse ne fit [on] onques tirer canon ne culverine' (see n. 1 above): and by Simon Worthier, in 1436, accusing Jean de Valu of surrendering Houdent without siege: 'en may darrein passe le defendant sans siege assault donner ou canon gelter parlementa a Girault de la Palliere ennemy' (Arch. Nat., X¹a 4797, fo. 314).

habitants were regarded as forfeit.[1] If lives were spared, it was only through the clemency of the victorious captain; and spoliation was systematic. The prospect of this free run of his lusts for blood, spoil and women was a major incentive to a soldier to persevere in the rigours which were likely to attend a protracted siege. Charles the Dauphin in 1358 certainly found a ready method of boosting recruitment by promising those who would follow him the plunder of rebellious Paris.[2] And we saw in the last chapter how at Fronsac in 1451 certain persons unknown, fearing that a treaty would cheat them of the spoil of the town, staged an incident in order to ensure that it be taken by assault.[3]

The word 'assault' must not be allowed to convey the impression that these excesses, lawfully permitted in a conquered town, were necessarily committed in hot blood. All that 'assault' meant in law was that surrender was unconditional. Thus, when Calais capitulated in 1347, the men of the garrison marched out bareheaded with naked swords in their hands, and the burgesses with halters about their necks; this was a sign that even though it had not been stormed, Edward III had taken the town by force of arms unconditionally, and that the lives of those in it were in his mercy.[4] He could take his time to decide their fate, if he wished. In a similar way, when Luxembourg was taken by the Burgundians in 1463, it was not sacked forthwith. The troops remained with their standards until after Philip the Good had entered the conquered town, and had been to the Church of Notre Dame to pray and give thanks. Then, and then only, the word was given, and the whole town systematically plundered from one end to the other.[5]

[1] It was taken as great generosity by Richemont, that after the capture of Hau he 'fit rendre a ceulx de la ville la moitie de tous leurs biens' (Gruel, *Chronique d'Artus de Richemont* in *Nouvelle collection des Mémoires pour servir à l'histoire de France*, ed. Michaud and Poujoulat, Tome III, p. 202).

[2] *Chron. des Quatre Premiers Valois*, ed. Luce, p. 80.

[3] See *ante*, ch. VII, p. 112, n. 2.    [4] *Knighton*, R.S., Vol. II, p. 51.

[5] *Mémoires d'Olivier de la Marche*, ed. Beaune and D'Arbaumont (Soc. de l'histoire de France, 1883), Tome II, pp. 42–3.

et autant de prins, *desquel la plupart furent pendus*; puis entra le roy dedens, et deffendy sur la hart qu'on ne meffeist rien aux bonnes gens de la ville . . . quant a leurs personnes; mais quant au regard de leurs biens tout fut pillie *comme en ville conquise*'. (*Chroniques*, R.S., Vol. 4, p. 224.)

This cold-blooded and scientific pillaging may seem shocking to the mind of the twentieth century, and to accord ill with the high-flown ideal of the just war, fought according to rules based in reason and morality. In fact its very callousness indicates what was its theoretical justification. The goods, and indeed the lives of the inhabitants of a conquered town, were not regarded as mere lawful spoil; they were forefeit for the contumacious disregard of a prince's summons to surrender. Thus when Henry V took Falaise he commanded that the goods of those inhabitants who had consented to deliver the town, and theirs only, should remain entirely in their possession; whereas 'the goods of them that were obstinate and contrarious to this deliverance . . . were used at the King's pleasure'.[1] Hence the scientific pillaging of towns, and the careful division of their spoil 'by the sentence' of the king or his lieutenant,[2] for this spoliation was not an act of war, but the sentence of justice. In strict law all the goods taken in a conquered town were the king's. *Preda hostium in una civitate spectat regi* was the principle, as quoted by the advocate Jouvenel in the Parlement of Paris.[3] The king could divide the spoil as he wished, or even promise it in advance, but it was all at his disposition, because it was forefeit for rejection of his authority.

In contemporary eyes there was thus a great difference between the conquest of a town by force of arms, and a victory in the field. To accept a challenge to battle was to accept the judgment of God; it was also to accept one's adversary as of approximately equal standing to oneself. To refuse the summons of a prince who claimed a town as of right was quite another

[1] *First English Life of King Henry V*, ed. Kingsford, p. 103.

[2] Cf. Blondel's account of the division of spoil at Ponteaudemer in 1450: 'bona villatensium mobilia cuilibet militanti juxta virtutis praestantiam in praedam ceduntur, et corpora incolarum a captivitate necnon eorum immobilia a proscriptione *recta regis locumtenentis sententia* exemit' (*De Reductione Normannie*, R.S., p. 70). Compare Titus Livius account of the division of the spoil at Harfleur in 1415, 'post spoliis oppidi capti militi cuique juxta virtutem omnium et merita divisis a rege' (ed. Hearne, p. 11).

[3] Arch. Nat., X¹a 4799, fo. 230 (case of Laillier *v.* the King, 1443); compare statement of the King's proctor in the case of David Margnies (?) in 1417: 'ja soit que les meubles pris sur les ennemis soient a ceulx qui les prennent *in bello*, autre chose est de ce qui est pris en ville fermee et a le roy tresgrant interetz'. (Arch. Nat., X¹a 4791, fo. 210.)

thing; it was an insult to his majesty and punishable as such. This, however, was a principle which could cut both ways. If by refusing a summons one appeared to deny the right of one prince, by obeying it one indubitably injured the right of another. What then was the captain of a beleaguered garrison to do? If he surrendered, he acted treasonably by his former lord, in obeying his capital adversary. If he held out, he might be condemning the men in his charge, not to mention the unfortunate townsfolk, to death and destruction. In the open field of battle there was no stigma attached to surrender, and the law of arms protected the life of the Christian captive who had given his faith to an enemy. At a siege there were no such safeguards, either for the life or honour of the besieged.

If the rules observed in a conquered town were savage, they were equally very stern towards the captain who capitulated. To surrender a town without siege was treason. 'It hath been seen in many realms and lordships', declared the Duke of Norfolk in his indictment of Somerset in 1453, 'that for the loss of towns or castles without siege, the captains that have lost them have been dead and beheaded, and their goods lost.'[1] The sign that siege had been laid to a town was the firing of cannon or siege engines; if there had been no bombardment there had been no siege, and there was *prima facie* evidence of treason. Hence Talbot's indictment of Stafford in the Parlement in 1433, on the ground that he had lost La Ferté Bernard 'sans assault et sans engins . . . et de raison et par le droit darmes il a tout confisque et s'est rendu indigne'.[2] The last three words of this charge are worth notice. The king's majesty had been injured because a town which was his had been lost to his enemies; but the captain was dishonoured because he had broken the oath he made when he took his office, that he would not render up the town to any but the king or his representative. Thus he was false to his faith and dishonoured. It did not matter how the fort was taken or whether the captain was there when it fell, for it was still he personally who had covenanted to keep it for the king. When Berwick was taken by the Scots in 1356, Lord Greystock, its captain, was still responsible, although at the time he had been serving, *com chivalrous homme*,

[1] *Paston Letters*, no. 191 (ed. Gairdner, London, 1872, Vol. I, pp. 260–1).
[2] Arch. Nat., X¹a 4797, fo. 106vo.

with the king in France. He had sworn to the king to guard his town and castle, and because he had failed in this charge, judgment of life and limb was passed on him, not upon the lieutenant whom he had left there.[1]

Robert Ogle, Greystock's lieutenant, had not surrendered without siege, but had done his best to repel the Scots attack. So had William de Weston, condemned to death in the Parliament of 1377 for having traitorously surrendered the castle of Outhrewyk. As he was careful to point out in his defence, Weston and his men had withstood the enemies' cannonade. What really told against him was that money had passed when the castle was surrendered, and that the payments included a sum for supplies left in it, a sure sign that he could have held out longer.[2] This was the key point. The law was severe, but not inexorable; it did not demand that a man should hold out to the last, but that he should not surrender while there was still a chance of making reasonable defence. Here there was more room for debate than in the case where no formal siege had been made. William Chamberlain, for instance, though charged with treason for surrendering Meaux in 1439 while it was still supplied, was in the end acquitted; his position had been hopeless, because the English attempt to break up the siege had failed completely. It was clearly in order to remove doubt and debate on this matter, that a good many indentures made with captains of towns stipulated a term for which he should be bound to endure siege. Thus in Hotspur's indenture for the captaincy of Berwick in 1385 it was agreed that 'si siege soit mys a laddite ville . . . et rescous n'en soit fait dedeinz sept sepmaignes apres que garnisement en soit fait au Roy . . . que alors le dit Henry soit deschargie quoique avaigne a la dite ville'.[3] It is worth remarking that in one of the very rare French military contracts

---

[1] *Rot. Parl.*, iii, pp. 11ᵇ–12ᵃ; Greystock was in fact pardoned in 1358 at the request of Queen Philippa, *C.P.R.*, 1358–61, p. 18.

[2] *Rot. Parl.*, iii, pp. 10–12. Weston also was later pardoned, cf. *C.P.R.*, 1377–81, p. 124.

[3] P.R.O., E101/73/2, no. 29: compare nos. 37, 38, 39 and 41 in the same bundle, all of which include the same clause, and two indentures made for the captaincy of Berwick temp. Henry IV, E101/73/3, nos. 44 and 47. For an example of this clause in an indenture for service in France, see B. Mus., Cotton MS. Julius F IV, fo. 266vo–267vo (Edward III and William de Bohun, 1345).

which have survived, struck between the Marshal of Burgundy and Francois de la Palu in 1431, a precisely similar clause is inserted.[1]

It was very important to get conditions on this point clear. Thus, when Simon Worthier in 1436 charged Jean de Valu with surrendering Houdent treasonably, the first action of the court was to demand to see the indenture they had made, in order to establish its precise terms.[2] For an indenture was not a commission but a contract, which a captain entered into in the hope of securing thereby profit to himself. If his town was taken by assault, he stood to lose his goods, his profits of war, and perhaps his life as well; it was therefore very tempting to him to sell out to an enemy who, given the expense a siege involved, was likely to offer an advantageous price for his surrender. There would not be anything particularly heinous about such a transaction in a soldier's eyes. He was merely selling his rights in the town, in which, while his captaincy lasted, he probably looked on himself as a kind of feudal *seigneur*.[3] The captains of free companies certainly acted like petty feudal lords in the forts they held; they also made a steady profit by selling these forts as if they were their property.[4] Men like the captains of Despenser's host in 1383, who had seen a good deal of this kind

[1] Arch. dep. de la Côte d'Or, B 11740. 'Item s'il avenoit, que dieu ne veuille, que le dit seigneur de Varembon [Francois de la Palu] ou ses gens fussent assigiez des ennemis . . . en aucune des places de mon dit seigneur, le mareschal sera tenu de lui bailler secours dedens ung mois apres ce qu'il en sera requis'.

[2] Arch. Nat., X¹a 4797, fo. 314.

[3] For their (captains') activities, e.g. raising tribute from local countryside, sending challenges in their own name, avenging offences to themselves and their relatives, see ch. XII *infra*. One of the objects of Bedford's reorganisation was to limit the powers of captains to the military sphere, and prevent them interfering with civil jurisdiction within their captaincies, see Miss Rowe, *Discipline of the Norman garrisons under Bedford E.H.R.*, Vol. 46 (1931), p. 204 (Bedford's ordinance of 1423).

[4] Hence, for instance, the stipulation in Ramonet de Sort's contract to serve the Count of Armagnac (1389) that 'lo dit Ramonet ne sas gens no laissonar ne vendran las fortallessas que preses auran estan al servici deldit Mosenhor lo Comte ses la voluntat de Mondit Senhor lo Comte' (Bib. Nat., Coll. Doat, Tome 203, fo. 286vo). The Count knew well that as captain of a free company fighting in the name of the English, Ramonet had constantly sold forts as if they were his own, e.g. Roquenaton, evacuated for 5,000 francs in January 1388 (Monicat, *Les Grandes Compaignies en Velay*, p. 84).

SIEGES

of unofficial war in their time, were therefore not likely to have
very high standards in this matter.[1] The king or lord who contracted with a captain did not therefore rely primarily on his
sense of public loyalty, but rather on the personal oath which
he made on his honour when he entered into the contract, and
it behoved him to make its terms precise.

In an age which understood the implications of the solemn
oath of a knight more easily than the idea of public allegiance,
this was a more effective sanction. Since a point of honour was
involved, not only the king but any knight or soldier could
charge a man with treason because he had traitorously surrendered a fort. The most famous instance of such a private
prosecution was the charge which Richard Annesley brought
against Thomas Catrington and subsequently proved on his
body in a duel, that he had sold St. Sauveur le Vicomte to the
French.[2] A similar charge was brought in the Parlement of
Paris in 1395 by Jean Bouquin against Jean de la Touche,
whom he accused of selling the fort of Argento, and challenged
to a duel. This was a remarkable case, because all the events in
question took place in the Duke of Anjou's war in Italy. It
came into the French king's court not because treason had been
committed against him, but because the honour of two of his
subjects was involved.[3]

The defence of Jean de la Touche, which seems to have been
ultimately accepted, was that Argento had only been surrendered after three months' siege. For, provided that he had
made a reasonable attempt at defence, the captain of a castle
or town was free to treat with the enemy. Whatever treaty he
then made, it had the same force as an international agreement,
as a truce or an agreement to pay ransom. The terms obviously
varied according to the military situation. If this was favourable
to the besieged, he might hope to march out with his garrison

[1] For the charges brought against these men in Parliament in 1383, see
*Rot. Parl.*, iii, pp. 156–8.
[2] *Chronicon Anglie*, ed. Maunde-Thompson, R.S., 1874, pp. 261–4. The
accusation against Catrington was brought in the Court of Chivalry, cf.
*C.P.R.*, 1377–81, p. 485.
[3] Arch. Nat., X²a 12, fo. 244 (11 March 1395). The court reserved the
case for consideration; the charge was presumably dismissed as it does not
come up again.

127

under safe-conduct, to carry away his spoils of war,[1] and even to be paid a large sum for evacuation. If on the other hand his stronghold was on the point of being overrun, he could expect much harsher terms: for his own men and the burgesses to be prisoners, for named persons to be reserved in the mercy of the enemy, and to lose all his goods and gains of war. This sort of treaty could be made verbally in the heat of an assault. Fulk Eaton, one of the captains of Ponteaudemer in 1450, made his treaty with the Count of Dunois on the stairs of a fortified house to which the remnants of his garrison had retreated. All that Dunois did was to quote his terms, and Fulk touched him to signify consent; from that moment the treaty was binding on both sides.[2]

There was one pattern of terms for surrender which was followed so commonly, however, that it demands special treatment. This was where besieged and besiegers struck an agreement to cease all hostilities for a given period, at the end of which the town would be surrendered, unless a relieving force had arrived in the meantime. The rules which licensed plunder and rapine in a conquered town would not apply in this instance. Instead, detailed conditions for the surrender would be laid down in a solemn legal instrument, of which each party would have a copy sealed by the other, and which established what some writers call the *lex deditionis*.[3] Such an agreement was likely to be to the advantage of all parties. It guaranteed the lives of the citizens and of the garrison, saved the town from plunder, and the besiegers from the expense of a laborious and costly operation.

The minor details of agreements of this kind did vary, but the general pattern was regular. A future date was fixed, which might be anything from a few days to six months or even

---

[1] All these conditions were allowed in, e.g. Jean de Luxembourg's appointment with the garrison of Roye in 1419, Monstrelet, Lib. I, ch. 218 (ed. L. Douet D'Arq, Tome III, p. 368).

[2] Bib. Nat., MS. Fr. 4054, fo. 148 (from the report of an enquiry into the capture of Ponteaudemer, by the Chancellor, the Marshal de Lafayette, and Theodore de Valpergue).

[3] Cf. for example Blondel, *De Reductione Normannie*, R.S., p. 95: 'et decima septima Septembris strenuus Britonum dux . . . quietam oppidi Sancti-Laudi possessionem cepit, a quo barbari ducenti *lege deditionis*, facultatibus necnon personis intactis, expulsi abeunt'.

a year ahead, on which the town or fort was to be given up, if not relieved. The nature of the relief was usually detailed; the relieving force would most likely have to appear ready to give battle, perhaps at an agreed spot. In the meantime, a strict truce was always imposed, and all military operations were put into suspended animation. Neither besieged nor besiegers, that is to say, were to revictual, except for current needs, and they could not construct new engines or defences, or repair old ones.[1] All must be kept exactly as on the day the agreement was struck. The town might even be put into the hands of an impartial commission, who would hand it at the end of the term fixed to whichever party had better right according to their treaty.[2] Besides these points, arrangements would be made in detail about the rights which the garrison soldiers might retain in their baggage, spoil, and prisoners; about any sums to be paid by either side, in respect of the agreement or of goods left in the town; and so on. Any major breach of the agreement by either party would of course render it invalid. Hostages would be given by both sides to guarantee it.

The conditions concerning the relief of the town were usually the most detailed. The relieving force must be in strength, ready to give battle, on the appointed day. If a battle did ensue, the garrison was not normally permitted to take any part. The field for it would have been carefully chosen; at Grancey in 1434, for instance, it was stipulated that the two armies must face each other in 'the place above Guiot Rigoigne's house on the right hand side towards Sentenorges, where there are two trees.'[3]

This exaggerated formality is revealing. The careful choice

---

[1] For two good examples of detailed agreements, see that made between Prince Henry and Rhys ap Llewellyn for the surrender of Aberystwyth in September 1407, *Rymer*, Vol. IV, pt. I, p. 120; and that between Jean de Luxembourg and the garrison of Guise, September 1424, full text in Monstrelet, Lib. II, ch. 22 (ed. Douet d'Arq, pp. 199–205).

[2] E.g. in 1441 Tartas, which Huntingdon had been besieging, was put in the hands of two commissioners, one French and one English. On May 1442, the French were in greater strength before the town, and it was handed over to them (Waurin, *Chroniques*, R.S., pp. 355–6, and 361–2).

[3] *Appointement* between Jean de Vergy, and Pierre du Chier and Jean de Bruneval, captains of Grancey (Bib. Nat., Collection de Bourgogne, Tome 103, fos. 142–9).

of a field of battle, the ban on the garrison's participation, and the insistence that all be maintained in the precise order, as it stood when the treaty was signed, all had the same purpose, to secure absolutely fair conditions for a judicial duel. They are all thus part and parcel of the contemporary belief that battle was an appeal to the judgment of God. Every possible precaution had to be taken to thwart any attempt on the part of wicked men to weight the scales of divine justice. In witness of this attitude one may quote the anathema invoked by Etienne de Vignolles, captain of Vitry, to sanction his treaty of surrender: 'If we do not surrender on the day appointed', he declared, 'we hold ourselves false, wicked and for traitors, denying God's law and taking to us that of the Devil, which God forbid. And if there is any fault on our part, they (the Burgundians) may hold us and each one of us dishonoured, so that as dishonoured men we shall have no excuse to make against this reproach before lord or prince, knight or esquire.'[1] Once again it was on the honour of Christian knights that men relied, not on any notion of the sanctity of international agreements.

The hostages for an agreement to surrender were in effect pledges to the honour of their party. They were in much the same position as sureties for the payment of a ransom, who in the case of default by the principal became prisoners themselves. In one important respect, however, their position was different. Prisoners were given the privilege of ransom to avoid the shedding of Christian blood, and could not be killed, but at sieges, as we have seen, no quarter was given. The sureties for a surrender could therefore not only be made prisoners if the agreement was broken; they could be put to death with impunity. In 1417 the Burgundians of Senlis went back on their agreement to surrender, on seeing that the Count of Armagnac had dismantled his siege engines and that they were no longer in danger of assault; so the Count put to death all but two of their hostages, 'as the laws of war allowed'.[2] Though surrender by

---

[1] *Appointement* for the surrender of Vitry-en-Perthois, 1424 (Arch. Nat., J 646, no. 22).
[2] *Chronique du Réligieux de St. Denis*, ed. Bellaguet, Tome VI, p. 194: 'bellorum jura proditores fedifrages aut fidejussores eorum capite plectendes tradunt'. Other examples include the execution by the English of Alexander Seaton, hostage, when Berwick was not surrendered in 1333 (*Scalacionica*,

treaty was a means of obviating the savage consequences of the laws of siege warfare, the moment a treaty was broken the rule of war to the death once more came into operation.

It is worth considering for a moment what were the reasons for this special severity of the law in the matter of sieges. One reason for it is obvious enough. Sieges were among the most important of all military operations in the Hundred Years War. By comparison with the results of famous sieges, such as those of Rouen in 1417 and Orleans in 1428, the military consequences of even such a victory as Agincourt could be questioned. It was no wonder that the rules should have been severe where so much was at stake. No land could be reduced until the fortresses on it were taken (the realisation of just this point was the secret of the success both of Henry V and Du Guesclin). It was therefore certain that an invader would use every inducement available in the way of threats or bribery to reduce these strong-points as quickly as possible. The terrible consequences of assault certainly made his task of reduction easier; most men were ready to listen to terms when they were reminded of them. In antithesis, it was necessary to invoke the utmost severity of the law against commanders who did surrender, because the inducements to do so were so great. Mere fear, quite apart from the prospect of profit from sale, was a sufficient argument for capitulation. Nothing short of the threat of personal dishonour and a traitor's death was likely to ensure that forts were properly defended.

To this extent the severity of the law did no more than recognise the realities of the military situation. But there was another cause for it, equally if not more important. A prince who had once summoned a town had committed his reputation and honour to entering it. What this meant was that any attempt to thwart him was an offence against his 'majesty'; and offences against majesty were not to be taken lightly. The men of the fourteenth and fifteenth centuries may not have had any very clear idea of what such words as 'nation' or 'nationality' implied, but they had no doubt whatever about the respect due

---

Maitland Club, 1836, p. 163); the execution of the hostages of Derval in 1373 when Knollys would not surrender as appointed (Froissart, *Chroniques*, ed. Luce, Tome VIII, p. 159).

personally to those of high social standing. Regnault de Mont-ferrand did not heed bombardment, or mines tunnelled under his fort of Verteuil, but when the man with whom he was fighting hand to hand in the mine told him that he was Louis, Duke of Bourbon, he was overcome by the honour done him and surrendered his fort forthwith.[1] His surrender in fact extri-cated Louis from a ticklish position, for Charles V had sum-moned him to join him, and though he knew he could not honourably neglect his sovereign's summons, he knew that having once laid siege to the place, he could not leave it except to his own dishonour.[2] It was for this same reason that when, in 1436, Philip the Good withdrew from before Calais, the first thing which he wished men to know was that he had never laid formal siege to the town: he had sent no herald to summon it, nor had he fired his cannon against it. He had been before Calais only *par maniere de logis*, and his honour was therefore unsmirched by his retreat.[3]

This was not just the pose of a prince who was well known to be meticulous in points of honour. Everyone knew that a siege involved personal honour. One of the leading questions in the law of arms which Geoffrey de Charny in 1353 put to the knights of the Order of the Star for decision was whether, if a man had laid claim to a town, it was to his greater dishonour to fail to win it, or to decline a challenge to battle in the field during his siege.[4] The gauge of the seriousness of a siege was the social standing of those conducting it: '(this) town', wrote an English-man at the siege of Sens in 1420, 'is worthily besieged; for there lie at that siege two kings, two queens, and four dukes, with my Lord of Bedford when he cometh hither'.[5] The phrase *siège de prince* came indeed to be used almost as a technical term, and where, for instance, indentures mention a period after which a commander may surrender without blame, it was understood that such a siege was implied.[6]

---

[1] *Chronique du Bon Duc Louis de Bourbon*, ed. A-M. Chazaud, pp. 150–1.

[2] Ibid., pp. 147–8.    [3] See p. 120, n. 4 *ante*.

[4] Bib. Nat., MS. Fr. (Nouvelles Acquisitions) 4736, fo. 16.

[5] Rymer, Vol. IV, pt. III, p. 177.

[6] Simon Worthier, in his charge against Jean de Valu (*supra*, n. 23), for instance describes Houdent as 'imprenable sans siege de prince'. For evidence that this is the kind of siege which a party to an indenture envisaged, see for instance Henry IV's indenture with Northumberland for the Captaincy of

To defy a prince was a bold act, and by no means necessarily an admirable one. Even his opponents admitted that Henry V's life had been a pattern of chivalrous conduct; but he had no kind words for the heroism of those who had defended Rouen against him, only blame for their obstinacy.[1] It was very largely on account of this entanglement of the authority and personal honour of the lord or captain commanding in the success of a siege, that such ferocious reprisals were permitted against those who resisted him. They were to be punished for disobeying majesty. Once again we are reminded that when we speak of the law of arms as an international law, we must guard against thinking of it as a law governing the conduct of warring nations. It was not this: it was a law governing the conduct of men who fought to settle by arms quarrels which were in nature private, and whose importance was judged by the social status of the principals involved. In this context, rules, which seem to us cruel and inhuman, could appear just and natural, for nothing was more just than the punishment of contumacy.

[1] Titus Livius, *Vita Henrici Quinti*, ed. Hearne, pp. 67-8.

Berwick in 1402: 'en cas que *poiair royale* des ennemis se taille par terre ou par mer d'assailler la dite ville, . . . adonques en fera le dit Henri certifier a notre dit seigneur le Roy et il dedeinz sys semaignes apres . . . ferra remoever tiel assiege . . . et autrement sera le dit Henry excusez' (P.R.O., E101/73/3 no. 44).

# PART III

# The 'Incidents' of Just War

# IX

# GAINS OF WAR AND THEIR DIVISION

Hitherto we have been concerned in discussion with three main topics. We have examined firstly, what sort of a law the law of arms was, secondly, the methods by which it was enforced, and thirdly, what conditions rendered it applicable. Throughout, there has been constant reference to rights in the 'gains of war'. The time has now come to examine rather more carefully the legal position of such rights.

At the outset, we may distinguish three main sources of 'gains of war'; plundered goods, the ransoms of prisoners, and 'ransoms of the country'—the *appatis* paid by villagers and peasants for immunity from hostilities. With regard to such gains, the basic principle of the civil and canon lawyers was that in a just war 'prisoners may be made slaves, and goods taken become the property of the captors'.[1] As has been said, however, the rule under which captives were reduced to slavery did not operate in wars between Christian princes;[2] instead they were ransomed, a process involving complex legal principles which demand separate attention. For the moment it must be enough to say that a captor acquired a property in the person of his prisoner, but not that absolute property which servitude would imply. Ransoms of the countryside were also

---

[1] Bartolus, *Comment. in Dig. Nov.*, XLIX, Tit. 15, l. 24. Compare Raymond of Pennaforte, *Summa de Poenitentia*, Lib. II, cap. 5 §17; and Johannes Andreas, *in II Decretal.*, Tit. 11, cap. 29.

[2] John of Legnano, *Tractatus*, cap. 60.

property in a sense. An individual captain could sue in court
for sums outstanding on this account, just as a landlord could
for an unpaid rent,[1] and he might be bound to pass on certain
shares in them, as in his other spoils of war.[2] But *appatis* might
equally well be treated as payments in lieu of wages or to
supplement them, and were as often demanded by soldiers in
country of their own allegiance as in hostile territory.[3] In this
sense they were not spoil, but a charge on the subject,[4] and by
military custom the payment of *appatis* was often held to be
evidence that local people were subject to the enemy and could
be plundered.[5] Ransoms of the country were thus something of
an anomaly, necessary, no doubt, in an age when war was
fought with the aid of independent and unpaid *routiers*, but

[1] See for example Thomas de Uvedale's prosecution of Pierre Tournebu
and others in 1366, for payment of certain *appatis* which had been owed to
Chandos and Henry of Lancaster, in the Parlement (Arch. Nat., X¹a 21,
fo. 73 et seq.). The defence alleged that the *appatis*, or sums owed on their
account, could not be demanded after the peace; but the court clearly
upheld de Uvedale's argument that the debts were private, as on 13 March
1368 it gave an arrest against de Tournebu (ibid., fo. 211).

[2] See for example the conditions concerning division of spoil in Du
Guesclin's contract of brotherhood-in-arms with Clisson, 1370, printed by
du Cange, *Dissertations sur l'histoire de St. Louis*, no. 21 (des adoption d'honneur en frère): 'item voulons et consentons que de tous ou quelconques
proufitz et droits qui nous pourront venir . . . tant de prisonniers de guerre
. . . comme de *pays raenconne*, vous aiez la moitie entierement'. (*Glossarium*,
ed. L. Favre, 1887, Tome X, p. 70.)

[3] See the speech of the captain of Crathor in the *Jouvencel* (ed. Lécestre
and Favre, Tome I, p. 95): 'Et s'ainsi est que, pour avoir autres affaires ou
moyennant le conseil d'aucuns, il [le Roi] soit trouble et desconseille ou
maniere qu'il ne nous puisse donner provision de payement ou de gaiges, il
nous faudra lever de nous mesmes vivres et finances, *tant sur ceulx de notre
obeissance* comme sur nos ennemys'.

[4] Cf. the comments of E. Cosneau, who shows that after the 1439 army
reforms, the taxes for the upkeep of the 'compaignies de grande ordonnance'
were in reality *appatis*. He quotes the Registers of the Cour des Aides on the
good effect of the regulations: 'les tailles qui sont mises en lieu des appatiz
empeschent les courses . . . le Roy a voulu que toutes manieres de gens y
contribuent'. (E. Cosneau, *Le Connétable de Richemont*, Paris, 1886, p. 363,
n. 3).

[5] Cf. for example Perrinet Gressart's letter to the Chancellor of Burgundy,
7 June 1426: 'Le pais de Berry est content de moy donner vivres, mais les
dessusdiz (La Tremoille's French captains) dient que s'ils me baillent, ils
leur ferront guerre et les appellent Bourgignons' (Flamare, *Le Nivernais
pendant la Guerre de Cent Ans*, no. XLV, Tome I, p. 297).

potentially a source of serious injustice. It is not easy to say whether they should be regarded as spoils of war, or not.[1]

This leaves for detailed consideration goods captured from the enemy, and it is with this sort of spoil that we shall be chiefly concerned in the present chapter. Goods, by long legal tradition, can be of two kinds, moveable or otherwise; and it was to the former only that the rule of civil law, which was quoted above, applied. Lands and tenements did not become the property of the captor, but of the prince for whom he fought,[2] and the people who lived on conquered lands became subjects (if they remained there), not slaves or prisoners.[3] In practice, however, this rule was not quite as precise as it sounds. As we have seen already, captains of free companies, though they held their forts in the name of the prince who avowed them, often behaved as if these forts were their own property;[4] and as we shall see shortly, they had a certain legal justification for doing so. In the case, however, where soldiers had proper terms of service and were on an official payroll, the rule applied straightforwardly, and a good many English indentures in fact make the point explicit. Lands, towns, and castles, however taken and wherever, belonged to the king.[5] It was therefore in moveable loot that the ordinary soldier was chiefly interested, and it was important for him to establish properly his title thereto.

His first concern was to be able to show that his booty was *prise de bonne guerre*, that is, taken in just war. If it was not taken in these circumstances, restitution could be demanded. The term, however, gave him sufficiently broad scope for pillage, for it did not just mean 'taken on the battlefield'. A soldier might

[1] On the general question of the legal standing of *appatis* see Appendix.

[2] Cf. Christine de Pisan, *Book of Fayttes of Armes and Chyvalrye*, pt. III, ch. 15 (Caxton's translation, ed. A. T. P. Byles, *E.E.T.S.*, 1932, p. 219): 'the whyche thynge were neither good nor just that they (the soldiers) with the money of the kynge or prynce and had at hys expenses shulde get for theyre own behove eny grounde'.

[3] Baldus, *Comment. in 1 Decretal.*, Tit. 34, rubr.: 'Quaero an civitates captae ab hostibus efficiantur servae hostium? Respondeo quod non efficiuntur servae, sed subdite'.

[4] *Ante*, ch. VIII, p. 126, n. 4.

[5] A clause to this effect is almost always inserted, for example, in indentures of war made late in Edward III's reign: e.g. P.R.O., E101/68/4, nos. 92, 93, 94 (46 Ed. III).

plunder civilians just as freely as men in arms, because they gave 'aid and countenance' to the war of their party. 'If on both sides war is decided upon by the councils of two kings', wrote Honoré Bonet, 'the soldiery may take spoil from the [opposing] kingdom, and make war freely.'[1] The law also favoured the soldier's right to spoil in other ways. Any goods being taken to the enemy (with the obvious exception of ransom money) were lawful prey,[2] whether or not the carriers were insured under safe-conduct.[3] A safe-conduct in any case only gave immunity from spoliation when it was given by a captain or commander who had direct authority over a soldier; he was not bound by the safe-conduct of another captain of his own party.[4] Even if a truce was arranged, a soldier might still be able to take spoil, if he could get himself excluded from its terms,[5] and in any case there would almost certainly be an interval after its signature and before its terms became operative when he could make a final drive for booty.[6] An ancient custom of the sea gave full forty days' grace, after a truce had been cried, during which prizes could be lawfully made.[7]

[1] Bonet, *Tree of Battles*, pt. 4, ch. 48 (Coopland's translation, pp. 153–4).

[2] Cf. defence of Waleran de Camberon, accused by Gualo le Campscherat of illegal spoliation of eight tuns of wine: 'dictus Wale dicta vina ipsis (quadrigariis) tradiderat pro vendendo inimicis et propter hoc dictus miles et sui socii ceperant dicta vina . . . et reddiderant equos et quadrigas licet totum retinere potuissent' (Arch. Nat., X¹a 19, fo. 74vo, arrest in favour of Waleran dated 2 April 1365).

[3] Cf. case tried before Jean de Neuville, Lieutenant of the Marshal d'Audreham, at Corbeil in 1359, concerning the spoliation of goods of Jean du Chapel Rouge, which had been taken, although he had 'bon saufconduit de mondit seigneur le regent' on the ground he was taking goods to the English (Arch. Nat., JJ 90, no. 232).

[4] Bonet, *Tree of Battles*, pt. 4, ch. 59: 'a captain has power to ensure safe conduct . . . only in regard to men of the captain's own country who are under him' (Coopland's translation, p. 162).

[5] See, e.g. the letter of Perrinet Gressart asking for exclusion from truces, 1426, quoted *ante*, ch. VI, p. 82, n. 1.

[6] See, e.g. the clause in the truce between French and Burgundians, signed at Nevers, 6 February 1435: 'por ce que de present l'en ne peut bonnement advertir les capitaines estans en forteresses faisans guerre d'un coste et d'autre . . . la dite abstinance quant a cassation de guerre sera suspendue jusques au huitiesme jour de mars prochain venant'. (Arch. dep. de la Côte d'Or, B.11918)

[7] Cf. the case brought before the Parlement by Kel Donas and other Gascon merchants trading from London, plundered in the summer of 1360

These rules sound adequately simple. In practice, they were far from being so. We have seen earlier that it was not always easy to be certain what places and persons were in the war, or even what war they were in. Was the town of Braisne, for instance, for Armagnac or Burgundy in 1419? And if it had been Armagnac, and so *de guerre* to the Burgundians, what sort of security was it that Hector de Saveuses gave the townsmen?[1] Were goods taken at Carentan in 1450 taken inside the wall, where the town's treaty of surrender secured them from pillage, or were they taken in the suburbs, which were stormed, and so lawful spoil?[2] In these instances, it was particular local conditions and agreements that muddied the issue. In others it was hard to say whether the normally accepted principles ought or ought not to apply. The rule that goods being taken to the enemy could be seized sounds fair enough; suppose, however, that part of a ransom was demanded in kind, what then? Was a man already in debt to the enemy to be plundered by his own side?[3] And what of the goods of a neutral merchant, loaded

[1] Case of the Seigneur de Torcy *v.* Philippe de Saveuses, Arch. Nat., X$^1$a 4800 fo. 85 et seq. (14 March 1444, referring to events of 1417). Saveuses, a Burgundian, was accused of unlawful spoliation, and his advocate replied that Braisne 'estoit en guerre en frontiere de guerre'. Torcy's advocate replied that Braisne was 'du party de bourgogne', because it had given obedience to the King and Duke of Burgundy, when summoned by Hector de Saveuses and Jean le Fosseux, and they had signed a 'scedule' to this effect. Philip's advocate replied that this was not a certificate of obedience, but a safe-conduct, which did not bind him: 'len leur avoit baille argent afin que ne assaillissent la place mais portant nestoit liez le duc de Bourgogne et autres gens de guerre'. The case was postponed, for another hearing, of which the register has no trace.

[2] See *ante*, ch. VIII, p. 120, n. 1.

[3] Technically it was forbidden to supply the enemy, even by way of ransom, but this rule was difficult to enforce, as it was impossible to prevent the enemy demanding ransoms in kind. Usually men involved in such cases were pardoned and arrests on their goods lifted. Cf. case of Beraud de Taillat, 1377, who was pardoned for trading 'chevaux et autres choses . . . qui

by seamen of St. Valery, who refused restitution, because of an established custom 'quod illi qui sunt in mare tam ex una parte quam ex altera, fiunt extra treugas et tractatus hujusmodi usque ad finem quadragesime diei a publicacione ipsarum . . . et si aliquid conquestum seu captum fuerit . . . ad victorem spectat et remanet tanquam in facto bone guerre' (Arch. Nat., X$^1$a 17, fo. 97 et seq.).

in the same ship or cart as goods belonging to enemy merchants?[1] Faced with problems such as these the courts could do little more than attempt to do justice on the individual merits of a case. To their credit they observed principles which presumed innocence rather than guilt; the cases of merchant strangers,[2] and of those who sued to avoid loss (*de dampno vitando*)[3] were always favoured. But they could not hope to do more than rough justice. In the frontiers of war it was not easy to distinguish which side even soldiers were on, and, as always where the law is involved, too often widely different tales were told by the two parties.

Where, as was most often the case, immunity from war (either by reason of a safe-conduct, or some other privilege) was alleged as grounds for a charge of unlawful spoliation, the court could only hope that it gauged accurately who told the truth about the immunity or lack of it. There were, however, two other grounds on which a right to spoil might be contested, in which particular legal principles were involved. One arose

[1] Cf. the case of Berant van der Zolte v. Adam Louvel (Arch. Nat., X¹a 4791, fo. 158vo–9). Berant, who had been despoiled, claimed he was a merchant of the Hanse 'qui n'est pas de la guerre d'angleterre et de france'; Louvel and his companions replied that his goods were lawful prize, because they were loaded in the same ship as English goods. The case was referred to the Council.

[2] Cf. for example the upholding of a safe-conduct under the seal of Edward IV, in spite of a technical infringement of English rules in failing to supply a list of men on a ship, by judgment of the Chancellor in 1473: 'merchants shall not be bound by our statutes, and though they are come into the kingdom by this (safe-conduct) . . . but this shall be according to the law of nature . . . which is universal throughout the world'. (*Select cases in the Law Merchant*, ed. Hubert Hall, Selden Soc., 1930, Vol. II, p. lxxvi.)

[3] Cf. case of Desmoulins v. Chartreux of Le Parc, in which the Carthusians claimed their right to the beasts they had recovered from enemy raiders was favourable because '*ipsi certant de dampro vitando* et est le bestail sien et a este arrete en leur possession' (Arch. Nat., X¹a 4797, fo. 50). Compare the statement in a ransom case, that of Buxton v. Dorot (ibid., fo. 215 et seq.): 'est le fait de Dorot bien favorable et *certat de dampno vitando* et Buxton *de lucro captando*'.

---

estoient expressement accordees en sa dite rancon' (Vaissette, *Histoire de Languedoc*, Toulouse, edn., 1872–6, Tome X, cols. 1594–5). Compare the case of Pierre de la Heruppe, pardoned for the same reason in 1359 (Arch. Nat., JJ 89, no. 40).

from the principle that goods were lawfully spoil only if taken *in actu belli*. By denying that they were so taken, a man might question the captor's right. This was not a very important principle, because, as we have seen, the plunder of civilians was allowed to be *in actu belli*, but it did help to limit indiscriminate looting well behind the lines.[1] The other possible objection to a captor's right to spoil was by invoking the principle of *postliminium in preda*. This allowed an owner who had been pillaged to ask for the return of goods which had been recovered from the enemy and treated as spoil. He could only succeed in his action, however, if he could show that the enemy had failed to establish their right to the spoil, because they had kept it for so short a time that it was as if he had never lost it. According to the doctors of the law, spoil only became the property of the captors once they had got clean away with it to a 'safe place' (*intra praesidia*).[2] This was a rule not easy to apply where, for instance, spoil was taken on an extended raid into enemy territory, when soldiers might not come to a 'safe place' for weeks on end. The courts therefore applied a rather simpler rule, that an owner lost his title to goods which remained in enemy hands for over twenty-four hours.[3] In the interval, they were not lost, and he could demand their return from those who recovered them.

[1] Cf. statement of the King's proctor in a dispute over a man taken behind the lines in Paris (plaidoirie of 18 March, 1417), that he cannot accept, as a precedent for a private captor's claim, the rights allowed to captors in prisoners taken 'quant Robin Canolle passa pres de Paris', because this was *in actu belli et in expeditione* (Arch. Nat., X¹a 4791, fo. 210).

[2] Bartholomew de Saliceto, *Super VIII Cod.*, Tit. 51, l. 12. 'In . . . rebus mobilibus et in omnibus dico, quod antequam sunt ductae intra praesidia hostium, non efficiuntur eorum, sed remanent sub dominio eorum, sub quo erant ante capturam, arg. *d. l. postliminii*.'

[3] Cf. Angelus of Perusia, *Disputatio*, inc., 'renovata guerra': 'si per unam diem preda fuerit in campo detenta per hostes . . . intelligitur capientium facta'. A good example of the rule being invoked is the case of Volo du Vris *v.* Huguet de Rieux and others, January 1430. Huguet was claiming goods as his; Volo asserted that they were given him by Jean ( ? Jacques) de Chabannes, in compensation for wrongful infringement of safe-conduct by him. If the goods had been Huguet's, he declared, 'elle avoit este depuis acquise en la main des ennemis qui lont tenu plus de XXIIII heures, voire plus de XXIIII jours; et si ont perdu la possession et seigneurie' (Arch. Nat., X¹a 4796, fo. 178vo).

A much more serious issue was raised when someone other than the captor challenged his right to spoil, or demanded a share in it. Such claims were alleged often, and were often allowed. This implies that the principle, that goods taken in just war became the property of the captors, was not absolute, and this is an implication that we must investigate.

In fact, almost every lawyer who quotes this principle un-says it later. The result is the confusion which Honoré Bonet noted. 'In truth,' he wrote, 'the law on this matter is involved. . . . According to one law it is thought that the chattels a man wins should be his, but another law says that if a man comes into possession of chattels in war, he must deliver them to the duke of the battle. For my part I say that what a man gains from his enemies belongs to him, if we bear in mind that previously it belonged to his enemies, who have lost their lordship over it; but it does not belong to the captor to the extent that he is not obliged to hand it over to the duke of the battle, and he should share the spoils out among his men, to each according to his valour.'[1] Bonet is here merely repeating what almost every doctor before him had said, and their statements seem as contradictory as he says they were. Bartholomew of Saliceto, however, clears up at least one obscurity in a parallel passage: 'goods become the property of the captor', he says, 'as far as those who had previous lordship are concerned, but not as regards the host to whose common profit they are seen to be taken, and so they should be handed over to the duke of the battle . . . for where the danger is common, the profit should be common too'.[2] Bartholomew is still uncertain, it is true, whether this principle applies to goods taken by raiding parties foraging in the countryside, but at least he has made an attempt to rationalise the seeming contradictions of the law. Bartolus adds a comment illuminating for its reference to contemporary practice: 'the captor is bound to hand over his spoil to the duke of the battle', he says, 'and we see this rule observed in practice, for after a victory all the goods taken are gathered together, and they are called *the booty*; and afterwards they are sold and the profits shared among the soldiers'.[3]

[1] Bonet, *Tree of Battles*, pt. 4, ch. 43 (Coopland's translation, p. 150).
[2] Bartholomew de Saliceto, *Super VIII Cod.*, Tit. 51, l. 12.
[3] Bartolus, *Comment. in Dig. Nov.*, XLIX, Tit. 15, l. 28.

Among these statements, the really revealing one is that of Bartholomew of Saliceto, that spoil is taken to the common profit of the host. It reminds us that war, properly so called, was a public affair, waged on the authority of a prince, which meant a 'public' person with responsibilities toward the common weal of his subjects. True, this situation was no longer as clear cut as it had been in the time of the Romans, whose law Bartholomew was glossing; for the wars of the Romans were waged on behalf of the Roman people, and the Roman soldier was the servant of the state. Neither the cause nor the service of a medieval sovereign was 'public' in this sense. Nevertheless it was he, in his capacity as a public person, who undertook the major risks of war, and common justice demanded he might bespeak some of its advantages. Since the war was waged on his behalf, the private interest of the individual soldier could not reasonably be permitted to prejudice his 'public interest', and this principle, as Jean de Beuil pointed out in the *Jouvencel*, could be applied to rights in spoil.[1] Important prisoners, as 'great captains' and princes of an adversary's blood, were for this reason at the disposal of the 'head of the war' without any reserve.[2] He could indeed reserve to himself any prisoner for reasons of state, provided he was prepared to compensate his master for the loss of his ransom.[3]

---

[1] *Le Jouvencel*, ed. Lécestre and Favre, Tome II, p. 10: Jean de Beuil is discussing the loss of rights in a prisoner, through failure to notify the captain when lodging him in a town. It is true that this is hard on the captor, he says, but officers must have control over the movements of enemy personnel, even under parole, in their towns, and the rule is therefore just, because 'ung bien particullier n'est pas a preferer a la chose publique'.

[2] This rule is mentioned in nearly all English indentures of war, in the clause which regulates shares of spoil. For an example of the wording see, e.g. Lord Willoughby's indenture, 47 Ed. III: 'Et aura notre dit seigneur le Roi devers lui les *prisoners roialx* comme le roi son adversaire ses freres et chevetayn de guerre lieutenant du dit adversaire . . . per fesant convenable regard a ceux qui les auroient pris' (P.R.O., E101/68/6, no. 122).

[3] For a good example of the exercise of this right, see the statement of the plaintiff in the case of Yvo de Puy *v.* the Count of Maine, concerning certain prisoners taken at La Ferté, 'Le Conte de Mayne . . . vint la et fist mettre les noms du dit Menton et des autres (the captors) en escript et ne demanda que Cliqueton que le Roy vouloit avoir pour la raencon du Sire de Goncourt' (Arch. Nat., X¹a 4801, fo. 399, plaidorie of 26 February, 1448). The English king's right to control all prisoners is well illustrated by the royal

It is already clear that the word 'public', as here applied to medieval political conditions, does not carry the same full force of meaning that it did in Roman times. This becomes yet more obvious if one looks at the position from the soldier's point of view. The Roman soldier was paid and kept and ultimately pensioned; but very often the medieval soldier was not even paid. If he had the misfortune to be taken prisoner, it was as a private person that he gave his faith to his captor, and this private obligation stood, even if he was rescued by his own side. From public service he derived far fewer benefits than the Roman soldier, and as a private individual he ran greater risks. If common justice demanded that the prince should have a lawful interest in the advantages of war, it therefore demanded equally that the common soldier's interest in them should also be legally protected.[1] The law in fact did its best to cater for both parties. Its seeming contradictions were really a compromise; the soldier was bound to assign his gains to the 'head of the war' or 'duke of the battle'; but the latter was bound equally to divide these profits according to merit. This compromise was based on principles of justice and reason, its object being to adjust rights in spoil to the extent of involvement in the risks of its capture.

The man who ran the greatest risk in war was clearly the prince. Consequently, the prince had certain definite rights in its 'advantages'. The plunder of towns stormed in his service was his,[2] as were all prisoners of 'public' standing. In addition, there was a royal portion to be paid from all booty. This portion varied according to the customs of different countries;

---

[1] Cf. Christine de Pisan, *Book of Fayttes of Armes and Chyvalrye* (Caxton's transl., ed. A. T. P. Byles, *E.E.T.S.*, 1932, p. 219): 'the prynce wyl gye to them of a specyall grace (a share of spoil), the whiche grace to say trouthe wel and largely hit behoveth them, as to them that setten in adventure so dere a catell as is the blode the lymes and the lyfe'.

[2] See ch. VIII *ante*.

---

bans on ransoming them after Neville's Cross (Rymer, Vol. III, pt. I, p. 1), and after Homildon Hill (ibid, IV, pt. I, p. 36). A demand for compensation for a prisoner called Macbeth, lost as a result of this ban after Neville's Cross, had to be investigated by the Sheriff of Northumberland, to establish whether the king was liable (P.R.O., C145, File 161, no. 15).

in England it was a third,[1] in Spain a fifth,[2] in France (where the right does not seem to have been often exercised) it was that portion of any *booty* which exceeded 10,000 francs.[3] These were customary rules which could, of course, be altered by mutual agreement. After the prince, the captain clearly ran a more serious risk than any other: and accordingly he too had his customary portion. In England his share was the same as the king's, a third;[4] in France he could claim a tenth;[5] and in Spain either a seventh or a tenth, according to his standing.[6] After these shares had been reserved, the remaining spoil was divided among the soldiers according to their rank; a mounted man had more than a foot-soldier, and he again more than an archer.[7] In order to ensure that the rules were observed, the

[1] This rule seems to have enjoyed general currency from at least the 1350s onwards, cf. D. Hay, 'The Divisions of the Spoils of war in Fourteenth Century England', *T.R.H.S.*, 5th series, Vol. iv (1954), pp. 91 et seq. It could of course be varied by written agreement, as in the indenture of Gregory van der Meer and Obert Gay (1372), where a half is substituted (P.R.O. E101/68/5, no. 117).

[2] See *Las Siete Partidas del Rey don Alfonso el Sabro*, pt. II, Tit. 24, l. 4 (Madrid edn., 1807, Tome II, pp. 275–6).

[3] Cf. Christine de Pisan, *Livre des Fais d'armes et de Chevalerie*, pt. 3, ch. xv, 'Autrefois tout le butin appartenoit au roi, maintenant ce qui depasse le prix de 10,000 francs'. We find Jean d'Armagnac modelling his terms on this French custom in his contract with Ramonet de Sort for service in Aragon in 1389, agreeing that he shall only have a portion in booties and ransoms of 'dets milla francs o daqui ensus' (Bib. Nat., Collection Doat, Tome 203, fo. 287vo).

[4] Claims by captains to thirds appear early in our period; cf. that on the part of Walter Bentley in 1351, mentioned by Professor Hay, op. cit., p. 103; and the demand by Gournay and Jean de Lou for a third of the spoil taken at Arselay, referred to arbitration in 1360 (P.R.O., E101/68/4, nos. 78–80).

[5] Cf. the claim of Robert Floques in 1450, to this share in an English prisoner taken by Jean de St. Waast, his soldier: 'or les capitaines ont grand droiz comme le X$^{me}$ sur chacun prisonnier' (Arch. Nat., X$^{1}$a 4802, fo. 198). This portion seems to be of ancient standing, as it is mentioned in the thirteenth-century romance of Eustace the Monk, ll. 960–77, cf. especially Eustace's message to the Count of Boulogne, his lord, ll. 975–7:

'Di li c'Uistaces li envoie
La dime de toute sa proie.'

(*Roman d'Eustache le Moine*, ed. F. Michel, Paris, 1833, pp. 35–6.)

[6] *Las Siete Partidas*, etc., op. cit., pt. II, Tit. 26, l. xiv. A seventh was paid to a captain who was also a 'natural' lord, a tenth to any other.

[7] This system puzzled Geoffrey de Charny, who in his list of problems in

standing orders of great hosts often laid down that all booty should be brought in to a central hoard;[1] it was then auctioned, and the profits shared according to rank. This is the custom which the lawyer Bartolus remarked on. Similarly, the names of all prisoners had to be provided by their captors as soon as they were taken, in order to ensure that the king and the captain could claim their portion of the eventual ransom.[2] Anyone who attempted to conceal spoil or prisoners forfeited his right thereto. Rights in spoil were thus not absolute but partial, and conditional on the captor's proper behaviour with regard to the common interest involved.

The rules which have been outlined so far applied wherever soldiers were in service under a king or captain, and were paid wages, or were mounted and armed by him. Where this was not the case they had not the same justification. As the soldiers were not deriving any direct benefit from the lord who avowed them, it was hard to argue any direct obligation towards him. The free companies who fought in central France in the 1370s and 1380s in the name of the King of England could hardly be said to be in his service, for he gave them nothing but his name, and so they did not pay him thirds of their gains of war. They were not really part of his host at all, but private hosts in themselves, and they were thus more in the position of allies than of ordinary soldiers. Internally, such companies observed the same kind of rules about division of spoils as did royal hosts;[3] externally,

[1] Cf. Salisbury's Perche Orders §3: 'And if so be that anie man have anie of the enemies goods the which he wolde selle that he bringe it into the common markett and proclaimed by the officer of the Marshalcie' (B. Mus., Cotton MS. Julius F IV, fo. 322). Compare Henry V's Agincourt orders (Upton, *De Officio Militari*, ed. Bysshe, p. 139, *de equitationibus generalibus*), and Archibald Douglas Orders for Scots hosts in the March, §2 (*Acts of the Parliament of Scotland*, Vol. I, Appendix IV, p. 350).

[2] E.g. Richard II's Durham ordinances, 1385, §xix (*Black Book of the Admiralty*, R.S., Vol. I, p. 456); Henry V's Mantes Orders, 1419, §20 (ibid., p. 465).

[3] Cf. for example Villani's description of the system in the company of Fra Moriale (*c.* 1353), which is the best account of the organisation of a

the law of arms, asks what share a foot soldier, who, when men are *à butin*, captures a horse and fights on it, should have. Does he thereby become a mounted soldier for the purposes of division? (Bib. Nat., MS. Fr. Nouvelles Acquisitions, 4736, fo. 24.)

however, they had no obligations and what they took was their own without restriction.[1] Their rights extended even over *immobilia*, though not absolutely. Roughly speaking, the rule seems to have been that though the towns and castles which they took in the cause of a prince became part of his lordship, he could not justify complaint if they afterwards lost or sold them, since he had not laid out anything to win his right. Sale in such case was not regarded strictly as purchase, but as a ransom which a captain was entitled to demand, because he had won a fort or town at his own peril. Thus, after Brétigny, English captains who held forts in northern France could not demand such ransoms for evacuation, because their forts had been taken in the *service* of Edward III, and he had renounced his right in them.[2] But the free companies who fought in the *name* of Richard II could and did demand whatever they could get from Jean de Blaisy in 1390, in return for the evacuation of their strongholds;[3] and no one suggested they had betrayed the King of England when they did so.

This adjustment of rights in spoil to terms of service and risks run seems to have been the general practice of the late medieval period. It also operated conversely, with regard to liability to spoliation. Thus for instance, when a man armed

[1] Hence Edward III's counsel to Philip of Navarre (*c.* 1358), his lieutenant in Normandy: 'Item au quart point du tierz de gain de guerre, semble que Mons. Philippe ne poet cela demander si les gentz ne feussent a ses custages' (quoted by Professor Hay, op. cit., p. 104, from B. Mus., Cotton MS. Cal. D III).

[2] Cf. protest of the French, December 1361 'que . . . les chasteaulx et forteressez occupeez en roialme par les Angloys . . . n'ont pas este voidies et deliverez par la manere ne au temps que se devoit faire . . . [et] ce qad este delivere ne a pas este delivere ne voidie au frais du Roi Dengleterre come se devoit faire, mes par grantz *ransons* d'argent'. See also the reply of the English 'les paiementz si qels estoient faites, ne furent mye *ransons*, mes ils estoient restatz qels furent duwes au roi et a ses subgez [i.e. outstanding *appatis*]'. (P. Chaplais, 'Some Documents regarding the fulfilment of the Treaty of Brétigny', *Camden Miscellany*, Vol. xix, pp. 12–13 and 15.)

[3] Cf. J. Monicat, *Les Grandes Compaignies en Velay*, pp. 87 et seq.

free company which I have found: 'molti soldati . . . senza volere piu soldo traevano a Fra Moriale . . . ed egli li faceva scrivere, e con ordine dava a catuno certa parte al bottino etc.' Villani also describes the public auction of all common booty on which these fixed shares were paid. (*Cronica di Matteo Villani*, ed. Ignazio Moutier, Florence, 1825, Tome II, p. 146.)

himself as a subject or a servant, without any wages and on the mere command of his lord, he could demand compensation if he was taken and ransomed.[1] On the same principle, when soldiers in their contracts of service stipulated that the prince or lord who paid them should ransom them if they were taken, they also usually undertook to hand over to him all their gains of war, without reserve.[2] It was much the same with regard to the captain of a company. Even when he paid his men no wages, he had a certain responsibility towards them. A company was a *societas*,[3] a corporate body of itself; and he was its head, the leader of a common enterprise.[4] As such he could be held liable for unauthorised pillaging by his men,[5] and it was he who mounted and armed them at his expense.[6] He might even, by

[1] Cf. Angelus de Perusia, *Comment. in Dig. Vet.*, Lib. XIV, Tit. 2: 'ubi propter communem utilitatem unus damnum sentit, debet onus communiter contribui'. But this applies to citizens and subjects acting on command, 'qui non habent stipendium, nisi aliud pacto convenerit, nam tunc pacta servanda'. Thus Charles VII in 1426 granted to La Tremoille all subsidies raised in his own lands to pay his ransom to Perrinet Gressart, as he was taken on the King's errand (Flamare, *Le Nivernais pendant la Guerre de Cent Ans*, no. XLVIII, Tome I, pp. 301–2).

[2] Cf. contracts of Philip VI with the Archbishop of Cologne, and the Counts of Juliers and Gueldres for war service, May 1332 (*Oeuvres de Froissart*, ed. Kervyn de Lettenhove, Tome XVIII, no. ix, pp. 22–5); and of Philip VI with Adolph of Cologne, 20 July 1337 (ibid., Tome XVIII, no. xvii, pp. 42–5). The same rule is laid down in the *Statuta Delphinalia* for war, 1367 (*Ordonnances des Rois de France*, Tome V, p. 39).

[3] See *Le Jouvencel* (ed. Lécestre and Favre, p. 216), where Jean de Beuil justifies the powers of a captain because they are 'pour le bien publique de la compaignie'.

[4] Cf. Villani's description of the internal regulation of Fra Moriale's company, quoted p. 148, n. 3, with its detailed rules for common booty, and its own internal system of justice and administration under him. 'E ordino camarlingo che riceva e pagava, e fece consiglieri e segretari con cui guidava tutto, e da tutti i cavalieri e masnadieri era ubbidito come fosse loro signoro, e mantanea ragione tra lore.'

[5] Cf. for example the prosecution of Raimon de Rabastans in 1428, on the ground that he was a captain and responsible for pillaging by his men (Arch. Nat., X¹a 9199, fo. 18). The rule that the captain was responsible for his men was strongly stressed in Charles VII's ordinance of 1439 (*Ordonnances des Rois de France*, Tome XIII, pp. 306–13, especially §18).

[6] This was the essential point as regards rights to shares in spoil, cf. the statement of Robert Floques in the case quoted *ante*, p. 147, n. 5: 'quant les archiers sont montez et armez par les capitaines lors les capitaines avoient les droiz dont parlent parties' (i.e. a tenth).

the terms of his contracts with his soldiers, be bound to ransom them when they were taken.[1] Therefore he could demand his right as a captain even when no wages were paid, for it was he who took the risks, and after all he himself in this case had no wages either. Thus we find that in 1351 the English soldiers in Brittany who were not at the King's wages had to pay their thirds to their captains notwithstanding.[2] A hundred years and more later the same rule was still being applied in the courts; Jean de Ferrières in 1475 could claim his captain's tenth in all the winnings at Montreuillon of those whom he had mounted and armed.[3] The idea of reciprocal obligation, which we see here expressed, was very deep-rooted in medieval social thought; it was the presupposed basis of feudal customs far older than the rules we are discussing.

So far the rules with which we have been concerned have all appeared to have some sort of rational explanation. There were, however, a variety of further rules about the division of spoil which were observed simply because custom gave them legal force. These can be listed, but not explained. The Marshal of

[1] This was clearly the case with Hugh de Rigney, taken at Brignais, as he claimed full compensation for the 'grant somme d'argent dont il havoit estey domagie et fraye tant pour ly comme pour ses compaignons . . . tant en raencons, perte des chevaulx, et d'autres biens'. (Arch. dep. de la Côte d'Or, B11885: there is another similar claim in this bundle from Robert de Grancey, for compensation for the ransoms of 'Odet mon fils et ceulx de sa compaignie', taken at Vanoy in 1326.) Froissart tells us that Perrot le Béarnois would only ransom his men if taken in his personal company (*Oeuvres de Froissart*, ed. Kervyn de Lettenhove, Tome XIII, pp. 57 and 60).

[2] Cf. Edward III's instruction to Walter Bentley: 'Nostre seigneur le Roi voet que de ceux qui ne voillent demorer a ses gaiges en Bretayn, que le capitayn illoeques eit le Tersage de lour gain et de lours prisoners' (*Oeuvres de Froissart*, ed. Kervyn de Lettenhove, Tome XVIII, no. LXXIX, p. 341). Compare Richard II's Durham ordinances §xvi 'qu chascun paie la tierce a son seigneur ou mestre, de toute maniere de gaigne d'armes, et ce auxi bien ceux qe ne sont point a soulde' (*Black Book of the Admiralty*, R.S., Vol. I, p. 456).

[3] Baluze, *Histoire de la Maison d'Auvergne*, Tome II, pp. 463–4. Jean de Ferrières claimed the 'jura decimae . . . capitaneis super redemptionibus prisonariorum per eorum servitores in bello cui praesunt captorum ex usu belli debita', in respect of Anthoine de Luxembourg, whose captor, Jean de Sandeville, was in Ferrière's company 'cujus expensis et sub ejus servitio et conductione militabat'. Ferrières was leading men raised by the *ban* and *arrière ban* in Auvergne.

England, for instance, claimed a right to all gelded beasts taken as prey on a royal expedition.[1] The Constable of France had a right to horses and harness taken in a town.[2] Another right, which is frequently mentioned in cases in court, is the right of a brother-in-arms to a half share in all the gains of war of his companion,[3] and to inherit on his death any booty made in their common enterprise.[4] This rule was founded in knightly custom; but it made possible the adaptation of what was in essence a chivalrous association to form the basis of a purely commercial partnership in gains of war. The partnership could indeed include more than two persons: we hear, for instance, of four soldiers, one of whom had as his prisoner the Marshal of Burgundy, who on the field of Montreuillon in 1475 swore 'all four to be brothers-in-arms and live and die by one another'.[5] The words have a high-sounding echo, but what was really constituted was a limited company to exploit rights in a particularly profitable prisoner.

This is a useful reminder that a great deal of booty was not even originally captured by individuals, but by groups of foragers. What they gained might be put into the common booty and divided according to rank. But groups could take spoil independently (and where two independent companies, for instance, were co-operating, they normally would do). In this

[1] Cf. the customs of Thomas of Brotherton (B. Mus., Cotton MS. Nero D6, fo. 85 and vo): 'quant ils chivachent, des proies qui seront pris avera le connestable tous les bestes decornuz et tous les chivaux deferrez et les porcs et le marechal avera toutes les bestes verrez' (this document is not official; it is a list of customs, probably produced at the time when Margaret Brotherton claimed the right to appoint a lieutenant to act as Marshal at Richard II's coronation, as this claim is mentioned earlier, fo. 65vo).

[2] Cf. customs of the Constable de Clisson (again unofficial) (Bib. Nat., MS. Fr. 4604, fo. 4vo): 'si lon prend chastel ou forteresses ausquelz se rendent chevaulx harnois d'armes vivres et autres choses que l'on treuve dedans, sont au Conestable'.

[3] For examples, see those I have quoted elsewhere: Keen, 'Brotherhood in Arms', *History*, Vol. 47 (1962), pp. 8–9.

[4] Cf. the statement of Simon, advocate for claimants to the ransom of the seigneur de Chateauvillain, in the Parlement in 1450: 'par l'usage de guerre la part du feu Fort Espice appartient au bourg de Mascaras, par ce que estoient freres et compagnons d'armes, et ce qu'ils gaignent ensemble vient au survivant' (Arch. Nat., X¹a 4802, fo. 138).

[5] Baluze, *Histoire de la Maison d'Auvergne*, Tome II, p. 464.

case, the method of division was regulated by certain cries, whose meaning was generally understood and which could if necessary be shouted in the heat of a pursuit when all were scattering in quest of spoil. The most common cry was *à butin* which meant that spoil was to be shared according to rank, as normally. But the cry could be *à prix d'une esguillette*, in which case portions were strictly equal, or *à bonne usance*, which meant that what each man took was his own.[1] 'The commander or captain has merely to give the cry,' wrote Jean de Beuil, 'for he may make booty in whatever way seems good to him, and it is enough that his words are heard by those around him.'[2] Words in the heat of battle had the force of law, as we are here again reminded.

With such multiplicity of rules it must be clear that legal disputes over rights in spoil could be very involved. By way of illustration, one might quote the circumstances of a case which came before the Parlement in 1428, over rights in a prisoner named Rohan who had been taken at the recovery of Le Mans three years previously.[3] The case originated in a quarrel between two squires, John Winter and Roger Pelerin, who both claimed this man as their captive. When their case came before Lord Scales, William Glasdale appeared to claim a third share in the prisoner, as Roger's captain, and with him came Thomas Rampston, John Popham, and William Oldhall, who had been companions *à butin* with Glasdale in the assault. Talbot, Winter's commander, then took his man's part as he too had a claim, in his right as a captain. This gives seven claimants when the case came before the Parlement on appeal, plus two more who appear to have been *à butin* with Winter, making nine in all. But the list of interested parties is not yet exhausted. The king still had his right to a third of whatever the captains obtained finally, and besides this we know independently that

---

[1] It is clear from Geoffrey de Charny's question about the shares of men who are *à butin* that shares were then by rank; see *ante* ch. IX, p. 147, n. 7. For the other two cries, see the definitions given in the *Jouvencel* (ed. Lécestre and Favre, Tome I, p. 65). Where men are *à bonne usance*, 'qui plus y travailleroit, plus y prendroit de prouffit'; where they are *à prix d'une esguillette* 'chacun s'attendroit a son compagnon', i.e. the whole band worked as one.

[2] *Le Jouvencel*, ed. Lécestre and Favre, Tome II, p. 215.

[3] Arch. Nat., X¹a 4795, fo. 324vo–5.

Winter had a brother-in-arms, Nicholas Molyneux, who there-fore had rights in half of any sum obtained by him.[1] The issue was further complicated by Winter's claim that firstly, Glasdale was not a captain and therefore had no possible right in a third, and secondly, that Glasdale, whom he admitted was by him when Rohan was taken, had promised in the heat of the affray to be *à butin* with him. The final decision of the court is not recorded, but it is clear that no individual had much prospect of establishing an absolute right to the prisoner. He was no longer being treated as if he was a living person, but as a capital asset in which a large number of people might hold shares.

The complex web of rules concerning rights in gains of war, which this case illustrates, bears witness to the importance which the law of arms acquired as a result of the military commercial-ism of the fourteenth and fifteenth centuries. The use and steady extension of ancient military customs, often no doubt of local origin, won it acceptance as an international code of war, because the very large financial stakes at issue made such a code both useful and necessary. In their turn, the pressure of these financial considerations was gradually altering the nature of the law; though terms of service and association were still spoken of in the language of chivalry and honour, their meaning was becoming more and more rational and commercial. At the same time, owing to the increase in litigation over rights ac-quired in war, another rationalising influence was being brought to bear. This was the influence of the professional lawyer, whose outlook was conditioned by his studies in Roman and canon law, not by the social rituals of a knightly education. From these studies he learnt that war was not just an acceptable and adventurous profession, but the prosecution of a public quarrel, and that rights arising out of war must be looked at in the light of this premise. If they were not reasonable, they had no standing in law. Conversely, what was reasonable must be lawful also; hence, if a man paid wages and undertook liabilities, he must be understood to have a lawful claim to some share in the advantages of those who benefited by him.[2]

---

[1] A copy of their contract of brotherhood is preserved; Magdalen Coll., Oxon., Southwark Deed 213.

[2] Cf. Christine de Pisan's justification of the rule that booty be assigned to the duke of the battle: 'For syth that the men of warre are at the wages

This application of rational principles was at the end of the middle ages changing men's outlook on war. The conditions and attitudes of the fourteenth century made possible the activities of the free companies, and endowed individual free-booting with a halo of romance. But the fifteenth century saw the rise of the standing army, and the necessity of regular pay and fixed conditions of service being urged on all sides.[1] Frois-sart was the last chronicler who could describe the events of war in terms of the private adventures of individual knights and still write convincingly. By the time of Malory this condition could only be pictured in a past golden age. At the end of the Hundred Years War the quest for commercial gain and the rationalism of the lawyer had left little of the idea of chivalry but an old-fashioned pose.

[1] Cf. for example, William of Worcester, *Boke of Noblesse* (ed. J. G. Nichols, Roxburghe Club, 1860), pp. 30, 71 et seq.

---

of the kyng or prynce what somevere they take . . . ought to be to the lorde after the lawes'. (Caxton's translation, ed. Byles, op. cit., p. 219.)

# X

# THE LAW OF RANSOM

F AR and away the most valuable gains of war were the ransoms of prisoners. Because a prisoner was a living person, and a Christian with a free will of his own, the rules controlling rights in this kind of spoil were necessarily much more complicated than those governing the capture of chattels. In addition, because more disputes were brought into court over ransom money than over any other kind of spoil, we know more about them. As a result, the examination of these rules will be an involved affair, and for this reason, the present chapter is divided into three sections. The aim of the first will be to examine the legal status of a medieval prisoner of war and his relation to his master. The second will be concerned with the questions, how a captor established his right to a prisoner's ransom, and what steps he could take if his prisoner failed to pay it? In the third section the grounds on which a right to ransom might be legally contested, and the answers which could be returned thereto, will have to be examined.

I

The Roman law laid down that persons taken in a just war became the slaves of the enemy. As we have seen, however, it was generally agreed that this rule did not apply in wars between Christians. 'According to the practice of the present day and the customs anciently observed among Christians', says John of Legnano, 'the rule of *postliminium* does not apply to persons, and persons are not sold, and do not become slaves.'[1] Unfortunately neither he nor Honoré Bonet, usually the two most reliable authorities on the law of arms, will go much further than to say that prisoners instead are now permitted to ransom themselves. They do not explain what a prisoner was if he was not a slave, or what a ransom was if it was not a sale. Most of the authorities seem content with similar statements.

Three lawyers do, however, make some attempt to explain what the legal position of a prisoner, taken in a war between Christians, was. They are Angelus of Perusia, Bartholomew of Saliceto and Paris of Pozzo. The relation of a prisoner to his master, these three suggest, is best understood by comparing it with the essentially similar relation of lord and vassal.[2] It was not servile, but contractual. 'When a man surrenders, and his victor accepts him as a prisoner', says Paris of Pozzo, 'then he makes a contract with him, that he shall be a captive and shall not be killed.'[3] This contract, like a feudal agreement, imposed obligations on both parties.

As in the case of a fief held by feudal service, the right of the captor in law was founded in the oath which his prisoner made him, when he was taken. This oath imposed a 'natural obligation',[4] guaranteed by the rule of the immutable *jus gentium* that all true contracts must be observed. Also as in the case of the lord of a fief, what the captor acquired was not an absolute property in his prisoner, but a lawful interest. That interest was the benefit of the service done the prisoner, by an act of capture which saved his life. 'A prisoner is not held as a slave', says Bartholomew of Saliceto, 'but as a pledge for the price of his ransom.'[5] On this principle, the captor could do anything to a

[1] John of Legnano, *Tractatus*, cap. 9; compare Bonet, *Tree of Battles*, pt. 4, ch. 47 (Coopland's translation, p. 152).

[2] Cf. Paris of Pozzo, *De Re Militari*, Lib. IX, cap. 2: 'sicut vassallus obligatur victori ratione juramenti et fidei praestitae, sic iste capitvus obligatur ratione fidei et captivitatis' (Zilletus, *Tractatus Juris Universi*, Tome XVI, fo. 421vo). Compare Angelus of Perusia, *Disputatio, inc.* 'Renovata Guerra': 'captivi captivantibus sunt astricti ad certam quoddamodo speciem homagii seu fidelitatis'.

[3] Ibid., Lib. IX, cap. 1 (Zilletus, op. cit., Tome XVI, fo. 421).

[4] Ibid., Lib. IX, cap. 5: 'ubi est bellum justum . . . ibi est obligatio naturalis, cui accedit juramentum' (Zilletus, Tome XVI, fo. 422vo).

[5] Bartholomew of Saliceto, *Super VIII Cod.*, Tit. 51, l. 2 (Venice edn., 1586, fo. 162vo).

prisoner which might in reason seem necessary to obtain due payment. He could keep him under lock and key, or even in irons,[1] but he could not threaten him with death,[2] or demand that he do anything contrary to law or his honour.[3] This would constitute a *delictum turpis quaestus*, and the prisoner would be freed by it from his obligation,[4] just as a vassal could defy his bond if his lord made unreasonable demands on him.

At least as far as the prisoner was concerned, his obligation was a purely private one, because he made his oath personally to his captor and to no other. The extent of his obligation is not so easy to define. When Gregory IX, for instance, asked Edward III that 'in accordance with the law of arms' a lower price be fixed for the ransom of Roger Belfort than that demanded by his captor, Jean de Grailly,[5] what exactly did he mean? The answer is not very clear. Bonet defines the correct price as being one which was not beyond the resources of a man's patrimony,[6] and tradition among knights was that the sum should be roughly equivalent to a year's full revenue of the captive's estate.[7] In practice no fixed rule seems to have been observed. The captor made a rough assessment of what his prisoner could at a pinch pay, threw in what his wealthier con-

---

[1] Cf. Bonet, *Tree of Battles*, pt. 4, ch. 56 (Coopland's translation, pp. 159–60). Jean de Beuil, in the *Jouvencel* describes a case in which a prisoner claimed to be free because 'son maistre lui avoit miz une cheisne aux piez', which claim was duly rejected; such action, he explains, was quite lawful for the master (ed. Lécestre and Favre, Tome II, p. 153).

[2] Cf. Bonet, *Tree of Battles*, pt. 4, ch. 46 (Coopland's translation, p. 152).

[3] Paris of Pozzo, op. cit., Lib. IX, cap. 2: 'non poterit victor . . . demandare, ut cum eo accedat ad loca inhonesta, vel ad hostes, aut proditionem committendam' (Zilletus, Tome XVI, fo. 421vo).

[4] Bartholomew of Saliceto, *Super VIII Cod.*, Tit. 51, l. 7: 'delictum turpis quaestus, redemptoris, privat ipsum a nexu pignoris, et pretio redemptionis'. (Venice, 1586 edn., p. 163.)

[5] See Gregory's letter of 7 October 1371, Rymer, Vol. III, pt. II, p. 185.

[6] Bonet, *Tree of Battles*, pt. 4, ch. 47 (Coopland's translation, p. 153). Cf. also Innocent VI's letter to Edward III (1358) complaining that the ransom of Charles of Blois is 'ultra vires sui patrimonii' and so excessive Denifle, *La Désolation des Eglises*, Tome II, p. 293).

[7] Cf. Monluc's remark, about the ransom he hoped for from Mark Anthony Colonna, a Roman knight: 'si je le povois attraper, j'estois riche a jamais, car pour le moin j'en aurois quatre-vingt mille ecus de rancon, qui estoit son revenue d'un an'. (*Commentaires de Blaise de Monluc*, ed. A. de Rublé, Soc. de l'histoire de France, 1866, Tome II, p. 179.)

nections were likely to add to this, and asked for as much as he thought he could get. The resulting demand was nearly always excessive; for the heads of many great families, as for instance those of Rodemack and of Chateauvillain, the payment of a ransom brought about in the end the ruin of their whole inheritance.[1]

Though a captor might, as we saw in the last chapter, have obligations to pay shares on a ransom to others, his right to payment from the prisoner was as absolute as a right to such property as a fief (which, it should be remembered, could be given in money just as well as in land). As in that case, the right was heritable, and so was the obligation to pay. In the early days of the Hundred Years War an older view seems occasionally to have been pressed, that a ransom was a purely personal obligation. Pierre de Tournebu quoted judgments of the marshals of France to this effect in the Parlement in 1363,[2] and Geoffrey de Charny consulted the knights of the Star as to whether it was legitimate to avoid a heavy ransom by enfeoffing one's heirs with one's whole estate.[3] Pierre de Tournebu's precedents were not upheld, however, and such persons as Edward III, Henry of Lancaster and the Captal de Buch all successfully passed on to their heirs rights in the ransoms of prisoners taken in the 1350s and 1370s. Though the older rule was still sometimes mentioned after this time, it was never allowed. 'The captive belongs to the son if he is his father's heir', writes Paris of Pozzo, 'although some knights unreasonably deny this, and I myself have won for a son the right to ransom a man whom his father took in war, and released on his faith.'[4]

On this same basis of the equation of rights in ransoms with property rights, any injury to the prisoner was a trespass against

[1] The struggles of these two families to discharge crippling ransoms are discussed by A. Bossuat, 'La Rançon de Jean Seigneur de Rodemack', *Annales de l'Est*, 1951, p. 145 et seq.; and 'La rançon de Guillaume de Chateauvillain', *Annales de Bourgogne*, 1951.

[2] Arch. Nat., X¹a 21, fo. 73: 'dicebant etiam quod de ratione jure armorum usu et consuetudine in facto guerre notorie observata, si ille cui sint obligationes capcionis fortaliciorum personarum vel redempcionum moriatur, obligati per euis mortem sunt liberati, sicut de Johanne de Charniaco milite contigisse dicebant et in pluribus aliis casibus per constabularium et marescallos Francie consimiliter fuisse judicatum'.

[3] Bib. Nat., MS Fr. (NA) 4736, fo. 29.

[4] Paris of Pozzo, op. cit., Lib. IX, cap. 11 (Zilletus, Tome XVI, fo. 423vo).

his master. The man who kills another's prisoner must pay his ransom, ruled Archibald Douglas, Warden of the Scottish March.[1] When forty-three English prisoners rioted against the terms of their prison at La Ferté in or about 1448 and were all killed, their gaoler, Etienne du Plessis, found himself being sued by their other captors for their share of the ransoms.[2] Similarly, those who took traitors, who had to be handed over to justice, had a right to compensation, and could sue for it.[3] The right of the captor was also protected by the law in other ways. A prisoner became a non-combatant[4] and enjoyed a more or less automatic right to safe-conduct[5] (which is why, when heralds were not available, prisoners were often used as diplomatic agents). In addition, a prisoner's lands, from the revenues of which he must pay his ransom, became technically

[1] Archibald Douglas ordinances §8 (*Acts of the Parliament of Scotland*, Vol. I, Appendix IV, p. 351a).

[2] Case of Yvo du Puy *v.* E. du Plessis, Arch. Nat., X$^1$a 4801, fo. 398vo–9. Compare with this the case of Jean de St. Venant *v.* Pierre de Bausserée and others, who had killed 'un prisonnier anglois appelle Hannequin de la Haie lequel estoit raunsome au dit escuier (Jean)'. They settled in the end with John out of court: cf. Arch. Nat. X$^1$c 15B/268 (18 December 1365). See also Gilet Prevost *v.* Colin le Barbier (9 March 1433); Prevost was suing le Barbier, gaoler of the *conciergerie*, for damages, for having allowed Perrin Blondeau, prisoner, to escape. (Arch. Nat., X$^1$a 4797, fo. 47vo–8.)

[3] Cf. case of Jean Bourdin *v.* Provosts of the merchants at Paris and Jacob Bernadin (3 July 1430). Bourdin sued to obtain compensation for ransoms of men taken by Lord Willoughby at La Chasse, who had been put to death at Paris (Arch. Nat., X$^1$a 4796, fo. 225). Compare Monstrelet's remarks on the execution of Burgundian prisoners taken in Auxerrois in 1414 'Lesquelz prins furent menez a Paris et mis en Chastelet, et depuis en y'eut d'executez. Mais paravant le Roy paya leurs rancons a ceux que pris les avoient'. (Monstrelet, *Chroniques*, ed. Douet d'Arq, Tome III, p. 57.)

[4] Bartholomew of Saliceto, *Super VIII Cod.*, Tit. 51, l. 2: 'nec ante posset militare, quam liberetur ab hoc jugo (i.e. from his ransom)'. (Venice, 1586 edn., fo. 162vo.) See also Jean de Melun's statement about Henry Pomfret (Melun *v.* Pomfret, March 1366, Bib. Nat., MS. Fr. 21717, fo. 144 et seq.): 'Henry . . . etoit prisonnier d'un escuier francois, et par ainsi selon droit d'armes ne pouvoit faire fait d'armes'.

[5] Jean de Beuil speaks of 'the signs which prisoners and others under safe-conduct carry' (*Le Jouvencel*, Tome II, p. 236). A prisoner had of course to have an official safe-conduct, but its grant was more or less automatic. A captain's routine powers included the right to give safe-conducts to his own and his men's prisoners, cf. Rymer, Vol. IV, pt. III, p. 192 (Salisbury's powers as captain of Alencon, 1420).

immune from war.[1] Thus the siege laid to Orleans in 1428 was in strict law unjustifiable, because Duke Charles, the lord of the town, was a prisoner in England. This was duly pointed out by the defence advocates, when in the 1480s the exiled Lancastrians, as heirs to the right of Charles's masters, sued his Duchess in the Parlement for the unpaid residue of his ransom.[2]

The rights of a captor in a ransom were thus as complete as rights over a freehold. As has been said, his rights over the person of his prisoner were more limited. The captive was not a slave. Nevertheless, they were very extensive. 'One who is a captive on his faith must come whenever his master summons him', writes Paris of Pozzo, 'and he is said to be *on parole* according to military usage'.[3] The obligation could override even the bond of allegiance, for his liege lord himself could not lawfully forbid him to obey his master's summons.[4] Moreover, if a prisoner could not pay a ransom, his master could demand service from him instead.[5] This was a dangerous custom, as such service could all too easily involve treason, but the Court of Chivalry did not question its legality when William Gerard sued before it for his prisoner, Hannequin Lower,[6] whom he had forced to serve him. Actual armed service against one's

---

[1] Cf. Perrinet Gressart's letter of 16 September 1427, informing the Chancellor of Burgundy of the warlike preparations of the Count of Clermont, whose lands have so far been in peace: 'Monsieur de Bourgogne luy faisoit tenir ses pais en seurete et paisible . . . veu que monseigneur son pere (Bourbon) est en Angleterre et qu'il est bien besoing que tiegne ses pais en seurte pour sener la finance pour mon dit Sgr son pere' (Flamare, *Le Nivernais pendant la Guerre de Cent Ans*, Tome I, no. LXV, pp. 328–9).

[2] Cf. defence argument against the Duchess of Somerset: 'fault avoir regard ausdits violences et ausdit [lettres] originaux et *causam obligationis* et non pas a l'obligation simple'; i.e. that the original obligation of Orleans, seeing it was made by him as a prisoner, was invalidated by the English wasting of his lands; and the formal terms of the letter of obligation were therefore not any longer germane (Arch. Nat., J 919/31, fo. 25vo).

[3] Paris of Pozzo, op. cit., Lib. IX, cap. 2 (Zilletus, Tome XVI, fo. 421vo).

[4] Ibid., Lib. IX, cap. 3 (Zilletus, Tome XVI, fo. 422). The argument is that as the lord in question makes the war, he is bound by any result of the war, e.g. his vassal being taken prisoner; 'cui permittuntur praecedentia, videntur etiam permitti sequentia'.

[5] Cf. Bartholomew of Saliceto, *Super VIII Cod.*, Tit. 51, l. 20: 'non solventes per quinquennium redemptoribus servire tenentur'.

[6] P.R.O., C47/6, no. 5. Hannequin promised to serve Gerard for twelve years, in lieu of a ransom of 150 francs.

own side was of course illegal,[1] and strictly speaking a demand for such unreasonable service freed the prisoner from his bond. Even here, however, there was room for doubt about the priority of obligation. When Guillaume de Brue was charged at the Chatelet in 1389 with treason, because he, a French subject, had ridden with the king's enemy, Geoffrey Tête-Noire, captain of Ventadour, he replied that he had been taken prisoner by one of Geoffrey's men, and, because he could not pay a ransom, had 'made an oath to his said master to serve him against all men who might live and die'. So, though he had many opportunities to escape 'he was advised in his conscience, that if he parted from the said Tête-Noire and his master without their leave, and without being quit by them of the faith he had pledged, he would be a perjurer and a traitor to his faith, and to save his word he served his said master and returned every day to the Castle of Ventadour'.[2] Guillaume de Brue was hanged for his offences, but clearly his problem of divided allegiance was a serious one, and one cannot withhold him a little sympathy.

When a man could be bound to keep close prison or to do service for a man whom he called his master, we may well think that this master's right came very near to making him a slave. And indeed the lawyers in the courts often spoke of prisoners as being 'slaves of the enemy', in spite of the theoretical objections to this,[3] and their statements were seldom queried.[4]

---

[1] See p. 158, n. 2. For examples of pardons to men who had served instead of paying ransom, and so committed treason, see, e.g. those given to Guillaume le Houlois for serving the English, September 1359 (Arch. Nat., JJ 87, no. 167), and to Henry Feure, August 1359, (Arch. Nat., JJ 90, no. 237).

[2] H. Duplès Agier, *Régistre criminel du Chatelet de Paris*, Tome I, pp. 23–4. Guillaume de Brue's case was very similar to that of Jehan le Restis (ibid., pp. 119–25), who was unable to pay a ransom to Perrot le Béarnois, who, therefore, 'lui fist promettre et jurer qu'il le serviroit bien et loyaument contre toutes persons'.

[3] Cf. defence of Jean Bause in Bause *v.* Guy de la Tremoille (21 February 1381): 'si Bause fu oblige ce fu li estant en prison [des Anglois] . . . et si estoit *servus hostium*' (Arch. Nat., X¹a 1471, fo. 439vo–40): and of Robert Floques in Floques *v.* Jean de St. Waast (dispute for rights in an English prisoner, 3 March 1450): 'l'anglois est prisonnier et *servus nec in judico stare potest*' (Arch. Nat., X¹a 4802, fo. 198).

[4] The only case I have noted where the claim was challenged in principle is that of Buxton *v.* Dorot (22 December 1434). Buxton claimed Jehan de la

The problem posed by this apparent contradiction between the views of theoretical and practising lawyers is resolved by the English writer, Nicholas Upton. 'A man can be noble and non-noble at the same time', he writes, 'as witness the case of English gentlemen taken in the kingdom of France, who while they are in the hands of the enemy are their slaves and captives; in England, they remain free and noble as they were before.'[1] In order to understand the implication of this statement, one must remember that to men of Upton's time nobility was not a national but an international status; gentle birth had the same significance throughout Christendom, wherever a man was born. What Upton is expressing is therefore a legal compromise similar to that struck by the law in the case of the unfree peasant, who was not a slave and was free in relation to ordinary men, but had no legal rights against his lord.

It was in the manner described by Upton that the courts applied the law regarding prisoners. As a defendant in the courts of his own country the prisoner was a free man, and he could defend himself freely before a court of knighthood, as we saw earlier in the case of the Marshal d'Audreham.[2] But in the courts of his master's allegiance he had no standing, and was legally incapable.[3] He could appear as a witness, if the court admitted him, but his testimony was not to be weighed against that of a native.[4] Without his master's leave he could make no valid contract with any other person of that party,[5] because among them he was not a free man. He could not challenge

---

[1] Upton, *de Officio Militari*, Lib. I, cap. 1 (ed. Bysshe, pp. 3–4).   [2] *Ante*, ch. IV.

[3] See the statement in the case of Floques *v.* St. Waast, *ante*, p. 162, n. 3, 'nec in judicio stare potest'.

[4] Cf. Archibald Douglas ordinances, §10 (*Acts of the Parliament of Scotland*, Vol. I, Appendix IV, p. 351b).

[5] Cf. statement in the case of Bause *v.* La Tremoille (cited *ante*, p. 162, n. 3): 'se Bauses fu oblige ce fu li estant en prison . . . a autre que son maitre et ne pas pour racheter sa franchise et se obligeoit *ex falsu causa*'; and further in the case of Buxton *v.* Dorot (*ante*, p. 162, n. 4), 'pour ce que La Haie . . . estoit prisonnier de guerre et serf, par l'usage de guerre ne povoit s'obliger au prejudice de son maitre et sans son consentement'.

---

Haie as 'son serf et prisonnier de guerre'; Dorot, who objected because he had other claims on La Haie, replied that prisoners 'ne doivent etre reputez mors ne cerfs *quia hoc jus non utimur*'. The court gave no ruling (Arch. Nat., X¹a 4797, fo. 215 et seq.).

any of them to a duel; for, as Owain of Wales pointed out to Thomas St. Aubyn, who offered to fight him when he insulted the captured Earl of Pembroke, the duel was a privilege of those of noble blood, but a prisoner was not even his own master on captor's soil.[1] It was not that a prisoner was without legal rights; we have seen that there was a limit to the terms of his captivity. No more for that matter was an unfree peasant, who was protected by the custom of his manor; what he and the prisoner both lacked was the legal standing to assert their rights in a public court.

The status of prisoner of war was really peculiar to itself. In certain ways it resembled the free status of a vassal; it even conferred privileges, as the immunity of the prisoner's person and lands from war. In other respects it was servile. A prisoner's captor was his master, to whom he owed obedience and even, possibly, service, and in whose regard he was not free. For want of a better word to describe their relation, it may be called a close chivalrous bond. This description can claim a certain accuracy, since the bond could only be established in the chivalrous business of war, and was guaranteed by an oath, breach of which was treason to the chivalrous code of honour.

## II

Because a ransom could be a very valuable asset, a captor was anxious to establish his right incontrovertibly. In a way, no doubt, his best guarantee was his possession of the person of his prisoner. This did not protect him, however, against rival claimants of his own party; and he was besides likely to find it in his interest to release his prisoner on parole, to negotiate with his relatives and advisers about raising the ransom money. His master therefore needed to protect his title carefully.

Ultimately the foundation of this title was the verbal promise of his prisoner, given on the field of battle. 'Simple words suffice', says Bartholomew of Saliceto; a man had only to say 'I yield myself your prisoner', and a firm bond was established.[2] This

[1] Froissart, *Chroniques*, ed. Luce (Soc. de l'histoire de France, 1888) Tome VIII, pp. 48–9.

[2] Bartholomew of Saliceto, *Super VIII Cod.*, Tit. 51, l. 12; and compare Angelus of Perusia, *Disputatio inc. Renovata guerra*. I suspect that Bartholomew is here using Angelus as his source.

view sounds adequate only between the covers of a law book. Let us switch the scene to the closing moments of the Battle of Poitiers in 1356. 'There on all sides you could see the French scattered, and the English running and making prisoners', says Chandos Herald.[1] Among these Frenchmen stood the Count of Dammartin, dismounted, it would appear, and probably more or less immobile in his heavy armour. First, as he stood thus, an esquire of the Black Prince's household called John Trailly came up and demanded his faith, which he gave him 'in such wise that he should save me'. Trailly took his bacinet and his gauntlets, and while he was doing so another man rushed up and cut the strap of his sword, which the count asked Trailly to keep, as he preferred him, rather than any other, to have it. Trailly then handed him over to a yeoman of his, who however quickly disappeared in quest of private gain. After this a Gascon came up, to whom also the count gave his faith, and who took an escutcheon of his armour. He too then moved on, and as he went the count called after him that since he was leaving him, he would give his faith to anyone else who might appear and would offer to save him. Finally, a man of Sir John Blank-mouster arrived on the scene, who stayed with him and took him to his master and the Earl of Salisbury.[2]

When Salisbury and the Black Prince both claimed the count as their prisoner before the Constable,[3] it was thus not at all easy to decide to whom he had pledged his faith. He had been much too liberal with it for that. To avoid this sort of problem, the courts demanded better evidence than conflicting memories of verbal promises. The first man to receive the faith of a prisoner, they ruled, was in law his captor, but on two conditions. Firstly, he ought to establish his capture in the proper way; he should be the first man to seize the prisoner's right

---

[1] Chandos Herald, *Le Prince Noir*, ll. 1576–80 (ed. H. O. Coxe, Roxburghe Club, 1842, p. 108).

[2] *Black Prince's Register* (London, 1930–3), pt. IV, p. 339.

[3] There is no record of the trial in the Constable's court, but it is clear the case was to be heard there, as the preceding document in the register (p. 338) is a notification to the Constable and Marshal of an order given by the Black Prince before Poitiers 'that no man should linger over his prisoner', which is clearly intended to strengthen the Prince's case with them.

gauntlet, and to put his right hand in his.[1] Thereafter, the gauntlet served as a token of his right.[2] Secondly, he must have made some attempt to fulfil his contract to his prisoner, to protect his life. If he simply abandoned him on the field, he lost his right to him. He must therefore either put the prisoner in the charge of someone who would look after him, or he must escort him to a safe place behind the lines. Otherwise the prisoner was still a free man, and to protect his life might give his faith to whom he chose.[3] No doubt it was on this last ground that the Count of Dammartin was in the end adjudged the prisoner of the Earl of Salisbury.[4]

With these provisoes, the prisoner's verbal promise to his master was strictly binding. If the master subsequently wished to transfer his rights, or if the king claimed his prisoner by royal right, he had formally to quit him his faith, and the prisoner then renewed his promise to his new master. Thus when Henry V made it a condition of the treaty of surrender of Meaux in 1422 that the garrison should free their prisoners, each master had to quit his faith severally to each individual prisoner.[5]

---

[1] Cf. Richard II, Durham ordinances §xxii: 'si aucun prent un prisonnier, qu'il preigne sa foy, et aussi son bacynet ou gaunt destre de li en gage' (*Black Book of the Admiralty*, Vol. I, p. 457). Compare the evidence given in the Parlement by Jaques de Chabbennes, to show that Bernard de Belbezin was the captor of the Marshal of Burgundy at Montreuillon: '[Marescallus] se ejusdem de Belbezin prisonarium, fidem suam et in illius signum manum suum dexteram et cyrothecam ejusdem eidem de Belbezin tradendo reddiderat' (Baluze, *Histoire de la Maison d'Auvergne*, Tome II, p. 464). The importance of touching in the right hand is stressed by Jean de Beuil, *Le Jouvencel*, Tome I, p. 220.

[2] Cf. Durham ordinance, op. cit., and Archibald Douglas's ordinances §13: 'Item it is fundin statut and use of merche that it is lefull til ilk man to tak alsmony presoneris as he may . . . sua that he leid theim within the strenth of Scottismen and to tak ane takin of his presoner with him at may be knawin sufficiand'.

[3] Ibid.; and compare the judgment given by the *Jouvencel*: 'tant qu'on est sur le champs et en payz de guerre que chascun garde son prisonnier, car qui le pert de vue . . . il est gaignie et acquiz a celui qui le treuve'. (*Le Jouvencel*, Tome II, p. 94.)

[4] No judgment is recorded; but Salisbury must have won as there are subsequent references to Dammartin's payments to him in the Parlement Registers; cf. judgment of 31 August 1370 in Dammartin v. St. Pol, Arch. Nat., X¹a 19, fo. 397.

[5] Rymer, Vol. IV, pt. IV, p. 65.

For once a man had given his faith only his master could acquit him of it, and neither the capture of his master, nor any defeat of the enemy could free him. 'Once a man has given his faith', says Bartholomew of Saliceto, 'even if he is rescued by his own side while the battle still continues, he is not freed from his captivity or from the faith he has pledged.'[1] Thus when, eight years after he had been taken, the Lord of Barbasan was freed from his dungeon in Chateau Gaillard, when the French retook the castle in 1430, he would not regard himself as free. The English captain, who was leading his garrison away on the terms of an *appointement*, had to be called back to quit him his faith, before he would consider himself released from his obligations.[2]

The prisoner's word of honour was given in the heat of war. Under the law of arms it was therefore a binding contract, but once he had got his man away to a safe place, the captor would not be slow to provide himself with more reliable evidence of his title. This would take the form of a solemn deed or charter, in which the captive gave three main undertakings.[3] First he promised to be a good and loyal prisoner to his master, and to obey him in all things reasonable. Here the close personal relation with this master was underlined; the promise seems similar in spirit to the promise of the holder of a fief to be a good and loyal vassal, or of a retainer to be a good and loyal servant. Secondly the prisoner solemnly renounced any right which he might use to dispute his master's title to ransom. He promised to take no advantage of any sentence given in any court, whether of prince or Pope, or of any vow, such as that of a crusader, or of any legal quibble about his status. Thirdly he

---

[1] Bartholomew of Saliceto, *Super VIII Cod.*, Tit. 51, l. 12.

[2] *First English life of King Henry V*, ed. Kingsford, p. 171. With this may be compared Froissart's story of the Duke of Gueldres' insistence on returning to his master, the squire Conrad, after he had been rescued from prison by the Master of the Teutonic knights in 1388 (*Oeuvres de Froissart*, ed. Kervyn de Lettenhove, Tome XIII, pp. 292–3).

[3] For two good examples of such charters, set out in the manner here described, see those given by John the Good (June 1360) promising to be 'en toutes pars loyal prisonnier' to Edward III (Kervyn de Lettenhove, *Oeuvres de Froissart*, Tome XVIII, no. CIII, p. 436); and by the Captal de Buch (September 1364), promising to be good and loyal prisoner to Charles V (Secousse, *Recueil de pièces sur Charles II Roi de Navarre*, pp. 211–14).

invoked savage anathemas against himself if in any way he failed his obligations. He was to be held to be a perjurer, a traitor to his faith, to stand dishonoured in every court or company in Christendom, and his master might take action against him as such, and in sign of it might display his arms reversed or humiliate him in any other way he chose.[1] This solemn charter would then be sealed with the captive's seal, and if possible witnessed by an apostolic or imperial notary.

Two further matters might be agreed in this charter, or might alternatively be dealt with in a second deed. First and most important of all, the arrangements for paying the ransom must be detailed. The capital sum must be fixed (part of this might be demanded in kind), and also the terms and the places at which it was to be paid.[2] It was usually understood that the captive was also liable for his keep as a prisoner, and for any expense in which his master became involved in order to obtain payment. Often penalties were also stipulated, if payment should not be forthcoming at any of the terms: Eudes de Champdenay, for instance, agreed with Ralph Salle that if he did not pay in five weeks his ransom was to be doubled.[3] The prisoner also, if possible, named sureties or pledges to his faith, who must answer for him if he defaulted, even to the point of constituting themselves prisoners in his master's power.

Besides these regulations for payment, the conditions of the prisoner's captivity might be agreed in writing. These could

[1] For a full and detailed series of renunciations and anathemas, see the letter of the Count of Vendosme, promising his faith as a prisoner to Henry V (22 March 1417), Rymer, Vol. IV, pt. II, p. 197. A notary is to witness the letter, the Count states.

[2] See for example the arrangements for the payment of the ransom of Charles of Blois, set out in a separate document of 10 August 1356, Rymer, Vol. III, pt. I, pp. 126–8. In the case of the Count of Vendosme, however, the promise to be a prisoner and arrangements for payment were all set down in one document (cited above), as also for instance in Ingergier d'Amboise's agreement with his captors after Poitiers (Arch. Nat., X[1]c, 33/264).

[3] Copied on the Treaty Roll for 1366, P.R.O., C76/49, m 15. This penalty was supposed to be a substitute for expenses, cf. the case of Robert de Commercy v. Monsard d'Aisne (1455). Monsard complained that the increase of his ransom by 120 ecus per annum after the term was usurious. Robert replied that 'dicta pena loco interesse apposita fuisset', and that it was therefore lawful (Arch. Nat., X[1]a 84, fo. 225).

vary widely. The Count of Foix, for instance, was very lenient to Berard d'Albret and his brother after Launac; he promised not to 'martyr their bodies' with close imprisonment, and to treat them 'graciously'. From sunrise to sunset they might wander and hunt in the forest anywhere in his country; they had only to be back each evening at their 'prison', in the town of Masères.[1] Others were less fortunate; Ingergier d'Amboise had to submit his body to prison wherever his captors, Gaillart de Saliers and Bascon de Mareuil, chose.[2] Two conditions were however nearly always mentioned. One was that the prisoner remained a prisoner 'rescued or not rescued'. The other was that as long as he remained a prisoner, he was not to arm himself against his master or those of his party. Occasionally, this ban was lifted and the prisoner permitted to arm in the personal company of his sovereign[3]; more often it was general.[4]

Once these matters were agreed there began the slow business of raising the ransom, and paying down instalments to the captor. This very often involved the temporary release of the prisoner, to go home on parole and negotiate with his connections. If he allowed this, the master might insist on yet another letter from his captive, setting out the terms of the parole and fixing a date for his return.[5] This was a wise precaution, for otherwise the prisoner might claim that he had been freed. 'It is arguable that a captive who is released (*licenciatus*) by the enemy is not bound to return', says Baldus, 'unless it be proved that he has agreed otherwise.'[6] Thus one of the many

---

[1] Bib. Nat., Collection Doat, Tome 195, fo. 34 et seq.

[2] Arch. Nat., X¹c 33/80.

[3] As appears to have been the case with the Marshal d'Audreham's agreement after Poitiers, cf. *ante*, ch. IV; probably this was also why Ingergier d'Amboise was able to arm at Poitiers, although already a prisoner (see p. 168, n. 2 and p. 164, n. 2 *ante*).

[4] Cf. the promise of Charles of Blois to Edward III that 'il se tendra nostre loial prisonner et ne se armera contre homme du mounde' (Rymer, Vol. III, pt. I, p. 127). But note that if he was killed by an Englishman in arms, the whole contract was dissolved; the ban was reciprocal.

[5] Cf. letters promising to return given by Thomas Percy to Charles V in 1370 (Kervyn de Lettenhove, *Oeuvres de Froissart*, Tome XVIII, no. CXX, p. 506); by Archibald Douglas to Henry IV in 1408, P.R.O. E101/69/2, no. 323; by Charles d'Artois and Artus de Richemont to Henry V in 1419, Rymer, Vol. IV, pt. III, pp. 112–13 (both notarially attested).

[6] Baldus, *Comment. in Decretal.*, Lib. I, Tit. 3, cap. 25.

arguments that Jean de Melun raised in 1366 to refute Henry Pomfret's claim to his ramson was that 'Henry had allowed him to go home from Provins without any (further) promise on his part, and in three days he was back in Paris'.[1] The essential distinction between this and proper discharge is indicated by another case in which Gaudri de Balorre and Galois d'Achy disputed their claims to the ransom of Robert Chesnel before the Parlement. The Englishman (Chesnel) had been taken on two separate occasions, and by Gaudri in the first instance; but whereas Gaudri claimed he had released him on parole (*licentiam dederat . . . ad partes suos eundi*), Galois claimed Gaudri had quit him his faith (*liberavit de sua potestate*) and had no further claims on him by law of arms. As a result Gaudri was never able to re-establish his preferential right to ransom, which shows how important it was to have one's arrangements cut and dried, and in writing.[2]

For the same reason, it was vital to the prisoner, when he had finally discharged his ransom, to get back his letters of obligation. Otherwise an unscrupulous master might all too easily question the quittances given for instalments of the ransom,[3] and demand further payments for any which he could get disallowed. The return of the letter also protected the prisoner against his own pledges, who might otherwise trump up some tale that they had been distrained for his ransom, and sue him for damages.[4] The returned letter of obligation showed that he was quit of his faith and had no further commitments. With it to hand he could rebut any claim made against him.

[1] Melun v. Pomfret (Bib. Nat., MS. Fr. 21717, fo. 144 et seq.): 'Henry le lessa aller de Provins en sa maison sans aucune promesse, et bien revient en trois jours a Paris . . . conclud par ce que dit est que Henry n'a cause ne action de faire ses conclusions, doit estre Melun absols'.

[2] Arch. Nat., X¹a 21, fo. 108 (23 February 1367). Chesnel was taken in 1364 by Gaudri; he was retaken by Galois shortly after, and an arrest was finally given in Galois's favour on 5 August 1368 (Arch. Nat., X¹a 19, fo. 300).

[3] As the Duchess of Somerset attempted to do in the case of the Orleans ransom (Arch. Nat., J 919/31 and 32).

[4] Cf. the case of Pierre de St. Bon v. Gilete des Forges (23 January 1431). Pierre was a pledge for the ransom of Gilete's uncle to one Jean de Blaisy; Gilete paid it, and Jean burnt the letter of obligation. Pierre sued her for the return of the letter of obligation, and had her imprisoned (Arch. Nat., X¹a 4796, fo. 257vo).

Here, if all went smoothly, the matter ended. Because the price demanded for a ransom was nearly always excessive, however, it very often did not. The first sign that things were amiss would probably be a default on one of the instalments of the ransom, and the captor's first reaction would be to bring pressure to bear on the prisoner's sureties. If the person of one of these had been left in his hands, he had no difficulties, and the longer the delay in payment, the harsher the conditions of this man's prison would become.[1] Even if he had none of them in his power, the captor still had certain advantages when dealing with the pledges. When they agreed to stand surety for the prisoner, they submitted themselves to the same penalties as he in case of default;[2] in effect, they were then to be treated as prisoners also. In addition, it was understood that by law of arms all sureties for a prisoner pledged themselves each and individually for the whole of his ransom,[3] and so the captor could treat with all or any one of them as suited him. They had no more rights against him than the prisoner himself, though if they sustained loss they could recover it from the prisoner[4]— supposing that he could pay them.

[1] Cf. for example Anselin de Pommelain v. Jean de St. Gaubert (4 March 1362). Anselin pledged himself for Jean's ransom to his English master, James Seaman, when both were his prisoners. When Anselin failed to return on his day, their master 'fecerat ponere dictum militem [Anselin] in duobus paribus ferrorum et incontinenti in aliis ferriis ponderis quinquaginta librorum faciebatque dare solummodo panem et aquam' etc. In the end James took pity on him and freed him, but he sued him before the Marshal for Jean de St. Gaubert's ransom and obtained judgment, and so Anselin sued for compensation. (Arch. Nat., X¹a 14, fo. 532vo.)

[2] Cf. for example the promise of Jean d'Armargnac's warrantors to the Count of Foix after Launac to submit themselves to the same penalties and give the same renunciations as he. (Bib. Nat., Collection Doat, Tome 195, fo. 49vo. et seq.)

[3] Cf. statement in the case of Grandelin v. Nalin (13 January 1429) that 'par l'usance de guerre quant ung plege prisonnier seschappe tous les autres demeurent pour le tout' (Arch. Nat., X¹a 4796, fo. 33); and in the case of Thibaut des Termes v. the Lord of Chateauvillain (27 August 1439) that 'selon l'usage de guerre chacun des obligez est principal' (Arch. Nat., X¹a 4798, fo. 108).

[4] Cf. the case of Anselin de Pommelain v. J. de St. Gaubert (ante, p. 171, n. 1); and of Ogier de Dongeaux v. Erard de Tintaville (2 April 1365). Ogier was a pledge for Erard, and on account of his default had to put himself a prisoner in the hands of Erard's master at Neufchastel in Lorraine. He was in prison

If neither principal nor pledges responded, the captor would have to take further steps. In this case he could proceed in two ways, either by *voie de fait*, or *voie de justice*. The problems involved in the latter course, as to where he should bring an action and how, have been dealt with in an earlier chapter.[1] As was then said, however, the problems of instituting legal proceedings in a time of open war were likely to be considerable. For this reason *voie de fait* might be the preferable course, and we must therefore examine this alternative way of proceeding.

*Voie de fait* provided two possible courses of action. In the first place, the captor might try to take reprisals on the lands and goods of his prisoner (or his pledges), which hitherto had been in theory immune from war. Thus in 1382 we find the French *routier* Jean de Vica threatening reprisals against the consuls of Millau, if they would not pay the ransoms of two townsmen taken in English company;[2] and of Perrinet Gressart at La Charité[3] and the English captain of Ste Susanne[4] levying marque for ransoms in the 1430s. These men were all of a type, more or less independent *routiers*, and this indicates one limit on the usefulness of this remedy. It assumed that taking reprisals was a viable military proposition, which was probably the case where free companies (most of whose prisoners were civilians taken locally) were concerned, but might be much less easy for say, a native Englishman against an Auvergnat. The usefulness of reprisals was also limited in another way: it clearly prejudiced any future action which a captor might hope to bring at law. He could not very well sue in court for money to which he had already helped himself. Usually, therefore, reprisals were taken

---

[1] See *ante*, ch. III.

[2] Rouquette, *La Rougergue sous les Anglais*, pp. 331–2.

[3] Cf. letter of Perrinet Gressart of 1 March 1434, explaining to the chancellor of Burgundy that his raids in Bourbonnais have been 'soulz umbre et couleur de la finance de Barillet', who had not paid his ransom. (Flamare, *Le Nivernais pendant la Guerre de Cent Ans*, Tome II, p. 87, no. CXCIX.)

[4] Cf. complaint in the Parlement June 1433, against the relatives of Guillaume de Labreville, that because he did not pay his ransom to Colin Harz of St. Suzanne 'les anglois coururent sur les habitans de houssay (his pledges, who are sueing)'. (Arch. Nat., X¹a 9200, fo. 166vo.)

---

600 days and paid the ransom, and received damages in consequence (Arch. Nat., X¹a 19, fo. 75).

only in the last resort, when, as in the case of the Denia ransom,[1] all other methods of obtaining payment had failed over a long period.

A much more effective method of distraining a prisoner was to proceed against him or his pledges by dishonour (*deshonnoirement*). The captor caused to be made a painting of the prisoner's arms reversed, or of the prisoner hanging by the heels or in some other undignified position. This he exhibited in some public place. Thus Thibaut des Termes and his companions hung pictures which dishonoured the Lord of Chateauvillain, their defaulting prisoner, at the gates of Berry,[2] and La Hire rode on campaign with the reversed arms of Robert de Commercy, a pledge of his prisoner Monsard d'Aisne, hanging at his horse's tail.[3] Such an insult was deadly; so deadly that Du Guesclin without ado hung the captain of Montcontour, who had slandered him with breach of his prisoner's faith after Najera, from his own battlements in full armour.[4] Because the insult was deadly, it was effective; only a prisoner who was very sure of himself would remain recalcitrant when threatened with dishonour. In particular, dishonour was effective when the action was taken against pledges. By insulting them mortally, it prompted them to take strong action in the courts of their own party, to force the prisoner to pay.

The procedure of dishonour, being a *voie de fait*, was of the standing of an act of war. Just as a prince alone could levy public war, only he could confer public honour; therefore one had to have his licence, or that of his constable in order to dishonour a man.[5] Dishonour was, however, a much more advantageous course of action than reprisals or acts of war proper. The risks and expense were much smaller. If old enemies became allies (as for instance Burgundians and French after 1435), their alliance would foreclose reprisals, but dishonour was

[1] Reprisals were granted against the Aragonese to recover debts of the Count of Denia on 23 and 25 October 1393, Rymer, Vol. III, pt. IV, p. 91.
[2] Cf. arrest of the Parlement of 6 March 1444, Arch. Nat., X¹a 74, fo. 91.
[3] Cf. arrest of the Parlement of 14 May 1455, Arch. Nat., X¹a 84, fo. 225: 'dictus La Hyre . . . in vituperium seu dedecus dicti deffensoris ipsum depicta ac etiam arma ipsius depicta ad caudam sui equi deportando processerat'.
[4] *Chronique du Bon Duc Louis d'Anjou*, ed. A-M. Chazaud, p. 89.
[5] See ch. IV *ante*, p. 55, n. 4 and 5.

'tolerable even among persons of the same party'.[1] Moreover, although it required the same authority as an act of war, dishonour was not an alternative to payment, and did not prejudice the captor's right at law. Both Jean de Melun in 1363, and the Lord of Chateauvillain in 1441 attempted to argue the contrary, but this view was not normally upheld.[2] Dishonour was thus probably the captor's most valuable weapon against a defaulting prisoner.

Its frequent employment is also significant for two other reasons.[3] In the first place, since the injury inflicted was in no sense material, it shows how very seriously soldiers of the later middle ages regarded any matter which technically affected their 'honour'. In the second place, since dishonour was the penalty for treason to a sovereign lord, it confirms the view that breach of faith was seen as the equivalent of this crime, and that a prisoner's master stood in the same kind of relation to him as his lord did.

### III

So far we have been dealing almost entirely with the rights of the captor against his captive. At law, however, it was not

---

[1] Cf. statement in the case of des Termes v. Chateauvillain (May 1441): 'deshonnoirement est tolerable *etiam* entre gens d'un mesmes party, et . . . ce droit de deshonnoirement ne lui [des Termes] est tollu par le traictie de paix [i.e. the treaty of Arras]'. (Arch. Nat., X¹a 4798, fo. 350.)

[2] Cf. statement of Chateauvillain's advocate: 'car ils [des Termes and his friends] ont comme dit est procede de fait, dit qu'ils ont perdu leur droit se aucun en avoit' (Arch. Nat., X¹a 4798, fo. 376vo); and of Jean de Melun (Melun v. Pomfret, op. cit.): 'Henry a injure, fait renverser les armes Meleun, et estoit *alternativa obligationis* . . . il a renuncie l'obligation d'argent'. Pomfret's reply puts the orthodox view clearly 'l'argument de Meleun que les armes ont este tournees et qu'il est quitte . . . ne vaut *quia non liberatur debitor a principali debito* ne tourner les armes ne sont pas *alternativa obligationis* ne ne peut introduire exception de non payer le principal, mais selon ly semble agir *de injuria quam allegat*'. This is true; dishonour was an injury, and compensation could be demanded, cf. Guillaume Blondel v. Thomas le Pois (30 May 1376), where Blondel demanded damages because Le Pois had detained him at Rheims, thus preventing him from paying his ransom to Henry of Lancaster, who reversed his arms (Arch. Nat., X¹a 25, fo. 133).

[3] For other examples of the procedure of dishonour see Arch. Nat., X¹a 4795, fo. 125vo (Charles de Servolles dishonouring Guy de Bar, July 1427); Arch. Nat., X¹a 4796, fo. 110 (captors of Pierre de Villiers dishonouring Charles d'Estouteville, June 1429); Arch. Nat., X¹a 78, fo. 271–2 (Yvo du Puy dishonouring Colard Mailly, September 1449).

only the prisoner who might dispute his title; the captor might also have to defend himself against rival claimants of his own side. What we must now examine are the grounds on which either of these parties might seek to impugn his right to a ransom.

Rival claimants of his own side might challenge a captor's right in three principal ways. In the first place, they might lay claim to an interest in the ransom as their lawful share in his spoils of war. The rules under which shares in spoil might be claimed were outlined in the last chapter, and there is no need to repeat details of the rights which lords, captains, or companions *à butin* might demand. Rights in prisoners could also be contested on other grounds mentioned earlier, as for instance that they had not been taken *in actu belli*; the same rules here applied to ransoms as to any other spoils.

In the second place, a rival claimant might demand a prisoner on the ground that the captor had forfeited his right by breaking rules which controlled the capture and retention of such persons. He might claim that the captor had failed to guard his prisoner in the field, and sue in the right of one who had later found him armed and uncaptured, and taken him.[1] Or the captor might forfeit his right by failure to obey regulations, because he had failed to give his prisoner's name to his superior[2] or had lodged him in a town without the captain's leave,[3] for instance, or because he had broken an ordinance of the host concerning prisoners. Thus before the Court of Chivalry in 1394 John Chamberlain claimed that William Gerard had forfeited all his rights in Hannequin Lower, whom he had captured on Despenser's crusade, because when he lodged him in prison at Calais he did not ask permission from the captain's lieutenant, William Beauchamp, as by law of arms he was bound to.[4] In the same way, Talbot at Bordeaux in 1453 judged that Louis de Berthalot had lost his right to his prisoner, Oliver de Coitevy, for all that Oliver had given him his faith, because

---

[1] Cf. *Le Jouvencel*, quoted p. 166, n. 3 *ante*.

[2] Cf. Richard II's Durham ordinances §19 (*Black Book of the Admiralty*, Vol. I, p. 456); Henry V's Mantes Orders §20 (ibid., p. 465).

[3] Cf. *Le Jouvencel*, Tome II, p. 10: 'l'usance a este telle que, qui met ung ennemy, soit prisonnier soit a sauf conduit . . . sans le congie del cappitaine et des officiers, qu'il est confisque a luy'.

[4] P.R.O., C47/6, no. 5.

he had made a townsman of Bordeaux, Arnaud Bec, his companion in the ransom, thus breaking Talbot's ordinance that no one who had been in French obedience should be allowed to take prisoners.[1] The object of the rules invoked in cases such as these was to protect the common interest of the host or garrison; which shows that the same view was taken with regard to ransoms as to other spoils, that they were taken in the common interest. Though the prisoner's obligations were to his master personally, if his master failed to consider his obligations to his own side, his right escheated to the king or to the commander whose interests were affected.

The third ground on which a rival might claim a prisoner was that he had taken him lawfully on some subsequent occasion. This ought never to have happened, for a prisoner was supposed to be immune from war until his ransom was paid. Nevertheless there are undoubted instances where ransoms for two different captures were demanded from the same man simultaneously, as from Ingergier d'Amboise, who through the 1360s was facing one prosecution in the Parlement for his ransom after Poitiers,[2] and another in the courts of Aquitaine for a ransom promised to Gaillart de Saliers in 1352.[3] The case of Robert Chesnel, claimed in 1365 by both Gaudri de Balorre and Galois d'Achy, shows how this could legally come about; Galois, though he admitted his capture was subsequent, had the appearance of a legal title because he claimed that he had captured Chesnel in arms 'with his gauntlets on and his sword drawn'.[4] If this was true, the fault was with Balorre, because he had failed to prevent his prisoner arming himself anew, and it was no defence that he had never given him permission for this; it only showed negligence. If, of course, a man had been given leave to rearm (for instance in his sovereign's company), both ransoms were lawful.

Alternatively a second ransom might be claimed by those

[1] Baureins, *Variétés Bordeloises* (Bordeaux, 1784), Tome I, pp. 199–205.

[2] Cf. Arch. Nat., X$^1$c 15$^B$/263, accord of the Parlement between the two parties over the payment of an instalment of this ransom.

[3] P.R.O., C61/81, m. 3 (entry on the Gascon Roll, appointing a commission to try the appeal in this case from the courts of Aquitaine, 16 October 1368).

[4] Cf. interim arrest in this case, 23 February 1367, Arch. Nat., X$^1$a 21, fo. 108.

who recaptured an escaped prisoner. There were strict rules about such escapes. A man who escaped on the battlefield could be retaken by another, and his first captor lost his right. But a man who escaped in peace or behind the lines was not lost; he remained the property of his captor, and had to be returned, as a stray cow would have to be.[1] Unless, that is, he had previously defied his bond to his master, which, like a feudal vassal, he had a right to do if his master outstepped the agreed conditions of his prison. Thus when in 1370 Simon Burley escaped from the prison of the Lady of Dampierre and gave his faith on recapture to Ralph de Rayneval, the legal point disputed was whether or not he had had just grounds for defying his bond to the Lady. In the end it was decided he had not, and he was returned to her, but only after long discussion and when knights learned in the lore of chivalry had been called in to advise the judges in the Parlement.[2]

This affair of Simon Burley introduces the other question, of the possible objections which a prisoner might raise against a demand for ransom. Foremost among these was the allegation which Simon actually made, that his bond was dissolved because his master had broken its agreed conditions.[3] This allegation could raise serious problems, because conditions of imprisonment were by no means always put in writing. In principle, we have seen, a master was entitled to take any step which he deemed necessary to secure his ransom, which included close imprisonment of his captive. The question was therefore whether the rule governing the tenure of fiefs, that a change in

[1] Cf. *Le Jouvencel*, Tome II, p. 95: 'en pays de paix, ung homme qui perdoit son prisonnier, il le peult poursuir par toute l'obeissance de son party . . . car c'est son meuble. Si ung homme de son partie l'a trouve et il l'ait pris et garde, celui a qui il est eschappe n'en doit payer que le depens'.

[2] The Lady of Dampierre *v.* Ralph de Rayneval, Arch. Nat., X¹a 22, fo. 259 et seq. (9 August 1371.)

[3] Cf. presentation of Rayneval's case, *cit. sup.*: 'quamvis dictus Simo pacta et convenciones predicta quantum in ipso erat . . . de facto adimplevisset, dicta tamen domina . . . eosdem convenciones et pacta pro sua parte noluerat observare sed prisionem ipsius Simonis de die in diem graviorem faciebat. Propter que eisdem domine et domino de Rambures [her associate] pluries dixerat quod se ipsum liberaret quam citius posset: ipse vero certa nocte premissa considerans per certum locum de dicto castro exiverat, prout sibi licuerat et licebat de jure et communi usu armorum'.

the established conditions of tenure dissolved the bond of lord and vassal, could be applied also to the conditions of a captive's prison. The rule that it should do was upheld, says Paris of Pozzo, by a court of knights in favour of Robert of St. Severino;[1] and both Rifflart of Flanders in 1367[2] and Lord Scales in 1436[3] claimed the same benefit by law of arms in the Parlement of Paris. Neither of their claims were upheld, however, though there were clearly serious doubts about the decision, since in both cases the court attempted to avoid judgment by getting the parties to settle out of court. The rough rule would seem to have been that conditions could be altered only as far as the written agreements explicitly or implictly allowed. If they did not forbid close prison expressly, good treatment did not constitute a 'custom' inhibiting it. If they did forbid it, however, any attempt to impose it freed the prisoner from his faith.

There was another important condition which a prisoner might invoke against his master. Some prisoners when taken only gave their faith conditionally, saying not just 'I give you my faith', but 'I give you my faith if I may be lawfully taken', or some such words. This put the onus of proof on the captor. Thus when Thomas Stafford claimed as his prisoner the Lord of Camprémy, who had been taken outside Paris in 1359, Camprémy said he had surrendered on condition that he could be lawfully taken;[4] and as Thomas was subsequently unable to

[1] Paris of Pozzo, op. cit., Lib. IX, cap. 2 (Zilletus, Tome XVI, fo. 421vo). They judged that Robert was bound to return to his master, but not to endure close prison.

[2] Jean Werchin, Seneschal of Hainault, *v.* Rifflart of Flanders (Arch. Nat., X²a 7, fo. 386 et seq.), argument of Rifflart's case: 'si aliquis miles prisonarius aut alius facto guerre captus prisionem in aliquo loco tenere jurabat, tale juramentum censeri et reputari debebat factum fuisse et esse sub tacita condicione, videlicet condicione in eodem statu remanente et quod prisio prisonarii detenti tempore juramenti facti non mutaretur . . . Et si contrarium fieret . . . talis prisonarius licite . . . absque denigracione seu blasffemia persone vel honoris sui a dicta prisone discedere poterat.'

[3] Galoby de Panassac *v.* Lord Scales, pledge for Thomas Cusac (Arch. Nat., X¹a 69, fo. 141 et seq.), argument of Scales: 'Dicebat autem idem appellans dictam condicionem [of giving Scales safe-conducts for making payments] non fuisse completam et sic posito quod nichil solvisset dictus Cusac subtili ingenio secundum jus armorum abire licite et impune poterat'.

[4] Jean de Camprémy *v.* Thomas Stafford (13 March 1365, Arch. Nat., X¹a 1469, fo. 45), *plaidoirie* of Camprémy: 'il se rendi par condicion cestas-

satisfy the court on this point, the case went against him. Or the prisoner might mention some other condition. One of Rifflart of Flanders' objections to his master's title was that he had given his faith to the Seneschal of Hainault on condition that he was not handed over to the Count, who, he feared, would put him to death.[1] When he was threatened with this transfer, he therefore defied his bond; and when he was thrust into close prison, he made off through the latrine window. There was, however, a limit to conditions which a prisoner might make, that they should be reasonable;[2] and it was hard to see how the Seneschal could be bound against the Count, whose officer he was. No doubt this was one of the reasons why the court, after lengthy discussion and consultation, gave judgment against Rifflart.

Rifflart's whole case was based on his fear that the Count would put him to death. A master could never put his prisoner to death (after all, he only surrendered to save his life), except in two circumstances; if he had committed treason against him or his lord,[3] or if his life endangered the public weal.[4] By this last argument the deaths of Conradin and Pedro the Cruel, for instance, could be justified.[5] But the threat of death normally

---

[1] Werchin v. Rifflart cit. sup.: 'qui Rifflardus ipsam prisionem tenere juraverat sub condicione et covencione tali videlicet quod predicto duci Alberto [Albert of Bavaria, Count of Hainault] . . . non traderetur seu deliberaretur'.

[2] Cf. Rifflart's own argument: 'tam de jure scripto civili et canonico, quam de omni ratione usu et consuetudine, obligaciones, pactiones, seu convenciones quecunque impossibilitacionem aut contradictionem facti continentes, facto sub condicione impossibili . . . nulle ac nullius efficacie seu valoris existebant'.

[3] Cf. the case of Marshal d'Audreham, ante, ch. IV.

[4] Bonet, Tree of Battles, pt. 4, ch. 46 (Coopland's translation, p. 152).

[5] Bonet, Tree of Battles, pt. 4, ch. 13 (Coopland's translation, p. 134), specifically quotes the case of Conradin in support of this rule. The accounts of the death of Don Pedro are confused, but it is clear that he was taken prisoner under security, and that this was broken.

---

savoir ou cas qu'il povoit estre pris par bonne guerre non autrement'. Compare the claim of Henriet Gentian, in Gentian v. F. le Palu (Arch. Nat., X¹a 4798, fo. 190, 28 April 1440): 'le dit demandeur [Gentian] ne se voult rendre prisonnier ou cas que prisonnier ne devoit etre, dont le defendeur fut content'.

released a prisoner from his bond, as did imprisonment in un-
healthy and dangerous conditions.[1] When Henriet Gentian reported that he had counted 'eighteen serpents and other
reptiles' in the dungeon in which Francois de la Palu had cast
him at Romenay, he therefore had a very sound *prima facie* case
against his master.[2]

This was not the only argument which Henriet Gentian employed. Francois had also sent a letter to the Duke of Bourbon
and others among Henriet's connections, warning them that if he
was not paid promptly he would pull Henriet's teeth out. When
they did not respond, he knocked out a few with a hammer and
circulated them to show that he meant what he said. This
showed, said Henriet, that his obligation was extracted by
force and fear, and was therefore invalid, because it was not a
voluntary pact. This was a very common objection to claims
for ransom.[3] At first sight it would seem a problematical one;
the imminent fear of death was, after all, what induced a man
to give his faith as a prisoner. Bartholomew of Saliceto resolves
this difficulty. Fear, he says, is the natural condition of the
battlefield, and so it is a natural and lawful condition of all
contracts to pay ransom.[4] Off the field, however, fear is an unnatural condition, and a contract made in fear is then in-

---

[1] Bonet, *Tree of Battles*, pt. 4, ch. 55 (Coopland's translation, p. 158).
On the same principle, if a man agreed to go *à butin* with a fellow soldier in
a ransom, because the other threatened the prisoner's life, his agreement to
share could be abjured, cf. Richard II Durham ordinances, §xiii (*Black
Book of the Admiralty*, Vol. I, p. 455); and Archibald Douglas ordinances §8
(*Acts of the Parliament of Scotland*, Vol. I, Appendix IV, p. 351a).

[2] Gentian v. Le Palu, Arch. Nat., X¹a 4798, fo. 190.

[3] Cf. statement of Jean Bauses in 1381, case of Bauses v. La Tremoille
(cited *ante*, p. 162 n. 3): 'les anglois fi par force et contrainte obligier Bauses devant deux notaires . . . et par paour de mort se consenti . . . pour ce que les
notaires le dirent que l'obligation ne valoit riens'. For other instances see,
e.g. cases of Jean de Vienne and his wife v. Jehan de St. Ligier (Arch. Nat.,
X¹a 4795, fo. 197vo, January 1428), in which Vienne's wife claimed her
father's obligation to St. Ligier was null, as obtained 'par crainte et force';
and of the Sieur de Menon v. Guillaume des Ages (Arch. Nat., X¹a 4791,
fo. 9, 1415), in which Menon denied obligation to des Ages on the same
ground.

[4] Bartholomew of Saliceto, *Super VIII Cod.*, Tit. 51, l. 12: 'nec obstat si
dicant, hoc factum est metu . . . quia respondebant quod ille textum non
habet locum in actu guerre publicae, seu in actu bellico, quia in actu illo
licitum est caedere, vulnerare, et caeteros cruciatus corporis committere'.

voluntary, and so invalid.[1] This rule was important, because soldiers were pretty ruthless about the methods which they used to screw excessive ransoms out of prisoners. Jean le Gastelier, one of Robert Chesnel's men, admitted to the judges at the Chatelet that his job in the company had been to beat prisoners 'until they could stand no more', to encourage them to promise the largest possible sums.[2] It was just as well to make sure that, at least as far as the courts were concerned, such action should be self-defeating.

A prisoner could also contest the legality of his contract on the ground that it was void because his capture itself was illegal. He could assert this on two grounds, firstly that he was immune from capture, or secondly that he had not been taken in a just war. Immunity could be claimed either on grounds of privilege of safe-conduct, or because the prisoner was of the same party as the captor. A man with a written safe-conduct could not be taken, even by way of marque, unless he had infringed its terms (for instance by entering a walled town without notifying the captain).[3] Clerks and others who were not in the war, such as prisoners and heralds, were also immune from capture, but this protection was lost if they took arms. 'A clerk taken in arms is to be treated as a soldier.'[4] This was the rule of the courts, and if he armed himself a clerk could not claim clerical privileges or ask to be tried in an ecclesiastical court, but must face the military judges.

---

[1] Cf. Paris of Pozzo, op. cit., Lib. IX, cap. 2 (Zilletus, Tome XVI, fo. 421vo), 'ubi vellet [victor] eum maletractare, aut torquere pro redimendo in pecunia, non debet sibi licere'.

[2] Duplés Agier, *Régistre Criminel du Chatelet de Paris*, Tome II, p. 95.

[3] As for instance in the case of Philip of Burgundy *v.* Jean Dedham (Arch. Nat., X¹a 4796, fo. 301vo, January 1432); Dedham was captain of Montigny and argued that Louis Bournel had broken Philip's safe-conduct: 'pour ce qu'il trouva que sans le congie de lui et de son lieutenant il y [i.e. Montigny] estoist entre, lui dit qu'il avoit enfreint son sauf-conduit et qu'il devoit estre prisonnier'.

[4] Cf. statement of Budes in the case of Geoffrey Budes *v.* Jean de Paine Vaire (Arch. Nat., X¹a 1470, fo. 249vo, 17 March 1377): 'Gefroy dit que Jehan tenoit partie des ennemis du royaume et estoit capitaine et homme d'armes chevalier et par force d'armes et tout arme fut pris en fait de guerre dont la cognoissance appartient au connestable entre toutes personnes'. Jean had claimed he was 'homme d'eglise' and not bound to answer in a secular court, but he was sent back (fo. 289) to answer before the Constable.

Where, on the other hand, a prisoner claimed he was on the same side as his master, the courts could only do their best to get at the facts. There was a great deal of litigation over this issue, because profiteering captains took prisoners indiscriminately and used any method to justify their capture. One of their favourite ruses was to interpret the possession of an enemy safe-conduct as evidence of communication with them, which would legalise capture;[1] another was to carry prisoners to a stronghold outside the realm (for instance from France into the Empire), where they themselves could not be adjourned.[2] But the only reasonable excuse which could be pleaded in these circumstances was that offered by John Fastolf in his action against Denis Sauvage and Henry Lidam, that he had discharged their full ransom to the enemy, and so had the same rights over the released prisoners as their masters had had. Even so, the court would not let him keep the men in prison after they had given pledges for their debt; they were not strictly speaking prisoners of war.[3]

If a prisoner was taken in an illicit war, he could claim that his obligation was void *ex falsu causa*. In this case his letter of obligation, as those of his pledges, could be abjured as a *bonus dolus*, a fair trick to overcome an unfair one.[4] It was by this action that Du Guesclin's heir rebutted the claim of Garcia

[1] See *infra*, ch. XI, pp. 198–9.

[2] Cf. cases of the curé of Harcourt *v.* soldiers of Humbert de Bulgneville (Arch. Nat., X²a 8, fo. 55, June 1368), who took the curé and ransomed him in Lorraine; of Giraud de Bucy *v.* Bernard de Lissade (Arch. Nat., X²a 8, fo. 118, July 1369), who raided his lands and men and took them across the border into Aquitaine; of the Sire de Fiennes *v.* Jean de Noyers (Arch. Nat., X¹a 1471, fos. 152 and 155vo, January and February 1379), who raided Fiennes's men and carried spoil into Lorraine; of Gentian *v.* Le Palu (*cit. sup.*), who carried Gentian off to prison in Savoy.

[3] Fastolf *v.* Denis Sauvage and Henry Lidam (Arch. Nat., X¹a 4793, fo. 384vo–5, 28 February 1424), argument of Fastolf: 'les marchans furent pris par la garnison de Pacy . . . lors lesdits marchans firent a Fastot pour leur delivrance et pour paier leur finance . . . et fist delivrer lesdits marchans qui s'obligerent envers lui . . . Fastot a le droit sur eux tel que avoient les ennemis'. But on 22 August 1427 the court ordered that if Fastolf had no opposition to raise, they were to be freed from prison on caution (Arch. Nat., X¹a 8302, fo. 247). They were ultimately released from all obligations to him by an arrest of 31 January 1428 (Arch. Nat., X¹a 66, fo. 61vo).

[4] Cf. Angelus of Perusia, *Disputatio inc.* '*Renovata guerra*': 'in quantum captivans esset hostis reipublice non est dubium quod ei non est servanda fides, et in observantia fidei est dolus bonus et approbatus'. It is clear that he

Raimond d'Aubeterre, founded in the pledge that the Constable
had given for the ransom of a prisoner taken in an illicit war in
Auxerrois.[1] The only possible reply to this objection, if the
legality of the war could not be proved, was that the captive
had been acting as if in open war. Thus Henry Pomfret claimed
that, truce or no truce, Jean de Melun was fairly taken because
he was riding at the head of his men with pennons displayed.[2]
It is worth noting one of Melun's replies in this connection, that
Pomfret being himself a prisoner at the time could not arm and,
therefore, truce or no truce, he could not justly take part in any
war.[3] This is a useful reminder that war could be illicit on
purely personal grounds, as well as public ones.

In the last resort, the strongest foundation of the captor's
title was his written letter of obligation, with its formal renunciation of any right to object, and he could call on his prisoner to
acknowledge or deny his seal. Even so, the prisoner might have
an answer, as that his seal had been taken from him or counter-
feited.[4] A wise captor who had any doubts about his title did

[1] Molinier, *Etude sur la Vie d'Arnoul d'Audreham*, Pièce Justificative, no.
XCIV (plaidoirie in Parlement of 6 January 1391, in de Longueville *v.*
Aubeterre): 'de la premiere obligation (of du Guesclin), qui parle d'un
prisonnier appelle Pierre Langlois, dist qu'il ne fait a recevoir, car il ne lui
[Garcia] loisait de le prendre pour ce qu'il estoit pais, et ainsi fu *turpis
causa*, et se Messire Bertran se obliga se fu *bonus dolus*'.
[2] Melun *v.* Pomfret (*cit. sup.*), argument of Pomfret: 'Melun et ceux de
sa compaignie chevauchoient a penon desploye, qui etoit vraye signe de
guerre entre les gens d'armes'.
[3] Ibid., argument of Melun: 'au temps que Henry le prist il etoit prisonnier d'un escuyer francois, et par ainsy selon droit d'armes ne pouvoit
faire fait d'armes de prendre prisonnier'.
[4] Cf. for example Isabel de Thouars *v.* Guillaume des Bordes (Arch.
Nat., X¹a 25, fo. 3, 21 November 1375). Guillaume sued in the right of
Gaillart de Saliers for the ransom of her father Ingergier d'Amboise (see
*ante*, p. 168, n. 2, 169, n. 2, and p. 176, n. 3); Isabel stated that Gaillart had
seized his seal, and the court would not force her to acknowledge or deny
it. The same argument was employed by de Longueville in Longueville *v.*
Aubeterre (Molinier, op. cit., pièce justificative, no. XCV, plaidoirie of 19
January 1391): 'il n'est tenus de nier et cognoistre, allegue l'arrest du Sire d'
Amboise contre Messire Guillaume des Bordes'.

---

means by 'hostis reipublice' one who is the enemy of all Christians since he
levies unjust war, as he says later 'sinautem guerra est licita, tunc captura
est licita, et tunc tales capti quia juste capti si aliquid promittunt captivantibus servare tenentur'.

not wait for it to be queried in court. He resorted instead to craft. Thus, when in 1363 Michel Amoines was taken prisoner by Yvonet le Galoet, a Breton *routier*, in Auvergne, Yvonet, 'fearing that as he could not lawfully keep him he would lose his ransom if he held him longer',[1] allowed Jean de l'Espine to pay on Michel's behalf. He then freed Michel, and gave John a receipt for 3,244 florins, a much larger sum than he had actually paid. On the strength of this receipt, Michel was forced to acknowledge a debt for 3,244 florins to John, and when he did not pay, John prosecuted him as an ordinary debtor. If he had not been found out, he would thus have secured a substantial profit on the transaction. Meanwhile Yvonet had his money safely in pocket, and did not need to worry any more about the illegality of his ransom. The safety and simplicity of this ruse was such that it was popular even in perfectly lawful war; the captors got a quick and secure profit, and the man who settled the ransom obtained a debt for more than he had paid, and which it was much easier for him than for an enemy to recover.[2] It is not surprising to find men who did quite a business in ransoming prisoners, like Bernard, the 'rich English merchant' who by his own account (before the Parlement in 1447) 'was always doing favours to the French'.[3] We may be sure that he was charging a concealed interest on his favours: they were not free.

There were ways of getting round the law of arms, but there are ways of getting round most laws. Indeed, the very fact that men bothered to find ruses to circumvent it shows that they had a certain respect for the law, and recognised the usefulness of its

---

[1] M. Amoines v. J. de l'Espine (Arch. Nat., X¹a 21, fo. 351vo, 6 May 1368), argument of Amoines: 'Sciebat enim dictus Yvo quod licite eum detinere non poterat, et si ulterius detinuisset, fuisset absque financia expeditus'.

[2] Cf. for example the case of Pierre de Villiers v. Charles d'Estouteville (Arch. Nat., X¹a 4796, fo. 181vo, 23 February 1430). D'Estouteville bought Villiers from Gilet de Ricarville, as he had been told 'que s'il pouvoit avoir Villiers il y povoit avoir grand prouffit'. He seems probably to have paid down 200 ecus, to have tried to obtain 800, and in the end to have taken an obligation for 300, giving him 33⅓ per cent profit.

[3] Case of Jaquot du Vergier and Walter Bernard v. Jean Martin (Arch. Nat., X¹a 4801, fo. 289vo, 12 June 1447): Martin was sueing to be free of his obligation to Bernard, who had paid his ransom to the English.

regulation of their military commerce. That it was the letter of the law rather than its spirit that men obeyed is only what we should expect. Just because ransoms were often excessive, we need not suppose that the rules of honour which controlled the relation of prisoner and master were hypocritical and a mere cloak for profiteering. The man of honour did not mean for a medieval soldier an ideal human being, but a person of a particular social status and calling who kept on the right side of certain technical rules. These rules were general; idealism lay beyond them in the realm of personal choice. They merely set the limits within which the individual decided how far he would sacrifice ideals to a profit in cash.

What the law of ransom usefully reveals is not the wickedness of medieval soldiers, but, once again, the limits of the medieval conception of international law. To explain the law, the legists compared it with the rules governing feudal tenures, which created purely private and personal relations. A prisoner was not bound to his enemies generally, but to his master personally, and the public fortunes of war could not compromise his master's right, which was private. The effective sanction which protected that right was not a public code based on principles of general utility, but a code of personal honour. The chivalrous relation of prisoner to master could even, we have seen, override the bond of allegiance. The law of arms bound both of them not as servants of their states, but as men who followed an 'honourable' calling in Christian society, and it was only international because the calling of arms was so.

# PART IV

Interludes in War and Peace

# XI

# IMMUNITY FROM WAR

An objection which was very frequently raised in the military courts against demands for ransom was that the conditions of the war in question did not allow the taking of prisoners, because it was unjust, or because it was only a feudal war. A still more common objection was that the captive was for one reason or another immune from war. Immunity from war could be claimed on three principal grounds. It could be claimed on account of the captive's standing or profession; or because he enjoyed the security of a safe-conduct; or because he was taken in time of truce. In this chapter these three kinds of immunity will be discussed in turn.

I

No one, in the middle ages, believed that war among Christians ought to be total war. Its extent was limited by its legal purpose, to establish right by appeal to divine judgment, and it should not disrupt the unity of Christian society. Within that society the canon law, in which the law of arms was in part founded, had universal currency, and therefore the laws laid down by the Church to prevent the dislocation of Christendom were in theory generally received. By these laws certain classes of person enjoyed 'canonical truce', a complete immunity from war.[1] In the first place, for obvious reasons, churchmen and their goods were *hors de guerre*.[2] Secondly, all pilgrims, *conversi*

---

[1] Cf. II Decretum, 24, q. 3, cap. 25; I Decretal., Tit. 34, cap. 2.

[2] Ibid., and see Hostiensis, *Summa Aurea*, Lib. I, 34 §6 (quot sunt species treugae); and Upton, *De Officio Militari*, Lib. II, cap. 13 (ed. Bysshe, p. 90).

and hermits, were immune from acts of war.[1] So, thirdly, were 'oxherds, husbandmen and ploughmen' when they were carrying on their business: 'because', says Bonet, 'those who cultivate the soil plough and work for all and everybody, and all manner of folk live of their labour'.[2] The protection of such people, it was argued, was essential for the welfare of society as a whole: their business was irrelevant to war, and so the law of the church put them outside its limited scope. Besides these, and on rather different grounds, persons such as heralds and ambassadors were immune from war by law of arms.

The unity of Christendom, as we know, was an unattained ideal, and so were the rules to protect that unity, which have been described. The theoretical legal immunity of the labouring man was a dead letter from the start. Upton, who states the rule with due citation from authority, sums the matter up in a single laconic comment: 'but all this was never observed in my time in France'.[3] Bonet is more rhetorical: 'in these days all wars are directed against poor labouring people', he says, 'the man who does not know how to set places on fire, to rob churches . . . and imprison priests, is not fit to carry on war'.[4] Elsewhere, however, he indicates how the law was circumvented in this matter. Those who give 'aid and countenance' to their sovereigns in war, he says, lose their immunity, whether they arm or not: 'and if sometimes the humble and innocent suffer harm and lose their goods, it cannot be otherwise'.[5] For his 'sometimes' we may substitute 'almost always'. Here and there, it is true, an exceptional commander made some attempt to protect the non-combatant. Henry V's orders for his armies acknowledged the principle of their security[6] and where he himself was present we gather that the worst sort of excesses were prevented.[7] There are also some tributes to the good conduct of Charles VII's

---

[1] Ibid.

[2] Bonet, *Tree of Battles*, pt. 4, ch. 100 (Coopland's translation, p. 188). Bonet is simply expanding the references given above.

[3] Upton, *de Officio Militari*, Lib. II, cap. 13 (ed. Bysshe, p. 90).

[4] Bonet, *Tree of Battles*, pt. 4, ch. 102 (Coopland's translation, p. 189).

[5] Ibid., pt. 4, ch. 48 (Coopland's translation, pp. 153–4).

[6] Henry V's Mantes Orders, §33 (*Black Book of the Admiralty*, R.S., Vol. I, p. 469).

[7] Cf. *Chronique du Religieux de St. Denis*, Lib. XXXVI, cap. 8 (ed. Bellaguet, Tome V, p. 556).

soldiers in the 1450s.[1] One or two other commanders as well, such as Dagworth,[2] Edward III's lieutenant in Brittany, and Perrot le Béarnois,[3] are praised for their clemency to churchmen and civilians by the chroniclers.

But the observance of the rules was much more remarkable than their breach. In areas overrun by armies, civilians were treated as enemies, and the miseries which they suffered were usually far more inhuman than any hardship a soldier might have to face. Occasionally official investigations note the capture of 'labouring men at their labour',[4] in a manner which shows that this was technically an offence. But if one reads such documents with any care, one must conclude that, if this was all, they were lucky labourers indeed. Normally captains took labouring folk as their prisoners of war, and because they were not gentlemen they treated them much more harshly than their military prisoners. Hideous brutalities were constantly perpetrated in the hopes of wringing money from the poor. The brief marginalia of enquiries into the excesses of *routiers* tell the story best: there is no need to expand such entries as *femme violee, gens crucifiez, rotiz et penduz, homme roty.*[5]

Under Bonet's broad saving clause, that those who give aid and countenance to war may be despoiled in the same way as soldiers, the French peasantry suffered untold miseries in the Hundred Years War. As they also undoubtedly contributed to the expenses of war, the immunity of churchmen could be eliminated on the same ground, and any reader of Denifle's

[1] Blondel, *De Reductione Normannie*, R.S., p. 49.
[2] Cf. the French poem quoted by Luce:
'En son vivant Dagorne avoit pour certain ordonne
Que menues gens de villes, ceulx qui gaignent ble,
Ne seroient des Englois plus prins ne guerroie.'
(Bib. Nat., MS. Fr. 1555, fo. 51, quoted S. Luce, *Histoire de Bertrand du Guesclin*, Paris, 1876, p. 105.)
[3] Cf. Kervyn de Lettenhove, *Oeuvres de Froissart*, Tome XIII, p. 72.
[4] Cf. for example, the report made in 1445 on the excesses of Robert Floques and his men on Burgundian territories: 'item, ont prins . . . deux laboureurs qu'ils ont prins *en leur labourage faisans* lesquels ils tiennent a grosse raencon et sont nommez Hugot Quaillart et Jehan Arnoste' (Arch. Dep. de la Côte d'Or, B 11906).
[5] These marginalia are a sample from a report on the excesses of the Dauphin's soldiers in Luxeuil and Faucogney in 1439 (Arch. Dep. de la Côte d'Or, B 11881).

two volumes on the desolation of the French church in these years would be entitled to conclude that it was equally disregarded.[1] The estates of churches and abbeys were overrun and forced to pay *appatis* to avoid further spoliation. Their buildings were invaded, and frequently used as fortresses by bands of raiders. Their treasures were pillaged. Even the communion plate was not spared; an eye-witness in 1373 deposed that he had seen more than a hundred chalices used as drinking bowls at a supper by the English knight John Harleston and his companions.[2]

It would be useless to deny the accuracy of the gloomy picture, which has been painted by Denifle and others, of the Church's sufferings at the hands of the soldiery. All that can be said is that there is a reverse side to it. The immunity of the Church and of churchmen was not disregarded as universally as that of the peasant was. Henry V's orders for their protection were so effectively enforced, indeed, that the peasants of Normandy are said to have donned clerical disguise whenever English soldiers were in their area, and even to have tonsured themselves.[3] As always, the worst excesses were committed not by organised armies, but by the free companies and the *écorcheurs*. From the point of view of legal history, the significance of their outrages is debatable. Such men took very little notice of any law, and their piracy sheds no more light on the law of arms than would the conduct of a Caribbean buccaneer on the history of civilised maritime law. What is important is not that the law of arms tolerated outrages (which it did not do); but that it was not effectively enforced throughout most of the Hundred Years War. It was only after Charles VII and the Constable de Richemont took matters in hand, and set about trying the *écorcheur* captains for war-crimes before drumhead courts martial, that conditions began very slowly to improve.[4]

[1] Denifle, *La Guerre de Cent Ans, La Désolation des Églises, Monastères et Hôpitaux en France*, 2 Tomes (Paris, 1897-9).

[2] E. de Fréville, 'Les Grandes Compagnies au Quatorzieme Siècle', *Bibliothèque de l'École de Chartes*, Tome V (1843-4), p. 246.

[3] Walsingham, *Historia Anglicana*, R.S., Vol. II, p. 322.

[4] Cf. cases of Henry Bourges, tried and executed for war crimes by the Constable in 1434 (Gruel, *Chronique d'Artus III Comte de Richemont*, ed. Michaud and Poujoulat, p. 202); of Bouson de Failles, tried and sentenced by the Prévot des Maréchaux in 1438 (ibid., p. 211); of the Bastard of

What the courts even before this time did attempt to do, when cases came before them, was to enforce the personal immunity of churchmen. They do not appear to have made any effort to uphold the immunity of church lands, as the church would have wished them to.[1] No doubt this was impracticable. But the Parlement of Paris in 1438 was even willing to allow English churchmen who had been taken prisoner to plead before it, although as prisoners of war they had no standing there.[2] Long before, its judges had thrust Watier Mazelandre, a valet of Rifflart of Flanders, into prison in the Chatelet, when he was charged with making a clerk prisoner:[3] and they had refused to allow the goods of Philipot de Serixe to be taken under letters of marque, because he was a cleric.[4] The only arguments which they were prepared to allow against the plea of clergy, were either that a churchman had in his private capacity stood surety for a ransom,[5] or that he had forfeited

[1] The Church occasionally attempted to invoke this immunity, cf. Innocent VI's letter to Edward III, forbidding him to ask the Scottish Church to pledge its revenues for the ransom of David Bruce, 11 July 1358 (Rymer, Vol. III, pt. I, p. 168); and of Gregory IX to Edward III, 7 October 1371, pointing out that Roger Belfort's clerical relatives should not be expected to use their ecclesiastical revenues to help him with his ransom (Rymer, Vol. III, pt. II, p. 185). But the courts did not generally uphold this view of things.

[2] Amboise de Lois v. Richard Unascues (?), an Englishman, 14 February 1438. Richard had been taken while on his way to the Council of Basle, and when he complained the Parlement was prepared to give him 'distribucion de conseil procureur et avocatz tant que suffire lui devra'. (Arch. Nat., X¹a 1482, fo. 63vo.)

[3] Cf. Pierre de Braly v. Watier Mazelandre (December 1365–January 1366), Arch. Nat., X¹a 1469, fos. 107vo and 112.

[4] Cf. Philipot de Serixe v. Etienne de Bailly (9 December 1374), Arch. Nat., X¹a 24, fo. 208.

[5] Cf. Martin Hurtel, Aubertin Cochelin and others v. Abbot and Convent of Notre Dame de Chartraine, on appeal from the Constable of France, 22 February 1422, in which the Abbot was being sued as the surety for a ransom: he clearly accepted the Constable's jurisdiction, as it was Martin and his companions who appealed. (Arch. Nat., X¹a 4799, fo. 32.)

Bourbon, tried and sentenced by the Prévot des Maréchaux in 1441 (ibid., p. 216). Richemont and the King also intended to proceed in the same way against Guillaume de Flavy (cf. P. Champion, *Guillaume de Flavy Capitaine de Compiègne*, Paris, 1906, p. 219) and Antoine de Chabannes (cf. *Chronique Martinianne*, ed. P. Champion, Paris, 1907, p. 47).

his clerical privilege by taking arms. A clerk who took arms was treated as a soldier, and as a soldier he could be ransomed;[1] and if he defaulted he could be sued in the military courts. Nevertheless, the courts always allowed him to plead his clergy, even if he was a prisoner.[2] If he was proved to have been in arms, then he was treated as the subject of a hostile sovereign. But a clerk in his habit was the subject of the universal church,[3] which was not a party to the war, and the cloth of his order protected him.

Heralds enjoyed immunity from war on much the same grounds as churchmen, that they belonged to an international order. The difference between the herald and the clerk was that the former's immunity was founded not in the canon law, but in the civil law and the *jus gentium*.[4] It therefore held good, not

[1] Cf. Bonet, *Tree of Battles*, pt. 4, ch. 97 (Coopland's translation, p. 187). For examples of cases see Geoffreoi Budes *v.* Jean de Paine Vaire, 17 March 1377 (plea of the King's proctor against Jean who claimed his clerical privilege): 'Le procureur du roy dit que au connestable appartient cette cognoistence et allegue de plusieurs prelaz et gens deglise qui ont este pris *en guerre* et mis a raencon' (Arch. Nat., X¹a 1470, fo. 249vo; Jean was alleged by Geoffreoi to have been taken in arms). Compare the case of the Seigneur de Chivre *v.* Baudrain de Harnel, 4 August 1393, in which Baudrain claimed his clergy; de Chivre replied that 'si tot qu'un homme . . . delaisse son habit de clerc pour prendre le fait et estat d'armes *illo casu* il renonce a son prive-lege . . . et s'il est prins *non incidit in canonicum*' (Arch. Nat., X²a 12, fo. 182). The point is well founded in canon law, cf. III Decretal., Tit. 1, c. 2 and 16.

[2] Cf. case of Jean de la Ferté and Guillaume Mucy *v.* Tanguy Cousinet, 12 May 1418. Jean and Guillaume accused Tanguy of despoiling them of their prisoner Guillaume Maradon, who claimed clerical privilege against both parties and was admitted to plead it: 'dist qu'il ne doit point estre compris en la guerre' (Arch. Nat., X¹a 4792, fo. 48 and vo). Cf. also cases of the Bishop of Paris and Jean Lyenne, *v.* the King, 20 April 1444, in which Jean's clergy was pleaded against his capture as a prisoner of war (Arch. Nat., X¹a 4800, fo. 106vo–7), and of Pierre des Villiers *v.* Charles d'Estoute-ville, 6 September 1430, in which Villiers pleaded clergy similarly: 'dit qu'il est homme qui n'est point compris de raison en la guerre *quia clericus et clericaliter vivens*' (Arch. Nat., X¹a 8302, fo. 247).

[3] Cf. Bonet, *Tree of Battles*, pt. 4, ch. 98 (Coopland's translation, p. 187).

[4] Cf. B. Mus., MS. Cotton Nero D 2, fo. 255 (*livre de la creacion et fondacion des heraulx*) 'se aucuns excercisans et usans de lour office leur faisoient aucunes injures qu'ilz furent reputez et jugez naturellement contre toutes bonnes coustumes qu'entre toutes bonnes gens et nascions estoient . . . comme silz avoient fait injure contre les sains aussi comme dient les droiz en

only in the wars of Christians, but (in theory at least) in all wars. Though they were created by territorial princes and magnates, the allegiance of heralds was not to their masters alone, but to the order of knighthood at large,[1] and so they could not be treated as the subjects of the enemy. When, for instance, in 1417 an English herald was taken prisoner by the French, there was thus no need to bring a case in court, because there could be no defence: a herald's coat of arms was sufficient safe-conduct for him in all places. All that the other English heralds had to do was to write to their French companions and ask them to see he was released.[2] They all, English and French alike, belonged to one single and special fellowship, with its own rules and ranks and ceremonies. Throughout the battle of Agincourt the heralds of both sides stood together on a hill, away from the fighting in which their order had no part;[3] and afterwards, it was Mountjoy King of Arms of France who told Henry V that the day was acknowledged his.[4]

The immunity of heralds was much better observed than any other. The reasons for this are obvious enough. In the first instance, soldiers were likely to respect their immunity, because they were part of the apparatus of their own chivalrous profession. They knew them well, for heralds were attached for duty to every major host. The main English garrisons in France nearly all had their own *pursuivants*,[5] and even *routiers* like the

---

[1] Cf. 'Othe of the Pursvant' (*Black Book of the Admiralty*, R.S., Vol. I, p. 299), 'Item ye shalle dyspose you to be lowly, humble and servisable to all estates of gentilnesse that cristene beth'.

[2] B. Mus., MS. Stowe 1047, fo. 220.

[3] Lefèvre de St. Rémy, *Chronique*, ed. F. Morand (Soc. de l'histoire de France, 1876), Tome I, p. 268.

[4] Monstrelet, *Chronique*, ed. L. Douet D'Arq (Soc. de l'histoire de France, 1859), Tome III, p. 111.

[5] Cf. G.E.C. Complete Peerage (London, 1949), Vol. XI, Appendix C, pp. 48–9.

---

la glosse qui s'appelle *Glossa de Offic: Lega:*'; cf. also B. Mus., MS. Stowe 668, fo. 796: 'quiconques donneroit empeschement aux heraulx faisans leur office soit tenu pour ung villain entre les noble et devroyt estre pugny et constraint come de tres grief delit et deshonnorable trayson'. The authority behind these statements is *Digest*, L, Tit. 7, l. 18 'si quis legatum hostium pulsasset, contra jus gentium id commissum esse existimatur'.

Archpriest[1] and Rodrigue de Villandrando[2] had private officers-of-arms. Soldiers knew, too, what savage reprisals were likely to be taken against those who did violence to such persons.[3] In any case, heralds were too generally useful to be plundered. They carried out endless essential duties in war; bringing the summonses of captains to towns before a siege, and the challenges of princes to pitched battle; obtaining safe-conducts for ambassadors, and for soldiers to parley or joust with the enemy; and helping to negotiate ransoms for prisoners with their relatives at home. The strict rules of the heralds' order forbade them to give away secret information which their profession might reveal to them,[4] and these rules seem on the whole to have been well obeyed. They were familiar and useful to every soldier, and they were treated with respect.

Certain other persons, besides clerks and heralds, enjoyed a more or less automatic immunity from war. Ambassadors were protected by the same rules of the civil law as heralds;[5] and prisoners of war and *bona fide* pilgrims[6] were also secure from hostile acts. But these people all required written safe-conducts to guarantee their security. Their situation was therefore more like that of peasants and local people who could prove immunity from spoliation only by producing either quittances for *appatis* they had paid, or 'bullets'[7] or signs of safe-conduct which they

[1] Cf. Kervyn de Lettenhove *Oeuvres de Froissart*, Tome VI, p. 413 (description of the Captal's interview with Prie, the Archpriest's herald, before the Battle of Cocherel).

[2] Cf. J. Quicherat, *Roderigue de Villandrando* (Paris, 1879), p. 113.

[3] Cf. for example the statement of one Guillaume Ascarot, whose father was executed at Senlis in 1417: 'aucuns tuerent aucuns des heraults et messages du connetable (d'Armagnac) lequel pour ce fist decapiter IIII desdits hostages (de Senlis) dont l'un fut Ascarot' (Arch. Nat., X¹a 4801, fo. 313vo).

[4] Cf. statement of Anjou King of Arms: 'Et quant au tiers point si ung herault avoit revele une embusche chevauchie ou ontreprise . . . a ce repons que oncques ne vit mettre tel cas en jugement (mais) . . . est contre le droit de l'office et toute raison' (Bodleian, MS. Rawlinson C 399, Treatise 7, fo. 1vo).

[5] See *ante*, p. 194, n. 4.

[6] Cf. Bonet, *Tree of Battles*, pt. 4, ch. 99 (Coopland's translation, p. 188): 'I declare to you that all pilgrims, or Romers, whatsoever . . . are under the safeguard of the Holy Father, and can travel in time of war and truce'.

[7] On the use of these 'bullets', cf. Waurin s.a. 1419 'si furent (les habitans de Rouen) contrains de non issir hors de leur ville sans avoir chascun une

had bought from their conquerors. If people such as these were plundered, their status aggravated the crime of breaking a formal safe-conduct, but they could not claim security on the strength of their status alone. They could not like heralds go where they would unquestioned, but were bound by the formal terms of a security which could not ordinarily be refused them.

## II

Written safe-conducts were granted frequently, and for a wide variety of purposes. As has been said, no one supposed that public war in Christian lands meant total war, and consequently safe-conducts were given, and often, to merchants wishing to pass through hostile territory on business, to students bound for foreign universities, to knights on their way to tournaments, and so on, as well as to pilgrims, prisoners, and diplomatic envoys. That such persons should be given security seemed necessary for the preservation of reasonable social relations within the frontiers of Christendom.

Written safe-conducts could be of two kinds, *saufconduit de grace* and *saufconduit de guerre*. Of the two, *saufconduit de grace*, gave a much wider protection; it secured the holder not only against acts of war, but against any prosecution or arrest. It could only be given by a prince,[1] and it bound all his subjects. Its only disadvantage was that they alone were bound. This was not of importance if the prince was a sovereign without superior; but it did matter where the prince concerned was a man such as the Duke of Burgundy or Brittany, who himself had a sovereign. Raoul Cardon for instance, found in 1449 that his

---

[1] Statement of Dedham in Louis Bournel *v.* Jean Dedham (January 1432): 'le roy est empereur en son royaume et a cause de sa couronne et souverainte peut donner sauf conduit de grace' (Arch. Nat., X¹a 4796, fo. 301vo).

---

bullette du Roy, et aussi en convenoit avoir tous autres du pays qui estoient en la domination du Roy d'Angleterre, et coustoit chascune bullette quatre soulz de Flandres' (Waurin, *Chroniques*, R.S., Vol. II, p. 265). Cf. also Salisbury Perche Orders §6: 'Also that noe man take no prisoners of men billeted of that said ground patized nor childe having billett upon him in paine to loose horse and harnois and theire bodies at the Kinges will'.

*saufconduit de grace* from the Duke of Brittany did not bind the sailors of Dieppe, who plundered the goods he was shipping from St. Malo to Rouen quite lawfully.[1] In his case, an ordinary safe-conduct of war from the Admiral or the Constable of France would have given more effective protection. The King's *saufconduit de grace*, however, was the best security a man could have.

A safe-conduct of war gave a more ordinary protection. It was a sealed document,[2] and, like other sealed documents, was usually paid for. The degree of security that it gave depended on the authority of the person under whose seal it was given. Almost any captain could give safe-conducts (though only for certain purposes), and the form of the document differed little, whether it was given by a Seguin de Badefol or an Edward III.[3] But a safe-conduct of war only bound those

[1] Cf. statement of Simon, advocate for Chrispian du Four and Jean Falaise, who had plundered Cardon (26 January 1450): 'disoit party (Cardon) qu'avoit sauf-conduit du duc de Bretaigne; eulx au contraire disoient que ne s'en vouloit aidier, maiss aussi que ce serait sauf-conduit de grace et que ne povoit toucher que les subgez de Bretaigne et non de Dyepe' (Arch. Nat., X¹a 4802, fo. 183).

[2] Cf. Upton, *de Officio Militari*, Lib. II, cap. 10 (Bysshe, p. 85): 'Sciendum est quod salvus conductus sive securitas tribus modis prestatur . . . tercio per scripturam vel signi aut tituli appositionem'. The form of a safe-conduct was that of a patent letter, and a sum was paid for the seal. This was a profitable source of revenue; John Fotheringhay, as Captain of Creil *c.* 1359, is said to have made 10,000 francs on the sale of safe-conducts (Denifle, *La Désolation de l'Englise*, Tome II, p. 219). Often clerks overcharged for the seal; and there are records of a long case between Fastolf and his clerk Thomas Overton, whom he charged with this offence, in the Parlement (cf. Arch. Nat., X¹a 68, fos. 26vo, 111; X¹a 4797, fo. 222vo–3).

[3] A good example of a routier's safe-conduct, given by Seguin de Badefol, is printed by G. Guigue, *Les Tards-Venus en Lyonnais* (Lyons, 1886), p. 107. It is addressed 'a touz mes biens vullans, alliez, et subgiez'. This brings out the difference in the powers of different captains. Seguin, as a free soldier, speaks independently to those who will obey him. A captain employed under contract could normally give safe-conduct to his own and his men's prisoners, but to give them for general purposes he required a commission empowering him to do so (for examples see Rymer, e.g. Vol. III, pt. II, p. 163; Vol. IV, pt. I, p. 182; Vol. IV, pt. IV, p. 173 etc.). A man who had the rank of '*Dux Belli*' (approximately the equivalent of King's Lieutenant) had automatic power to give safe-conduct, cf. B. Mus., MS. Stowe 1047, fo. 248 (*de gubernatione ac principali capitaneo exercitus*): 'octavo datur potestas salvos conductos ubique quibuscumque personis concedendi'.

under the authority of the man who gave it:[1] the safe conduct
of, say, a Burgundian captain like Jean de Luxembourg did not
bind an Englishman like John Cornwall, even though they
were both operating on the same side and in the same area.[2]
We therefore find there was a good deal of questioning of the
authority for the grant of safe-conducts, and that sometimes
additional securities were requested before they were used. The
safest security that a man could get was the safe-conduct of the
King, or of his Constable or Lieutenant-General, but even so
the bearer had to be wary, as there might be some catch in its
terms. Francois de Surienne, for instance, asked for himself to be
excluded by name from the security of all English safe-conducts
in 1441,[3] so that anyone who wanted protection from his men
would have to apply to him personally. Things were still more
difficult in an area where free companies were operating: a man
who wished to travel there had to obtain a whole series of safe-
conducts from their various independent captains.[4]

Every written safe-conduct laid down detailed conditions of
tenure. It supplied the name of the bearer, listed the number of
persons he was allowed to have in his company, and the arms
and goods which he might carry, and also gave any necessary
details concerning the route he was to follow and the places
which he was or was not allowed to enter.[5] Any goods not

[1] Bonet, *Tree of Battles*, pt. 4, ch. 59 (Coopland's translation, p. 162): 'a
captain has power to ensure him safe-conduct only in regard to the men of
the captain's own country who are under him'.

[2] Cf. Monstrelet, *Chronique*, ed. L. Douet d'Arq. Tome III, pp. 369–71.
He describes how John Cornwall rode down and took prisoner the Dau-
phinois of the garrison of Roye, who had surrendered by *appointement* to
Jean de Luxembourg and were travelling with his safe-conducts (1419). In
spite of Luxembourg's protest, the English would not regard his safe-
conducts as binding them.

[3] Sir H. Nicolas, *Proceedings of the Privy Council*, Vol. V, p. 149.

[4] In 1358, for example, a traveller from Valognes to Coutances needed
three safe-conducts; one from the English at St. Sauveur, one from the
Navarrese at Valognes and one from the French at St. Lo; cf. Luce, *Du
Guesclin*, p. 271.

[5] Upton, *De Officio Militari*, Lib. II, cap. 12 (Bysshe, pp. 87–9), gives a
good exemplar of a safe-conduct, on the model of those given by Salisbury
in his army. It details the goods taken under safe-conduct (compare, e.g.
*Rot. Scot.*, Vol. II, p. 346); the number of persons under security, the route,
and the places they are not to enter (compare e.g. Rymer, Vol. IV, pt. IV,
p. 199, a safe-conduct for a French legation in 1433).

expressly secured in the safe-conduct could be taken from him as spoil; thus Froissart tells us that the Navarrese in the 1350s would never put 'hats of beaver, ostrich feathers, and spear-heads' into their safe-conducts, but always plundered them.[1] If the bearer directly infringed any condition of his safe-conduct, he could be lawfully taken prisoner. Thus Jean Deschamps in 1415 in the Parlement claimed four Englishmen as his lawful prisoners, because they were taken on land between Harfleur and Dieppe, whereas their safe-conduct was from the Admiral to go by sea.[2] It was therefore important to examine carefully the conditions of security in a safe-conduct, and we find that care was duly taken. When, for instance, John Le Scrope and John Melton in 1410 looked into their safe-conduct from John the Fearless, they found that it bound them, on entering his lands, to make an oath before the *bailli* of Flanders, that they would seek to do no harm there. As they thought it was 'very obscure' who the *bailli* was, they wrote off at once, asking that he be named before they used the safe-conduct.[3] This was a wise step, for, as Bonet says, soldiers 'are much more pleased to find flaws in one or many safe-conducts than to find full guar-antee in them'.[4]

Certain general conditions were besides always understood to govern the security given by safe-conducts of war, whether or not they were mentioned in writing. This was just as well, as a good many of those who used them must have been unable to read. Firstly, the security given by the safe-conduct was under-stood to give protection not only against open war, but against letters of marque too, even if these had been granted in reprisal for the breach of another safe-conduct.[5] Secondly, a safe-con-

---

[1] Kervyn de Lettenhove, *Oeuvres de Froissart*, Tome VI, pp. 98–9.

[2] Case of Jean Deschamps *v.* Guillaume Watier (6 February 1416), Arch. Nat., X¹a 4791, fo. 34 and vo.

[3] Cf. letter of Thomas Pikworth, of Calais, to the Chancellor of Bur-gundy, 13 April 1410 (?) (Arch. Dep. du Nord, B 18843, pièce 29484). The archives at Lille contain several other letters asking for the authority of safe-conducts to be confirmed: e.g. letter of R. Aston, Lieutenant of Calais, 19 February 1406 (?), asking for a confirmation of the Duke of Burgundy's safe-conduct from Orleans, as Captain General in Picardy (Arch. dep. du Nord, B 18823, fo. 85).

[4] Bonet, *Tree of Battles*, pt. 4, ch. 58 (Coopland's translation, p. 162).

[5] Cf. *Le Jouvencel* (ed. Lécestre and Favre), Tome II, pp. 28–9: 'Et pour

duct to travel to a place in enemy territory automatically gave
security for the return journey, provided this was made within
the period for which security was given.[1] Thirdly, the bearer's
security could not be forfeited for breach of local regulations,
of which he could reasonably plead ignorance.[2] These conditions all favoured the bearer. Like other promises, a safe-
conduct was to be interpreted according to the intention of the
man to whom the promise was made[3] (provided his intention
was honest). This principle was both fair and just, and it was
essential to uphold it if safe-conducts were to give any meaningful
security.

Similarly, the bearer's conduct was expected to be in conformity with his supposed good intentions. He was bound to
show his safe-conduct to anyone who might legitimately ask to
see it. He could not bring outlaws or personal enemies of the
grantor into his country under its cover.[4] Moreover, as the safe-
conduct was given to him and his company, he could not
introduce into that company a person of higher status than
himself, for then he would no longer be the principal in the
party.[5] Perhaps most important of all, before entering any
strong town or fortress he had to ask leave of the captain or his
lieutenant to do so; otherwise he could be taken prisoner.[6]

[1] Bonet, *Tree of Battles*, pt. 4, ch. 57 (Coopland's translation, pp. 160–1).

[2] Cf. the judgment of Morton, acting for the chancellor of England, in
1473: 'though they (merchants) are come within the kingdom by this (safe-
conduct), the king has jurisdiction of them . . . but this shall be according
to the law of nature . . . which is universal throughout the world; and
'merchants shall not be bound by our statutes, which are introductive of new
law'. (*Select Cases in the Law Merchant*, ed. Hubert Hall, Selden Soc., 1930,
Vol. II, intro., p. lxxxvi.)

[3] Bonet, *Tree of Battles*, pt. 4, ch. 57 (Coopland's translation, p. 161):
'the safe-conduct must be interpreted according to the intention of the man
to whom it is given and granted'.

[4] Ibid., pt. 4, ch. 96 (Coopland's translations, p. 186).

[5] Ibid., pt. 4, ch. 58 (Coopland's translation, pp. 163–4).

[6] Cf. *Le Jouvencal* (ed. Lécestre and Favre), Tome II, p. 10: 'qui met ung
ennemy, soit prisonnier, soit a sauf-conduit ou a quelque seurte que ce soit,

vous advertir touchant le fait des sauf-conduitz, beaucoup de gens y veullent
donner des abuz et y prendre marque; ce qui ne se peult ne doit faire, pour
ce que celluy qui prent le saufconduit est ton ennemy, et si n'estoit pas ton
ennemy, il n'achetteroit pas ton sauf-conduit . . . marque sur autre saufconduit n'auras tu point'.

Soldiers made use of every opportunity and every ruse in order to infringe safe-conducts and take valuable prisoners. Richard Young, bishop of Rochester, was taken prisoner in 1405 because he had not got his safe-conduct about him.[1] Coppin de Fiennes was taken prisoner in 1406 because he was travelling under the safe-conduct of a man of humbler rank than he.[2] The sureties of Guillaume de Chateauvillain were taken prisoner because they travelled through Barrois, which was off the route laid down for them.[3] These were fair captures, at least according to the letter of the law; other men were taken by blatant sharp practice. The seigneur de Hangest was arrested in 1414 on the ground that his safe-conduct did not expressly secure him on his return journey.[4] Philippe de Cassel and Giraud des Bégués (c. 1448) followed Richard King, a rich English merchant, on his travels in Flanders, and the moment he came near to Calais and left the lands of the Duke of Burgundy, whose safe-conduct he carried, they took him prisoner.[5] John Dedham's men lured Louis de Bournel into Montigny-le-

[1] Cf. letter of Nicholas Rishton concerning this capture, May 1405, and the replies of the Burgundian envoys (Arch. dep. du Nord, B 18823, fos. 13, 15, 16, 18, 21); a copy of the safe-conduct itself is given (ibid., fo. 118), dated at Bruges, 8 May 1405.

[2] Cf. letter of Richard Aston, Lieutenant of Calais, 3 March 1406 (?), which states that Coppin was taken travelling 'par vertu du sauf conduyt donne a une garson prisonnier de Hammes qui au temps de sa prinse estoit en sa compaignie' (Arch. dep. du Nord, B 18823, fo. 88).

[3] Cf. statement of Simon, advocate for des Termes in the case of Thibaut des Termes v. the Seigneur de Chateauvillain (July 1441): '(les hostages) enfreignerent leur sauf conduit car sans licence et le fait savant ils entrerent en barrois pour quoy ils furent arretes' (Arch. Nat., X¹a 4798, fo. 376vo).

[4] Monstrelet, *Chronique*, ed. L. Douet d'Arq (Soc. de l'histoire de France, 1858), Tome II, pp. 220–1.

[5] Case of Raoul de Gaucourt (and Guillaume Juvenel des Ursins, both suing in the right of Giraud and Philip) v. Conte de Joigny (and the Duke of Burgundy), 26 November 1450. Gaucourt tried to suggest that the safe-

sans le congie del cappitaine et des officiers, il (l'ennemy) est confisque a luy. Pour ce dit-on aux sauf-conduiz qu'ilz n'entreront en ville ne en chasteaux sans avoir congie des personnes ad ce ayans pouvoir.' Compare the statement in Louis Bournel v. Jean Dedham (*cit. ante*, p. 197, n. 1): 'il y a aussi saufconduit de guerre mais toutesvoiez soubz umbre de tels sauf-conduiz nul ne doit ne peut entrer en villes ou forteresses et se perd le benefice de tels sauf-conduiz en plusiers maneres'. Bournel was alleged to have lost his safe-conduct by entering Montigny without leave.

Roi for a drink, and at the town barrier one of them said he was the captain's lieutenant; and as soon as Louis was inside it they made him a prisoner, and claimed his safe-conduct was voided because he had entered the town without permission.[1] It was all too easy to question safe-conducts, and many soldiers were very unscrupulous about infringing them.

A safe-conduct was in any case a dangerous document. Even if the enemy observed it, it was very likely that soldiers of the bearer's own party would claim that its possession showed he was of enemy allegiance, and so lawful prize. Thus, when Jean Sarradin and Thibaut Cale (both French soldiers) brought Jaquot le Breton before their captain in Normandy in 1359, they gave evidence that he had two Navarrese safe-conducts and no French ones; and the captain judged that there was therefore a 'presumption' that he was an enemy.[2] So he was made their prisoner. This principle, that a man who had an enemy safe-conduct could be taken prisoner, was often upheld,[3] and may appear unjust. It was not, however, quite as unreasonable as at first sight it would seem to be. In the permanent confusion which reigned in the frontiers of war, allegiance was not easy to gauge. All kinds of local people were in the pay of the enemy for one purpose or another, and were given safe-conducts to go about their nefarious business. It was therefore perfectly reasonable to take them on suspicion. A sensible and

[1] Case of Louis Bournel v. Jean Dedham, cit. ante.

[2] Arch. Nat., JJ 90, no. 549.

[3] Cf. for example case of Seigneur de Laval v. Arnoul de Beaufort (5 August 1368), in which Laval claimed that certain carters whom he took near Chateau-Thierry were lawful prey to the French because they had safe-conducts of the free companies (Arch. Nat. X¹a 21, fo. 344); of the King v. Etienne Cordelois (13 April 1361), who was charged with treason, the possession of an English safe-conduct being quoted as evidence (Arch. Nat., X¹a 17, fo. 288); and of Jean de La Ferté v. Guillaume Montfiquet (23 November 1418), in which Jean claimed Guillaume to be taken as a lawful enemy 'par ce qu'il a pris saufconduit des angloiz' (Arch. Nat., X¹a 4792, fo. 91).

conduct ceased to apply once King was on English soil, but Joigny and the Duke rebutted this by appealing to its intention: 'de la licence du Roy il (le duc) peut donner aux marchans sauf-conduit qui communiquerent en Flandre . . . or en y alant et venant doivent joyr du sauf-conduit autrement ne poroient aler ne venir pour communiquer' (Arch. Nat., X¹a 4803, fo. 9).

loyal person not only carried a safe-conduct in enemy territory, but also letters of protection from his own party to show that his business was lawful.

It is clear now that the protection given by safe-conducts was not very effective. What, we must therefore ask, was the basis of the guarantee given in them, and what actions were available to those plundered while travelling under their security? The basis of a safe-conduct was, as Bonet says, the solemn oath of the grantor to give the bearer such protection as he could afford.[1] This oath was made on his personal honour, as witness the words of Master Jean Bienaissis in the *Jouvencel*: 'guard well the king's honour in his safe-conducts, as you would your own.'[2] Nicholas Rishton's pleas to the Burgundians, after Bishop Young had been taken when under safe-conduct, are in the same spirit: 'for the sake of your lord's *honour*', he wrote to them, 'we beg you to write . . . and ask him to free the bishop and restore him his goods'.[3] The guarantee of a safe-conduct was thus a personal matter; for a safe-conduct was a public instrument only in the contemporary sense, in so far as the person who gave it was a man of public standing. In essence it was a private agreement, and men phrased its legal guarantee in this sense: 'a lord is bound to honour his safe-conducts by law and in good faith'.[4]

The breach of a safe-conduct therefore gave rise to two actions. The bearer's action lay against the grantor, who had promised him security. The man who had an action against those who had actually infringed the safe-conduct was the grantor himself.[5] Thus when John Hawley of Dartmouth plundered merchants under the safe-conduct of Jean des Roches,

[1] Bonet, *Tree of Battles*, pt. 4, ch. 59 (Coopland's translation, pp. 161–3). Bonet states the grantor of a safe-conduct may be held 'false and disloyal', if 'within the limit of his power', he does not try to enforce its observance.

[2] *Le Jouvencel*, ed. Lécestre and Favre, Tome II, p. 28.

[3] Letter of Nicholas Rishton, 20 May 1405, to the Burgundian envoys (Arch. dep. du Nord, B 18823, fo. 18). Compare the letter of the Burgundians of 18 May: 'notre tresredoubte seigneur . . . en verite voldroit en ce et en toutes autres choses garder son honneur a l'expedition de ceulx qui sur son sauf-conduit seroient dedens les mettes de sa siegneurie' (ibid., fo. 16).

[4] Ibid., fo. 18: 'dominus tenetur ex honestate et de jure suum salvum conductum defendere'.

[5] Cf. for example case of the Duke of Alençon *v.* Jacques de Clermont, leiutenant of Louviers (14 August 1450). Alençon sued Clermont for breaking his safe-conducts, and won his case (Arch. Nat., X¹a 80, fo. 171vo–2).

lieutenant of the captain of Brest, it was des Roches whom the merchants sued, and the Earl of Arundel, in his court as captain of Brest, awarded them damages. It was then des Roches's turn, and as Hawley was not under Arundel's jurisdiction, he sued him for damages in the Court of Chivalry, and ultimately obtained judgment in his favour.[1] Alternatively, the grantor and the bearer of the safe-conduct might sue together, as Philip the Good and Louis Bournel together sued John Dedham.[2] The bearer, naturally, could only sue the grantor if he was despoiled by men under the grantor's authority. As Queen Catherine pointed out in 1430, when she was sued by the merchants Jean Coq and Jean Delboeuf, she could not be bound to insure anyone against brigands of no allegiance.[3] This case illustrates a further point, because it was not Queen Catherine's safe-conduct that had been broken, but one she had purchased for the merchants from the French, so that they could transport supplies for her household. In these circumstances it was her business to see that the safe-conducts were good;[4] the merchants

---

[1] Case of Jean des Roches v. John Hawley of Dartmouth, in the Court of Chivalry (P.R.O., C47/6/4, Roll 1, evidence for des Roches, shows the basis of his case; the note on the sentence to be given in his favour, by Adam of Usk and John Hisperton, attached to Roll 4, shows he won).

[2] Bournel and Burgundy v. Dedham, cit. ante. Philip the Good was very careful about his safe-conducts; he also joined in the action to uphold his security in the case of Gaucourt v. Joigny (ante, p. 203 n. 1); see also p. 211 n. 3 for another instance. When the King's safe-conduct was broken, as for instance in the case of John de Berkeley's safe-conduct in 1357, his proctor normally joined in the case with the injured party or parties (for the Berkeley affair, see S. Luce, Histoire de Bertrand du Guesclin, Pièce Justificative, no. XI, p. 526 et seq., where the Parlement's arrest of 18 January 1358 is printed).

[3] Queen Catherine v. Jean Coq and Jean Delboeuf (20 June 1430), case for the Queen: 'les merchans in ipso contractu ont confesse avoir eu les sauf-conduiz et sont les sauf-conduiz bien faits; et se on n'y a obey et on les a enfreint . . . ne leur (la reine et ses officiers) doit estre impute et n'estoient en la puissance de la royne de promettre qu'ils n'auroient point d'empeschement nec potuit factum alienum promittere . . . et n'est mie tenu des faits des brigans ou d'autres qui avoient enfraint les sauf-conduiz' (Arch. Nat., X¹a 4796, fo. 220).

[4] On this point, see also the case of Jean Petit, Simonet Gautier and others, carters, v. Jean Sac and Jean Coq, merchants of Paris (15 December 1429). The merchants had purchased the safe-conducts, and the carters were plundered of their carts and horses while carrying for them, and sued for damages claiming that 'on doit imputer aux marchans si leur sauf conduit n'estoit bon ou ils ne l'ont monstre' (Arch. Nat., X¹a 4796, fo. 146).

were acting as her *mandatarii*, and so, if they suffered loss by her negligence, they could obtain redress from her by an *actio mandati*.

The grantor's action against those who broke his safe-conducts was good, whether or not he had to recompense those plundered. The infringement had caused him to break his promise, and injured him in his honour. The gravity of the crime of breaking safe-conducts was therefore gauged by the estate of the grantor: thus according to Henry V's Mantes Orders those who broke the Constable's safe-conducts were to be punished with death, but those who broke the King's were to be hanged and drawn.[1] These last were the penalties of treason, and breach of the King's safe-conduct could easily be construed as such because it injured his honour and majesty.[2] It was judged to be a treason in the famous case of the murder of the Genoese ambassador, in the English Parliament in 1380,[3] and was declared a High Treason by the Statute of Truces in 1415.[4] But the crime was of such frequent occurrence, and extenuating circumstances (as that the accused had himself been plundered under safe-conduct) were so usual, that the law was seldom rigorously enforced. On the French side, in such cases as we know of, imprisonment or a fine were more frequently the punishment than death.[5] When so many ingenious pleas could be used to impugn the validity of safe-conducts, this final penalty was obviously too severe.

### III

A truce and a safe-conduct are, says Upton, very much the same thing.[6] As far as law is concerned, he is right. The main

---

[1] Mantes Orders, §22 (*Black Book of the Admiralty*, R.S., Vol. I, p. 466).

[2] Cf. Upton, *De Officio Militari*, Lib. II, cap. 13 (Bysshe, p. 89): 'nunc quero de qua pena punietur qui frangit talem securitatem? . . . alii . . . volunt quod puniri debent pena lese majestatis . . . sed dicendum est credo quod talis pena sit in arbitrio judicis supremi illam securitatem concedentis'.

[3] *Rot. Parl.*, III, p. 75.    [4] 2 Hen. V, Stat. 1, c. 6.

[5] Damages and imprisonment were for example the penalties imposed on those responsible for the spoliation of John Berkeley in 1387 (see p. 205, n. 2 *ante*); damages alone were awarded in the case of Jean le Galois *v.* Jean de Ploisy (Arch. Nat., X¹a 14, fo. 435).

[6] Upton, *De Officio Militari*, Lib. II, ch. 13 (Bysshe, p. 90): 'et nota quod ista securitas multum assimilatur treuge'.

difference between the two was that, whereas a safe-conduct secured a person against war, a truce put a whole area, possibly even a whole country, in security.

A truce was not a peace, but an interlude in war. 'When a truce comes to an end', says Martin of Lodi, 'we do not say that there is a new war, but that the old one continues.'[1] Baldus is of the same opinion: 'if a truce is made even for one day', he says, 'then the war sleeps, and neither side may make any changes in its dispositions'.[2] This is perhaps the most striking fact about a medieval truce: it was not an intermission so much as an absolute suspension of war. During a truce no one was permitted to build new forts, or even to repair old ones, let alone move troops, within an agreed distance of the frontier. Indeed in 1340 the English and French were so anxious to preserve the *status quo* of the day on which the truce was made, that they agreed that wherever places were under siege, seven men from each side should be chosen to take stock of the garrison's supplies and muster the men, 'to the end that, on the day of the ceasing of this truce, the said towns, castles and strongholds . . . be set in such store of victuals and men as they shall be found by the said fourteen persons'.[3] Such meticulousness was rather exceptional, but the principle involved was a firm one, as witness the stream of French complaints a hundred years later, in the 1440s, at the English refortification of St. Jacques de Beuvron.[4] Behind the principle we discern the medieval idea of war as being a kind of lawsuit; if the case be

---

[1] Martin of Lodi, *Tractatus de Bello*, quaest. XXIX (Zilletus, *Tractatus Juris Universi*, Tome XVI, fo. 324vo): compare Baldus, *Comment. in Decretal.*, Lib. I, Tit. 34, *rubr*: 'finita treuga videtur tacite actum, quod remaneant in guerra'.

[2] Baldus, *Comment. in Decretal.*, Lib. II, Tit. 24, cap. 29.

[3] *Chronicon Henrici Knighton*, R.S., Vol. II, p. 21 et deq. The French text of the truce is given by R. Avesbury, *De Gestis Mirabilibus Regis Edwardi III*, ed. E. Maunde Thompson R.S., 1889, p. 319. Similar conditions were stipulated in the truce of 1343, cf. Avesbury, p. 347.

[4] J. Stephenson, *Letters and Papers Illustrative of the Wars of the English in France*, R.S., 1861, Vol. I, pp. 211–12, 233, 245, and *Chronique de Mathieu d'Escouchy*, ed. G. du Fresne de Beaucourt, Tome III (Preuves), pp. 226, 227, 232, 236, 245. Compare the demand made to the Scots in 1405 that the 'castra et fortalicia, contra formam treugarum hujusmodi facta seu reparata' be destroyed (Rymer, Vol. IV, pt. I, p. 77).

adjourned, it should reopen at just that point where previously
the advocates closed their debate.[1]

While the war was thus suspended, the land in which the
truces operated was strictly neutral ground. The description
usually given is that it was *hors de guerre*, for the word neutral
was seldom used in the middle ages. The idea of neutrality was
not well understood; indeed it could not be, as long as the
decision to fight in a war was regarded as a private rather than
a public one. But in one sense at least a truce did establish a
genuine neutrality: within the area where a truce ran acts of
war done elsewhere had no standing. It was dangerous to take
prisoners or spoil there, because one might thereby lose one's
right in them. Thus Henry VI's councillors in 1427 claimed that
prisoners taken by a Spaniard off the Irish coast and landed in
Scotland, which was in truce, should be freed without ransom.[2]
For the same reason, Odinet de Beuderet in 1444 was unwilling
to land wounded Englishmen at Boulogne 'because he did not
know whether those of Boulogne were in the war against the
English, and feared he might thus lose his prisoners'.[3] Legally,
this principle had solid foundation, because a man who took
spoils of war to any place which was in truce had clearly not
brought them *intra praesidia*, which, as was seen earlier, he had
to do to make good his right.[4] In effect he was taking unfair

[1] Plenty of further examples can be given of the condition that forts be
not repaired, reinforced or built during a truce. See for example Rymer,
Vol. III, pt. III, p. 30 (truce of 1375); ibid., p. 32 (St. Sauveur codicil,
ordering that conditions there be kept as on the day truce was cried); ibid.,
Vol. III, pt. IV, p. 29 (truce for Aquitaine, 1388); ibid., p. 117 (truce of
1396, which stipulates no repairs, etc. within seven leagues of an enemy
strongpoint); ibid., Vol. IV, pt. I, p. 124 (Guyenne truce of 1407, repeating
seven league condition); ibid., Vol. IV, pt. II, pp. 63–4 (truce of 1414).

[2] Rymer, Vol. IV, pt. IV, p. 131. Compare Richard Aston's letter from
Calais, 22 November 1405, demanding that during the truce the Flemings
should be obliged to restore all spoils 'amenez en aucuns des portes de
Flandres . . . ou mys a terre' (Arch. Dep. du Nord, B 18823, fo. 65).

[3] Case of Odinet de Beuderet *v.* Jacques de Villars and Jean Lause
captain and lieutenant of Boulogne (28 January 1445). Odinet took his
prisoners at sea, and then sailed near to Boulogne, where 'le dit Villars
manda a Odinet que mieulx seroit en la ville, et ses prisonniers. Odinet lui
dist que en faisoit doubte, car il ne savoit se ceulx de Boulogne estoient *de
guerre* avec les anglais, et par ce ne feust empesche en ses prisonniers'.
(Arch. Nat., X¹a 4800, fo. 230.)

[4] See *ante*, ch. IX, p. 143.

advantage of aids other than those of lawful war to secure spoils taken by the right of war, and so his title to them could be questioned.

Apart from these two special aspects—the suspension of war in the *status quo* and the neutrality of the soil—a truce gave a security very similar to that given by a safe-conduct, except that it had wider application. For this reason, higher authority was needed to make a truce. A truce, says Bonet, is a 'royal surety'.[1] An ordinary captain in the king's pay could not, therefore, make a truce in the proper sense; this required the authority of a *chief de guerre*.[2] Such at any rate was the opinion of the heralds, the known experts in the law of arms. *Chief de guerre* implied roughly a rank equivalent to that of a king's lieutenant. Others who from time to time made truces locally (as for instance the Wardens of the Scottish March) needed specific grant of powers in order to do so. The only point where there was room for serious debate was over the right of powerful feudal lords to make truces. By the middle of the fifteenth century the fact that he had made truces with the English without the king's permission could be urged as a treason against the Count of Armagnac.[3] This however was a sign of the changing times: in earlier days great lords had freely made their own truces with enemies both private and public.[4]

Like safe-conducts, truces could be either general or particular. A general truce, like a *saufconduit de grace*, bound all the subjects of the princes who made it, and all those who fought in their name (though there was some doubt as to how far it covered private rancours, which had previously been pursued

---

[1] Bonet, *Tree of Battles*, pt. 4, ch. 103 (Coopland's translation, p. 189).

[2] Cf. Martin of Lodi, *Tractatus de Bello*, quaest. VIII (Zilletus, *Tractatus Juris Universi*, fo. 324).

[3] Cf. Armagnac's letters of remission from Charles VII, August 1445, which mentions, among his treasonable acts, that he had made truces with the English 'sans avoir de nous congie et licence'. (*Chronique de Mathieu d'Escouchy*, ed. G. Du Fresne de Beaucourt, Paris, 1865, Tome III, p. 129.)

[4] See for example the truce of William Douglas with Humphrey de Bohun, Easter 1356 (Rymer, Vol. III, pt. I, p. 122); of Armand Amanieu d'Albret with John Neville, King's lieutenant in Aquitaine, 22 June 1380 (Bib. Nat., Collection Doat, Tome 201, fo. 5 et seq.); of Armand Amanieu and Berard d'Albret with the Lord of Duras, 5 August 1388 (Bib. Nat., Collection Doat, Tome 203, fo. 257), etc.

under cover of the main quarrel).[1] A particular truce only covered a certain given area, and might even be limited to protect only a certain kind of person; many of the English truces with Flanders, for instance, were *trèves marchandes*, giving security to merchants but not suspending military operations.[2] In this case only genuine merchandise was secured by the truce; military supplies were lawful prize, in the same way that goods not expressly mentioned in a safe-conduct were.[3] Other conditions similar to those of safe-conducts were often specified in truces; as that persons entering strong towns must notify their captains, or that travellers under its security should only carry personal weapons.[4] Most important of all, a particular truce, like a safe-conduct of war, bound only those under the authority of the commander who made it. Thus when Jean de Melun objected to his ransom on the ground that he was taken in time of truce, Henry Pomfret answered that he was not bound by the truce in question, because he was not under the command of Henry of Lancaster, who made it.[5] To avoid problems of this kind, when the French and Burgundians made their truces in the 1420s and 1430s, the latter found it expedient to circularise captains who were fighting indiscriminately for them and the English, to ask if they wished to be included.[6]

[1] Cf. Martin of Lodi, *Tractatus de Confederatione, Pace, et Conventionibus Principum*, quaest. LXIII: 'qui promisit pro suis adherentibus, intelligitur promittere occasione guerrae, non autem pro inimicis singularium personarum hominis ad hominem'. (Zilletus, *Tractatus Juris Universi*, Tome XVI, fo. 303.)

[2] See for example the terms of the truces between England and Flanders of 1370 (Rymer, Vol. III, pt. II, p. 172), and 1408 (ibid., Vol. IV, pt. I, pp. 133–4). The second of these truces was not for merchants only, but was to hold good for them even if war broke out again.

[3] See the terms of the truce of 1370, *ut supra*.

[4] Limitations such as these are very frequent. See for example the conditions of the truce between England and France of 1375 (Rymer, Vol. III, pt. III, p. 30); of the truce for Guyenne of 1407 (ibid., Vol. IV, pt. I, p. 124), of France and England in 1414 (ibid., Vol. IV, pt. II, pp. 63–4), etc.

[5] Pomfret v. Melun, *cit. ante*: argument of Pomfret: 'n'y avoient treues sinon ceux que le duc de Loncastre de luy et de ses gens qui ne porroient lier Henry ne ses compagnons qui guerroyoient pour le Roy d'Angleterre'.

[6] Cf. for example Arch. Dep. de la Côte d'Or, B 11942, nos. 172 and 202 (letters of the Council at Dijon to various captains asking them if they wish to be in the truce, January 1432). Complicated problems could arise over this question of inclusion, cf. for example the letter of Chateauvillain of

For if a truce did not bind a man personally, or if its conditions were broken, spoil could be taken as in war, since it was a condition of war, not of peace.[1]

Again as in the case of safe-conducts, the ultimate guarantee of a truce was the personal promise of the prince who made it, or of his proctors for him. 'To the keeping of this truce we oblige all our goods', wrote John Neville, the king's lieutenant in Aquitaine in 1380, 'and it is our will that we be bound to uphold it before all judges, secular or ecclesiastical, and that [if it is broken] we be held traitors to our faith, and we renounce in particular all rights by which we might seek to avoid responsibility for repairing damage done [while it lasts].'[2] This is a promise on knightly honour, of the same kind that a man made when he promised to pay a ransom, or gave security to an individual. As in that case, any attempt against the truce was an injury to him personally, and to his honour. When Philippe de Ternant, a companion of the Golden Fleece, infringed the truces with England in or about 1448, it was therefore before the chapter of the Order that he was called to account, because by breaking them he had injured the honour of its sovereign, the Duke of Burgundy.[3] The same attitude can be seen reflected in the personal guarantee of Anglo-French truces in the 1350s, which provided that, in case of major breaches, certain great lords of either party were to put themselves prisoners in the hands of the enemy.[4]

[1] Cf. for example the letter of the Abbot of Vézelay to the Council of Burgundy at Dijon, 1 June 1431, in which he mentions that it will be difficult to obtain restitution of prisoners taken by Pierre de Morimont, when the love-day is held at Montbéliart, because Pierre was not in the truce (Arch. Dep. de la Côte d'Or, B 11942, no. 121).

[2] Bib. Nat., Collection Doat, Tome 201, fos. 11vo–12.

[3] Régistres de la Toison d'Or, i, fo. 34vo (chapter of 1451). As Philip had already been imprisoned by the Duke, he was allowed to earn full pardon by a pilgrimage to Compostella.

[4] E.g. the truces of 1353 (Rymer, Vol. III, pt. I, p. 83), and of 1354 (ibid., Vol. III, pt. I, p. 95). The guarantors for the English in 1353 were the Earls of Lancaster and Arundel, and for the French the counts of Angoulême and Montfort; in 1354 Bartholomew Burghersh was added for the English, and Robert de Lorris for the French.

---

22 February 1432, including himself in the Franco-Burgundian truce, but reserving the right to 'faire guerre aux ennemis de sa personne' (Plancher, *Histoire de Bourgogne*, Tome IV, Preuves, p. cxi).

The personal nature of a truce is also emphasised by the fact that it only covered one quarrel at a time, that of the principals to the agreement.[1] This is well illustrated by the terms of the truce agreed between the lords of Duras and d'Albret in 1388. Armand Amanieu d'Albret and his allies promised that if, on any *chevauchée* they made with the people of their sovereign, the King of France, any goods of the Lord of Duras were taken or any of his men made prisoner, they would restore them. At the same time, they were free to take spoil as they pleased from any other person of the English party.[2] Private truces of this kind were particularly a common feature of war in those areas where feudal provincialism died hardest, as in southern France and the Rhineland, for in these parts personal and family quarrels were heavily involved in the general war.[3] But the same sort of facts complicated the maintenance of truces elsewhere too. We have seen already how the companies in northern France fought sometimes in the name of England and sometimes of Navarre, and how the Norman privateers broke the truces in Henry IV's time under the avowal of the King of Scotland.[4]

Matters were further complicated because the legal principles which were generally accepted as governing the maintenance of truces, often did not materially assist in preventing breaches. A truce was an agreement with an enemy, and it was therefore guaranteed by the acknowledged principle that contracts were binding, even with an enemy. Equally acknowledged, however, was the principle that sworn contracts were not binding on the one party if the other broke its word.[5] This principle posed serious problems in an age when the idea that acts of war had a public nature was at best half understood, because truces, unfortunately, were usually broken not by parties collectively but by individuals. A third legal principle confused the issue still further, that public agreements, such as truces were, could not

[1] Cf. Martin of Lodi, *cit. ante*, p. 210, n. 1

[2] Bib. Nat., Collection Doat, Tome 203, fo. 257 et seq.

[3] Cf. the remarks of the Seigneur de Chateauvillain, *cit ante*, p. 210, n. 6. The quarrels of the families of Vergy and Chateauvillain caused great difficulties to the Burgundians over the keeping of the truces in the early 1430s.

[4] See *ante*, ch. VII, p. 114, n. 5

[5] Cf. Baldus, *Comment. in Decretal.*, Lib. II, Tit. 24, cap. 29: 'fides etiam firmata servanda non est ei qui frangit fidem'.

prejudice the rights of private persons.[1] The three-pronged legal problem which resulted may be stated roughly as follows. If X plunders Y in time of truce, is X responsible personally, or is his party collectively liable? And if X personally is responsible, have Y's party any right to prevent Y taking reprisals, because they have pledged their faith to uphold the truce? And if, because public agreements cannot prejudice individuals' rights, they cannot prevent Y doing so, can one say that such a public agreement as a truce has any meaning at all?

The first of these questions is discussed by Baldus, who comes to two conclusions. Firstly, he decides that if an individual breaks a truce, then the others of his party are still bound by it. The opposing party, he however goes on to say, are no longer bound towards the individual offender, and may lawfully take reprisals against him.[2] In practice, there was obvious difficulty in containing reprisals which were to be taken against a single individual; what was actually done, therefore, was to license reprisals against the offender's party, for the recovery of damages equivalent to those he had inflicted. Such action was not merely lawful; unless men were prepared to compensate the injured individual out of public funds, his party was *bound* to take such reprisals if restitution was not made.[3] By doing so, however, they in turn injured other innocent individuals, and

[1] Cf. Martin of Lodi, *Tractatus de Confederatione, Pace et Conventionibus Principum*, quaest. I: 'quando fit pax et remissio damnorum inter principes, non intelligitur in prejudicium privatorum', (Zilletus, *Tractatus Juris Universi*, Tome XVI, fo. 302.)

[2] Baldus, *Comment. in Decretal.*, Lib. II, Tit. 24, cap. 29. The terms of the truce of Bourbon Lancy, 6 December 1427, between France and Burgundy, show this principle applied in practice: 'le conservateur desdites abstinences . . . sommera et requerra . . . celui qui aura faicte la dite enfraincte et s'il ne le repare, celui qui sera enfrainct et dommagie pourra par toutes manieres a luy possible et que bonnes luy sembleront recouvrer sa place sans que ceulx du parti contraire puissent ne doivent aidier, conforter et secourir le rompeur et infracteur'. (Bib. Nat., Collection de Bourgogne, Tome 99, fo. 235.) See also ch. XII *infra*, p. 236, n. 1.

[3] Cf. clause in the truce between Armand Amanieu d'Albret and the Lord of Duras (*cit. ante*, p. 212, n. 2): 'nos avant dut Armand Amanieu et Berard de Labrit . . . em tenguts de prendre merqua en lo quaus que a nous avan dit Arnaud Amanieu et Berard de Labrit ne fos (los domnatges) restitut dedens oeyt joins'. Compare the similar clause in the truce between Henry VI and the Lord of Pons in 1426 (P.R.O., C61/122, m. 6). In the case of a general truce, a longer respite than eight days would of course be given.

thus began a chain reaction of reprisals and counter-reprisals, as a result of which the parties to the truce were driven inevitably towards the renewal of open war.

This brings us back to our third question; can one, given these principles, claim that a truce had any real meaning at all? Once again, it is Baldus who gives the clue to the correct answer. A truce is not void in law, he says, because of minor infringements; it becomes void only when it is broken on such a scale and in such a way as to be irreparable.[1] In practice this line could be hard to draw. Roughly speaking, however, a truce was reparable when only individuals were injured by its infringement, but public and flagrant breaches of a truce, such as the escalade of towns (that of Fougères is a good example) gave the injured party the right to abjure it.[2] This distinction is well illustrated by the terms on which the English and French warrantors stood surety for the truce of 1354. They pledged their honour to its maintenance, and if either side broke the truce its sureties were bound to surrender themselves prisoners to the other. But they were only bound to do this if the truce was really broken, if towns were taken or armies clashed in the field.[3] Their honour was pledged to the keeping of the whole truce; and, since the injuries done by individuals to individuals did not make it void, they were not to be held responsible for them.

No medieval truce was ever properly observed, and, as the foregoing indicates, no one expected it to be. The true guide to the effectiveness of truces is not, therefore, the success of the

[1] Baldus, *Comment. in Decretal.*, Lib. I, Tit. 34, *rubr*: 'non tamen intelligo eam ruptam pro qualibet occasione, sed per magnam et evidentem'.

[2] The distinction is made firmly in a letter of the English ambassadors to the French in 1405, comparing St. Pol's attacks on the English coast with their minor infractions of the truce: 'cum primum non sit reparabile . . . ac faciliter potest inducere occasione infracturae treugarum; secundum enim est reparabile juxta formam treugarum' (B. Mus., Add. ch. 12507).

[3] See p. 211, n. 4 *ante*. The kind of offences which would constitute a major breach are thus listed: 'prise de chastel ou forteresse, ou de ville, ou d'aucune notable parsone, clerc ou autre, qui eit mille livres turnois de rente ou de terre'. The warranty was quite effective; cf. order, 15 January 1355, to Roger Beauchamp, Captain of Calais, to arrest John Danseye, who took and burnt the bastide of Guynes in breach of the truce, 'per quod dilecti consanguinei et fideles nostri Henricus Dux Lancastrie et Ricardus Comes Arundellie sunt graviter impetiti' (Rymer, Vol. III, pt. I, p. 111).

parties to them in keeping the peace, but the efforts which they
made to repair the breaches which were always committed.
Breaches of a truce were considered at periodic love-days, when
representatives of the sides involved met on or near their borders.
These representatives might be either commissioners or conservators of the truce, the difference being (roughly speaking,
for their functions often overlapped) that a conservator was a
judge, and therefore concerned with the suits of individuals,
whereas a commissioner was a diplomatic agent, concerned with
the public liabilities of his party. The nature and limits of the
jurisdiction of conservators of truces have been discussed in an
earlier chapter.[1] Commissioners went about their business in a
different way. They arrived at their meeting with lists of the
breaches of the truce alleged by their party,[2] which were then
read over, and each charge was discussed.[3] If the other party's
commissioners denied the charge, it would have to be set aside
for a special enquiry, or else turned over for the conservators to
judge between the individuals involved.[4] If it was admitted,
reparation was due, unless reprisals had been taken. In that
case, if persons had been made prisoner, both sides must release

[1] See *ante*, ch. III.

[2] In the inventory of the articles to be taken by the Burgundian commission to the love-day at Rheims in 1445 is mentioned 'ung livre ou sont
escriptes les informacions faictes sur les domaiges et ranconnemens faiz es
terres de Faucougney et de Luxeu depuis la traitie' (Arch. dep. de la Côte
d'Or, B 11906). The list survives separately, a *cahier* of 124 fos. (ibid.,
B 11881). A good many other such lists survive, e.g. ibid., B 11880 (list of
excesses of the garrison of Montigny 1425–6); ibid., B 11882 (list of excesses
of the *écorcheurs* in Rethelois, 1445); see also A. Tuetey, *Les Écorcheurs sous
Charles VII* (Montbeliart, 1874), Tome I, pp. 84–93; and H. de Flamare,
*Le Nivernais pendant la Guerre de Cent Ans*, Tome II, no. CXCIII.

[3] For a good account of such proceedings, see the record of those taken
by the English and French commissioners in 1402 (Arch. Nat., J 645ᴬ, no.
18), in which individual charges are listed and answers given. Another
excellent record is that of the meeting of the commissioners of Burgundy
and Savoy on 8 November 1420, which gives details of the enquiries made
as a result of the infractions alleged, and of the compensation paid (Plancher,
*Histoire de Bourgogne*, Tome IV, Preuves, pp. VII–X).

[4] See for example the arrangements made by the English and French
commissioners in 1402: 'vero que tunc propter debatum seu controversiam
partium reparari non poterunt . . . que in terra facta sunt coram con-
servatoribus treugarum utriusque partis . . . remittentur'. (Arch. Nat.,
J 645, no. 19.)

them without ransom:[1] if goods only were involved, reparation was due only for damage in excess of the reprisals. Responsibility for recovering the prisoners from their captors and making up the excess damage was the collective liability of the offending side. It was the business of their internal authorities to track down and punish those who had infringed the truce, and to compensate those damaged. These last could also take action against those, for whose offences they had been plundered, in their domestic courts.[2]

Commissioners normally had powers to quash all preceding letters of marque, and, when necessary, to renew the truces. Thus their meeting put some brake on the cumulative effect of reprisals and counter-reprisals.[3] In addition, this diplomatic method of repairing truces had the advantage of making responsibility for the compensation of injured individuals a domestic and internal one, which made it a much easier task to supervise. It would be rash, however, to suppose that commissioners often achieved very much. When one reads records of their debates what one is most struck by are the endless evasions. 'This was done before the truce', the commissioners answer to one charge; another they seek to avoid because the plaintiffs have given insufficient evidence; yet another, they say, is denied by the men accused of breaking the truce, who have offered to prove their innocence and must go before the conservators.[4]

---

[1] Cf. for example John the Fearless' letter to his commissioners concerning the release of six English fishermen without ransom, in order to obtain release of six fishers of Dunkirk taken in reprisal. The precise balance of reprisal and offence is noteworthy (Arch. dep. du Nord, B 18824, fos. 184 and 194, *anno* 1404 or ? 1405).

[2] Cf. case of Reginald of Pons *v.* Jean de Beaufort (December 1412). Reginald was conservator of truces; Jean during the truce took prisoner the Bourg de Campaigne, of English allegiance, and reprisals were taken, for which Reginald was held responsible. He therefore sued Jean, successfully (Arch. Nat., X²a 16, fo. 222).

[3] Cf. Henry V's statute regulating marque, which guarantees this remedy for all injuries, where such action has *not* been banned by an agreement that all preceding marque shall be abolished (4 Henry V, Stat. 2, c. 6). It was a normal condition of truces, especially at their renewal, that all marque should cease.

[4] These examples are all chosen from among those given by the English commissioners in reply to the French charges in 1402 (Arch. Nat., J 645ᴬ, no. 18).

Breaches of truce were so common, and seemed so venial, that most commissioners were inclined to take more care to defend the individuals of their party who were accused of infringing them, than to indemnify injured aliens. Public envoys that they were, they still saw the whole business in terms of individuals' rights and injuries. Their efforts may have been a little more effective than those of conservators, whom plaintiffs of the opposing side were very often simply unable to find. But they were not effective enough to prevent almost all truces miscarrying in the end, as a result of cumulative infringements.

The fact of the matter is that all forms of security against war (with the exception of the immunity of heralds) were pretty ineffective. Partly this was due to the general unscrupulousness of soldiers, but the trouble was not really so much that they had no respect for law, but that the laws were inadequate to achieve their purpose. It was all too easy to observe them in the letter and break them in spirit. The laws were aimed at controlling and protecting the rights of individuals in limited individual quarrels, but the Hundred Years War was becoming, more and more clearly as time went on, a war of nations which was all but total. In these circumstances, the emphasis of the law on private and personal obligations merely made it easy to evade. It was too simple for the soldier to claim that he personally was not bound by a truce or a safe-conduct, or that he was justified in breaking them to avenge a personal wrong. He thus had plentiful excuses to infringe immunities, and the private rights which he could thus acquire in spoil gave him every inducement to do so. The law of arms was too old-fashioned, its rules too concerned with private rights and duties. Things were changing fast in the time of the Hundred Years War; young nation states were growing up steadily within the framework of an older society, whose bonds were personal rather than national. The idea of the chivalrous soldier was a heritage of this earlier, more individualist order of things. This meant that his law, the law of arms, could still give very adequate protection to the rights of individuals in the spoils of war. It left too much, however, to the individual to give effective sanction to security granted under public authority.

## XII

# LETTERS OF MARQUE AND
# DEFIANCE

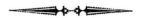

T HE discussion of truces inevitably brings up the subject of reprisals, or marque. Reprisals were the very antithesis of truces, for they legalised acts of war in time of security. Their object, as has been seen, was to obtain compensation for injuries or hostile acts, done by aliens who could not be brought to justice. They could only be licensed in cases where for one reason or another legal redress could not be obtained. They could be levied on account of any injury to the right of an individual; to obtain compensation for spoliation or because he had been taken prisoner, or even to recover a debt. In particular they were often granted on account of breaches of a truce, which were too minor to justify repudiation of the truce itself, but as a result of which individuals had suffered loss. They thus enabled these men to obtain compensation by force, without breaking the truce and plunging all and sundry into the horrors of general war. They licensed a sort of limited war, to recover goods, chattels, or persons to the value of the loss originally sustained. Reprisals therefore permitted the taking of spoil, but only in payment as it were of a specific debt, not as gains of war proper.[1]

Reprisals were a very important remedy in an age when pillage and piracy were common. A full review of the subject

---

[1] Cf. Baldus, *Comment. in Decretal.*, Lib. II, Tit. 28, cap. lv: 'Represalie autem vocantur pignorationes, quae extenuant sortem . . . sed bella appellantur depraedationes. . . . et non extenuant quicquam debitam, sed lucra fiunt'.

would demand far fuller treatment than can be given in a single chapter, and it would not be the rules of the law of arms only that would have to be considered, but also those of the law merchant and the law of the sea. Here, however, we are concerned only with the use of reprisals in warfare on land, and this limits the nature both of enquiries and of conclusions. It will be wise to make it clear at the very beginning what limitations are involved, as otherwise it may appear that too much is being claimed. On the high seas, piracy may occur almost anywhere; on land, however, unauthorised pillage is most likely to take place in certain special areas, where, in our period, rather exceptional conditions prevailed; that is, in disputed frontier lands. Here local lords and commanders habitually acted (as indeed they had to) with greater independence than was permitted to their fellows in other places. It must be stressed that what is said here of them should be taken as applying to them only, and not to their fellows in other places, whose problems (and in particular the problem of their relations with their sovereigns) were rather different. Because we are dealing with these particular people, a further difficulty arises. Frontiers were disorderly places, and systematic records of doings on them were seldom kept. A number of the documents which are used in this chapter came to hand quite by chance, and it is therefore impossible to produce full supporting evidence for some of its conclusions.

In broad outline, however, the law regarding reprisals is not hard to establish. There is a very full legal literature on the subject.[1] Easily the most important single work on the subject is Bartolus's *Treatise of Reprisals*, which is the ultimate source of most that other writers, such as Bonet, John of Legnano, and Nicholas Upton, have to say of them.[2] The first point which Bartolus emphasises is that reprisals, because they involve the use of force, constitute a desperate remedy, only to be employed

[1] Printed in Bartolus, *Commentaria in Jura*, Basle edn., Tome 5, pp. 593 et seq.

[2] See Bonet, *Tree of Battles*, pt. 4, chs. 79–90, 98–9 (Coopland's translation, pp. 173–82, 187); John of Legnano, *Tractatus de Bello*, pt. 5 (Holland's edn., pp. 155–74); Nicholas Upton, *De Officio Militari*, Lib. II, chs. XIII and XIV (Bysshe, pp. 91–6). Among other writers who deal with the question, the most notable are Baldus and Jacobus de Bellovisio, to whose commentary Bartolus and John of Legnano both refer.

when all other means of obtaining justice have failed.[1] Every legal channel must have been tried, and every court of appeal must have had its chance to settle the case peaceably before they can be granted.[2] From this it follows that reprisals can only be granted by a judge whose jurisdiction is final—that is, by a prince who has no superior.[3] The same conclusion follows also from the fact that the laws which permit reprisals are the *jus divinum* and the *jus gentium*, the same laws which permit public war.[4] For only such a war, waged on the authority of a prince, will permit the taking of spoil, and reprisals likewise involve the spoliation of innocent persons.[5]

For just this reason, Bartolus is at pains to labour the safeguards against irresponsible grants of reprisal. He is well aware of the very real danger, that if reprisals are granted on inadequate grounds, those injured will resort to similar means to recover their losses.[6] He therefore lays down a careful procedure to be followed in cases where reprisals are requested. First, the injured individual ought to seek redress from a judge with authority over the man who injured him.[7] If he does not get it, he must have recourse to his own sovereign lord. This sovereign will then inspect the evidence presented to him, and if he is satisfied that injustice has really been done, he in turn will demand redress in a legal manner.[8] The accused parties

---

[1] Bartolus, *Tractatus de Represaliis*, quaest. II, ad IV. He says reprisals are 'odious'.

[2] Bartolus, *Tractatus*, quaest. II, ad III: and also Upton, *De Officio Militari*, Lib. II, ch. XIII (Bysshe, p. 91).

[3] Bartolus, *Tractatus*, quaest. III, ad II: 'ex parte concedentis repraesalias, requiritur quod sit talis qui superiorem non habet'.

[4] Ibid., quaest. III, ad I: 'rationes et jura quae ad hoc cogunt, sunt magis de jure divino et de jure gentium, quo bella licita permittuntur, quam de jure civili'.

[5] Bartolus, *Tractatus*, quaest. VI, ad IV: 'in illo bello etiam innocentes capiuntur'.

[6] Ibid., quaest, IV, ad I: 'sed periculum est, quia gens illa contra quam fit haec concessio poterit eodem jure uti contra concedentes'.

[7] Ibid., quaest, II, ad III. Bartolus throughout labours that the only justification for reprisals is the 'delictum domini negligentis facere justitiam'. This delict cannot be established unless application has been made to the lord for justice.

[8] Ibid., quaest. IV, ad I. Because he is a sovereign, Bartolus says, the man who grants reprisals need not proceed formally ('cum omnia in potestate concedentis'), but he believes formal procedure to be advisable:

must also, if possible, be given an opportunity to state their defence.[1] If, and only if, after all this justice is still denied, the sovereign is bound to license reprisals on behalf of his subject. The loss is then to be recovered from the subjects of the lord whose judge has failed to do justice.

This is, in fact, precisely the manner in which reprisals or letters of marque were sought and granted in France and England in the later middle ages. In England the procedure was regulated by statute in the fourth year of Henry V.[2] The plaintiff had first to submit his claim, and when this had been considered, letters were issued under the Privy Seal, requesting justice from the overlord of the man who had done the injury. If this was refused, letters of marque were then issued by the Chancellor, under the Great Seal. In France requests for grants of reprisals were judged in the Parlement. The plaintiff appeared and gave his case and, if it was judged just either letters would be sent to request justice,[3] or the proctors of the nation involved would be summoned to show cause why reprisals should not be taken. If they did not answer, or if their defence was not adequate, letters of marque under the King's seal would be granted.[4] The two commonest defences against a request for

[1] Ibid., quaest. IV, ad I: 'item quod eis, contra quos conceduntur, sit salva defensionis facultas, quod est de jure naturali vel gentium, quod per principem tolli non potest'.

[2] 4 Henry V, Stat. 2, c. 7.

[3] See for example letters of the Parlement, Arch. Nat., X$^1$a 15, fo. 339 (12 July 1354, demanding reparation on behalf of two merchants of Montpellier from the Podesta of Genoa, and threatening reprisals in default); Arch. Nat., X$^1$a 26, fo. 31 vo–32 (28 February 1377, demanding reparation on behalf of three merchants of Abbeville from Ferrand of Portugal, and threatening reprisals), etc. The facts were normally certified before the Parlement, and where the aliens involved did not retain a proctor in the court, letters under the seal of the Parlement were sent demanding justice.

[4] The Parlement registers record a large number of cases, arising out of requests for grants of reprisals. See for instance Arch. Nat., X$^1$a 15, fo. 335 (11 July 1354; marque upheld against Genoese in favour of a merchant of Montpellier); Arch. Nat., X$^1$a 17, fo. 73 (4 September 1361, grant of marque upheld in favour of merchants of Aigues-Mortes against the

---

'tutius est quod processus fiat super hoc, et redigatur in scriptis, ut cesset omnis scrupulositas'. Upton repeats this, more or less verbatim (Bysshe, p. 93).

reprisals were either to deny the facts stated (not a very promis-ing line), or to claim the spoliation in question was a justifiable act of war. In 1348, for instance, the Aragonese proctors claimed that reprisals could not justly be granted to certain merchants of Montpellier, because they had laded the goods pillaged in a ship of Genoa, which was at war with Aragon, and what was taken was therefore lawful spoil.[1] Besides this right of defence, the persons injured by reprisals would of course also have an action in the courts of their own country, against the man whose acts had caused marque to be granted.[2]

Where possible (as was very often the case when merchants had been despoiled) reprisals were taken by putting an arrest on the goods of other merchants of the offending allegiance, which could be seized either at the ports or elsewhere in the land.[3] This was a relatively civil procedure, which involved no true act of war and gave ample room for negotiation both before and after the letters of marque had been issued. An example of such action may be worth quoting to illustrate this point. In the year 1446 Erard Capdorat, the Dauphin's subject and his *Maître d'Hotel*, was passing peaceably through the lands of Philip of Burgundy, when, near Besançon, he and his men were set on, robbed and spoiled by certain subjects of the Duke. As Erard's 'ardent prosecution' of his right failed to obtain any justice in the courts of Burgundy, he took his case to his master, the Dauphin, and was granted letters of marque against the Duke and his subjects. The Duke's council, anxious to avoid the effect of these letters, immediately offered a settlement, which was agreed: but as no cash had been paid at the agreed term (16 October 1446) Erard put his letters into effect, and the

[1] Arch. Nat., X¹a 11, fo. 223vo.

[2] Cf. case of Reginald of Pons v. Jean de Beaufort, 1412, cit. *ante*, ch. XI, p. 216 n. 6.

[3] For some examples of this procedure see *Select Cases in the Law Merchant*, ed. Hubert Hall (Selden Soc.), Vol. I, pp. 94–5; Vol. II, pp. 73–6 and 81–3.

---

Genoese, whose proctor did not appear to defend the case when sum-moned); Arch. Nat., X¹a 17, fo. 82vo (28 June 1361, marque upheld in favour of merchants of Narbonne against the Provencals, whose excuses, sent in writing by their seneschal, were not accepted); Arch. Nat., X¹a 1470, fo. 88vo (June 1373, *plaidoirie* in a case where Castilian merchants were complaining against a grant of marque to Frenchmen), etc.

goods of various Burgundian subjects were seized in Dauphiné. These men, as was to be expected, complained, and once more the Duke's council went into action to obtain a settlement. In the end Erard agreed to accept the sum originally offered (2,000 *écus*, considerably less than his own estimate of his loss), with 400 *livres tournois* thrown in for his expenses. In return for this he promised the Duke a full quittance for all liability.[1]

If Erard's case had been typical, there would be no need now to do more than refer back to Bartolus's treatise. For in this instance all his principles were duly observed; there was first the application by Erard to the courts of Burgundy, followed, in default of justice, by reference to his lord the Dauphin, who examined the case and in the end gave him letters of marque. These were executed with the minimum of violence. True, neither the Dauphin nor the Duke of Burgundy were *de jure* independent sovereigns; they were imperial subjects. But Bartolus is careful to explain that the reason why reprisals are now so common, is that the Empire has fallen on evil days; there is no longer, *de facto*, a single secular ruler to whom recourse may be had in all disputes.[2] Even here therefore there is no real deviation from legal principle. The trouble about Erard's case, as an illustration of current practice, is that it was not typical. Reprisals could indeed provide a useful remedy, as on this occasion they did; but much more usually they simply gave legal cover to an endless series of raids and counter-raids in quest of loot.[3] Such reprisals, moreover, were often taken on the authority of persons whom no stretch of the imagination could describe as sovereigns.

If one reads what the lawyers have to say about reprisals

[1] See copy of the official record of the case, Bib. Nat., Collection de Bourgogne, Tome 23, fo. 114vo.

[2] Bartolus, *Tractatus*, preface. John of Legnano also stresses this point (*Tractatus*, cap. 123).

[3] See ch. XI *ante*. For a good illustration of the kind of situation which could arise, see the Parlement case of Thomas Aymusson *v.* the King's proctor (17 January 1420). During the foregoing truce the Armagnac garrison of Montlhéry had made a raid near Chartres; by way of marque, certain merchants of Orleans were taken prisoner. By way of 'contre-marque' Thomas and certain other merchants of Chartres were imprisoned at Orleans making three raids in series. He was suing to be free of his obligation (Arch. Nat., X¹a 4792, fo. 176).

with care, it begins to be clearer why this unhappy state of affairs came about. One of the first things that strikes one is their obvious discomfort about the legality of reprisals. What worried them was that reprisals caused the innocent to suffer for the guilty. The Church therefore condemned them,[1] and Bonet at least thought it was right to do so. 'On this point', he wrote, 'you must know that this kind of war is by no means permitted, and the law does not allow its exercise; for on this theory one person suffers loss for another, and receives damage and molestation for the deeds of another, which ought not to be, either according to reason or written law'.[2] Even Bartolus admitted that by many standards the right of reprisal appeared to be contrary to natural law.[3] He and others got over the obvious difficulties by looking at the question from another angle—the duty of the community to protect the rights of its individual members.[4] But *in foro conscientiae* they were clearly unhappy about this resolution.

The difficulties which the lawyers encountered in explaining the legality of reprisals arose because of their own premises about the nature of law. Something has been said of these in earlier chapters, but it may be as well to remind ourselves of them. For the legist of the fourteenth or fifteenth century, law was not based in sovereign command; rather it was the expression of certain moral principles which were immutable and eternal, to which the will of the sovereign could give at most (in St. Thomas's words) a *vis coactiva*.[5] The object of law was therefore a higher one than mere social utility; it must be framed to meet the demands of absolute justice. This object implies that there can be no ultimate conflict between social utility and private right, a view which few today would care

---

[1] See the Decretal. Sext., Lib. V, Tit. 8, cap. unic. On the general subject of their condemnation in church law, see R. de Las Matrie, 'Du Droit de Marque', *Biblothèque de l'École de Chartres*, 6th series, Tome II, pp. 544–6.

[2] Bonet, *Tree of Battles*, pt. 4, ch. 79 (Coopland's translation, p. 173).

[3] Bartolus, *Tractatus*, quaest. I, ad I: 'alius pro alio non potest capi: praeterea, non licet in foro conscientiae facere id quod repugnat naturali rationi, sed istae (i.e. repraesalie) naturali rationi repugnant'.

[4] Ibid., quaest. I, ad II: 'ob tutelam unius civis, potest civitas indicere bellum'.

[5] Aquinas, *Summa Theologica*, I 2ae, quaest. 96, Art. 5, ad 3.

to countenance, but much easier to accept in an age when Augustine's interpretation of history was widely received. For him history was the story of the working of the divine purposes of an almighty and rational god. There was no room in this context for any ultimate miscarriage of justice, for, as Bonet put it, *Dieu est vray justicier, et oncques faux jugement ne fist.*[1] As war was therefore to be regarded as an appeal to a judge who was neither human nor fallible, to sacrifice legitimate private interests for the sake of peace was not only wrong, it was pointless. On this basis a very cogent justification, not only for reprisals but also for the feudal right of private war, could be constructed. If injury was to genuine right, to take no step to redress it would be to tolerate, and so tacitly encourage sin.

Attitudes based on these assumptions are clearly behind a great deal of medieval legal thought about truces and reprisals. It is only in the light of a quest for absolute justice that principles such as that of Martin of Lodi, that a treaty cannot bind to the prejudice of private persons, make sense. The same quest makes it clear why the grant of reprisals was not regarded as a discretionary power of the prince, but, in default of justice, as a right of the injured subject.[2] It was as a right or privilege that Henry V promised to give his subjects the remedy of marque in 1417;[3] and we have seen earlier how signatories to truces *bound* themselves to take reprisals if injuries were not amended.[4] To avenge injuries unjustly inflicted was not only a right; it was a positive duty. To quote once more from Bonet, 'The King of France . . . could not refrain from making war on the King of England without mortal sin . . . if he were to allow his men to be killed and pillaged, and his Kingdom robbed and destroyed'.[5]

---

[1] Bonet, *Tree of Battles*, 'interpolation' (Coopland's edition, p. 296).

[2] Cf. Upton, *De Officio Militari*, Lib. II, ch. 13 (Bysshe, p. 91). He is discussing the case of an English merchant plundered of wines by the Bretons, which he resolves thus: 'Tu breviter dic quod dominus Rex Anglie *tenetur* prefato mercatori concedere martam sive represalias post debitas requisitiones factas Duci Britannie pro restitutione'.

[3] 4 Henry V, Stat. 2, c. 7: 'the King . . . hath declared in this present Parliament, that of all attempts made by his enemies upon any of his faithful people, against the tenor of the truces, . . . the same our Sovereign King will grant marque in due form'.

[4] See *ante*, ch. XI, p. 213, n. 3.

[5] Bonet, *Tree of Battles*, pt. 4, ch. 108 (Coopland's translation, p. 192).

On this basis, as has been said, one could justify with equal cogency the right of reprisal, and the feudal right of private war (though not, perhaps, the customary limitation of this right to the nobility). Examination will reveal that these rights were parallel in many ways, and often hard to distinguish. Indeed, in origin they were probably the same. The growth of a distinction between them is of some importance, especially with regard to the problem of controlling infractions of truces. It also illustrates strikingly the gradual change of attitude towards the legal problem of war, which was taking place in the later middle ages. It is with this subject that the remainder of this chapter will be chiefly concerned.

The objects of reprisals and of private war were the same, the protection of the rights of private persons. So, essentially, was their justification, *déni de justice*. They were both classified by the lawyers as species of 'particular war', as opposed to public war. The only difference lay in the authority on which they were levied, reprisals being taken in the name of a prince (a public person), whereas private war was declared by formal defiance in the name of an individual lord. Bartolus, however, introduces a qualification which makes even this difference hard to establish. Reprisals, he says, can only be granted by a prince who has no superior, but this authority may be dispensed with in exceptional circumstances, as when there is urgent necessity for action, or when it is impossible to obtain leave from the sovereign.[1] Very unfortunately, these 'exceptional circumstances' were very nearly the norm in unruly marchlands, which were the very areas where, on land at least, raid and counter-raid were most likely to disturb the peace. The border magnate, or the free soldier fighting in the name of the English king in Auvergne, were just the kind of people who might wish to employ reprisals to redress injuries done them. They were also just the kind of people who were most likely to find their sovereigns hard of access and urgent necessity pressing them. While they dallied, their lands might be being wasted, or their

---

[1] Bartolus, *Tractatus*, quaest. III, ad II. He explains that a 'civitas vel dominus subditus' can take reprisals on their own authority 'propter urgentem necessitatem', or 'quia superioris copia non potest habere'. John of Legnano gives an example, to illustrate the latter point: 'utpote imperator sit valde distans, et pars est pauperimma' (*Tractatus*, cap. 152).

prisoners defaulting on their ransoms. If in these circumstances they took redress on their own authority, how was one to tell whether they were invoking the right of reprisal, or making war on their enemies in their own names?[1]

The cases of a border magnate and a free soldier in Auvergne are here quoted as parallel. It might be thought their situations were different; for how could a free soldier, who was not a feudal nobleman, invoke the feudal nobleman's right of private war? In fact, their cases were not very dissimilar. A captain of free soldiers could call himself, like the nobleman, an independent *chief de guerre*, and because he was a soldier, he had at least a claim to nobility, for the profession of arms was itself noble.[2] In his own right he might have great wealth, for what he won in the way of goods and ransoms was his own. Moreover, the fortunes of war might make him something very like a territorial *seigneur*, because of the forts he won. It could not make him a sovereign, for these forts were in the technical sovereignty of the lord in whose cause he fought, but to all intents and purposes they were his own. He held them at his own cost and to his own profit, and he sold out to the enemy when it suited him.[3] As long as he was ensconced within his fortress, moreover, it was in the manner of a petty *seigneur* that he acted. He and his men lived off the tribute by which the local countrymen bought freedom from pillage, just as the seigneur lived off the dues of his peasants. For free passage through the land he con-

---

[1] There were, of course, technical differences in the layout of a letter of marque and a cartel of defiance. Thus, the hostilities licensed by the Bourg de Béarn in 1383 against St. Flour were clearly marque, as his captain, the Bastard de Garlans, later quashed his letters of 'merca' (M. Boudet, *Régistres Consulaires de St. Flour*, Paris, 1898, Reg. IV, p. 191). Rodrigue de Villandrando in 1427, on the other hand, sent the consuls a 'letra . . . de dezafiament', when his men were injured there (Boudet, *Villandrando et les Écorcheurs à St. Flour*, Paris, 1895, p. 26, n. 2). But these technical differences do not affect the question, how one can fault the defence to a charge of levying unauthorised war, that the relevant acts were no more than reprisals with authority which was legitimate in urgent circumstances.

[2] Cf. the words of the *Jouvencel* in Jean de Beuil's romance: 'nouse pauvres soudoyers . . . sommes de l'estat des nobles, et nobles de lignee la pluspart; et ceux qui ne sont pas nobles de lignee, le sont par exercice et mestier des armes, qu'ils suyvent, qui est noble de soy meme'. (*Le Jouvencel*, ed. Lécestre and Favre, Tome II, pp. 80–1.)

[3] See *ante*, ch. IX.

trolled he sold safe-conducts, much as a *seigneur* might charge tolls. And when the men of neighbouring towns or castles failed to pay their ransoms, or in other ways hindered him in the exercise of his rights, he defied them and enforced these so called rights by arms.

A good many examples of such action could be quoted. Thus, when in 1434 the Burgundian *routier*, Perrinet Gressart, was accused of breaking the truce with France, he excused himself on the ground that his quarrel was a private one, pursued 'under colour of the fact that Barillet had failed to pay his ransom'.[1] Significantly, at least some free captains claimed also the purely 'feudal' right of avenging injury to their family as well as to themselves. 'I have warned the Count of Clermont', Perrinet wrote to the Chancellor of Burgundy in 1427, 'that if men under his command do any harm to my relatives, I will make war with fire and sword in Bourbonnais'.[2] Perrinet's office at La Charité-sur-Loire was that of captain, but he had won the town by his own sword, unaided, and here he was claiming to exercise the

[1] H. de Flamare, *Le Nivernais pendant la Guerre de Cent Ans*, Tome II, no. CXCIX. Plenty of other examples of such private rancours pursued by captains and petty nobles could be quoted: e.g. the private war between Tristan L'Hermite and the men of Chastillon, 1431 (Arch. dep. de la Côte d'Or, B 11942, no. 175); between the people of Bassigny and Etienne de Salins, captain of Choisnel, 1431 (ibid., no. 146); between Guillaume de Flavy, captain of Compiègne, and the town of Noyon (P. Champion, *Guillaume de Flavy*, p. 184; Flavy's raid was nominally in reprisal for the death of a single soldier); between the Seigneur de Chateauvillain and the town of Troyes, 1431 (M. T. Boutiot, *La Guerre des Anglais—Un Chapitre de l'histoire de Troyes*, p. 7). Both these last wars were finally settled for sums down, to avoid further rancour, in much the same way that Erard de Capdorat's letter of marque was surrendered for a settlement; but they were technically levied under cover of letters of *defiance*, not of *marque*.

[2] H. de Flamare, op. cit., Tome I, no. LXV. For a similar example of free soldiers invoking such rights, see A. Tuetey, *Les Écorcheurs sous Charles VII* (Montbéliart, 1861), Tome I, pp. 56–8. He describes how in 1443 a group of *écorcheur* captains were defeated while plundering in Burgundy by the Count of Etampes, who was acting under Burgundy's orders. In reprisal, they attacked Etampe's kinsman, the Count of Nevers, i.e. claimed that their quarrel, like a feudal one, involved not only the principal opponent but his kin as well. The quarrel was made up next year; the captain returned Nevers his town of Clamecy, taken 'soubz couleur et pour avoir recompensacion', and he undertook not to pursue the matter further, 'par voye de droit, de fait, de guerre, de marque' (p. 58, n. 2).

right of a *seigneur*. Different captains gave different names to action such as this. Perrinet called it *contrevengement*; Jean de Vica, a French *routier*, warned the consuls of Millau that if the townsmen he had taken prisoner did not pay ransom, he would take *merca*;[1] others spoke of *défiances*, or *voye de fait*, or *represailles*. In effect, what all alike meant was private war, private in the sense that it was levied to avenge personal injuries. These free soldiers were claiming, under colour of reprisals, the rights of feudal noblemen, and it was as such that they thought of themselves. Witness the titles which, according to Froissart, Geoffrey Tête-Noire used in his safe-conducts: 'Geoffrey Tête-Noire, Duke of Ventadour, Count of Limousin, and sovereign lord of all the companies in Auvergne, Rouergue and Limousin'.[2]

As long as men like Perrinet Gressart and Geoffrey Tête-Noire could claim a legal right to avenge injuries done to them by reprisals levied in their own names, the chances that any truce would be properly kept were slight. Border lords behaved in just the same way as these free soldiers,[3] and the consequences were the same too. We have already seen what these were—how the chaotic tale of marque and counter-marque made it well-nigh impossible to preserve a truce. If reprisal and private war were indistinguishable, and no treaty could bind to the prejudice of a private person, what hope was there of controlling

---

[1] Rouquette, *La Rouergue sous les Anglais*, pp. 331–2. For another instance, see pp. 303–4, where the consuls' messengers were told (1379) by the 'English' companies, that booty taken from the townsmen was 'per merca', and so the truce was not infringed, properly speaking. The account of another similar incident, in the registers of St. Flour for 1382, makes this point explicitly, referring to 'li merqua de Bereta, engles deldit luoc de Salhens, la qual levet durant lodit pati' (M. Boudet, *Régistres Consulaires de St. Flour*, Paris, 1898, Reg. IV, p. 156). The word 'pati' in Languedoc meant 'truce', and the consuls of St. Flour had made a truce with local English *routiers*.

[2] *Oeuvres de Froissart*, ed. Kervyn de Lettenhove, Tome XIII, p. 352.

[3] For a good example, see the letter of William Douglas to the English Council, 1425, printed by Sir H. Nicolas, *Proceedings of the Privy Council*, Vol. III, p. 353. He complained that the men of Robert Tylliol and Thomas Lucy had raided his land, doing damage to the value of £5,000. He himself, he said, had never harmed the English, *except* that his men had 'ascunes foytz' taken goods and chattels by way of redress, i.e. they had taken no action except legitimate reprisal. This shows how venially such reprisals were regarded, but the exception is rather a large one.

the personal and private feuds which threatened the peace of every march?

Happily, although nearly so, marque and feudal war were not quite indistinguishable. The distinction rested on a fine legal definition, not easy to apply in practice: nevertheless, it was there. The essence of reprisals was that they permitted the seizure of the goods or person of one man for the offence of another. '(Ces) choses sont purement et proprement fait de marque', wrote Richard Aston to the Duke of Burgundy in 1404, alluding to French raids on the English coasts, 'comme en executant les innocentz pour le fait des coupables.'[1] Theoretical justice was claimed for such reprisals, on the ground that injured and innocent both were subject to the judge who had refused redress, and so all were party to the crime.[2] The case with feudal war was a little different. It was levied for the same end, to protect the right of an injured individual, but defiance only entitled the defier to take revenge on his opponent personally, or on his relatives and direct dependents. The quarrel was thus more strictly limited than in the case where marque was licensed.

An example may serve to make this point clearer. In 1431, a certain Erart du Chastelet wrote to the Council of Burgundy, complaining that Anthoine de Vergy, a subject of Duke Philip, had raided over his mother's lands and burnt a village. 'And therefore', he wrote, 'if we do similar injury in the time to come to the said Messire Anthoine and his people in Burgundy, I and my brother Philibert would wish to be held excused, as regards my lord of Burgundy and all the rest of his country.'[3] This is a very different story from that of Erard Capdorat, mentioned earlier; when he was robbed, he obtained letters of marque which entitled him to take compensation from *any* subject of

[1] Letter of R. Aston to the Duke of Burgundy, 18 March 1404 (Arch. Dep. du Nord, 18823, fo. 91).

[2] Cf. Bonet, *Tree of Battles*, pt. 4, ch. 80 (Coopland's translation, p. 174); compare Bartolus, *Tractatus*, quaest. I, ad II: 'propter delictum domini negligentis facere justitiam, potest indici (bellum) contra totam terram et omnes gentes subditas sibi'.

[3] Arch. Dep. de la Côte d'Or, B 11942, no. 117. Erart du Chastellet was a subject of René of Anjou, Bar, and Lorraine. He acted for René to conserve the truce with the Count of Vaudemont in 1436–7 (Bib. Nat., Coll. de Lorraine, Tome 8, fo. 18).

Burgundy. Erart du Chastelet, on the other hand, was claiming that if he defied Vergy, their quarrel would be quite private; he was to avenge himself on Vergy only, and though Vergy was a subject of Burgundy, he claimed that he could do this without prejudice to the right of the Duke, Vergy's overlord.

The distinction is a fine one, and in some cases, no doubt, it could be very fine indeed. Nevertheless I believe it is important. In order to see this, we must once again examine the legal principles underlying the different actions involved. In the case of private defiance these are clear. Any injury to the right of an individual (at least if he is of a certain social status) can be a *casus belli*. This means that all rights are assumed to be on a par; it does not matter whether the person injured is the King of England or a petty noble, except in that the King of England has more forces at his disposal to defend his right. But the right in both cases is sacred and absolute; no real distinction is drawn between public and private interests, only between the greater or lesser estate of the man injured.[1] The situation is quite different where action is taken under letters of marque. These are granted on the authority of a prince, and the assumption is, therefore, that it is the business of a prince to defend the interests of the members of the community he represents.[2] This indicates a more sophisticated attitude towards the functions and rights of public authority. How was it, then, that the distinction arose between these two essentially similar forms of action?

This is not an easy question to answer, but some attempt may be made. Originally, in all probability, no difference was discerned at all; the very word 'marque' is said to be derived from 'march', from the marcher's right to avenge his private wrongs by armed force.[3] A number of truces in the thirteenth century actually mention the right of those who had been injured to revenge themselves (*courir sus*) on their enemies.[4] Although by

---

[1] Cf. Bonet, *Tree of Battles*, pt. 4, ch. 16 (Coopland's translation, p. 136): 'according to natural reason a poor man has as much right to avail himself of the help of his own as a rich man has, *for every man is lord of his own*'.

[2] Cf. Bartolus, *Tractatus*, quaest. I, ad II: 'ob tutelam unius civis, potest civitas indicere bellum'.

[3] See E. Nys, *Les Origines du Droit International* (Paris, 1894), p. 71.

[4] Cf. R. de Las Matrie, 'Du Droit de Marque', *Bibliothèque de l'Ecole de Chartes*, 6th series, Tome II (1866), p. 538.

the outbreak of the Hundred Years War, the private right of defiance was being heavily criticised,[1] this view, that it was a valid right, still had some currency. That knights and free soldiers should have held it is perhaps not surprising; authority as high as that of Edward III could, however, still condone it. This is clear from his action when the Duke of Anjou, a hostage for the prisoner King John, broke his parole and escaped from England. His response is thus described in the *Chronicle of the First Four Valois*: 'The said King Edward commanded Sir John Jewel . . . that he should make war in France in his own name as John Jewel; and this was a private war.'[2] The last two words, as rendered in the French of the Chronicle, are *guerre couverte*; a technical term meaning feudal war. Clearly therefore Edward regarded private war as a legitimate means of taking reprisals.

In case it should be thought that the *Chronicle of the First Four Valois* has misinterpreted the facts, another instance may be quoted. On 4 December 1361, Edward wrote to King John, demanding the release of one William Bulmer, who had been arrested in France and imprisoned without trial, because 'he had ridden in arms in the Kingdom of France since the peace was made'. Edward questioned the truth of this charge, but supposing it was true, he said, there should have been enquiry as to whether Bulmer had been making war in order to recover sums outstanding on ransoms due to him, as he had a perfect right to do.[3] As he did not pretend to know whether this was Bulmer's real purpose, the King clearly had issued no letters of marque. Edward was therefore claiming that, although England and France were at peace, Bulmer had a right, if he could not get them to pay by any other method, to distrain French subjects who were his debtors by arms. He was also claiming that such distraint of French subjects was a personal affair between them and Bulmer, which did not affect the rights of the crown of France.

Edward III's claim for Bulmer has plenty of parallels. It was

[1] Especially this is true of the Church's view, but by the mid-fourteenth century the right was severely limited by public authorities in many places; see Nys, *cit. sup.*, p. 79 et seq.

[2] *Chronique des Quatre Premiers Valois*, ed. S. Luce, p. 129.

[3] P. Chaplais, *Some documents regarding the fulfilment and interpretation of the Treaty of Brétigny* (Camden Miscellany, Vol. XIX), p. 22.

basically the same as the claim of Erart du Chastellet, that his quarrel with Vergy did not affect the rights of the Duke of Burgundy, or that of Raymond of Turenne, that his war with Louis of Anjou did not touch the crown of France[1] (although Vergy was a Burgundian subject, and Louis a liegeman of the French king). What makes Bulmer's case striking is that as late as 1361 the legality of action such as his could be openly supported by a prince of the standing of Edward III. Nevertheless, by that time such an attitude was beginning to look old-fashioned. Edward was not prepared to make an issue of the affair, and Bulmer's acts cost him his life. He was executed on the same charge as Mérigot Marchès thirty years later, of levying un-authorised war.[2] In their judges' view, the actions both of Bulmer and Mérigot did touch the crown. It is clear, both from statutes and from trials such as these, that by this time, though it was not regarded as treason to defy a private person, to levy war against the king in his realm was so regarded,[3] for the king was not a private person, but public majesty.

In the late fourteenth century this principle seems to have been being gradually extended. It was no longer the king

[1] Cf. Raymond's letter of 7 July 1393 to Jean de Vienne who had accused him of treason to the King of France, because he had defied the king's kinsman and liegeman Louis of Anjou. This puts the point very clearly: 'Quant a ce que vous dites que les busoignes du Roy de France et du Roy Loys sont toutes unes, je ne le croy pas; car pouse que je suis homs du roy de France, pour ce ne suy je pas tenus de servir son linage se je ne me weul, ne s'ilz m'ont tort que je ne puisse bien demander le mien, ne s'ils m'accomencent guerre que je ne me doye deffendre et ne leur coure sus'. (Terrier de Loray, *Jean de Vienne, Amiral de France*, Paris, 1877, p. CLXXIII.)

[2] So we learn from the remark passed in the Parlement in the case of Mirabel *v.* Hannequin (8 March 1380): 'Boulemer nestoit que pillart et ne pouvoit faire guerre et fu executez pour ses demerites' (Arch. Nat., X¹a 1471, fo. 293). Mérigot's case is discussed in detail, *ante*, ch. VI.

[3] See Edward III's statute of treason, 25 Edward III, Stat. 5, c. 2. The sentence passed on Mérigot Marchès shows that the rule was the same in France: 'a icellui Mérigot, qui n'est pas chief de guerre, le Roy n'a aucune guerre formelle' (Duplès Agier, *Régistre Criminel du Châtelet de Paris*, Tome II, p. 207). This is also clear from John of Vienne's charge against Raymond of Turenne: 'il est bien vray que j'ay dit a aucuns de vos gens qui sont du royaume de France que en tant qu'ilz vous ont servi et servent contre le roy de Jherusalem, . . . attendu que son fait est le fait du Roy de France, mon souverain et le vostre, sont faux, desloaiux et mauvaix' (Terrier de Loray, op. cit., p. CLXXI).

personally who could not be defied by the individual, but also those who stood close to him, his servants and officers. For instance, when in 1396 the dispute between Pierre Craon and Oliver de Clisson was brought before the Parlement, Craon was charged with treason because he had defied Oliver, although he had defied him in his own name as Oliver de Clisson. Clisson's argument was that as Constable of France, a royal officer exercising public power, he bore the king's person, and the man who defied him defied implicitly the king also.[1] Such extension of the definition of *lèse-majesté* made recourse to private war even more dangerous than it had been before. On the other hand, it did not affect the right of marque if this was licensed by a sovereign. In that case he in effect avowed the action of his subject who took marque, and assumed himself the responsibility for the action.

The same point that was made in the Clisson case was made again, and still more clearly, by the ambassadors of Philip the Good at Paris in 1448, when they complained of the letter of defiance that Joachim Rouault, 'soy disant capitaine de gens d'armes pour le roy de France', had sent to the Marshal of Burgundy. The Duke's Marshal, they declared,

> . . . est son lieutenant general, et represente sa personne en fait de guerre, et mesmement ce qu'on veult dire avoire este fait dont icellui Joachim se plaint avoit este fait comme mareschal . . . et consequentement (que) icellui Joachim deffie en effet mon dit seigneur le duc.[2]

Here once more the 'representative' relation between sovereign and subject is stressed. The affair becomes more significant, moreover, when one compares this statement (with its implication, that Joachim was not a man of sufficient status to defy on his own authority the Duke of Burgundy), with the remarks of Philip's ambassadors about another dispute which was discussed on the same occasion. This was the action taken by another French captain, Alabre de Suze, against the Sire des Vaulx.[3] The ambassadors complained about this too, but they did not use the same arguments, because Alabre had letters of

---

[1] Case of Clisson *v.* Craon, December 1395 (Arch. Nat., X²a 12, fo. 320vo et seq.).

[2] Arch. dep. de la Côte d'Or, B 11907.    [3] Ibid.

marque, granted in his favour by Charles VII. Charles was a sovereign, emperor in his realm, and his right to grant such letters to an injured subject was beyond question. Therefore the ambassadors asked merely that the letters of marque be suspended[1], and the matter referred to justice, so that it might be shown that Alabre had no good grounds for his complaint. This matter was handled, therefore, in a quite different manner to the defiance of Joachim Rouault; his was a purely private action, but this had another, and much more impressive authority.

The distinction drawn here is between acts of war which have public, and those which have only personal authorisation. This distinction is carried to its logical conclusion in another statement, made by Philip the Good's representatives a few years later, at the love-day with the Austrians at Montbéliart on 17 November 1454. This is worth quoting in full.

Ja soit que mon dit seigneur (de Bourgogne) soit prince et souverain en son pays du conte de Bourgogne, et a le seignurie et jurisdiction de tous ses subgez, et puissance de les contraindre a faire raison a toultes gens qui leur voldroient aucune chose demander ou quereller, sans que par raison, puis qu'il est souverain comme dit est, nul estranger leur puisse ou doigt faire ne inferer guerre ou voye de fait quelconque; et se l'on fait le contraire, c'est au prejudice de mon dit seigneur; et a lui appartient de faire poursuite et aussi de garder sesdits [subgez] de toutes oppressions et guerres que estrangers ou aultres leur voldroient faire.[2]

This is a much more sweeping statement than that made in the case of Joachim Rouault. Whoever defies the subject, it says, defies the sovereign too. He personally is bound to protect his subjects against any attempt to distrain them by armed force, whether the issue be private or otherwise. There is no

[1] This action was in fact taken; the official letter quashing the letters of marque, dated at Tours 28 January 1449, is to be found in Arch dep. de la Côte d'Or, B 11882.

[2] Arch. dep. de la Côte d'Or, B 11933. Another indication of the changing attitude towards reprisals about this period is the petition of the States General of Tours in 1484, for measures to prevent the use of unauthorised letters of marque. An ordinance of 1485 laid down that the right to grant them belonged to the sovereign alone. See Nys, *Les Origines du Droit International*, p. 74.

longer any limitation; it is not just those in the sovereign's service, or in his personal company, that are so protected, but all his subjects. More important, there is no longer any chance of doing what Erart du Chastellet hoped to do, and invoking the principle *fides non tenetur fidem frangenti* in such a way as to limit the effect of private revenge to a purely personal issue.[1] In all the affairs of his subjects, the statement implies, the sovereign has an interest, and therefore all complaints made against them must be referred to him. This means that the only proper way of distraining them is by letters of marque, issued against his people generally, and these need to be authorised by someone who is his equal in status.

It would no doubt be misleading to attach too much importance to the dates at which the statements I have quoted were made. Philip the Good's ambassadors, as good diplomatists, were flexible in their approaches, and they must have known that they could go further in their claims when they were talking to Austrian noblemen, whose overlord was not a very effective ruler, than they could when they were meeting the representatives of Charles VII. If, however, one compares their remarks at Montbéliart and Paris with, say, Edward III's attitude in the Bulmer affair, one can see that between the two dates there has been a very considerable change of view about the authority required to legitimise acts of reprisal. If one turns from the statements of diplomacy to those of legal theory, one finds the same change reflected. Bartolus, writing in the mid-fourteenth century, left by his reservations wide scope for levying reprisals by means of private defiance. Nicholas of Cusa,

---

[1] This defence against a charge of breaking a truce was exceedingly common. See for example Clermont's reply to a Burgundian complaint about the capture of Vitry in time of truce (letter of 31 July 1433): 'ceulx des garnisons de votre cote, tant de Marcigny que Rosemont, Cuffi et autres places . . . ont fait et font incessamment chacun jour courses, dommaiges et maulx innumerables es pais et subgiez de montres redoubte seigneur et pere, dont plusieurs gentilzhommes, qui par les dictes courses ont este destruiz et domaiges, m'ont plusieur fois requis leur donner congie d'eulx revanchier . . . Finablement leurs diz qu'ils se desdommaigassent sur ceulx qui leur faisoient cesdiz domaiges' (H. de Flamare, *Le Nivernais Pendant la Guerre de Cent Ans*, Tome II, no. CLXXXII). For other examples, see *ante*, p. 228, n. 1; this one is striking, in that it shows Clermont, the conservator, avowing private reprisals by men of his party.

writing a hundred years later, left the reservations out. All private defiances, he says, are illegal, *supremi judicis consensu non interveniente*. 'What virtue do you believe there is in the cartels of defiance you concoct', he asks the nobleman, 'that you should believe that when you send this little letter, all laws human and divine should cease in their effect?'[1] The reference to laws human and divine shows what is in his mind. Wars and reprisals are *de jure divino* and *de jure gentium*, and only the *placet* of a sovereign can legitimise such hostile acts as taking spoil from strangers. No private defiance can make such acts legal.

Of course feudal noblemen still claimed the right to defy their enemies and make war in their own names after the mid-fifteenth century. As we have seen already, at that time no one in practice claimed that such sovereign acts as making public war implied the absolute independence of the sovereign;[2] the very Duke of Burgundy, whose ambassadors put forward such sweeping claims at Montbéliart, was himself a vassal. Further, the employment of letters of marque in preference to private war, as a means of obtaining personal redress, implied no questioning of the absolute nature of private rights; this was the justification of reprisals, just as much as it was of feudal war. Nevertheless, the principle which then for the first time was being urged with force in actual disputes, that any sort of hostile act requires sovereign authority, was an important one. It indicates a shift of outlook on the question of war's legitimacy. The crucial question is no longer the justice of the cause, but the authority on which war is levied. The redress of wrong is no longer to be regarded as a matter of private enterprise; it is the business of the public authority which represents the members of the community, individually and collectively, in all relations with foreigners. This is a much more modern concept of sovereignty than any we have encountered so far.

The principle, that the proper way to obtain redress for injuries inflicted by aliens is through letters of marque is therefore important for three reasons. In the first place, it brings into much clearer relief the distinction between public and private war. In the second place, it made it much easier to control

---

[1] Nicholas of Cusa, *De Concordantia Catholica*, Lib. III, ch. 31 (Basle edn., 1565, p. 813).
[2] *Ante*, ch. V.

marches and enforce the observation of truces. If the sovereign so wished, he could still of course make nonsense of a nominal peace; English corsairs, operating under letters of marque, achieved just this in the reign of Elizabeth. But if he did not so wish, he could be sure that at least on his side there could be no legitimate violence except by his leave, and he might reasonably hope that his adversary's liegeman would equally hesitate to break the peace unless they had his support—in which case, the peace might not be worth very much. In effect, the proper observance of the law of marque drew the sting from the principle that treaties could not bind to the prejudice of private persons. It also, and lastly, affected the position of the soldier. A soldier who could not act except on the command of a sovereign could no longer be regarded as a knight errant whose vocation was the pursuit of just quarrels. A new order was emerging, in which the soldier was becoming a mere servant of the state, who was not asked to reason why. In this new order of things, the law of arms, which bound soldiers on the personal honour of their knighthood, could have little meaning. The only people who had any further use for it were heralds, whose antiquarian mystique kept its memory alive.

# XIII

# CONCLUSIONS

'THE notion of a law of nations was preceded and prepared for by the chivalric ideal of a good life of honour and loyalty.'[1] The conclusions which stem from a study of the law of arms form in effect an extended commentary on this statement of Huizinga. For this military law of the fourteenth and fifteenth centuries bridges the gap between his two theses. It reveals the chivalrous obligations of a soldier formalised in a law, which was applied in the courts as a part of what was then understood to be the law of nations, the ancient *jus gentium*.

Because it bound men irrespective of their allegiance, one may perhaps call the law of arms an international law. But it was very different from any international law known to the modern world. The extraordinary variety of the legal matters which it regulated make this clear, and make it clear further that in the late middle ages the categories into which laws were classified were different from those now in use. The law of arms governed alike the conduct of soldiers towards enemies (a matter now regulated by agreed international convention), the discipline of armies (military or martial law in our sense), rules concerning rights in spoil (which appear to be modelled on the law of property), and armorial disputes (which would probably now be regarded as a branch of peerage law). Of the distinction which today is drawn between public and private international law there is no hint here. The rulings of the law of arms quoted

[1] J. Huizinga, 'The Political and Military Significance of Chivalric Ideas in the Late Middle Ages', *Men and Ideas* (translated James S. Holmes and Hans van Marle, London, 1960), p. 203.

by individuals who were claiming, for example, rights in ransoms, suggest that it was an early prototype of private international law. But when Charles VII's advisers told him that by law of arms the English seizure of Fougères in 1449 constituted a *casus belli*,[1] they were applying this law to a public issue, and labelling the English action (to use modern phraseology) a breach of public international law. The same law was taken to govern public and private relations in war.

What this apparent confusion of terms indicates is the difficulty of applying a definition such as 'international law' to the customs of a society which did not think in terms of nationality. The distinguishing feature of a nation, as we understand the word, is its independent sovereign status, which makes it, legally, a unique and self-sufficient society. In legal theory, the kingdoms and principalities of the later middle ages were neither unique nor self-sufficient. The only society which was so was the society of Christendom, a supra-national society of which Christian kingdoms were dependent members. His allegiance to this society was the one overriding obligation of the Christian soldier. Various ties of personal loyalty might attach him to a whole series of secular masters; to one man, perhaps, he was bound by a sworn contract to serve him for a stated period, to another because he wore his order of chivalry, to others again by the tenure of fiefs. Each of these allegiances was based in an individual relationship, and for this reason conflicts of loyalty were a problem for the individual, defying resolution on the basis of any guiding principle of nationality. The only obligations which were universal were those which bound all Christian men alike, such as the rules of chivalrous conduct, for allegiance to the honour of knighthood was not limited by place or time. The rules of chivalry applied, in Ayala's words, 'wherever there was war'.[2]

This points the way to a first and most important conclusion. Because the society called western Christendom had no visible head, its unity (at least in the later middle ages) is often treated as chimerical. That one law could be accepted as binding on soldiers throughout its length and breadth shows that this was not the case. This law was something more than a vague set of

[1] R. Blondel, *De Reductione Normannie*, pp. 37–8 and 41.
[2] *Cit. ante*, ch. IV, pp. 52–53.

principles of loyalty and honour. It was a law which was accepted and enforced in properly constituted courts, and whose intricacies were argued by trained lawyers. It had a sound authoritarian basis in the written laws of Rome, the canon and civil laws. These laws had general validity because the equation of Christian society and the Roman people was assumed as a historical fact. The absence of any visible head to this body politic did not matter, since its members were bound together by their common obedience to 'mother church', whose lord was God himself. The sovereignty of this unseen master did not seem remote or ineffective to men who believed that the direct inter-play of natural and supernatural forces was the key to historical causation. Thus, just as the principle that kings should rule under God's law was the rallying cry of constitutionalists among their subjects, so too the principle that *dei lex est major legi principis*[1] gave force, in the late middle ages, to the belief that the relations of the subjects of one king with those of another ought to be 'constitutional' also.

As has been said before, chivalry in the fourteenth and fifteenth centuries was regarded as a Roman institution. To the people of that period, the difference between the rules of chivalry and the discipline of imperial Roman armies was merely chronological. The law of arms was thus a professional law, the common law of all soldiers in the world of Roman Christians. But these people viewed Roman history through the distorting lens of contemporary conditions. To the descendants of the barbarian invaders of the Roman world profession and status went hand in hand, and were alike hereditary. Thus when Charles VII's council, spurred to reflection by the out-rages of the *écorcheurs*, attempted to diagnose reasons for the general indiscipline of his soldiers, they attributed it to the fact that of late the King's armies had become filled with 'artisans, labourers and other idle folk', who could never be expected to live up to the high standards of chivalry.[2] Fighting was a busi-ness for those of gentle birth. This is why armorial disputes came within the view of the military courts; for men of this age, banners and blazonry, which were inherited, had the same sort

---

[1] See *ante*, ch. II, p. 18.
[2] Document quoted by Tuetey, *Les Écorcheurs sous Charles VII*, Tome I, p. 131.

of significance as badges of rank today. This brings us to a second important conclusion about the law of arms. It was not just the law of a certain Christian profession, but also the law of a hereditary noble class.[1]

This is a quite different idea of what an international law may be to any with which we are now familiar. It does, however, serve to illustrate how real the unity of Christendom seemed in those days; class solidarity transcended the boundaries of kingdoms. It also helps to explain why the law of arms was respected. 'In the middle and lower classes', said Taine, 'the chief motive of conduct is self-interest; with an aristocracy the mainspring is pride.'[2] As regards the greater nobility, at least, of the later middle ages, there is much truth in this statement. Princes, such as Philip the Good or Henry V, were jealous of their good fame, and punctilious in discharging obligations in which their honour was involved.[3] It is true, no doubt, that it was chiefly the very great who were as careful as they, and that this was partly because they had to play to a wide audience—they knew that every action they took would be observed, and judged by severe critics. Obligations upon honour clearly weighed much more lightly with ordinary knights and professional captains, as is shown by the subterfuges which they adopted in order to avoid them. Nevertheless, the example of their social superiors was not completely lost on them. Nowadays we hear so much of class strife as an overriding force in history that we may sometimes forget how strong, in most periods, has been the natural urge of men to ape their betters. Certainly, just as they were often more impressed by the outward appurtenances of rank than by its obligations, professional soldiers were as a rule more concerned with the letter of their chivalrous code than with its spirit; but this does not mean that chivalrous obligations meant nothing to them. When Seguin de Badefol, one of the worst of the *routiers*, swore to keep his treaty with the Dauphin of Auvergne, or otherwise 'to be

---

[1] It is very difficult to distinguish the professional from the hereditary elements in the factors which made soldiering a noble profession. On this, see Appendix II, *The Peerage of Soldiers*.

[2] Quoted by Huizinga, *cit. supra*, p. 205.

[3] See ch. XI *ante*, especially p. 190, n. 6 and 7 (Henry V), and p. 203, n. 1., p. 205, n. 1., p. 211, n .3 (Philip the Good).

held forever false and wicked, attainted of treason and perjured on his faith in all courts and before all lords',[1] he may not have intended to keep his word, if he could find an excuse to break it. But it is surely significant that even in dealings with a man of his stamp, the Dauphin still regarded a solemn promise on knighthood to be the best guarantee he could get.

In fact, in their dealings with their equals and superiors, the conduct even of the free companies and the *écorcheurs* will stand up to scrutiny. Here at least pride of place had its beneficial effect, and not surprisingly, for it was in this sector of society that ambitious soldiers wished to impress. For those in arms generally, the law of arms did a great deal to ensure a humane standard of conduct. Gentlemen prisoners were usually treated well, and allowed to go free on parole. The practice of taking men for ransom also helped to prevent unnecessary bloodshed in the field. But the story was different in the case of the non-combatant. The civilians, and above all the humble, suffered untold hardships in war. The awful tales in descriptions of the *écorcherie* of men hung, roasted, or dragged behind horses in order to extract a few pennies of ransom from them, testify to conduct which can only be described as barbaric and inhuman. One or two exceptional commanders (Henry V is a famous example) acquired a good reputation for enforcing the rules which protected the common people of the country over which war was raging; the average captain simply did not regard them. 'A man may not torture a prisoner to extort money from him by way of ransom', says Paris of Pozzo, 'but it is different in the case of peasants, at least according to the custom of mercenaries.'[2] This is a very wide exception, and a very important one. In its light, the whole theory of chivalry, of an order of knighthood whose Christian duty is the protection of the needy and defenceless, becomes meaningless.

The trouble with professional soldiers was not that they failed to take the obligations of their chivalrous rank seriously, but that they did not take them seriously enough. Rank can indeed foster in a class a sense of obligation, but it can also foster a sense of exclusiveness. Too many soldiers treated their obliga-

[1] *Spicilegium Brivatense*, ed. A. Chassaing (Paris, 1886), p. 366.
[2] Paris of Pozzo, *De Re Militari*, Lib. IX, cap. 2 (Zilletus, *Tractatus Juris Universi*, Tome XVI, fo. 421vo).

tions as such as applying only to their relations with their equals in the field of battle. This attitude is understandable, but it is not endearing. For here there were stronger grounds for taking their responsibilities in earnest; it was very much in their interest to do so. If one did not pay one's own ransom to the man who took one prisoner, he or his friends might all too easily serve one in one's own coin. One observed enemy safe-conducts, because to infringe them without excuse might easily lead to reprisals. Pride was a potent force in keeping soldiers to their word of honour, but it was clearly much more potent when it was backed by self-interest.

One cannot, indeed, help wondering whether the law of arms would have meant anything if it had not been for the financial stakes at issue in battle. In all the legal problems of war, as we have studied them, the question of profit has been in one way or another involved. Among other things, this is the reason why matters of discipline and disputes between soldiers of different allegiance were governed by the same law; in contemporary conditions, such questions were inseparable. It was essential for a commander to have power to limit the plundering of his soldiers; otherwise his army was likely, in the hour of victory, to dissolve into a disorderly rabble in the quest for loot. Thus disobedience of standing orders could be held to invalidate a man's title to a ransom, because by law of arms a captain was entitled to make ordinances which his soldiers were bound to obey.[1]

This matter of the spoils of war may have had a still more crucial importance. Financial interest was not only a reason why the law was obeyed; it seems likely that it was the key factor in its development and achievement of general recognition. There had always been local rules about conduct in war,

---

[1] Cf. Upton, *De Officio Militari*, Lib. I, cap. 16, and Lib. IV (ed. Bysshe, p. 32 and p. 133); see also B. Mus., Stowe MS. 1047, fo. 248 (on the powers of a commander, heraldic MS.), 'quinto datur [principali capitaneo] potestas faciendi statuta, et proclamationes faciendi, et executionem demandandi'. A good example of a disciplinary ordinance being quoted in a dispute over ransom is the case of Chamberlain *v.* Gerard in the Court of Chivalry, in which Chamberlain called the Marshal of Despenser's host of 1383, who testified that the ordinances he had made about taking prisoners made it impossible for Gerard to have taken the prisoner in dispute legitimately (P.R.O., C47/6/5).

such as those which are recorded by Beaumanoir for the Beau-vaisis, or the thirteenth century customs of the March of Scotland. But in the fourteenth and fifteenth centuries war had become a commercial concern at the international level; the ransoming of prisoners and villages, the sale of safe-conducts and strategically placed forts had become a legitimate means of making a living. Soldiering too had become international. A captain like Francois de Surienne had on his muster rolls men born in England, France, Brittany, and Germany, and they might find themselves equally easily fighting in any one of these lands, or in Italy or Scotland. In these circumstances, the need for a common soldiers' law was one which was felt. It was met by applying to the problems which conduct in war presented the principles of the only laws known to be generally accepted, the canon and civil laws. Where these laid down no rules, difficulties were resolved by applying principles drawn from other known laws. Thus for instance the rules governing rights to ransom were assimilated to those governing the tenure of fiefs. But if ransoms had not been so profitable, it is unlikely that any learned doctor would have bothered about defining these rules.

The law of arms was thus a product of the international wars of the late middle ages. As has already been said, though, the word 'international' must be used with caution with reference to this age. Its legal theories were dominated by ideas of 'right' which made little distinction between the rights of public bodies and those of private persons, its political relations by ideas of allegiance based in the sworn promises of one man to another. Its wars were fought over the rights of persons, rather than the interests of nations, and its soldiers fought as members of an order pledged to the defence of such rights. The rights which they in turn acquired in war, to ransoms and such-like, were allowed to be theirs individually, as the fair reward of the risks which they had run therein. It was this which made their profession so profitable. The rules of the law of arms were appropriate to this condition of things. They were formulated and applied with a view to the protection of the rights of individual soldiers, not to regulating the conduct of the troops of warring nations. In a society in which, under God, personal loyalties and heritable personal rights meant more than anything else, these rules gave the code of chivalry tangible force, sanctioning agreements made for private gain by allegiance to the honour of knighthood. Their effectiveness was due to their appeal to two most potent human motives, pride and profit.

Circumstances, however, were changing at the end of the Hundred Years War. The idea of chivalry, of a united order of Christian soldiers pledged to the armed defence of justice, was a legacy of the age of the crusades; it had little significance in the contemporary world of emergent nation states. By this time the open profiteering of professional soldiers had debased the old principle, that the spoils of war were the equitable reward of the man who risked his life in a just cause. It was not easy to justify their sort of profit on moral grounds, or to take much pride in the way it was won. From the very beginning of the Hundred Years War, moreover, signs of the pressure of standards quite other than those in which chivalry was founded had been apparent. The courts had always enforced the rule, that only rights won in a war waged on the authority of a 'public' power were recognised as justly acquired. This standard of judging the justice of war was a purely conventional one, and its recognition implied that there were more important calls on the loyalty of a soldier than his allegiance to an order of knighthood, pledged to defend eternal right. Once this supra-national allegiance no longer took priority, chivalry had no more purpose.

The law of arms, however, had more to it than a set of chivalrous ideals. It was a formal and generally accepted law, and its currency helped to establish two very important legal principles, which were remembered long after the idea that soldiering was the Christian vocation of a noble class had been forgotten. One was that war, in its proper sense, could only be waged by sovereigns. The consequences of this view were, in the period of the Hundred Years War, unclear, because it was not then clear what the precise definition of a sovereign ought to be. In early days, the word was taken to denote an individual whose high personal status entitled him to special rights, but more and more, as time went on, these special rights were associated with those whose status entitled them to speak on behalf of a collective body of men. Here are revealed essential links in the pedigree by which Grotius's principle, that only sovereign states may legitimately make war, may be traced back to its ancestry in the *droit de guerre* of the feudal *seigneur*. The other principle, which the enforcement of the law of arms by the military courts of the fourteenth and fifteenth centuries helped to establish, was that in war soldiers, though they served different lords, were yet bound by certain general and known rules of conduct. Once again it was on this belief, that there are general laws binding on all men regardless of nationality, that Grotius founded his theory of international law. Huizinga was right: the chivalrous conceptions of honour and loyalty of an age when the idea of nationality was not fully understood prepared the way for the notion of a law of nations.

# APPENDICES

# APPENDIX I

# THE LEGAL IMPLICATIONS
# OF 'APPATIS'

The word *appati* or *pati* is only one of a number of names used to describe agreements between local inhabitants and soldiers living off the countryside. They are also sometimes called *raencons du pays*, *abstinences* or *souffrances de guerre*, or, in Languedoc, *sueffras*. Though all the names describe agreements to pay money on the same sort of terms, their variety helps to bring out the variety of legal implications which such payments could bear, and which were sometimes conflicting.

From the point of view of the captain exacting them, they could be treated as ordinary spoils of war, as the phrase *raencons du pays* implies. On this ground he could be bound to pay shares in them, as in other spoils, to his superiors or his companions-in-arms.[1] When hostilities ceased, he could still claim outstanding sums, in the same way as he could still claim ransom money;[2] and, as in the case of ransoms, his heirs inherited his claims.[3] But whereas when a truce was signed men could not be taken prisoner anew and put to ransom, the obligation on country 'appatised' to make further payments did not necessarily cease.[4] The inhabitants might have to continue to pay, even though the hostilities which in theory they were buying off had become illegal. The rate of payment might be

[1] This is, for example, stipulated in the agreement between Du Guesclin and Clisson, quoted *ante*, ch. IX, p. 138, n. 2.

[2] Thomas de Uvedale, for instance, was still collecting sums outstanding for *appatis* owed to Henry of Lancaster and Chandos from the period before the treaty of Brétigny, in 1366 (case of de Uvedale *v.* Pierre de Tournebu and tohers, Arch. Nat., X¹a 21, fo. 73).

[3] Ibid.; the court did not uphold Tournebu's plea that *appatis* could not be inherited, and permitted de Uvedale to continue to act for Lancaster's executors.

[4] See, e.g. the arrangements for continuing their payment, in the truce of 27 May 1394, Rymer, Vol. III, pt. IV, pp. 95–8.

adjusted in these circumstances, or it might be continued at the old rate.[1] As active hostilities were what justified the taking of gains of war, such payments in times of truce cannot be considered as gains of war proper.

From the point of view of those paying *appatis*, they implied the purchase of immunity from war—hence the names *abstinences* or *souffrances de guerre*. Indeed, in Languedoc the word *pati* was often used to describe a quite ordinary truce.[2] Thus, as long as they made their payments at the proper time and did not aid their own side in any way, the inhabitants of 'appatised' country could not be plundered or put to ransom, nor could their lands be burned or wasted[3] (though, as always, they were only protected against soldiers under the command of the captain or officer with whom they had treated). But here again there is a difficulty. Where a captain levied *appatis* in lands whose inhabitants were of the same obedience as he, these payments could hardly in law be regarded as buying immunity from hostilities (though no doubt that was their effect). They were more like a form of purveyance.

The difficulties of both the definitions so far advanced are re-solved if one treats *appatis* as a form of tax levied on the spot for the upkeep of soldiers.[4] Taxes do not necessarily cease when hostilities do, and they can legally be imposed on those of one's own obedience. The fact that *appatis* were often taken in kind strengthens this view, that they were a form of tax or purveyance.[5] This definition, how-ever, fails just as much as do the others to be inclusive; it does not bring out the sense in which *appatis* could be treated as gains of war, or bought truces.

[1] In the above truce, for instance, the conservators were empowered to reduce the rate where it was excessive: but it normally remained at the previous rate. In 1445, on the other hand, Charles VII is seen instructing his envoys to try and get the rates increased if the truce is renewed (Bib. Nat., MS. Fr. 4054, fo. 41).

[2] The truce between the Lords of d'Albret and Duras of 1388 is for instance called by them a *pati* (Bib. Nat., Collection Doat, fo. 257).

[3] See the rules laid down by Salisbury, to regulate the conduct of his troops in 'countrie appatized', Perche Orders, cl. 2, 3, 4.

[4] They are sometimes explicitly referred to as such. Thus, one item of the agenda for the meeting of the 'Estates' of Senlis, with their local French captains, on 29 January 1432 was 'la provision des pastis pour le soustenne-ment . . . des gens d'armes' (Bib. Nat., Collection de Picardie, Tome 89, fo. 277).

[5] See, for example, the rolls recording payments of *appatis* in the areas of Vannes and Becherel, 34 Edward III, which show many parishes making payments in kind (P.R.O., E101/174, nos. 10 and 11).

The trouble was not so much that the same word was used to describe different practices, as that the normal practice could be interpreted in quite different ways. Thus the payment of *appatis* could be used as evidence that the man who accepted payment was acting in a hostile manner.[1] Equally it could be used in an opposite sense, to prove that those who paid them were contributing taxes towards the enemy war effort, and could therefore be treated as their subjects and plundered.[2] Thus the same evidence could be used to prove (*a*) that the inhabitants of a given stretch of country were in the obedience of one party, and suffering for it, (*b*) that they were in the obedience of the other and comforting him. The result usually was that they were expected to comfort both sides, and had to suffer at the hands of both.

[1] Thus in 1390 Jean de Blaisy undertook to get the English companies to cease 'toute maniere de guerre par patis, marque ou autrement' (Jacotin, *Preuves de la Maison de Polignac*, Tome I, no. 707). Quittances for payments of *appatis* were sometimes used as evidence of hostile action; see, e.g. Arch. dep. de la Côte d'Or, B 1180 (alleging illicit hostilities by the garrison of Montigny against Burgundian subjects, with the quittance for *appatis* attached).

[2] See ch. IX, *ante*, p. 138 n. 5.

# APPENDIX II

# THE PEERAGE OF SOLDIERS

That the soldier's calling should be regarded as noble seems to have been generally agreed.[1] No doubt this idea was largely an inheritance from the period when the *droit de guerre* (the right to defy one's enemies and make war on them) was held widely to be a privilege of the feudal nobleman.[2] It is very hard, however, to decide whether in our period this status should rather be regarded as hereditary or purely professional. People in the fourteenth and fifteenth centuries expected birth to dictate profession, and to some extent the problem is thus illusory; but this contemporary view inevitably ran into innumerable difficulties in individual cases. It is thus worth considering by what means, if any, these difficulties were reconciled.

Nobility was expected normally to be of the blood; any other kind of nobility was clearly found hard to explain.[3] 'Peerage,' says Caxton, 'is nothing else but honour (i.e. rank) anciently observed.'[4] How then do we allow for Jean de Beuil's statement that 'a man at arms with his bacinet on his head is noble, and of fit condition to do combat with a king'?[5] This was not just an individual view of

---

[1] See *Le Jouvencel*, ed. Lecestre and Favre, Tome II, p. 80: 'les armes ennoblissent l'homme quel qu'il soit'; and also the English *Knyghthode and Bataile*, ed. Dyboski and Arend, E.E.T.S., p. 11: 'ignobiles non sint milites'. A plaintiff in the Parlement of Paris in 1428 claimed that 'quant aucun est passe deux fois en monstres, est *deinceps* reputé noble' (quoted by A. Bossuat, *Perrinet Gressart et Francois de Surienne*, Paris, 1936, p. 2).

[2] See e.g. Beaumanoir, ch. 59 §6: 'autre que gentil home ne poent guerroier'.

[3] See, e.g. Upton, *de Officio Militari*, Lib. I, ch. 19 (ed. Bysshe, p. 63): 'Set istud non esset verum videlicet, quod ex vili patre ignobili possit descendere filius nobilis; sequeretur omnino, quod aut omnes, quod falsum est, aut quod nulli sunt nobiles, quia si primus parens fuit nobilis, sic et omnes ab illo descendentes'. It takes Upton a long time to get out of this difficulty.

[4] Caxton, *Book of the Ordre of Chyvalry*, ed. Byles, E.E.T.S., p. 58.

[5] *Le Jouvencel, cit. sup.*, Tome II, p. 80.

Jean's; it was widely held that on the field of battle, and in matters of war generally, all soldiers were peers. We have seen already, how, before a court of knights, the Black Prince and the Marshal d'Audreham were on an equal footing.[1]

I believe we may discern, behind these apparently differing views, the combined influence of two very ancient ideas. One is the belief (which had its ancestry in Teutonic custom) that a man's rank is part of his inheritance. The other is the belief that to fight a man is to put oneself on an equal footing with him before the judgement of God. This view is clearly indicated by the rules which governed admission to duels:[2] a party might decline a challenge on the ground that his challenger was not of sufficient status to fight him.[3] Now it is clear from the writings of lawyers, such as John of Legnano, that they saw no essential difference between such a contest, and a war of two kings. They were simply different kinds of wars, the one a *bellum particulare*,[4] the other a *bellum hostile*.[5] Thus, as admission to a duel showed that the two parties had equal standing, the fact that he was fighting in a battle was a tacit admission that a soldier had equal standing with all others so engaged, whether or not he was born as noble as they.

From the legal point of view, what this parity of estate meant was that, in war, one soldier had the same rights as another. In other places and at other times, this was not necessarily so. At Poitiers John the Good surrendered himself to Denis de Morbek, and Denis thus acquired the same rights over him as any master had over his prisoners of war[6] (until he transferred those rights to some-

---

[1] See ch. IV *ante*.

[2] Cf. for example Beaumanoir's remarks on appeals of battle (ch. 61.8): 'se chevaliers ou escuiers apele home de poeste, il se combat a pie, . . . ainssi come home de poeste: car porce qu'il s'abaisse en apeler si basse persone, se dignite est ramene en tel cas a tex armeures comecil qui est apeles a de son droit'.

[3] I cannot find authority for this rule in the legist's writings, though both Upton (Lib. II, cap. 6, and 7 *in fine*) and the author of the treatise on duels in the *Black Book of the Admiralty* (R.S., Vol. I, p. 330 et seq.) assume that the parties will be gentlemen. In practice the rule was observed; Du Guesclin objected to Felton's challenge because Felton's rank was insufficient (Felton *v.* Du Guesclin, Arch. Nat., X²a 7, fo. 145 et seq.), and Richard II, in order to enable John Kingston in 1389 to take up a challenge, raised him to the rank of gentleman (Rymer, Vol. III, pt. IV, p. 42).

[4] Cf. John of Legnano, *Tractatus*, cap. 168.　　[5] See *ante*, ch. V.

[6] Cf. testimonial letter of 20 December 1357, printed in Rymer, Vol. III, pt. I, p. 161, certifying that John surrendered to Denis and 'fist a lui tout ce que loial prisonnier doit faire a son maistre en tieu cas'.

one else). These were just the same rights as John would have had over Denis had their roles been reversed, for on the battlefield and as fighting men they were equals. But Denis could never have been the equal of John, when John acted as King of France. Similarly, Michael de la Pole could say to Bishop Despenser that, as a party to an indenture of war, he must be judged as one of the King's soldiers; as regarded his indentured commitments, the fact that he was a bishop was immaterial.[1] As a soldier, Despenser had the same rights as other soldiers and no more, though as a bishop, he undoubtedly enjoyed rights which they could never have.

Here it is the professional element in a soldier's status which comes out most clearly. But the soldier who was not a prince or a bishop did not lose his rank when he left the field of battle, or when old age led him to lay aside his calling. The privileges to which this rank entitled him might be fewer and less specific, but some remained; he could still use the same devices that he had worn in the field, and he could still, if his honour was impugned by an equal, vindicate himself in a duel. And in so far as he could do these things, so also could his children. The professional parity of soldiers cannot be divorced from a hereditary concept of nobility, because a soldier's descendants could base a claim to nobility on the ground of his service in war.[2]

In order to understand this equation of hereditary and professional status, one must bear in mind that, to men of the period under discussion, nobility was understood to mean something more than social rank. It was the outward and visible sign of greatness of spirit.[3] If they accepted birth as a passport to gentility, it was because they believed (and it would be hard to show them wholly mistaken) that mental as well as physical qualities were inherited.[4] But it was the quality of spirit that mattered, and they accepted as equally

[1] Cf. *Rot. Par.*, III, p. 156b; Pole's speech: 'le Roi notre seigneur vous ent purroit clerement mesner et jugger come persone temporele, a cause que vous vous avez et porter come persone temporele: qar par expres vous vous liez au Roi notre seigneur par vos endentures d'estre soldeour le Roi'.

[2] Cf. the claim made by Jean de Saulx in the Parlement in 1426, quoted by Bossuat, *cit. sup.*, p. 2, n. 5, that 'il est noble homme extrait de noble lignee, et furent deux freres Jehan de Sauls . . . dont yssi Guillaume de Sauls et Gautier de Sauls, dont yssi Odot de Sauls, pere de l'appelant, qui ont servi le roy et le duc de Bourgoigne es guerres et ont vesqui noblement'.

[3] Cf. Upton, *de Officio Militari*, Lib. II, cap. 19 (ed. Bysshe, p. 64): 'nihil aliud est vera nobilitas quam vita humana, clara virtutibus per electionem et habitum anime intellectualis exterius operantis'.

[4] Ibid. (ed. Bysshe, p. 66): 'animus illius qui ex nobilibus traxit originem facilius ad virtutes inclinatur quam alterius'.

noble with the born gentleman the man who had proved his worth on the field of battle, where human qualities are tested as severely as in any place. The children of a man thus proved to be noble were rightly accepted as noble too, for there was no reason to suppose him less capable than another of implanting his own virtues in his posterity.

This is not just an argument put forward by legal theoreticians, anxious to justify the social *status quo* in terms of metaphysical justice. Practice conformed to their theory. The reward of conspicuous gallantry in the field was, by law of arms, ennoblement, promotion to a hereditary status.[1] On the same principle, the punishment of cowardice or treachery by a soldier was, as we have seen, degradation from all honours.[2] The heirs of a man so disgraced could inherit from him no rank which was not theirs already.

Like so many curious rules of the law of arms, its definition of the status of a soldier would, therefore, be seen in terms of an attempt to achieve justice, rather than in terms of either hereditary or professional exclusiveness. This is not to say that justice was always done, or that exclusiveness did not, in practice, come into the picture; only that the rules were, given contemporary assumptions, both intelligible and justifiable.

---

[1] The rules on this point are discussed at length in the *Jouvencel, cit. sup.*, Tome II, pp. 112–14. Waurin gives an excellent instance, very similar to the one discussed by Jean de Beuil, of a soldier who was ennobled, 'luy et ses successeurs', for conspicuous bravery in the assault of Pontoise in 1441 (*Chroniques*, Vol. IV, p. 364).

[2] See *ante*, ch. IV.

# APPENDIX III

## Illustrative Cases

I have included as a final appendix the texts of the pleadings (*plaidoiries*) in three cases arising out of war, which were tried before the Parlement of Paris. The object is to give some illustration of how disputes under the law of arms were actually argued in the courts. It should be stressed that these texts are intended as illustrative material, and not as *pièces justificatives*. The case for including a wider selection of cases has really fallen to the ground since the publication of Professor P. C. Timbal's excellent selection of documents about the Hundred Years War, *La Guerre de Cent Ans Vue à travers les Régistres du Parlement*, 1337–1369 (C.N.R.S., 1961). This collection includes a large number of cases in which the law of arms was invoked; in particular in the long section on the status of prisoners of war (ch. IV, §3, pp. 305–74), and in the section on the activities of the free companies (ch. V, §3, pp. 467–501). A number of the cases which Professor Timbal publishes in these sections have been quoted in the text of this book. He includes, for instance, the full texts of the dispute arising out of the escape from his prison by Simon de Burley (discussed in ch. X *supra*), and of the dispute arising out of the re-purchase of the town of Poix from the Anglo-Navarrese (discussed in ch. VII *supra*). This collection provides a sample of cases far wider than I could hope to include here, and anyone who wishes to examine further cases should consult it. One point, however, should be made here. Professor Timbal and his collaborators, in their commentary on the texts they print, draw a sharp distinction between the law of arms and Roman civil law. For reasons which are set out at length in ch. II of this book, I believe that this distinction must be regarded as misleading. Roman civil law was accepted as the foundation of the law of arms.

For purposes of comparison, another recent publication may be useful. Mr. A. Rogers, in Vols. VI and VII of *Nottingham Medieval Studies*, has published the full text of the trial in the Court of Chivalry between 1390 and 1395 of the dispute over the ransom of the Count of Denia, one of the prisoners taken at Najera in 1367. This supplies an account of an English trial to set beside the French cases published by Professor Timbal.

A word should be said about the three cases printed here. Each concerns a quite different matter. In the first case, that of Pomfret *v.* Melun, a French knight is challenging the right of his English captor to a ransom. The Englishman bases his case first on the letter of obligation he has from his adversary, and demands that he acknowledge the seal on it as his; and secondly on the fact that Melun was taken by a lawful act of war, as understood by law of arms. Melun's defence is that he was not taken in lawful war, and that his obligation is void because extorted by force; interestingly, he also claims that he has in any case a papal (?) dispensation from the oath it records. Melun also claims that the reversal of his arms by Pomfret, when he (Melun) failed to meet his commitments, was unlawful and injurious, and claims damages. I have printed here only the *plaidoirie*; the text of the final arrest in favour of Melun is printed in Professor Timbal's book, pp. 308–12.

The second case concerns the capture of a soldier travelling under safe-conduct. The grantor of the safe-conduct, Philip the Good of Burgundy, and the grantee, Louis Bournel, a knight in the service of Charles VII, together sue Bournel's captor, John Dedham, captain of Montigny. Dedham claims that Bournel had infringed his safe-conduct by entering Montigny without the permission of himself or his lieutenant there, and so could be lawfully made prisoner, according to the rules of the law of arms concerning *saufconduits de guerre* (see ch. XI *supra*). Philip's advocate replies that this was not a *saufconduit de guerre* but a *saufconduit de prince*, and that as the Duke of Burgundy was the King's (Henry VI) lieutenant, this bound all of his party: moreover, he asks, is it likely that Bournel, himself a soldier and a captain, was so ignorant of the law of arms as to act as Dedham alleges? It would appear rather that he was tricked into entering the town. This case, which was heard in January 1432, was referred to the Council; no final decision seems to be recorded.

The third case concerns the status of booty recovered from the enemy. French troops, said to come from Maurepas, on a raid in July 1433 captured a booty of cattle; some of these were bought back by the Carthusians of Le Parc. Giles Desmoulins, however, who had also lost cattle in the raid, claimed that some of the beasts recovered were his, and had an arrest put on them. The question at issue was, supposing them to have been booty, had they become the property of the enemy? If they had, clearly the Carthusians, having bought them from their owners, had a cast iron case. Desmoulins therefore had to argue that they were not the property of the enemy; he argued this on the ground that they were not taken in a just war, and that the raiders in question were not properly speaking enemies but brigands, who had made the oath of allegiance to Henry VI; thus, no lawful title could be acquired by them to the stolen goods. The Carthusians replied that the enemies were true enemies, Frenchmen; that the war classed as a 'just and public war', and that in such a war we must attribute the same rights by the laws of war to the enemy as we claim ourselves. The whole question of just and public war and the rights which arise out of it is thus raised. It is worth noting two points in particular made by Desmoulins. He quotes on the one hand previous judgments of the marshals of France, on the other the opinion of the great canonist Hostiensis, an excellent reminder that the law which those marshals administer is founded *'tam per textus quam per doctores juris civilis et canonici'*. This case, like the preceding one, is referred to the Council, and again no final decision is recorded. It is worth mentioning that another case, in which almost precisely similar arguments were used, is printed by Professor Timbal, ch. V, §3, pp. 493–4.

1. *Case of Jean de Melun v. Henry Pomfret, plaidoire* before the Parlement, March 1365 (Bib. Nat. MS. Fr. 21717, fo. 144 et. seq.; collated with Arch. Nat., X¹a 1469, fo. 123vo, et seq.).

Entre Henry Pontfroit Anglois d'une part et Jehan de Meleun Sire des Bordes d'autrepart. Henry propose comment il a pris Messire Jehan et mis a rancon, et l'obligation qu'il en a de Messire Jehan de la somme de XVIᶜ escus sous son seel dont il a eu environ Vᶜ or VIᶜ escus, requiert que Messire Jehan cognoisse ou nie son seel et ly cogneu qu'il soit contraint ou condampne, et contraint a payer ladite somme de XVIᶜ deduit ce que Henry en a recu, et par les contraintes et paines contenues es lettres obligatoires retenues faites.

Meleun dit que au temps que Henry le prist de fait, et par avant, il etoit prisonnier d'un ecuyer francois, et par ainsy selon droit d'armes ne pouvoit faire fait d'armes ne prendre prisonnier francois; et par dessus les trieues prises entre les francois et anglois qui etoient au pais, par espie et mauvaisement Henry prist Meleun et par force de fers et contrainte de prison le fit mettre a rancon, et puisque tout le fait est tortionnier mauvais et dampnable par ce que dit est l'obligation pour cause de ce fait doit etre mise au neant, et mesmement que la dite obligation fut faite a Regennes qui lors etoit fort d'anglois, et comme par ce que dit est Henry ne put faire fait droit d'armes *quovismodo* ne prendre prisonniers: apres priant la forme et teneur de son arrest par lequel il doit proceder au principal, et des lors ne fit plaidoye ne juge sur la recognoissance ou ny de son seel qui etoit preparatoire du principal mais sur l'obligation tortionniere que Henry avoit fait commencier sur Meleun, et l'arrest dit *procedent ulterius partes in causa principali* etc., si ne doit etre abstraint a reconnoitre ou nier, et bien proteste qu'il n'entend a dire contre l'arrest: conclud a ce, puis retourne au principal et dit qu' il a eu novacion qui extint l'obligation. Car puis qu'il fut retourne a Beaufort il accomplet ce qu'il avoit promis, et apres s'en parti sans obligation, et par ce ly et ses pleges sont demeures quitte. Ce nonobstant Henry a injure fait renverser les armes Meleun, et c'estoit *alternativa obligationis*, en elisent cele voye il a renuncie a l'obligacion de l'argent par raison et droit d'armes comme l'obligation ne l'y reserve son recours, et sur ses injures requiert que Henry ait jour, et aussi sur la repetition de ce que Henry en a tortionnieres eu et receu, et qu'il donne caution *de stand jurio*. Apres propose une autre novacion de ce que Henry le lessa aller de Provins en sa maison sans aucune promesse, et bien reveint apres trois jours a Paris, et lors en pour-parlerent le Comte de Tanquarville et Chandos sans determiner et s'en alla Henry sans autre promesse et plus grand diligence a fait de luy mettre en raison que Henry; les droits d'armes dessusdits mets en fait, conclud par ce que dit est que Henry n' a cause ne action de faire ses conclusions, doit etre Meleun absols, et conclue aux dommages, depens et interets, ne doit nier ou cognoitre, et toutes voyes s'en rapporte a l'ordonnance de la cour. Et requiert adjournement comme dessus retenue faite.

Henry dit que le principal ou partie d'iceluy est connoitre ou nier le seel. Et en tant que Meleun le contredit par quelconque maniere que ce soit il vient contre l'arrest et le doit amender apres.

Henry replique et dit que Meleun et ceux de sa compagnie chevauchoient a pennon desploye qui etoit vray signe de guerre entre les gens d'armes, et par especial entre les anglois, et pour ce fut loisiblement pris, et n'y avoit treues sinon ceux que le Duc de Lancastre donna de luy et de ses gens qui ne pourroient lier Henry ne ses compaignons qui guerroient pour le Roy d'angleterre et si ne leur avoit le Duc signiffie ses treues, et se treues y eut vrayes, si les avoit rompues Meleun et ses compaignons par la maniere que dit est, et si attendoit Meleun l'arceprestre qui etoit a trois lieues pres pour debeller les anglois, et avant la bataille si meirent en aroy d'une part et d'autre comme esnemis, et fut pris Meleun, et se rendit et renconna sans alleguer treues ne autre chose, et se teint prisonnier en la compaignie Henry par le quart d'un an sans y mettre debat ne a luy renconner: ne fut contraint par violence de prison fermee ne autrement indeuement mais loisiblement selon le cas, et encore seroit la violence loisible en tel fait, et par ce ne vault ce que Meleun propose de l'obligation faitte a Regennes etc. Car n'estoit ja par plusieurs jours eslargir et retourner en ratifiant sa prison et rencon, et si etoit lors Regennes garde tant par francois comme par anglois a cause de traitie de la paix qu'on esperoit, et si en a entre Meleun en paye comme par sa lettre appert en ratifiant tout et si y a foy et serment contre lequel il n'est a recevoir, et contient l'obligation qu'il devoit aller a Beaufort prisonnier et payer etc., si ne l'acquitte pas d' y aller sans payer comme il propose. *Item*, l'argument de Meleun que ses armes ont ete tournees *quomodo* il est quittes comme ce soit *alternativa obligationis* etc., ne vaut, que *solutione posse non liberatur debitor a principali debito*, ne tourner les armes ne soit pas *alternativa obligationis* ne ne peut introduire exception de non payer le principal mais selon ly semble *agat de injuria quam allegat*, car Henry en a fait deuement ce qu'il a fait et pour la reverence du Roy Jehan seulement furent les armes remises. *Item*, Meleun ne peut opposer valablement contre Henry a empescher son droit que il fut prisonnier d'un autre, car il avoit conge de luy garnir d'epee et coustel et de greverl es francois etc. *Item*, se Meleun avoit eu congie de Henry ce que non si ne seroit il delivre de l'obligation, mais seulement de la prison, ne par ce n'y auroit eu novacion. *Item*, comme par l'arrest Meleun doit proceder peremptoire etc., et ce soit sur le principal, et a peremptoire de Henry cognoitre ou nier le seel et ainsy l'ait requis, et Meleun ne ait defere par confession ou nier; mais en a fait retenue qui n'a lieu en ce cas, encois par ce il appert que il doit etre repute et tenu pour cogneu, et Meleun cheu de ses deffenses et doit etre condampne, et contraint a payer, et comme la premiere instance soit finie, et il poursoit sa matere principale en requerant cognoitre ou nier etc., l'on doit avoir regard a la demande faite a present et non a l'autre combien que des lors il eut aussy requis. Si doit Meleun *ulterius procedere* etc., selon la teneur de l'arrest et si doit on proposer toutes ses peremptoires a une fois, et pour ce ly soit impetre s'il n'a cogneu ou nie. Conclud que Meleun ne face a recevoir *et aliter ut supra*.

Meleun duplique et dit que chevaucher arme ou a penon desploise, se il ni a fait dont lesion s'ensuive contre partie, treues ne devoient etre reputes enfreintes, et si les anglois ont use du contraire tant est leur fait plus dampnable, et dit aussi Meleun que lors il n'avoit aucun penon, et si etoient les treues toutes gardiees, et donnees par le Duc comme chef de la guerre qui etoit au pays pour les angloys, et si etoit lieutenant du Roy d'Angleterre, et leurs treues ratiffia le Roy et les donna aussi, ne Meleun et ses compaignons n'alloient prendre le fort de Fresnoy: mais s'en retournoient leurs bacines hors testes comme Henry confesse assez. Si appert que Henry ne dit chose qui soit vraysemblable. *Item*, Henry etoit prisonnier, et n'avoit conge d'armer, ne il n'en fait foy, ne par droit d'armes ne le pouvoit il avoir, et pour ce ne pouvoit faire ne acquerir Meleun ne autre son prisonnier. *Item*, considere le dampnable fait de Henry *in omni parte* il appert que Meleun a ete contraint *per justum metum qui cadit in constantem virum*, et tout ce qu'il propose pourroit seulement avoir lieu en fait de guerre loisible, ne (*sic*), et au temps de l'obligation Regennes etoit du tout en la puissance des angloys. *Item*, de ce qu'il a paye ce fut avant qu'il peust oncques partir des mains Henry ne oncques rien paya hors prison, et se il retourna a Beaufort ce fut pour la delivrance de ses pleiges, desquels il avoit pitie, et non pour ratifier l'obligation. Quant est de cognoistre ou nier le scel, d'etre tenu a proceder selon l'arrest etc., ce cheu en droit et s'en rapporte a la discretion de la cour. Quant a venir contre le serment etc., il montre dispensation et bien dit notablement en plaidoiant que en venant de Provins a Paris il s'en partit par conge et licence de Henry, si n'etoit tenu de retourner. *Item*, il n'y dut nantissement comme le seel ne soit cognu: conclud *ut supra*.

Henry dit outre que Meleun ne peut user la dispensation la ou le serment ou obligation n'est cognu, et en tant qu'il en use vault en son prejudice, il confesse l'obligation, se doit etre execute, et au moins garnir la main. *Item*, la dispensation est subreptice et ne tient juste cause d'octroy ne n'appert certainement qu'elle soit donnee sur la dite obligation. *Item*, il ne vient a temps a en suer apres duplique et il doit proceder par peremptoire.

Meleun a soutenu que la dispensation vaut par plusieu rsraisons de droit.

Appointez sont que quant aux requestes la court en dordener (?) au conseil et a present Messire Jehan cognoistra ou niera son seel et garnira la main de VIII^e et L escus comme Henry en ait resceu VII^e et L escus, et quant aux autres fins a conclusion la cour aura consideration aux raisons des parties et y fera droit par ordre et verra les lettres etc. Et tiendra Messire Jehan prison parmy la ville de Paris jusque a temps qu'il ait parmy la main la somme de VIII^e et L escus.

2. *Case of Philip of Burgundy and Louis Bournel v. John Dedham, plaidoirie* before the Parlement, January 1432 (Arch. Nat., X^1a 4796, fos. 298vo and fo. 301vo. These folios are torn, and where the text is missing I have left blanks: only a few words are lacking in each case).

Entre le duc de Bourgogne et Messire Loys Bournel chevalier demandeurs d'une part et Messire Jehan Dedham capitaine de

Montigny le roy en bassigny defendeur les demandeurs presupposent les prerogatives et lestat du dit duc et ditque le duc de bourgogne pour le temps qui estoit lieutenant pour le roy manda bournel qui tenoit forteresses et faisoit guerre en son pais de Charroloys et traicta ou fist traictier de le reduire et de mettre en ses mains ses fortresses / et selon le traictie delivra les fortresses aux gens du duc de bourgogne qui lui bailla saufconduit pour venir et passer par lengres lui VI$^e$ desarmez et y fu receu pour ce quil monstra son saufconduit et au partir trouva sept compagnons qui ne queroient que avantage (            ) ceoient quil avoit bahu robes et de bonnes bagues / et lui dirent quil convient quil venist boire du vin du capitaine de Montigny / et ly menerent non obstant toutez excusations / et quant il vint a la barriere / il dist quil ny entreroit point sans congie du capitaine / et eux qui ne queroient que lui faire quil perdie leffect de son saufconduit lui dirent que la estoit luy qui estoit lieutenant du capitaine / et quil lui en donneroit congie / et le bouterent dedens le chastel et prindrent males et bahu et toutes leurs bagues / si ont obtenu lettres dont recitent le contenu et selon ce proposent et conclu afin que le defendeur soit condampne a reintegrer ledit saufconduit et a remettre les prisonniers en la main du duc de bourgogne / ou au moins en justice / et a rendre et delivrer les biens et que de la valeur bournel soit creu par son serment / et que pour en savoir la verite que par provision le prisonnier soit amene ceans / et oultre ce soit le defendeur condampnez en telles amendes honnorables et proffitables selon la discrecion de la courte et quon lui face defence de partir de paris jusques a ce que le prisonnier soit par deca au moins jusques a ce quil soit delivre / et dit Maistre Jehan Luillier quil ne parle que pour le duc de bourgogne et quil eut provision de temoins *valetud. et affect.*

En la cause d'entre le duc de Bourgogne demandeur d'une part et Messire Jehan Dedham captaine de Montigny le roi en Bassigny defendeur qui dit quil vouldroit complaire au duc de Bourgogne et le servir / et autreffois a voulu tenir / et tendroit volontiers ce que le duc de Bourgogne bien informe en vouldroit ordonner / oultre dit quil est bon chevalier et a bien servy le roy et pour le bien de luy le roy lui a baillie la garde de Montigny et autres forteresses estans es frontieres et en la derreine bataille mena VI$^e$ combatans avec le mareschal et autres seigneurs de bourgogne / et fu la journee honorable et profitable au roy et au duc de bourgogne / dit oultre que le roy est empereur en son royaume / et a cause de sa couronne et souveraine puet donner saufconduit de grace / et ne puet ne doit aucun retourner en son royaume *inconsulto principe* / Il ya aussi saufconduiz de guerre mais toutesvoiez soubz umbre de tels saufconduiz

nul ne doit ne puet entrer en villes ou forteresses et se perd le benefice
de tels saufconduiz en pluiseurs manieres. Ce presuppose dit que
autreffois pour fair une grant entreprise il se mist sur les champs et se
trouva en grant compagnie de gens darmes et en renvoia une partie
a Montigny / avec lesquels sen ala bournel sans parler et sans dire
quil fust ennemy et sans dire qui il estoit entra en la dite forteresse
de Montigny et cuidoient que ce fut ung chavalier du pais / et aprez
furent paroles entre le lieutenant du capitaine et ceulz de la garde du
chastel pour savoir quil il estoit et qui lavoit boute dedens / et qui
lui avoit donne congie de y entrer / et pour ce quils trouverent que
sans congie et sans parler il sy estoit boute il fu retenu prisonnier et
fu bien logie pour ce quils trouverent quil estoit chevalier et homme
d'estat / Et au soir bien tard quand Messire Jehan Dedham retourna au dit chastel on luy dit ce qui estoit avenu / et lors fit venir
Bournel et l'interrogea / et pour ce quil trouva que sans le congie
de lui et de son lieutenant il y estoit entre / luy dit quil avoit enfraint
son saufconduit et quil devoit estre prisonnier / et neantmoins quil le
traitteroit bien et gracieusement mais quil respondist de ses gens / et
quil se tenist ainsi quil appartenoit / et quil en feroit ce que le roy
en ordonneroit / voire ce que le duc de bourgogne bien adverty en
diroit / si (?) dit oultre que asssez tost apres un de ses gens monta sur
les murs et descendi es fosses et se latita et depuis fu poursuy et
ramene / et si est vray que bournel apres la date de son saufconduit
(          ) a tenu et fait guerre sur les subgiez du roy en son pais / si
est son saufconduit enfraint / et combien que manages(?) et reduc-
tions d'ennemis soient assez favorables pour ce ny doit proceder
autrement que a point et ainsi quil appartient ne bailler saufconduit
de grace *inconsulto principe* / et se le duc de bourgogne avoit lors
lieutenance pour le roy / ce cas ny seroit mie compris *quia maiores
cause non transeunt* / et auroit enfraint son saufconduit par ce que dit
est et en auroit abuse / et furent a lengres mal contenz de bournel qui
parloit a plusiers personnes a part secretement / et apres se bouta
dans la compagnie des gens du dit chastel ou il entra sans congie du
captaine et sans parler au lieutenant et sans savoir comment il y
entroit / et navoir point de bahu / mais seulement avoit une vielle
mallete ou il ny avoit qu'une robe et chaperon qui ne valoient mie
dys frans et est tout en nature de chose et ny a riens distribue / combien que tout soit aquiz par droit de guerre et ne chiet point en
restitution / et demourra prisonnier et ne sera le defendeur despointie de sa possession / en ceste matiere qui nest point privilegiee /
et ne vit oncques le defendeur le saufconduit bournel et / lauroit
enfraint se saufconduit avoit et nauroit mie tenir prison ainsi quil
avoit promis pour luy et pour ses gens / et monstra bien le defendeur

par instrumens et autrement ce quil dit sil a delay pour ce faire / si conclu a fin d'absolution et a dispens.

Le duc de bourgogne en soubstenant sa demande ses preeminences(?) et ses prerogatives / dit quil avoit baille au bournel saufconduit pour cause honorable et profitable / et semblerent par le propos de parti adverse / que bournel et les gens du dit capitaine feussent enfans tres simples ou folz / daler et dentrer / et de recevoir en ung chastel / sans parler / et est le propos de partie tresmal colours / et doit on avoir presumption tout contraire et est tout presumption pour bournel qui estoit et est chevalier et savoit bien que c'est de guerre et de saufconduit / et nest mie vraisemblable quil se fut boute en ladite compagnie ne en leur chastel sans parler et sans congie / et sil neust eu saufconduit / le defendeur neust mie envoie en Rethelois depuis sa prise pour soy informer se bournel avoit fait aucuns courses et en verite il ny entra mie sans parler et sans congie et lui qui a este capitaine et garde de forteresses scet bien comment on y doit entrer et se ung de ses serviteurs sestoit eschape ce ne justifieroit mie la prise torcionnere de bournel / qui dit que son dit serviteur est devenue insense / oultre dit bournel quil avoit baillie les forteresses quil tenoit es mains duduc de bourgogne et quelque difference que face partie adverse de saufconduiz de grace et de guerre on ne peut ne doit dire quon puisse enfraindre la saufconduit baillie audit bournel pour le reduire / et a certifie le duc de bourgogne qui en a rescript au roy quil avoit donne le dit saufconduit / et le roy en a respondu et rescript et quil vouloit quil fust amene par deca et mis en la main de la court / si sera mis et amene ceans par provision *aliter* on ne porroit savoir le fait ne aussi bournel ne porroit autrement faire sa demande / si dura ladite provision et mesmement pour ce que le defendeur a offert den faire juge le duc de bourgogne.

Le defendeur dit quil nest mie vraisemblable que lui ne ses gens voulsissent sans cause faire chose desplaisant a ung si grant seigneur quest le duc de bourgogne / ne prendre ou retenir induement bournel qui voloit entrer oudit chastel *sub specie Walpina* / et se soubmist a tenir prison sur peine de perdre leffect de son saufconduit quil a enfreint / et est ennemy si naura provision / et ne sera despointie le defendeur et aura delay pour produire instrumens et lettres / et offert et offre den faire ce que le duc de bourgogne bien informe et adverti en vouldra ordener / mais cependant ne veult ne doit estre despointie et dit que bournel nest point favorable qui est ennemy et a moult durement traite les subgiez du roy.

Le defendeur interrogue ou giron de la court a respondu et afferme que oncques il ne vist le saufconduit dont se vante bournel /

mais bien a oy dire a son lieutenant quil lavoit veu / mais il navoit point donne congie a bournel de y entrer et y entra sans le congie de son lieutenant / bien a oy dire le dit defendeur que quand bournel fust es faubours de Montigny ou il navoit mie seur logis / il demanda a aucuns gens du dit chastel avec lesquels il estoit venu se il porroit etre logie au dit chastel / lesquelz lui respondirent que il y seroit bien logie / et apres ycellui bournel sans demander congie a lieutenant ne a autre se bouta audit chastel / et ne entra mie ainsi quon y doit entrer / oultre a dit ycellui defendeur quil nest mie venu a paris a loccasion de ce proces / mais est venu pour ce quil avoit este mande pour estre au sacre du roy et ny a apporte lettres ne autres enseignemens servans a cette cause.

Appoinctie que la court verra ce que les parties vouldront monstrer et considerera leurs raisons et au conseil fera droit sur la provision et sur tout et aura le defendeur delay jusques au XV$^{me}$ mars pour envoier ses lettres.

3. *Case of the Carthusians of Le Parc v. Giles Desmoulins, plaidoirie* before the Parlement, March 1433 (Arch. Nat., X$^1$a 4797, fo. 49vo et seq.).

En la cause d'entre maistre Giles des Moulins audiencier d'une part et les religieux Chartreux leiz pairs de l'autre part / Molins dit quen juillet CCCCXXXII les ennemis des forteresses de maurepas ou autres emmenerent son bestail et le bestail d'autres et lendemain les chartreux et autres de par eulx rammenerent en leur ostel une partie dudit bestail / pour ce Molins y envoia son frere et ung sergent qui arresta lxxiij de ses bestes signez a sa marque, mais le procureur respondi quil y avoit mises et despenses pour la recouvrance a quoy moulins ou son frere offry a contribuer raisonnablement et neantmoins les religieux non vouldrent faire delivrance et pour ce que le sergent en senlistenant(?) et contrainant son arrest volt emmener les bestes lesquels trouva aux champs les religieux en appelerent / recite le demene du proces et ce qui a este dit par arrest par le quel lappellation a este mise a neant et sont ceans sur le principal pour ce soubstient Molins son arrest et demande despens domages et interests.

Les celestins dient qu a la venue des ennemis ils perdirent iii$^c$ de leurs bestes / aussi peut estre que Molins et autres y perdirent / lesquels firent diligence de y envoier pour les recouvrer et n'y firent riens / aussi les religieux y envoierent et moiennant lxx saluz dor et autres mises, de iii$^c$ bestes ils en recouvrerent ix$^{xx}$ seulement / et ne sceurent riens se Molins a riens perdu et estoit le bestail aux religieux / et quoy que soit le bestail estoit acquis *hostibus jure belli* / et les ont les religieux des ennemis *titulo oneroso* | et ny avoit point de seing sur le bestail qui estoit nouvellement tondu | et est vrai que Molins envoia son frere aux chartreux faignant y venir por devotion et ainsi quil aloit en leglise envoia ung compagnon en la bergiere qui signa lxxiii bestes dune reye noire sur le dos | et lendemain retourna avec un sergent qui emmena le bestail a notre dame des champs | et tantost quil fust la vint un bergier qui en choisy lxxiii quil vouloit emmener mais les religieux surviendrent qui sopposerent | et estoient saisis et estoit le bestail en leur possession et ny avoit arrest valable et n'estoient en riens obliges envers Molins ne condamnez si ne povoit user par voie darrest et nest recevable et n'a cause ne action conclu a ce a despens dommages et interests et par provision leur sera delivre a caucion leur bestail.

En la cause dentre Maistre Giles de Molins audiencier demandeur dune part et les religieux Chartreux leiz pairs defendans dautre part Molins soubtient son arrest et dit que de raison et par usage ung chascun peut proceder par voie darrest sur ses biens meubles *quicquid sit de mobilibus* oultre dit que les lxxiii bestes quil fist mettre en arrest lui appartenoient et estoient signez a son seing qui fut recogneu par les bergiers et pour que le signe estoit sur loreille et nestoit mie bien apparent les bergiers du consentement du procureur des charteux leur firent une roye sur le dos pietre noire por les mieux cognoistre | et ne doit on mie dire que les bestes feussent des ennemis *ab hostibus* | *quia non erant hostes* et nestoient que larrons pillars labourerurs qui ne quererent que pillage | et ont fait le serment par deca | et suppose quon die que ce que nous prenons sur noz ennemis | soit nostre *in judicio nostro* pour ce que nous reputons *bellum nostrum justum* | mais por ce ne disons nous mie que ce que les ennemis prennent sur nous soit a eulz acquis *in judicio nostro quia non agunt justum bellum* | et ainsi le bestail ne povoit estre acquis aux pillars ou ennemis qui lont prins | et se on disoit *quod in mobilibus non habet locum jus postliminii* on le doit entendre des meubles qui sont occupez *per vim bellicam* | mais ainsi na mie este fait en cas | pour ce on doit dire que on les doit restituer *quia sunt in praeda* | *etiam si titulo oneroso habeantur* | *quia res est viciosa* | selon les opinions des maistres et de Hostiensis *in summa de penitentibus et remissione* | et se les religieux ont envoie devers les ennemis et non Molins | ce ne les excuse point car cest une chose de mauvaise exemple pour donner occasion aux pillars de retourner plus volontiers et plus souvent | et si est vrai que le procureur dist a Molins et aux autres quils emmenerent leur bestail en contribuant aux mises et offry Molins a contribuer et nen paierent les chartreux dix saluz en tout et se nen peuvent riens demander | et *imputari debet sibi* | et pour ce Molins doit avoir la recreance de son bestail / et ainsi a este dit ceans par plusieurs arrets dentre Jehan Aumont Vols du Vris Huguet de Riey et autres et en y a jugemens devant les mareschaux qui sont venuz ceans par appel / et offre peremptoirement informer que le bestail est sien / si lui sera delivre au moins aura la recreance et a ceste fin requert que soit fait examen de v ou vi temoins qui vaillent aussi a fin principal et conclu comme dessus.

Les chartreux *dicunt quod ipsi certant de dampno vitando* / et est le bestail sien et a este arreste en leur possession si leur sera restitue *quia etiam predo restituendus est* si auront provision et recreance et ny ot oncques rien Molins / et sont les bestes des chartreux signez par loreille / et communement toutez y sont signez par les bergiers pour les maladies et souvent aussi les chiens les prennent par les oreilles et les seignent / oultre recitent ce que on dit *de hostibus et de latrun-culis* / *quia latrunculis dicuntur a latrando et hostes dicuntur qui publice bellum indicunt* / or dient ils que a la prise du dit bestail estoient les capitaines de Chartres de Rambouillet et autres et par ce on doit dire que ce que les ennemis prennent sur nous est a eulz acquiz ainsi que nous est acquiz ce que nous prenons sur eulz *etiam in judicio nostro aliter judicium claudicaret* / et quoy que dit partie adverse le bestail estoit aquiz aux ennemis / et le peut on acheter deulz et retenir et *in foro contencioso et in foro conscientie* / toutes voiez on parle point cy *de foro conscientie* / et nest mie trop estrange de dire que encorez *in foro conscientie* on peut retenir ce quon achete des ennemis et allegue les *auctoritas* de la sainte escriptures / et ce qu'on dit de *usucapione* / Et ne font riens les religieux contre les arrets qui parlent *de tercia persona* qui n'avoit riens perdu du sien et |nestoit mie si favorable que les religieux qui ont perdu et rachete leur bestail et quant est du proces de Huguet de Rieux lempeschement et la delivrance advint par tatonneau(?) a cause de louage / et sont *casus diversi et non adversi* / et quant est des chartreux *ipsi certant de dampno vitando* / pour ce requierent la restitution de leur bestail au moins par recreance en cas de delay / car ils sont despointiez et a este prins en leur possession le bestail / si conclu comme dessus et a depens.

Appoinctie que la court verra ce que les parties vouldront monstrer au conseil.

# BIBLIOGRAPHY

## I. SOURCES

The sources available for the study of the law of arms and its working are very scattered. The only primary sources which give consistent information about its rules are the commentaries and treatises of the lawyers, and the records of court cases. As regards the latter, it is unfortunate that no consistent records of the decisions of military courts, in France or England, have survived. The registers of the Parlement of Paris, where appeals from them were heard, are the only legal records from which this aspect of the subject can be studied systematically. For England there survive only the records of commissions being appointed to hear appeals, which are entered on the patent rolls.

As a result, I have found it difficult to produce a list of sources which is informative. As far as manuscript sources are concerned, I shall therefore simply describe what kind of material is available in the various archives and libraries where I have worked. Printed sources I shall list under three heads: (*a*) Legal, Theological, and Chivalrous writings bearing on the law of arms, (*b*) Printed records useful for the study of military usage, and (*c*) Chronicle sources.

## MS. SOURCES

(a) *The Archives Nationales* (Paris). The records of the Parlement are the most important single source for the study of the law of arms preserved here. I have used documents from three different series: the registers of civil cases (Arch. Nat., $X^1a$, registers of *plaidoiries*, arrests and judgments): the parallel registers of criminal cases (Arch. Nat., $X^2a$): and the collections of accords made in the Parlement (Arch. Nat., $X^1c$), which contain useful copies of documents produced in cases heard there, e.g. letters of obligation to pay ransoms. The registers I have examined most systematically are those covering the years 1348–80, and 1415–53. The registers are uncalendared, and one has therefore to look through them examining the subject matter of each case as it comes up; there appear to be many fewer military cases in the registers for 1380–1415 than in those I have used more thoroughly.

Two other series in the Archives Nationales are of some value. These are the registers of the French royal chancery (Arch. Nat., JJ), which include large numbers of pardons granted to French subjects, which usually give detailed case histories of the crimes covered: many of these are connected with the events of the war. The *Trésor des Chartes* (Arch. Nat., J) contains a number of useful diplomatic documents, concerning for example the enforcement of truces, surrenders of forts and the like.

(b) *The Bibliothèque Nationale* (Paris). The most important material in the Bibliothèque is to be found in the great provincial collections of MSS.; I have used matter from volumes in the Collection de Bourgogne; the Collection Doat (Langeudoc); the Collection de Picardie; and the Collection de Lorraine. These collections contain enormous and very miscellaneous series of documents, some original, and some copied from local repositories. These include letters of soldiers and captains, diplomatic instruments, notarial and other deeds, records of judgments, and much else. As they are uncatalogued, my researches in them have been very haphazard, but I have found them valuable even so.

Besides these, I have used several collections of heraldic and chivalrous material; notably MSS. Fr. 1968 and 1983 and MS. Fr. (Nouvelles Acquisitions) 4396, which last contains the list of questions concerning points in the law of arms which Geoffrey de Charny submitted to the Knights of the Order of the Star for consideration. MSS. Fr. 4604, 7492 and 18541 contain some useful material on the offices and powers of the Constable and of the king's provincial lieutenants. I have also found interesting items concerning the war (especially two records of enquiries into irregularities committed on campaign in Charles VII's reign) in MSS. Fr. 4054 and 21717, and MS. Duchesne 108.

(c) *The Public Record Office* (London). Among the Chancery Miscellanea are preserved the only full records of cases tried before the Constable and Marshal of England (C47/6). Nearly all are heraldic cases, but two concern more strictly military affairs (Gerard *v.* Chamberlain, and Des Roches *v.* Hawley, both commenced *temp.* Richard II), and for these there are full records of proceedings.

The French (now called Treaty) and Gascon Rolls from time to time furnish useful information (C76 and C61). They record grants of powers (including judicial authority) to lieutenants, captains and commanders of garrisons; and orders to officials and commissioners to investigate or try military cases. Sometimes details of the cases in question are recorded; usually they are unfortunately sketchy.

Among the Exchequer records, the only really important series is the collection of indentures of war among the Exchequer Accounts Various (E101). These throw invaluable light on soldiers' terms of service, especially on rules concerning the division of spoil, royal rights in prisoners, and the obligations of garrison commanders under siege.

(d) *The British Museum* (London). A great deal of miscellaneous information about the history and activities of the Court of Chivalry can be gathered from various MSS. in the Museum; in particular from Anstis's notes for a history of the court (Add. MSS. 9021-2) and from Cotton's collections (especially MSS Titus C1 and Nero D6). Cotton's collections also contain a good many copies of indentures and other documents concerning the war. Add. MS. 33191 contains a copy of standing orders for an unspecified royal host (fifteenth century): and Cotton MS. Julius F IV a copy of Salisbury's standing orders of 1427 for his companies in Maine (referred to here as 'Perche Orders').

Among the Stowe MSS. are some useful heraldic collections (including notes by Anstis and Thynne); in particular I have drawn from MSS. 668, 674 and 1047.

I have found some useful material in the Collection of Additional Charters: but these are catalogued in such a way that it is only possible to use them systematically where a name, and not a subject is being pursued. What I have found has been largely a matter of chance.

(e) *Archives départmentales de la Côte d'Or* (Dijon). A great deal of useful material is to be found among the records of the *Chambre des Comptes* of the Dukes of Burgundy (Series B in the archives). Military and diplomatic records furnish information concerning prisoners of war and their ransoms, agreements to surrender towns, contracts between captains and the Duke or his Marshal, and letters of marque. They also contain several lists of 'excesses' (i.e. war crimes) committed by hostile troops on Burgundian soil. I have taken material from the following bundles: B 11735, 11875 and 11879-86. On truces and arrangements to ensure their observance there is most useful information in B 11906-7, 11918, 11920, 11923, 11929-30 and 11933. But the most useful source of all is the register of *lettres missives*,

B 11942. This contains many copies of letters (mostly dating from the time of Philip the Good) which passed between captains in the field, and the Chancellors and Marshals of Burgundy. They comment widely on everyday military problems involving the allegiance of forces operating in the various theatres of war, infractions of truces, reprisals, surrenders, terms of service and much else.

(f) *Archives départmentales du Nord* (Lille). The material to be found in the Archives at Lille (from the *Chambre des Comptes* of Flanders) is very similar to that to be found at Dijon. Five registers of *lettres missives*, B 18822–4 and B 18842–3, furnish much useful information; particularly interesting is the long series of letters between Burgundian officials and Richard Aston, lieutenant of the Captain of Calais, and other English officers there *temp.* Henry IV, mostly about infractions of truces and safe-conducts.

(g) *Private Sources.* Two sources which are in private hands have been of great use to me. Mr. C. A. J. Armstrong of Hertford College, Oxford, allowed me to use his micro-films of the *Régistres de l'Ordre de la Toison d'Or*, which contain full records of the order's proceedings at its early chapters. Professor G. W. Coopland allowed me to use Phillips MS. 10396, a valuable heraldic scrap-book, which was probably compiled at the court of Burgundy.


## PRINTED SOURCES

(a) *Legal, Theological and Chivalrous writings.*

Alfonso IX of Castile, *Las Siete Partidas del Rey don Alfonso el Sabro* (Madrid, 1807).

Andreas, Johannes, *In sex Decretalium Libros Novella Commentaria* (Venice, 1581).

Andrew of Isernia, *In Usus Feudorum Commentaria* (Frankfurt, 1598).

Angelus of Perusia, *Disputationes* (Pavia, *c.* 1490).

Aquinas, St. Thomas, *Summa Theologica.*

Augustine of Hippo, St., *De Civitate Dei.*
*Epistolae.*

Baldus of Perusia, *Lectura super Digesto* (Lyons, 1540).
*Consilia sive Responsa* (Frankfurt, 1589).
*In Decretalium Volumen Commentaria* (Venice, 1595).

Bartholomew of Saliceto, *In Novem Libros Codicis Commentaria* (Venice, 1568).

Bartolus of Sassoferrato, *Commentaria in Jura* (collected commentaries and treatises on civil law, Basle, 1562).

Beaumanoir, *Les Coutumes du Beauvaisis*, ed. M. le Comte de Beugnot (Soc. de l'histoire de France, 1842).

Beuil, Jean de, *Le Jouvencel*, ed. L. Lécestre and C. Favre (Soc. de l'histoire de France, 1887–9).

Bonet, Honoré, *The Tree of Battles*, ed. and translated G. W. Coopland (Liverpool, 1949) [also ed. E. Nys, Brussels, 1883].

Caxton, William, *The Book of the Ordre of Chyvalry*, ed. A. T. P. Byles (E.E.T.S., 1926).

*Corpus Juris Canonici.*

*Corpus Juris Civilis.*

Cynus of Pistoia, *In Codicem et aliquot Titulos primi Pandectorum Tomi Commentaria* (Frankfurt, 1578).

*Debats des Herauts d'Armes de France et Angleterre*, ed. L. Pannier and P. Meyer (Soc. des Anciens textes français, 1877).

Durandus, William, *Speculum Juris* (Frankfurt, 1612).

Gratian, *Decretum.*

Henry of Gorinchen, *Tractatus Consultatorii* (Cologne, 1503).

Hostiensis (Henry of Segusio), *Aurea Summa* (Cologne, 1612).

Innocent IV, *In quinque Libros Decretalium Commentaria* (Venice, 1578).

Isidore of Seville, St., *Etymologiae.*

John of Legnano, *Tractatus de Bello*, ed. T. E. Holland (Oxford, 1917).

*Knyghthode and Bataile*, ed. R. Dyboske and Z. M. Arend (E.E.T.S., 1935).

Martin of Lodi, *Tractatus de Confederatione, Pace et Conventionibus Principum* (printed in Zilletus, *Tractatus Juris Universi*, Venice, 1584, Tome XVI).

*Tractatus de Bello* (printed in Zilletus, op. cit., Tome XVI).

Monaldus, *Summa* (Lyons, 1516).

Nicholas of Cusa, *De Concordantia Catholica* (in *Opera*, Basle edn., 1565).

Nicholas of Tudeschi, *Lectura super quinque Libros Decretalium* (Lyons, 1524).

*Noblesse, Boke of*, ed. J. G. Nichols (Roxburghe Club, 1860).

Paris of Pozzo, *De Re Militari* (printed in Zilletus, *Tractus Juris Universi*, Venice, 1584, Tome XVI).

Pisan, Christine de, *The Book of Fayttes of Armes and of Chyvalrye* (Caxton's translation) ed. A. T. P. Byles (E.E.T.S., 1932 and 1937).

Raymond of Pennaforte, *Summa de Poenitentia* (Rome, 1603).

*Somnium Viridarii* (Paris, 1516).
Upton, Nicholas, *De Officio Militari*, ed. E. Bysshe, (London, 1654).
Valera, Diego de, *Tratado de los Rieptos y Desafios* (Madrid, c. 1500).

(b) *Printed Records.* The most valuable record evidence from which the law of arms can be studied comes from collections of diplomatic, local, and family papers concerned with the war. Those which I have found most useful are these.

*Acts of the Parliament of Scotland* (Scottish Record Commission).
Baurein, J., *Variétés Bordeloises* (Bordeaux, 1784–6).
Bentley, S., *Excerpta Historica* (London, 1833).
*The Black Book of the Admiralty*, ed. T. Twiss (R.S., 1871–6).
*The Black Prince's Register* (Record Commission).
*Calendar of Close Rolls* (Record Commission).
*Calendar of Patent Rolls* (Record Commission).
Chaplais, P., *Some documents regarding the Fulfilment and Interpretation of the Treaty of Bretigny* (Camden Miscellany, Vol. XIX, 1952).
Douet d'Arq, L., *Choix des Pièces Inédits rélatives au règne de Charles VI* (Soc. de l'histoire de France, 1863–4).
Du Fresne de Beaucourt, G., *la Chronique de Mathieu d'Escouchy, Preuves* (Tome III of the chronicle, Soc. de l'histoire de France, 1864).
Duplès-Agier, H., *Régistre Criminel du Châtelet de Paris* (Soc. des bibliophiles français, 1861–4).
Flamare, H. de, *Le Nivernais pendant la Guerre de Cent Ans* (Paris, 1913–25).
Hingston, F. C., *Royal and Historical Letters during the reign of Henry IV* (R.S., 1860).
Jacotin, *Preuves de la Maison de Polignac* (Paris, 1898–1906).
*John of Gaunt's Register*, 1371–6, ed. S. Armitage-Smith (Camden Soc., 1911), and 1379–83, ed. E. C. Lodge and R. Somerville (Camden Soc., 1937).
Nicolas, Sir H., *The Scrope and Grosvenor Controversy* (London, 1832).
*Proceedings of the Privy Council* (Record Commission, 1834).
*Ordonnances des Rois de France de la troisième race* (Paris, 1733–1847).
*The Paston Letters*, ed. J. Gairdner (London, 1904).
*Régistres Consulaires de St. Flour*, ed. M. Boudet (Paris, 1898).
*Rotuli Normannie*, ed. T. D. Hardy (London, 1835).
*Rotuli Parliamentorum* (London, 1767–1832).
*Rotuli Scotiae* (London, 1814).
Rymer, T., *Foedera, Conventiones et Acta Publica* (The Hague, 1745).
Secousse, *Recueil de Pièces sur Charles II Roi de Navarre* (Paris, 1755).

Stevenson, J., *Letters and Papers illustrative of the Wars of the English in France* (R.S., 1861–4).

*Spicelegium Brivatense*, ed. A. de Chassaing (Paris, 1886).

(c) *Chronicles*. In their accounts of campaigns, chroniclers frequently refer to incidents which raised legal issues, of which no record would otherwise survive. In order to track these down, there is no alternative to reading a chronicle from cover to cover. As it is impossible to read all the possibly relevant chronicles in this way, I can do no more than list the sample I have worked over systematically (others are quoted in the text, but I have not studied them with the same care).

Avesbury, R. de, *De Gestis Mirabilibus Regis Edwardi Tertii*, ed. E. Maunde-Thompson (R.S. 1889).

d'Ayala, P. Lopez, *Cronicas de Los Reyes de Castilla* (Madrid, 1779–80).

Berry, le Herault, *Le Recouvrement de Normendie*, ed., with R. Blondel *De Reductione Normannie*, by J. Stephenson (R.S., 1863).

Chandos Herald, *Life of the Black Prince*, ed. M. K. Pope and E. C. Lodge (Oxford, 1910): for the French text, see the edition of H. O. Coxe (Roxburghe Club, 1842).

*Chronicon Anglie*, ed. E. Maunde-Thompson (R.S., 1874).

*Chronicon de Lanercrost* (Bannatyne Club, 1839).

*Chronique des Quatre Premiers Valois*, ed. S. Luce (Soc. de l'histoire de France, 1862).

*Chronique des Règnes de Jean II et Charles V*, ed. R. Delachenal (Soc. de l'histoire de France, 1910–20).

*Chronique du Bon Duc Loys de Bourbon*, ed. A-M. Chazaud (Soc. de l'histoire de France, 1876).

*Chronique du Réligieux de St. Denis*, ed. L. Belleguat (Collection des documents inédits sur l'histoire de France, Paris, 1839).

*Chronique Martinianne*, ed. P. Champion (Paris, 1907).

*Chronique Normande du Quatorzième Siècle*, ed. A. and E. Molinier (Soc. de l'histoire de France, 1882).

Froissart, Jean, *Chroniques*, in *Oeuvres de Froissart*, ed. Kervyn de Lettenhove (Brussels, 1869–77).

Gray, Sir Thomas, *Scalacronica*. ed. J. Stevenson (Maitland Club, 1836).

Gruel, Guillaume, *Chronique d'Arthur de Richemont*, ed. A. Le Vavasseur (Soc. de l'histoire de France, 1890): quoted also from the edition of Michaud and Poujoulat (Nouvelle Collection des Mémoires pour servir à l'histoire de France, Tome III, Paris, 1837).

Jouvenel des Ursins, Jean, *Histoire de Charles VI*, ed. J. A. C. Buchon (Choix des Chroniques et Mémoires sur l'histoire de France, Paris, 1838).

Kingsford, C. T. (ed.), *The First English Life of King Henry V* (Oxford, 1911).

Knighton, Henry, *Leycestrensis Chronicon*, ed. J. R. Lumby (R.S., 1889–95).

La Marche, Olivier, *Mémoires*, ed. H. Beaune and J. d'Arbaumont (Soc. de l'histoire de France, 1883–8).

Le Baker, Geoffrey, *Chronicon Galfridi Le Baker*, ed. E. Maunde-Thompson (Oxford, 1886).

Lefèvre de St. Rémy, *Chronique*, ed. F. Morand (Soc. de l'histoire de France, 1876–81).

Livius, Titus, *Vita Henrici Quinti*, ed. T. Hearne (Oxford, 1716).

Monstrelet, Enguerrand de, *Chronique*, ed. L. Douet d'Arcq (Soc. de l'histoire de France, 1857–62).

Murimuth, Adam, *Continuatio Chronicarum*, ed. E. Maunde-Thompson (R.S., 1889).

Waurin, Jean de, *Chroniques*, ed. W. and E. Hardy (R.S., 1864–91).

## II. SECONDARY WORKS

No book has been written on the law of arms: and as a result some of the works I have listed here are not quoted in the text. I have mentioned some because they give essential information either on the intellectual background or on military history, others because they suggested useful lines of enquiry. As in the note on sources, I have separated as far as possible works on legal and chivalrous theory from works on the history of the Hundred Years War; and I have also listed separately general historical accounts and monographs on individual campaigns and careers. These last, especially the French dissertations, I have often used virtually as primary sources, because of the original documents which they print as *pièces justificatives*.

(a) *Works on Legal and Chivalrous Theory and Practice.*

(i) Books:

Anstis, J., *Register of the Order of the Garter* (London, 1724).

Ballis, W., *The Legal Position of War: Changes in its Practice and Theory from Plato to Vattel* (The Hague, 1937).

Carlyle, R. W. and A. J., *Medieval Political Theory in the West* (London, 1903–36).

Du Cange, *Dissertations sur l'histoire de St. Louis* (printed in the *Glossarium*, ed. L. Favre, 1887, Tome X).

Harcourt, L. W. Vernon, *His Grace the Steward and the Trial of Peers* (London, 1907).

La Curne de Ste. Palaye, J. B., *Mémoires sur l'ancienne Chevalerie* (Paris, 1759).

Mitchell, J. M., *The Court of the Connétable* (Yale, 1947).

Nys, E., *Le Droit de la Guerre et les précurseurs de Grotius* (Leipzig, 1882). *Les Origines du Droit International* (Paris, 1894).

Regout, R. H. W., *La Doctrine de la Guerre Juste de St. Augustin à nos Jours* (Paris, 1934).

Reiffenberg, Baron de, *Histoire de l'Ordre de la Toison d'Or* (Brussels, 1830).

Savigny, F. C. von, *Geschichte des Römischen Rechts im Mittelalter* (Heidelberg, 1815–31).

Squibb, G. D., *The High Court of Chivalry* (Oxford, 1959).

Vanderpol, A-M., *La Doctrine Scholastique du Droit de Guerre* (Paris, 1919).

Woolf, C. N. S., *Bartolus of Sassoferrato: his position in the history of Medieval Political Thought* (Cambridge, 1913).


(ii) Short Articles:

Audinet, E., 'Les Lois et Coutumes de la Guerre a l'Epoque de la Guerre de Cent Ans', *Mémoires de la Societé des Antiquaires de l'Ouest*, Vol. 9 (1917).

d'Alauzier, L., 'Une alliance de Seigneurs de Quercy en 1380', *Annales du Midi*, Vol. 64 (1952).

Bossuat, A., 'Un ordre de Chevalerie Auvergnat: la Pomme d'Or', *Bulletin Historique et Scientifique de l'Auvergne*, Vol. 64.

Coopland, G. W., 'Le Jouvencel Revisited', *Symposium*, Vol. 5 (1951).

Huizinga, J., 'The Political and Military Significance of Chivalric Ideas in the late Middle Ages', *Men and Ideas* (translated J. S. Holmes and H. van Marle, London, 1960).

Las Matrie, R. de, 'Du Droit de Marque', *Bibliothèque de l'École de Chartes*, 6th Series, Vol. 2.

Ullman, W., 'The Development of the Medieval Idea of Sovereignty' E.H.R., Vol. 64 (1949).


(b) *General Histories.*

Baluze, *Histoire de la Maison d'Auvergne.*

Delachenal, R., *Histoire de Charles V* (Paris, 1909–31).

BIBLIOGRAPHY

Du Fresne de Beaucourt, G., *Histoire de Charles VII* (Paris, 1881–91).
Luce, S., *La France pendant la Guerre de Cent Ans* (Paris, 1890).
Newhall, R., *The English Conquest of Normandy* (Newhaven, 1924).
Perroy, E., *The Hundred Years War* (translated D. C. Douglas, London, 1951).
Plancher, Dom. U., *Histoire de Bourgogne* (Dijon, 1739–81).
Vaissette, Dom. J., *Histoire de Languedoc* (Toulouse, 1872–6).
Wylie, J. H., and Waugh, W. T., *The Reign of Henry V* (Cambridge, 1914–29).

(c) *Monographs.*

(i) Books:
Bossuat, A., *Perrinet Gressart et Francois de Surienne* (Paris, 1936).
Boudet, M., *Villandrando et les Écorcheurs à St. Flour* (Paris, 1895).
Boutiot, M. T., *La Guerre des Anglais—un chapitre de l'histoire de Troyes* (Paris, 1861).
Champion, P., *Guillaume de Flavy, Capitaine de Compiégne* (Paris 1906).
Cherest, A., *L'Archiprêtre: épisodes de la Guerre de Cent Ans au Quatorzième Siècle* (Paris, 1879).
Clément-Simon, G., *La Rupture de la Traité de Brétigny et ses conséquences en Limousin* (Paris, 1898).
Cosneau, E., *Le Connétable de Richemont* (Paris, 1886).
Denifle, H., *La Désolation des Églises, Monastères et Hôpitaux en France pendant la Guerre de Cent Ans* (Paris, 1897–9).
Fréminville, J. de, *Les Écorcheurs en Bourgogne* (Dijon, 1888).
Gaujal, B. de, *Annales de Rouergue* (Limoges, 1825).
Guigue, G., *Les Tards-Venus en Lyonnais, Forez et Beaujolais* (Lyons, 1886).
Hewitt, H. J., *The Black Prince's Expedition of 1355–7* (Manchester, 1958).
Luce, S., *Histoire de Bertrand du Guesclin et de son Époque* (Paris, 1876).
Mazure, A., *L'Auvergne au Quatorzième Siècle* (Clermont, 1845).
Menard, L., *Histoire Civile, Ecclésiastique et Littéraire de la Ville de Nîmes* (Paris, 1744–58).
Molinier, E., *Étude sur la Vie d'Arnoul d'Audreham, Maréchal de France* (Paris, 1883).
Monicat, J., *Les Grandes Compagnies en Velay* (Paris, 1928).
Newhall, R., *Muster and Review* (Harvard, 1940).
Quicherat, J., *Roderigue de Villandrando* (Paris, 1879).
Rouquette, J., *La Rouergue sous les Anglais* (Millau, 1887).
Russell, P. E., *The English Intervention in Spain and Portugal in the time of Edward III and Richard II* (Oxford, 1955).

# BIBLIOGRAPHY

Terrier de Loray, Le Marquis, *Jean de Vienne Amiral de France* (Paris, 1877).

Tuetey, A., *Les Écorcheurs sous Charles VII* (Montbéliard, 1874).

(ii) Articles:

Bossuat, A., 'Les Prisonniers de Beauvais et la rancon du poète Jean Regnier, Bailli d'Auxerre', *Mélanges d'histoire du Moyen Age dédiés à la mémoire de Louis Halphen* (Paris, 1951).

'La rancon de Guillaume de Châteauvillain', *Annales de Bourgogne* (1951).

Fréville, E. de, 'Des Grandes Compagnies au Quatorzième Siècle', *Bibliothèque de l'École de Chartes*, 1st series, Vols. III and V (1841–2 and 1843–4).

Hay, D., 'The Division of the Spoils of War in fourteenth-century England', *T.R.H.S.*, 5th Series, Vol. 4 (1954).

MacFarlane, K. B., 'The investment of Sir John Fastolf's profits of war', *T.R.H.S.*, 5th Series, Vol. 7 (1957).

Perroy, E., 'Gras Profits et rancons pendant la Guerre de Cent Ans: l'affaire du Comte de Denia', *Mélanges d'histoire du Moyen Age dédiés à la mémoire de Louis Halphen*.

Rowe, B. J. H., 'Discipline in the Norman garrisons under Bedford, 1422–35', *E.H.R.*, Vol. 46 (1931).

Templeman, G., 'Edward III and the beginnings of the Hundred Years War', *T.R.H.S.*, 5th Series, Vol. 2 (1952).

de Velasco, A. Gutteriez, 'Los Ingleses en Espana', *Estudos de Edad Media dl la Corona de Aragon* (Saragossa, 1950).

# INDEX

* These references only cover *detailed* discussions of cases tried in the Parlement and references to the activities of the Court.